Racing With My Shadow

The Compelling True Story of America's First Leading Female Jockey

by

Karen Rogers

ISBN-13: 978-1542593366
ISBN-10: 1542593360

about the cover

This pastel, done in 1981, is of me in the paddock the day I won my first stakes race at Belmont Park. My mother is the artist. People from the racetrack who saw the pastel would ask my mom, "Why didn't you make her smiling?" After all, I was always so upbeat and happy at the track. However, Mom mostly saw me as the person in the pastel—serious—what I called "the real me."

www.racingwithmyshadow.com

To God,
Who revealed the truth and set me free.

To Mom,
who really did love me through it all.
I love you.

To fellow jockey and friend, Robbie Davis,
whose courage to come forward with his story
gave me the courage to face my own past.

To my friends, Alison Selby and Day Hellwig,
who read a very early version of this book,
were inspired by it, and encouraged me
to go public with my story in order
to help others.

To the track vet, Dr. Fritz,
who pulled my face out of the dirt
and saved my life.

To Dr. William Davis,
who "figuratively" pulled my face out of the dirt
and saved my life.

To Sergeant Striker,
who kept me from pulling the trigger.

"They can't conceive that a girl can come to a man's game and be one of the top." – Angel Cordero, Jr., Hall of Fame jockey

Quote taken from article by Janet Barrett, Parade Magazine, 6/28/81

Beating Angel Cordero, Jr. at Belmont Park

"My long-shot choice for the next woman star: jockey Karen Rogers, 17, probably the best girl rider ever and one of the best kids of either sex since the record rookie year of Steve Cauthen."

– Pete Axthelm, Sportswriter
Newsweek, 1/7/80

"She gets along with horses. They try for her. She'll be around for years to come."

– Bobby Lake, leading N.Y. trainer

Quote taken from article by Janet Barrett, Parade Magazine, 6/28/81

"Karen rode a winner for me the other day. The next morning she came to the barn with a big bag of donuts for the help and staked the groom of the horse that won. I don't think I've had a rider, especially a 'bug' rider, stake a groom since the late '50s."
– Budd Lepman, leading N.J. trainer

Quote taken from article by sportswriter Doug McCoy, Daily Racing Form, 8/79

"Karen can come back and tell me things about the mounts I put her on and a lot of 'bug' boys can't do that. She does the right thing, too. She won't offer an opinion; she'll wait for me to ask. Smart little lady."

– J.J. Crupi, leading N.J. trainer

Quote taken from article by sportswriter Doug McCoy, Daily Racing Form, 9/10/79

"Karen Rogers convinced whatever skeptics remained with a brilliant riding performance, winning three races in one day in New York. It was the second time this winter that Karen won both ends of double."

– John Piesen, Sportswriter New York Post, 3/80

"Most female riders, you could pick them out in a field of horses. But not her. She gets right down and rides like the boys. Whips left and right, takes chances, fights back. She takes care of herself."

– Freddy Stevens, N.Y. jockey agent

Quote from article by Janet Barrett, Parade Magazine, 6/28/81

"She's not a female rider. She's a very good lightweight rider."

– Frank Wright, top N.Y. trainer

Quote take from article by Dave Koerner, Courier-Journal 6/14/81

"She's terrific, she has style and class, the best girl rider I've ever seen."
– Chris McCarron, Hall of Fame jockey

Quote taken from James Tuite's "She's Riding With Courage" New York Times, 12/80

Leaving the gate at Aqueduct (middle - #5)

"That kid's for real. She can ride. At the Meadowlands you gotta come outta the gate fast, get the rail and be one-two or you're dead, most of the time. That kid's a good gate rider."

– Angel Cordero, Jr., Hall of Fame jockey

Quote taken from article by sportswriter Wes Gaffer, New York Daily News, 4/80

"Rogers, injured in spill Thursday, checked out of the hospital and rode four races. Toughest kid on the block."
– John Piesen, Sportswriter New York Post, 3/81

"She worked as hard as any rider I'd known. Anybody who'd been around her knew her personality was one in a million."

– Ed Rubenstein, jockey agent

Quote taken from sportswriter Doug McCoy's "The Cute Little Girl Who Could" The Horsemen's Journal, 3/80

"Good hands, good head, and such a good seat that you can't tell she's a girl."

– Angel Cordero, Hall of Fame jockey

Quote taken from James Tuite's "She's Riding With Courage," New York Times, December 1980

"She's as good as any boy. She tries real hard and likes all the horses. She doesn't have to ride the favorite. She rides a lot of horses that the boys don't like to ride. She's got a light touch. She handles a horse with more finesse than power. She rates a horse well. She whips real good, with her left hand as well as her right."

–Jack Bradley, N.Y. trainer

Quote taken from Elizabeth Wheeler's "A Day at the Races" Women's Sports Magazine, 1980

"She's a terrific kid with natural ability, great skill, and no fear. She's going to do well. All she needed was the start and now she has it. I'm going to be giving her more rides and I know other trainers will, too." – Bobby Lake, leading N.Y. trainer Quote taken from article by sportswriter Richard Mortlock, The Star, 2/80

Winter racing – ear muffs and gloves

Beating Jorge Velasquez at Aqueduct

"Karen has shown amazing ability to get horses out of the starting gate quickly and send them off to an insurmountable lead. She has also been able to boldly move her horses through tiny openings along the rail and overtake pace-setters!"

– Ray Brienza, Sportswriter
The Star-Ledger, 10/29/79

"If all this publicity has gone to Karen's head, you'd never know it. Karen, dubbed 'The Shirley Temple of Racing,' is just a nice talented kid who wants to ride, ride, ride. And this kid can ride."

–Bob Raimonto, Sportswriter
The Sunday Record, 12/16/79

"This kid is a good rider. The owners like her, I like her—and best of all, she wins."

– J. J. Crupi, leading N.J. trainer
Quote taken from article by Bob Harding, Star-Ledger, 9/21/79

"I sold her her first pony (Jack) years ago. I have reservations about girl riders. She certainly seems one of the best I've seen. I rode her and she won. You can't knock success."

– J. Willard Thompson, leading N.J. trainer
Quote taken from article by sportswriter Bob Raimonto, The Sunday Record, 9/16/79

Contents

Winning at Aqueduct

This book is a true story. Some of the identities, descriptions, and events have been changed to protect the privacy of individuals.

"...you will know the truth, and the truth will set you free."
– John 8:32 (NIV)

Finding the truth isn't easy. Without God, it's impossible. But praise Him that He can show us all truth and reveal past things that are so long buried. It wasn't until God helped me face my past and relive the painful memories that I could understand the truth and come out with the victory. And so it was that God brought even the most painful of these to mind, so that I could heal.

Prologue

In 2004, I decided to take my eleven-year-old son to Belmont Park Racetrack, so he could get to see what his mother used to do. Instead of watching the races, we went directly to the jocks' room, the place that was so familiar to me, my second home for some time. It had been fourteen years since I last rode a race. The old familiar faces in the old familiar places made me realize how far I'd come since then. Life wasn't always so peaceful and stable as it has been these past many years away from racing and walking with the Lord.

I greeted many of my old friends. There were agents, trainers, valets, and jockeys I had come to know so well. We talked about old times, the good old days. But, as good as the good old days were in racing, those days held some very difficult times for me personally. Back then I didn't know the Lord so well, nor could I have loved Him as I do now, after having survived so much adversity.

I count my blessings as I look back, seeing the Lord's hand through it all—the good *and* the bad. For it was in the hardships that I was drawn near to Him; God used all of it to draw me close. As it says in Romans 8:28:

> "And we know that God causes all things to work together for good to those who love God, to those who are called according to His purpose." – Romans 8:28

Let me tell you my story then. How it really was, from the very beginning: the good, the bad, and the ugly. And let me again praise God for where I am today, no longer a slave to anyone or anything, except Jesus Christ!!!

> "It was for freedom that Christ sets us free; therefore keep standing firm and do not be subject again to a yoke of slavery."
>
> – Galatians 5:1 (NASB)

Chapter 1
Who Did Vince Love?

I was ten years old. Dad had just moved out. Mom's friend, Vince, slept over sometimes now. He slept in the living room on the beanbag chair. I remember this one night. It surprised me, took me off guard. Maybe it happened more than once. I don't know. But I remember the first time Vince crawled into my bed.

He talked to me quietly for a while, and then he put his hands under my pajamas and touched my chest. It felt wrong—very wrong. What about Mom? Mom was asleep in her own room. Vince said he loved me, that I was the one he *really* loved. He stayed there in my bed. Vince and Mom weren't married yet, and Vince was supposed to be sleeping in the living room.

I was glad when Vince got out of my bed. He had felt warm beside me, but I had been very uneasy. I wasn't sure exactly why, but I felt like I had done something wrong. He left my room quietly. Where was he going? To sleep in his bed, on the beanbag chair on the living room floor, right? Or was he going to Mom's bedroom to love her the way he loved me? I was confused, yet curious. My mind was racing.

Who did Vince love?

Finally, I got out of bed. I peeked out my door and looked down the hall into the living room. Yes, Vince was there. He was lying there on the beanbag, sprawled out in his underwear, looking right at me. He was waiting there, in just his underwear. He smiled and winked at me knowingly.

I had my answer and went back to bed.

• • • • •

Growing up, I was a happy kid. My sister, Susan, one year my elder, was easy-going and kind. If we had an argument, she always let me win. She told me after we were grown that it was just easier that way.

I was a determined seeker of the truth. I always wanted to

know why things were. It wasn't enough to get the answer right. I had to understand why. My father often had to sit with me for hours to explain my schoolwork, say, from a science book. I always asked the questions what, how, and why, forever driving my parents crazy. Like the time we went to the movies to see "The Sting." I made it an unbearable experience for them with all my questions. Eventually they stopped taking us to complicated movies, sticking to simple films like "Charlie the Lonesome Cougar" or "My Side of the Mountain." It was a good thing Mom loved me and Dad had so much patience.

I was a straight A student, mostly because of my desire to know things and get them right. My mother and father never asked if I did my homework and barely looked at my grades. They didn't push me. I pushed myself. I had a strong will, for better or worse.

I don't remember doing anything wrong or bad as a kid, but I would get upset and frustrated when things didn't make sense. When I was about seven years old, Dad figured out that spanking wasn't the best way to deal with me. I just got more upset and angry. "Let's talk about it," he would say, quickly learning that this approach got much more positive results.

Mom was great. She did exciting things. She had projects going, and these were always interesting and fun. Mom loved animals. We had all kinds of animals: puppies, kittens, birds, gerbils, rabbits, and horses...always the horses. We got our first pony when I was three years old. Mom taught Susan and me to ride. She let us be responsible for things, which built our self-esteem. We put out our school clothes (dresses back then) before bed and made our own breakfast and bag lunches in the morning. We woke Mom only for help to cross our busy street on the way to walk to school, first and second grade.

Susan and I spent so much time at home doing fun things; we didn't have time or interest in other kids, or what they were doing. We were happy riding bikes, swimming in the pool, exploring in the woods, and climbing the apple trees. But always, Mom was the solid center of our world. We would rush home from school to see what she had been up to all day: making an old chicken coop into a playhouse, learning to play the guitar (then teaching us, as well), trying to get the Myna bird

Flower and me (3 yrs old)

to talk, or just fixing up the barn, transformed from an old garage. She was fun to be around. I remember wearing cowboy boots like Mom and learning to throw a lasso (this was in her cowboy phase). She made life exciting. We were proud of our mother. With her, nothing was impossible. Life was one big adventure.

I was eight years old and going into fourth grade when Mom discovered Bridleton, New Jersey. The beautiful horse country there held Mom captivated. In Bridleton, there was foxhunting, a sport Mom fell in love with. Along with a group of riders, she chased behind a pack of foxhounds, hunting a fox across the rolling countryside.

Mom was finding new friends among the horse people. Three days a week she would pull horse and trailer to Bridleton to foxhunt. Her heart was there, away from Dad. My father taught high school near where we lived, and as far as I knew, everything was fine between them. They never fought or argued, so I never knew that Mom had been unhappy with her marriage. Dad saw how much the horses meant to Mom, so when she found a house in Bridleton, we moved there.

Riding Flower in a horse show (4 yrs old)

Mom immediately converted the garage into a four stall barn. Susan and I helped take care of our horse and two ponies: our first little pony, Flower, and Catch Me, a bigger pony.

I was nine years old when I first met Vince. I was riding Flower with a group of Mom's riding friends at the time. They were all evaluating Mom's new young horse. I could tell that Mom really wanted the opinion of this tall, thin man with jet black hair. His name was Vince DeLuca, and he was a top show rider that Mom had met while foxhunting. I watched him try out Mom's horse, but didn't think much about it at the time.

Mom started spending lots of time riding with Vince. He came around the house, too. I liked him. He was fun. We would

Foxhunting – Flower and me (9 yrs old)
Mom and Susan behind me

all do things together while Dad worked. Vince was twenty-one but looked much older. Because of his dark complexion and deep sunken eyes, he looked closer to Mom's age, thirty-four. Vince helped me with my riding. One day Catch Me threw me off, and Vince, Mom, Susan, and I spent the whole day searching Bridleton for him. Vince never seemed too busy for us.

Years later Mom explained, "One of the reasons I liked Vince was that he was always so good with you and Susan. He spent so much time with you."

Mom, always being so creative, invented a board game called "Fox Hunt." Many afternoons Vince, Susan, and I helped Mom make the game pieces. We filled up molds for ceramic horses and riders, foxhounds and foxes, and then we painted them. Mom hoped to sell the game at a nearby tack shop. She also helped Vince with his college projects. She typed up his papers and even made a small model of the Parthenon for his Art History class. I remember going to Gino's, a fast food restaurant, where I stood on Vince's shoulders to get the correct measurements of the building, which Mom helped construct in a miniature version for his class.

Vince was becoming part of the family...sort of. He would stay on into the evenings when Dad came home. Sometimes he cooked dinner for all of us, or the five of us would go to the movies. It was awkward to see who was going to sit next to whom. It *was* kind of strange. Where exactly did Vince fit into our family? Mom seemed to like Vince better than she liked Dad, yet Vince didn't seem a bit uncomfortable with this. He seemed quite at home. I didn't know what my father was thinking, but I felt badly for him.

Years later, Dad told me he put up with the situation because he heard rumors that Vince was living with a gay man.

One night while Mom was out somewhere with Vince, Dad sat in the kitchen with us.

"Kids, I've got something to tell you," he said sadly. His voice broke with emotion. "I'm moving out. It has nothing to do with you two."

I was surprised, but not altogether unhappy for him. Actually, it amazed me that he had put up with things as they were for so long. I didn't want to see him continue to suffer.

"It's okay, Dad. We love you." Susan and I tried to comfort him with hugs as he broke down and cried. I had never seen my father cry before, and it bothered me that he could be so sad. Susan and I started crying, too.

"I love you so much. I'm really going to miss you both."

I knew this was the last time we would be together as a family. Because when Mom came home, Dad was leaving. Then Mom was all we would have left. We *had* to keep her happy...and Vince, too. Because when Vince was around, Mom was the happiest.

As time went on, my feelings were getting more and more mixed-up. One of my "crazy" feelings was that Mom didn't love me anymore. Vince would take me aside and tell me how selfish my mother was. He said all she cared about was herself. She didn't care how anyone else felt. This bothered me. I knew that Mom had always included us in everything. Mom never went anywhere without us. Even at three and four years old, Susan and I would ride in the back of Mom's old army jeep as it pulled her homemade horse trailer to a weekend horse show. She loved us, didn't she? And we still did everything together—Mom, Vince, Susan, and I. She still acted the same toward me. But Vince would tell me things that got me confused and angry. Still, he was the one who always gave me attention.

"I love you, even if your mother doesn't," he would say, putting me to bed. He always made me feel special. It was always in secret, away from Mom.

Vince acted as if he loved Mom when he was with her. But as soon as she wasn't looking, he would roll his eyes. Like *we* knew the *truth* about Mom and what a *jerk* she was.

Looking back, Vince's anger toward his own mother seemed to transfer into anger at my mother. He had an underlying hatred for his mother and often wished her dead. It appears that, to Vince, these two "mothers" were one and the same.

I was so mixed-up. I wondered who loved whom. It was all so confusing. Was Vince on my side or Mom's side? Who did Vince love? I wanted desperately for things to make sense, but I always felt like my insides were twisting up. Why was I always getting so angry and upset? Mom, Vince, and Susan all seemed fine. What was wrong with me?

I remember an incident when I was ten, before Dad left. Mom, Vince, and I had gone to a horse show. I don't remember exactly what set me off that day, but it had to do with Mom and Vince again. I had that awful feeling. I remember running, leaving the indoor ring where Mom was riding. I ran and ran as fast as I could. It was pouring rain, but I didn't care. I felt like I would explode, so I just kept running through the rain. I ran toward our truck and horse trailer. I felt crazy and *bad.* I crawled under the truck to be alone. What was wrong with me? I felt so alone, like nobody could understand my feelings. I didn't even understand them! I wanted to just scream, to tear the bad feelings out of my insides. *I don't care about my life anymore*, I thought as I lay there in the muddy wet grass under the truck. *If I have to feel like this, I just don't want to live anymore. I deserve to feel bad. I am bad.*

Vince must have followed, because within minutes he was crawling under the truck to be with me. He cared! Vince knew how I felt, he said. He felt the exact same way! I didn't have to feel so alone, he said. He understood, and he said we shared the same feelings. He told me the rain was like teardrops, our teardrops. We were soaked, but we didn't care. He rubbed my forehead and stroked my hair. As he talked, the bad feelings started to go away. I didn't understand my emotions, but Vince seemed to. He said things that made my crazy feelings go away.

After Dad moved out, my crazy feelings got more intense and frequent—especially when we were all together at dinner. That was when I felt the worst. Vince would give Mom those lovey-dovey coy looks, the same looks he gave me when we were alone. He called her "Babe." Vince would look at Mom like he loved her so much, and then he would look over at me to see my reaction. Of course, when I got upset, he would look at me like I was crazy. One time I got so mad at him that I threw mashed potatoes in his face. Most of the time, I just got upset. Mom couldn't understand, so usually she told me to leave the table. If we were out to dinner, she would tell me to go sit in the car. Knowing full well that he got me upset, Vince would tell Mom that he would take care of it. Then he would come out to the car to calm me down. Mom never did. It was always Vince. He would talk in that secret, special, understanding way. I quickly forgot that he was "against" me and "for" Mom at the table. When it was just the two of us alone, he was on my side and understood my feelings exactly. He would tell me that I was very special, that he loved me, and that he didn't love Mom.

Vince liked New York City and wanted to take us to a restaurant there called Trader Vic's. I don't remember much about the dinner, but I do remember running out of the restaurant and into traffic, wishing a car would hit me. I wanted to run away from all my crazy feelings. I ran through the New York City streets, crying. I hated Vince and Mom. I felt someone grab me by the arm and was glad that Vince had come to rescue me. When Mom and Susan caught up to us, however, Vince held the arm of my coat like a leash and taunted, "Look, I'm walking the dog!"

Pretty soon I started to believe that I was crazy. What was wrong with me? Why did I always have to get upset and ruin everyone's evening? Why was I the one who always made things crazy, while everyone else seemed perfectly normal and happy?

Remembering this traumatic time in my life has been extremely difficult for me. These memories came later in my adult life, when I was at a low point and didn't want to live anymore. Most of these painful events had been blocked from my memory in order to survive, but recalling them was crucial to discovering the truth, so I could heal.

Our house in Bridleton was a converted stable with a courtyard in the middle. It was one story, shaped like a horseshoe, and all the rooms had windows into the courtyard. Susan and I each had a bedroom on the one side of the courtyard, and it was easy for us to see into the rest of the house. One night I looked out my bedroom window and saw Vince and Mom kissing in the dining room. I felt awful, betrayed. I hated Vince for lying to me, and I hated Mom, too. But most of all I hated the way I felt. Jealousy and anger burned inside of me. I called Susan to come and see, expecting that she would feel the same way that I did. Didn't she feel just *awful* watching them kiss? Didn't she just want them to stop? I was surprised to find that Susan didn't feel angry or jealous. She told me nothing was wrong and that I had better calm down. Didn't anyone feel like I did? Then I just snapped and went berserk. I threw my chair across the room and toppled the desk over. I beat my fists into the wall, and then started to go for the window. I wanted to smash it to pieces. It was like a dam had burst inside me, and all my anger was pouring out. I slammed my door again and again and again. I wanted them to hear me. I wanted them to stop kissing, and I wanted to die, all at once.

Mom and Vince came running in. They yelled at me as if I

were crazy. Maybe I was. Mom seemed angry, but confused. She didn't know what to do. Vince did.

"I'll handle this, Babe," he said in his usual way. He told Mom and Susan to leave the room, and then he held me close until my anger subsided.

Later that night I swore to myself that I would never *feel* that way ever again. Being totally out of control really scared me. I was so angry, strong, and powerful, and yet so weak and helpless that I just wanted to die. I could have killed myself to stop those bad feelings. I would rather be dead than feel that way again! Something was definitely wrong with me. Why didn't Susan feel the way I did? I must be the bad one, the crazy one. I didn't want Mom to hate me.

That would be the last time I outwardly showed my feelings about Mom and Vince. I decided that from then on, I would hide those feelings because something really *was* wrong with me. I wouldn't feel those feelings anymore, or if I did I would turn them into a kind of self-loathing.

The "bad me" feelings didn't go away, though. They were there, under the surface. So, I chose not to acknowledge them. I would hide them so well nobody could ever find them, not even me. *They weren't going to be me.* I was going to be good. The bad me was angry and mean and horrible. The bad me *was* me, though, down inside. Yeah, the real me, the bad me. I would keep *her* hidden forever.

Chapter 2
Pleasing Vince

We had outgrown our ponies, Flower and Catch Me, so Mom sold them and bought us a bigger pony. His name was Jack. It was Vince's idea to have me race him. Not Susan. Me. He wanted to help me get him fit for the kids' "pony races," short races (with no jumps) which were part of the steeplechase racing circuit. We all looked up to Vince, the expert on horses. Not only did Vince excel with show horses, he also had experience with fox-hunting and training some steeplechase horses.

Vince would train Jack with me. We'd do it together, just the two of us. "Your mother and Susan don't understand," he explained. They weren't to be included. The venture was ours, Vince's and mine. I didn't know anything about racing, but Vince said he would teach me. Vince would get all the racing equipment and everything I would need to train Jack.

Years later Mom explained that at the time, she was very happy that Vince showed an interest in me and that he encouraged me to ride in the pony races. When she first became friends with Vince, she had told him that my father favored my sister Susan, and therefore I was the one who needed more attention.

I isolated more and more and focused my thoughts on the pony races. This way nobody could hurt me, nobody could let me down. And anyway, if anyone got to know me they would think I was crazy. Maybe I was. I didn't relate at all to the kids at school and couldn't wait to get home to Jack. Driven by the force that was splitting me apart, I obsessed on getting Jack ready to race. Jack knew no fear, and I loved him for it. Jack was very tough and independent, and out in the paddock he would boss around the new horse that Mom bought for Susan. Jack won my respect, which was getting hard to do these days. We got along because we understood each other. At least, Jack put up with me. When I wasn't riding, I did schoolwork rather than face my inner turmoil. I stayed busy every minute.

As promised, Vince helped me train Jack. He took Jack's training very seriously, so therefore, I did too. He got a calendar out and told me I would do well to follow his rigorous training schedule. I was to jog Jack for twenty minutes a day, gradually building it up to forty minutes a day. Vince said this would build a strong foundation on Jack. (The pony races were only 3/8 of a mile, but Vince would train Jack like it was the 1 ¼ mile Kentucky Derby!) After two weeks of jogging, I could begin to gallop Jack. I wanted to please Vince so much that I stuck to his schedule exactly. I was determined. Nothing could stop me! After three weeks of galloping, Jack's fast workouts began. This was the really fun part. I would let him run as fast as he could for short distances. Vince had me do this two or three times a week for the last two weeks leading up to Jack's race.

Chapter 3
My First Pony Race

One month before my first pony race, I had my twelfth birthday; it was the best birthday ever. I got a brand new lightweight racing saddle, fully equipped with aluminum irons (stirrups) and elastic racing girths. I was thrilled. But it got even better. Mom and Vince drove me all the way to Long Island to get another present. I couldn't imagine what it could be. We pulled into Thyben's Saddlery, a tack shop across the street from Belmont Park Racetrack. Mom had ordered a set of racing silks for me! I had been drawing designs of racing silks on paper, just for fun, and Mom had used one of my patterns! They were forest green with a yellow hoop in the middle, and yellow hoops on the sleeves. At standard jockey size they were quite big on me, but they were the *real* thing.

Vince encouraged me to try the new saddle on Jack, to get him used to the feel of the elastic girths. I couldn't wait to go fast in a workout using the new racing saddle. The feeling was incredible. No longer was I worried about Mom, Vince, or anything. With no bulky saddle between us, Jack and I were racing as one, racing like the wind! Pulling up, I could see Vince smiling. He seemed pleased with my efforts.

Finally, the big day arrived. Jack was fit. I was ready. Ricky Hendriks, who came from Pennsylvania, was riding a little undefeated mare called Twin Nora. Ricky was only nine years old, but he was riding a champ. Twin Nora was a real thoroughbred, but being a twin, she never grew over pony size. She was beautiful, a miniature racehorse. Then there was Ricky,

Twin Nora and Ricky, Jack and me (12 yrs old)

who looked and rode like a professional jockey. I idolized him. Ricky and Twin Nora looked like they had come straight from Belmont Park!

Jack had early speed. We broke on the lead, saved ground, and led for most of the race. Jack hung in tenaciously when Twin Nora challenged him, but he was no match for the sleek little thoroughbred. She blew by us and won easily. We finished second in the field of eleven ponies, and I was so proud. I loved the fact that, in racing, things were black and white. There was no confusion. Winning was winning, and losing was losing. It didn't matter anyone's opinion. It wasn't how well you rode, or how much Vince approved. I understood *this* game. Even though I had very little chance of winning against Twin Nora, I absolutely lived for the pony races. As crazy as things were at home, the pony races kept me focused and sane.

My first pony race
Ricky 1st on Twin Nora, me 2nd on Jack (center)

Chapter 4
Confusing Roles

Mom and Dad's divorce was official. I guess that was all Mom and Vince were waiting for to make their wedding plans. Somehow though, I couldn't really believe they would ever get married.

Vince told Mom that he wanted to be a trainer at the racetrack. He told Mom that in order to get horses to train, he needed to start a business for injured racehorses. He explained that he would need a farm for these horses to recuperate and start in light training. Vince convinced Mom to sell the house in Bridleton and buy a bigger place where they could start this business after they were married. I had mixed feelings about them getting married, so I didn't think about it. I did think about the new farm we bought where I would be around lots of racehorses, bigger versions of Twin Nora. I was thirteen years old and my world was rapidly changing.

The day before we moved to our new place, Mom and Vince got married. Their wedding ceremony was small, with just the four of us and the neighbors. Now that they were married, I figured that Vince would finally leave me alone. All our furniture (except for Mom's bed) had been moved to our new farm, which was twenty minutes away. However, after the wedding, Vince didn't feel like driving out there and suggested that the four of us sleep on Mom's bed; Vince slept right between Mom and me. It was their wedding night, and we were still doing everything together.

My feelings about Vince were very mixed-up. He was my new "step-father," yet he was also my "secret boyfriend." I wanted Vince to forget about me, and yet I still wanted his attention and approval. I didn't know what I wanted. It was all so confusing.

At thirteen I wasn't at all sexually developed and had no interest in boys. I wanted to be a jockey, to be forever small and thin like a jockey. I was afraid that if I ever developed a woman's body, Mom would see me as direct competition for Vince as his *girlfriend*. I couldn't bear the thought. I felt enough guilt as it was. I didn't want Mom to know, and Vince wanted me to keep it a secret. I wanted Mom to love me. I didn't want her to think of me as "bad." I loved her and wanted her to be happy. I didn't want her to hate me. But, what did Vince want? Now that Vince had married Mom, did that mean he loved her? He always told me that he didn't. It was all so upsetting. I didn't want to think about it. Instead, I turned my thoughts to the racehorses and the new opportunities to work with them on the farm; maybe I would even get to ride them.

Life on the new farm was exhausting. There was so much work to be done. With ten horses in the big barn (we built this structure specifically for injured racehorses, complete with an indoor walking ring) and four more horses of our own in the little barn, there was time for little else. We got up early to take care of the horses before school and were right back in the barn helping out when we got home.

Vince was hardly ever around. At four-thirty every morning he would drive two hours to Aqueduct Racetrack on Long Island, where he exercised racehorses for a trainer. Even though training hours at the track were over by ten in the morning, Vince didn't get home most days until after six or seven at night. He claimed he was "getting business for the farm."

Mom never complained, nor did she question him. She just worked and worked, trying to please Vince. Money was always a problem. Vince took many horses on "deals" in order to "get horses to train." Mom was afraid to question Vince about the lack of money because it made him very angry. With fourteen horses to feed and care for, we were working around the clock and sinking deeper and deeper into debt. Things were not looking good. A few times Vince came into my room and took the money I was saving up to buy Mom a nice Christmas present. I began to stash away any money I got from Dad or Grandma, and told Vince that I was broke. I don't know if he believed me. I dreamed of the day when I would be a real jockey—riding races, making lots of money—and Mom wouldn't have to worry anymore.

I took extra special care of Jack. After all, he was like a racehorse now. One day I discovered a small bump on his leg and was worried. I showed it to Vince. He said it would be a good idea to have a specialist look at it. He was planning a trip to New Bolton Center, a top equine hospital in Pennsylvania, to have a few of the injured racehorses evaluated. Would I want Jack to go along?

How could I pass up the very best for my pony?

Vince and I headed out for Pennsylvania in the horse van. It was a long trip, but it would be worth it—for Jack. He would be getting the same treatment as the racehorses! After we arrived, the racehorses were led inside the clinic. Jack stayed on the van. The vet never did come to look at Jack, but Vince said the vet had assured him that Jack was fine. It was nothing serious, just a little "splint" which would heal.

Jack and me

It was late when we headed home. Four hours of bouncing up and down in the cab of the van was exhausting, so Vince told me to put my head on his lap. I didn't object much to it, but it was awkward as the gear shift was constantly getting thrust into my face. I wasn't comfortable. The bumps sent me upward into the steering wheel, then back onto his lap. I started to sit up, but Vince pushed my head back down against his groin. If I tried to sit up, he shoved me back down again. I pretended I was comfortable, just to keep him happy.

Halfway home Vince pulled over. We had horses in the van, so it surprised me that he wanted to stop. He said we were going to have a "special" dinner together, just the two of us. Immediately I felt guilty. *This should be happening to Mom, not me. She never gets to do anything with Vince.* I told him that I wasn't hungry and asked if we could just keep on going home. Ignoring me, he pulled into the parking lot of a restaurant with a statue of a Black Angus bull out front. I felt so guilty. *Bad me. Alone with Vince. I am so selfish. All I care about is myself... and Jack. What about Mom? What about all the work at home?*

We went in and Vince ordered the most expensive thing on the menu. I cringed, but he insisted. It all felt so wrong. He sat very close, like he was my boyfriend. *It should be Mom that he loves, not me. It's my fault. It's my fault he loves me and not Mom.* I couldn't wait to get out of there.

Normally, I would have blocked out this trip from my memory as I had so many other times when I was "alone with Vince." The pain and guilt of what happened later was too much to bear, so most of the "alone with Vince" memories were buried. But this was no ordinary day in history, and Vince assured me of that. While riding home in the horse van, news of President Nixon's resignation came over the radio. Vince said to me, "Never forget this day. Always remember where you were and who you were with when President Nixon resigned." And so, I did.

Chapter 5
Just Like Steve

Vince brought home many racing magazines. There were articles and pictures, beautiful photos of jockeys on racehorses. Maybe other kids were reading *Teen* magazine, but I collected and read every horseracing magazine I could get my hands on. Vince talked about Steve Cauthen, the sixteen-year-old riding sensation who had burst onto the New York racing scene. "The Kid" was becoming a legend, winning races at an incredible clip. He was riding Affirmed, the two-year-old champion colt. (Steve and Affirmed went on to make racing history, winning the Triple Crown the following year, when Steve had just turned eighteen!) I would go through the magazines and cut out the pictures of Affirmed with Steve Cauthen on him, one of which I put on the inside of my locker at school. It kept me going.

Steve was so perfect with that unique riding style of his—low, cool, and smooth as silk. He was the best jockey in the world. What if I could be like him, winning races and setting records in New York? I wouldn't need anyone then. I could escape all this insanity. I would be in control. I would just ride and ride and ride. Nobody would hate me. Steve looked so happy. If I could be like him, then I would be okay. I would be good, not bad. At that moment, I made a decision. I would dedicate my whole life to this one thing: I would be a great jockey, like Steve. At sixteen, I would be riding in New York, riding at one of the best tracks in the world.

I thought ahead, planning it all out. I would have to double up on courses in high school so that I could graduate early. No longer could I just fool around riding Jack. I had to be *good*. I watched films of Steve to study his style. I practiced twirling my whip, practiced my "seat," and watched the television show "Racing from Belmont" every Saturday night without fail. I read everything on racing that I could get my hands on. I studied photos of Steve and Angel Cordero, the best jockeys in New York, so I could imitate their riding style. Yes, I would ride just like them. I would do it. Do it or die.

After school I would ride Jack, training him for his upcoming race, but now I wanted more. I asked Vince if I could get on any of the racehorses, and he picked out an easy one for me to start on. I would pull my stirrups up short like a jockey and go fast. I loved this. I still loved Jack, but I needed to move on. Jack just wasn't fast enough, and this frustrated me. I wanted him to keep up with my fanatical pace. *Come on, Jack! Go faster! I have to be a race rider soon!* I wouldn't be sixteen soon enough, the age when I could get a professional jockey's license. I wanted it all, and I wanted it now.

I tried to keep my lofty goal to myself. I wanted Vince to get me started, but that was it. I would make it *on my own.* However, when Vince asked if I would like to go into Aqueduct Racetrack with him, I jumped at the chance. I had never been to a real racetrack before and even though it was a dismal place, it seemed like heaven to me. This was where Steve Cauthen rode! I had seen all the pictures, and now I was actually *here.* I vowed that Aqueduct would be the place where I would make it as a jockey. Just like Steve. *Just like Steve!*

Chapter 6
A New Challenge: Royal Star

I felt sorry for Mom. Not only was she overworked and tired, but she found out she was pregnant. Vince was never around to help with anything. I knew she loved him, but I also knew that he didn't love her. When my baby sister, Amy, was born, she brought hope to our failing farm. She was an incentive for all of us to make things work. Mom managed somehow. She was so strong; nothing seemed to dampen her spirits. There was never a task too difficult for her.

At fourteen, I couldn't relate to anyone at school. I was well-liked, so that was good. But I knew the truth. I knew who I really was. I couldn't wait to get away from all this. I had a dream, a big dream that I just *had* to make come true; I had to become someone else, a great jockey, so I would be worthy of living.

With the next season of racing approaching, I realized with sadness that Jack was never going to beat Twin Nora. For three years (and fifteen races) he had kept me sane and focused, but it was time to retire him. I certainly didn't expect the call I got a few weeks later.

Alan McChesney, one of my racing competitors from Pennsylvania, called to ask if I wanted to ride his pony in an upcoming race! Alan also wanted to beat Twin Nora, and thought his pony, Royal Star, was good enough to do it. He explained that he had just turned seventeen, too old to compete in the pony races, and now he needed a new jockey for Royal Star! Alan disclosed a secret to make me a believer. Royal Star was by Buffoonery, a thoroughbred sire from Maryland. A small thoroughbred was just what was needed to beat Twin Nora! From what I remembered of Royal Star, he was bigger boned than Twin Nora. He was unruly in the paddock and had trouble making it around the course on several occasions. Alan explained that he just had "bad racing luck," but I needed no explanation and no further encouragement. Here, at last, was my chance to win a race!

Pony races – Ricky 1st on Twin Nora (center),
Alan 2nd on Royal Star (right), and me 3rd on Jack

There wasn't much time until the Unionville race meeting in Pennsylvania. I asked Alan if Star was fit, and he said he had been turned out in a field all winter! However, Alan told me not to worry. It didn't take much to get Star fit.

"You don't know Star," Alan explained. "If I get him too fit, he becomes a rogue. He gets unmanageable. I can bring him up to you right away. I just got my driver's license. Would that be good?"

I was astounded. It was a three hour drive from Pennsylvania. Not only that, a major snowstorm was on its way. Negotiating our mountainous roads in a snowstorm with a horse trailer would be no easy task, especially for a new driver.

"It's your call, Alan. If you're up to driving in this weather, it's fine with me. The sooner I get to work, the better."

Alan was *so* bold. And I was *so* lucky!

When Alan brought Royal Star to our farm, I realized his pony was nothing like Twin Nora. She was sleek and beautiful. He was the opposite. He had bad feet, a skinny long neck, and a big head. I noticed lots of bumps and scars on his legs; he was far from fragile. Star's coat was long and scruffy from being turned out during the brutal winter months, but as I brushed it—lo and behold—there appeared a silky coat underneath! This was the smooth undercoat that only a thoroughbred racehorse possessed! Yes, Star had potential.

Vince took no interest in training Alan's pony. I was on my own. I jogged Star for a week and then, because the fields weren't cleared of snow, I took him to a dirt road to finally let him gallop. I had no idea what I was in for. He was twice as fast as Jack! Once he got going, I couldn't get him stopped. He ran as fast and far as he liked, until I was weak as a kitten and gave up. I knew then that my hardest job was not getting Star fit, but keeping him under control before, during, and after his race. I would try a new training approach. Jog. Just jog.

Ever since I got Star, Vince didn't take an interest in the pony races. I was working with Alan, and therefore, Vince couldn't control the situation. He didn't seem to care what happened with Royal Star; he wasn't there for Star's races and only wanted to be involved when it was just the two of us.

On race day, Vince wasn't there to help. Alan was in California, but he told me not to worry if things went wrong. In the paddock, all the other ponies were calm. Ricky and Twin Nora were cool and collected. Star was an uncontrollable maniac. He tried to run us down as we put the saddle on. After I got on him, he stood straight up in the air and struck out with his front legs. I kept my balance and hoped he wouldn't flip over backwards with me.

We managed to make it down to the start, with Royal Star pitching and lunging the whole way. He was rearing up when the race began. The other ponies shot ahead. When he finally came down, he took off. Before we had gone ten strides, huge racehorse strides, we sailed past everyone including Ricky. I hadn't planned on being in front this soon; I wanted another pony on my outside to hold Star in around the sharp turn. Star kept going straight, as all the other ponies made a perfect left-hand turn behind us. I looked back and saw Twin Nora leading the way (the other way). Luckily, there was fencing up ahead to block our way, which caused Star to head back on course. We were so far behind, yet he was eating up the ground with every stride. Could we make it? It didn't seem possible. As we headed toward the stretch, I saw Ricky easing up on Nora. Ricky thought he had the race won, but Star was gaining ground with each huge stride up along the fence. Zoom! We sped past Ricky right at the finish line. Ricky looked over at us in shock. We had won! Twin Nora's winning streak was finally broken!

At last! We (right) beat Twin Nora!

When I called Alan with the good news he was so excited. "What? Star beat Twin Nora? I knew he could do it, Karen!" There were two more races coming up, but I didn't even have to mention them. "Why don't you just keep Star until after the Andrew's Bridge and Brandywine race meetings?" he said enthusiastically. "This time I'll be there to see it!"

One week after my big win, Mom, little Amy, Susan, and I were off to Pennsylvania again. Royal Star acted his usual unruly self, but this time I wasn't so lucky. Instead of turning, Star went crashing through the woods and up a hill. We never finished the race.

The next race in Pennsylvania proved to be a repeat of Star's bad behavior at the start. However, the turn wasn't as sharp and we managed to catch Twin Nora and win by seven lengths!

Most of the kids who rode in the pony races during this time went on with racing in one way or another. Ricky Hendriks, Bernie Houghton, and Benny Guessford became steeplechase jockeys. Later Ricky became a trainer. Alan McChesney and I were the only riders "light" enough to become jockeys at the racetrack. I'll never forget Alan. He put me on my first winner!

Tenth grade was almost over. It was a tough year academically, but all the work didn't bother me. I was a winning jockey now! To my delight, Vince was planning on training some horses for the summer meeting at Monmouth Park Racetrack on the Jersey shore. I looked forward to working at a racetrack so I could get the experience I needed to ride races at sixteen. My goal was finally in sight!

Chapter 7
Summer at Monmouth Park

Summer came and Vince had six horses to train at Monmouth Park. I would be going to the track every day! I felt guilty leaving Mom behind on the farm, but I was on my way to becoming a jockey!

I was able to work at fifteen by getting special working papers. And work I did. I did everything for Vince. I groomed and walked the horses, cleaned the tack, did the stalls, but best of all I got to gallop three of the horses on a real racetrack!

Around 11:30 each morning we would finish up and go to breakfast. Instead of making the two hour drive back to our farm, Vince said we had to wait until 4:00 to give the horses their evening feed. It occurred to me that it would make more sense to head home and pay someone else to feed the horses, but I never said anything because I liked hanging around the track. After breakfast Vince would go to sleep in the tack room, and I would go off to watch the races. I went over to the starting gate and watched race after race. I studied the jockeys to see who left the gate the best, and how they did it. The starter noticed my interest and let me sit on the inside stall of the gate so I could see up close. I loved it. After the start, I would run to a nearby building to watch the rest of the race and the replay on the television monitor. Sometimes I would go over to the grandstand to watch the finish of a race. After six or seven races I would head back to the barn, where Vince would still be sleeping, or starting to feed the horses. I would help him finish, and then we would head back home.

At fifteen, I looked more like a nine-year-old. But I felt old. The clock was running. Tick, tick, tick. I would be sixteen soon, and I had to be riding races by then! Time was running out. I wouldn't let myself think about Mom back on the farm. I told myself that *nothing* would get in the way of my racing dream.

I dreaded the end of summer. I didn't want to go back to school. I just wanted to ride. But, inevitably, September did come.

It was the last day I would be at Monmouth Park. I was so torn. I didn't want to be away from the track. How could I go back to school after *this*? How could I stand eleventh grade after being here? I loved riding racehorses. How could I possibly *live* through another year of school?

As I prepared to leave Monmouth Park for the last time, I was so sad and depressed. Vince noticed. Trying to ease the blow, he promised me that he would take the horses to Garden State Park Racetrack for the fall so that I could continue to ride them down there. I looked at Vince, confused. He explained that instead of moving back to the farm, he would live down at Garden State Park Racetrack with the racehorses, and that he would come pick me up on the weekends. That way I could continue to gallop at the track on Saturdays and Sundays! This was something to look forward to, but it wouldn't be the same as riding them every day.

Before driving home on that last day, Vince said casually, "Let's go down to the beach and watch the waves come in." He tossed the Frisbee into the back seat of the car.

It was freezing cold on the beach. Fall had definitely arrived. The wind whipped across the sand, and the ocean looked dark and hostile. Vince and I walked across the beach. He held me to try to block the wind. I started feeling uneasy. Vince hadn't been paying much attention to me all summer, for which I was glad. It made things easier on me because I didn't have to feel guilty about him giving me the attention that belonged to Mom. I didn't feel bad about being at the track as long as he left me alone. I had been able to just concentrate on riding. But now, all of a sudden, here on the beach, Vince was looking at me *that way* again. Like, he really *cared* about me. He had that lovey-dovey strange look in his eyes.

Putting his jacket and arms around me, he shuffling me off to a secluded spot behind a sand dune, where there was less wind. We sat down. It felt very wrong. I didn't want to be there. I didn't want to be alone on the beach with Vince. It wasn't right. I wanted to get up and leave.

Vince put his arm around me. I was shocked and numb as I felt his hands slip under my shirt and over my bare, flat chest. I pretended that I didn't notice what he was doing and started to get up, but he told me to sit back down.

"Boy, it's cold! Let's huddle together to stay warm," he said, pulling my hands over and trying to place them inside his pants.

I was shocked. This was *wrong*. I pulled my hands back. Before I knew what was happening, he took off my shirt. I sat there numbly as he lifted his billowy shirt and brought me underneath it "to keep warm." I was going numb. Why was this happening? Why now? Why me? I was just a kid. He was my *stepfather!* I didn't want *this*. I didn't *like* it. The panic that raced through me was overcome by my extreme coolness. I talked about the ocean, how cold the wind was and, trying not to panic said, "We really should *go!*"

He tried to get me to lie down to get more out of the wind. I jumped up quickly saying, "Quick! Let's go! I'm freezing out here!" I grabbed my shirt and started to run toward the car. He followed behind me.

All the way home my mind was racing. I kept telling myself that this would not happen again. Vince meant nothing by it. It *won't* happen again. It *can't* happen again. I'm going to have to see him on the weekends *all by myself* if I want to continue galloping at the track. Stop thinking! Forget it. Everything will be fine. Everything will be all right. Nothing really happened. It was all just a misunderstanding.

Chapter 8
The Secret

A week later, Vince was settled in at Garden State Park Racetrack. He told Mom he was planning on living there as it was too far to commute every day to the farm. Garden State Park was located in Cherry Hill, a good three hour drive from our farm. He told Mom he would come home on Fridays to pick me up and again on Sundays to return me in time for school. Vince showed no concern for Mom or the farm. I felt so guilty. I would be seeing more of Vince than poor Mom. *Well, never mind. I have to do this. I have to, in order to make my goal.*

Vince came to pick me up that first weekend. I brought all of my homework with me and planned on staying busy studying in the afternoons. (Garden State Park had no racing as the grandstand had burned down in a fire. It was only serving as a training track at this time.) I had my sleeping bag with me. *Maybe I'm just overreacting. Maybe he isn't going to try anything, after all. I'm so young. I'm a tomboy. What had I done to cause him to touch me that way?*

On the way to Garden State Park, the more we drove the more I realized that there really was nothing to be apprehensive about. *He wouldn't touch me. He had thought about it and realized that he was wrong, and he was going to leave me alone.* As we approached Cherry Hill, Vince discussed dinner. He said we should have a really special dinner at a nice hotel where we could stay. I started to panic. My skin crawled. I felt that numb tingling sensation that real fear brings on. I tried to talk myself through the cold sweat. *No, it will be okay. He COULDN'T touch me.* I was scared and the numbness that had filtered across my entire body like a coating was now penetrating my mind. Being numb, I acted as though everything was fine. My feelings of terror had retreated to a place deep inside me. All that remained was the outside of me, a shell. I was shielded, protected, so that my logical mind could continue to function. My emotions were separate from me now—numbed, sealed off, and hidden away.

I brought up Mom and the farm, hoping this would make Vince think more clearly; it would remind him that he was *married* to my *mother*.

Vince stopped the car in front of a hotel near the track. He explained that he had checked the place out, and that there was a nice restaurant inside. I still wouldn't accept that anything bad would happen.

We sat down to dinner. I felt strange. Vince was treating me special, like an adult. Like a girlfriend, like he was in love with me, the way he should have been with Mom. *Why? Why now? Why me?* He told me how special I was, and how I was such a good rider. He went on and on about how much he could teach me on the weekends. He told me he wanted to spend time with me because he *loved* me so much. It was all so confusing. I knew

I was in trouble, and I knew I was alone.

We finished dinner and went upstairs to the room. I hoped that there would be two beds. There was only one. One big bed. My fears were being realized. *This is really happening to me. This isn't just a bad dream.* I hadn't imagined that incident on the beach. This wasn't my imagination, either. *This is really happening to me. No! It can't be. I'm in trouble. How am I going to deal with this?*

I became numb. I was like a hollow shell, void of feelings. I felt like I was playing out a part in a play. I was really someplace else and my body was somebody else's, not mine. This was not really happening to me at all.

Vince told me to get into the bed. I said I wanted a bedroom with two beds, and that I was only comfortable in a bed of my own. He reassured me that everything would be all right. "Just relax," he said, disappearing into the bathroom.

I got into the bed with all my clothes on. I was frozen with fear. When I saw Vince come out of the bathroom, I was stunned. He was completely naked. I could see his "thing" sticking out. It was awful. I was appalled and scared and felt like he was a total stranger. He crawled into the bed next to me. He started to take off my clothes. I tried to stop him, to reason with him, but he took my clothes off anyway. I hated my body. *Why did I have to be there?* He touched me in places I started to hate. I hated my body. *Why did I have to be there, in my body?* I trembled but tried to stay cool. Stay cool. Don't panic. He tried to push himself inside me.

"NO! NO!" I yelled and pushed him away. "PLEASE don't do this. Don't do this to me!" My mind raced.

"Why not?" he asked.

How do I stop him? I had to stop him. "It's not right. You're married to Mom. I'm only fifteen. It's against the law!" I pleaded with him. I knew I would be sixteen soon, and this excuse would no longer be valid, but right now—just for now—I prayed it would work. I said anything I could think of as an excuse without hurting his feelings or getting him mad. I didn't want to hurt him, but I wanted him to *stop.* I had to do something to put off....the inevitable. *If I can just get him to stop, right now, maybe it would all go away.*

Vince said, "You might bleed."

I was so *frightened.*

I don't remember if he raped me that night or the next. I just told myself it wasn't really happening. I was bad, very bad, very bad. I was horrible, so horrible, so horrible. I remember looking in the bathroom mirror in that hotel room. Seeing myself naked, I hated my body. I remember trying to find a towel to wipe off the mess he made and to cover me, wanting to cry, but far too numb to do anything, to feel anything at all.

I became very good at blanking things out. It was the only way I could survive the unthinkable. There was me, awful me, and then there was Karen that everyone else saw differently.

The hotels stopped after the second weekend I spent with Vince. I guess he had decided that once he had me away from home, he could do anything to me anywhere he wanted to. His dirty, filthy tack room became the next scene of the crime, the place of all my hidden horrors.

During the week, I pretended as if nothing had happened to me. It was like what happened wasn't real. I tried to block it out of my mind; I tried to live on as if I were the same, as if nothing had happened and nothing would happen again. But I wasn't the same. Something had been torn out of my insides. I was just an empty shell. Could anyone tell? I still went to school. I still took care of the horses. I rode, but felt weak, very weak and out of control of my life. My urge to ride races was dampened, confused. I was in a dreamlike, surreal state. All I wanted to do was survive, get through every day of this nightmare. I couldn't face Mom. She would *hate* me if she knew. She would *kill* me.

When Vince would come to pick me up for the weekend, he would look at me in that lovey-dovey way—right in front of Mom! I died. What if she suspected? I couldn't look at Vince. I was so scared that Mom would know. I felt so guilty, so bad. All

I tried to think of was my purpose for going, to get on the racehorses. I blanked out the fear and reality of what else was going to happen at Garden State Park. I kept fooling myself into pretending he wouldn't touch me. I still brought my sleeping bag and school books along.

At Garden State Park Vince slept in the tack room of the barn. He slept on a dirty little cot with dirty horse blankets and an old smelly brown pillow with no cover on it. He smelled. The whole room smelled. In the dingy little room was Vince's cot, a little tape player on a shelf above the cot, and a little heater up by the ceiling in the far corner. He would always put the tape in with the song "Landslide" by Fleetwood Mac. The heater hummed away and made the place so hot and stuffy that everything—the smell, the filth, the confinement—choked me. My sleeping bag stayed on the floor, on the dirty floor. I couldn't convince him that I belonged *in the sleeping bag*, and *not* on his cot. The cot was too small, I would argue. I never won the arguments. In the mornings I would crumple up my sleeping bag in fear, so that if anyone looked in, the sleeping bag would look slept in. Vince would ask me in the morning if I was sore. *Of course I was!* I felt like I couldn't walk, let alone get on horses. But I did. I was determined not to let him ruin my riding career, as well. I would try to clean myself up in the filthy bathroom of the barn. There was no toilet paper or shower in the brown, damp, smelly place. There was just a toilet with no seat and a brown rusty sink. Actually, going to the bathroom hurt tremendously, so I would hold my breath and try not to cry.

Vince had his vet friend, Eric, come over and visit with us in the tiny tack room. They smoked pot together. I felt very strange, left out. I guessed they spent a lot of time together during the week when I wasn't around. I wondered if Eric "knew." I wondered if Vince had told him what he had been doing to me, and if they had laughed about it together. I wondered what Eric thought of me. What did he think when he left us alone together and locked in for the night? I was scared to death that we would be discovered. I studied Eric's expressions. Yes, he must have known. He smiled a lot. It was like Vince and Eric were conspiring together, maybe about what Vince was going to do to me next. Or, maybe he didn't know. I looked so young.

Vince drank Dubonnet, a type of wine, at the barn. He and "Bubba" the black groom who was also Vince's assistant trainer, took turns drinking out of the bottle. They kept the bottle hidden in a bag of oats in the feed room, not wanting Mary Sue, Bubba's wife, to find out about it. Mary Sue was totally opposite Bubba. He was quiet and even-tempered. She was big, had bleach blonde hair, and voiced her opinion about everything. Vince laughed at the fact that Mary Sue wouldn't approve of the Dubonnet. He liked the fact that they were "getting away with it" behind her back. It seemed like Vince had these little secrets with every person he came in contact with, me included. I was sure that Bubba and Mary Sue were unaware of what Vince was doing to me. They were both so nice. Mary Sue treated me like a daughter. In fact, a few years later I heard she had a little girl and named her Karen, after me.

One time Bubba and Mary Sue left for the weekend, and Vince convinced me to watch a football game in their room. Their room was next to Vince's, on the end of the barn. It was a bigger room and didn't smell as dirty as Vince's. There were no chairs to sit on, just a big bed with a television set. I didn't want to be on their bed, but didn't have a choice. We were watching the game. Vince raped me again, right there on their bed! I was so afraid. What if they came back and caught us? Walked right in, while...ugh. I couldn't bear it. I felt so horrible and ugly. I was scared to death of leaving a blood stain on their bed, or that somehow they would find out. I liked Bubba and Mary Sue and didn't want them to hate me. I couldn't have felt any lower than I did that day. Vince was totally unaffected by the whole thing, as if it were a perfectly ordinary thing to do on a Sunday afternoon. Nights were nightmares, but now even my days weren't safe.

After training hours, we had all day to kill. I remember one afternoon I was trying to do my homework in the tack room. I had pushed the door wide open so that if anyone passed by they would see me doing homework. I was reading a book that I had to finish for school. Vince knew how important my homework was to me. I was surprised when he came in and made me put the book down. He shut the door behind him. That day I was so afraid of being found out. Bubba and Mary Sue were in the next room, and Eric might stop in. Later that afternoon Vince took me into Cherry Hill. We went to a nice place for lunch. I felt like a secret lover. I was embarrassed to be seen with him. What did people in the restaurant think? Did they know? Could they tell from my face? Did they notice the way he *looked* at me? Did they think he was my father or my boyfriend? Of course, I knew they wouldn't ask.

On the fourth weekend I spent at Garden State Park, I turned sixteen. For my birthday, Vince gave me two pieces of jewelry. I hated them. They were *evidence*. I tried to figure out how I could get rid of the jewelry—so Mom wouldn't find out—and still keep the gifts so Vince wouldn't be hurt. I was appalled and confused by the whole thing. *How could he give these to me? Was he stupid? I don't have a boyfriend! Who can I say gave these to me? Mom will know!* One was an emerald bracelet; the other was a gold bracelet with little love hearts that made me feel sick to my stomach when I looked at them.

We had a small birthday party outside the barn: Vince and I, Bubba, Mary Sue, and another couple we knew. It was so awkward. I wondered what everyone thought when Vince gave me the jewelry and looked at me with that lovey-dovey face. I quickly put the bracelets away, hoping that nobody had paid much attention to the expensive gifts. I barely thanked Vince. I was embarrassed and amazed. He thought nothing of presenting this evidence—in front of everyone!

I don't remember every incident when Vince forced himself on me. As I said before, I was good at blanking things out, erasing them from my memory. I could block out what was happening even as it happened. When he was on top of me on that cot I would mentally leave my body. I would focus on the noisy heater in the corner, up by the ceiling. I pretended I *was* that heater, way up in the corner of the room, away from Vince. This distracted me from what he was doing. The physical pain was severe. He would tell me to relax. *Relax???* I was frozen with fear. Fear of the pain, fear of what he was doing, and fear of getting caught. Sometimes Vince wouldn't lock the door. What if someone walked in?

Vince would put his face *down there*...I felt *so* dirty. Then he would bring his contorted face up to mine—I couldn't bear to look at it—forcing his tongue into my ear, or into my mouth. When he stuck his tongue in my mouth, I used this as a diversion from reality. I would fight back, my tongue against his. I would push it away, then duck and dodge it, then push it away again. It would distract me from what was going on down there. My tongue fought and my eyes stayed fixed on the heater.

Arguing or pleading with Vince never worked. "What about Mom? Don't you love her? Shouldn't you be doing this to *her?*"

"I never loved your mother. I love you," was always his reply. Did this make it okay to do "it" to me because he loved me? I thought about how much Mom loved Vince and couldn't understand why he didn't love her back. She loved him so much. Why me? Why this? Mom would *kill* me if she ever knew.

I said to Vince, "If Mom ever finds out, I'll kill myself. I mean it. I really will." And I meant it more than anything. *I should be dead. How can I do this to my mother?*

I didn't know how to reason with Vince. I didn't know how to fight back mentally, physically, or emotionally. I couldn't get away, and he made it out that he was doing something wonderful! He knew I had to endure pain, yet it never once stopped him. Time and time again I told him that if Mom ever found out, I would kill myself. That didn't seem to bother him, either. He acted as though nothing was wrong. Why couldn't he love Mom this way, and just love me like a step-daughter? It was all my fault, that's why. I had taken away his love for Mom, and I *hated* myself for it.

Chapter 9
Meeting My Idol, Steve Cauthen

There was one highlight among my trips to Garden State Park. Steve Cauthen, my idol, was going to be there to film a Trident gum commercial! Five other jockeys were supposed to be part of it. One of them, Cash Asmussen, never showed up. I was ready! Having brought my racing silks from home, I hoped that maybe—just maybe—if one of the jockeys didn't show up, I could be involved. Vince and I went over to the starting gate where the commercial was to be filmed. There was Steve! He was standing next to a food table and talking with the camera crew. The other jockeys were milling around the table, too. Vince brought me over to meet Steve. Steve had these incredible hands, so large, as he reached out to shake my hand. As he withdrew his hand I watched him knock over a gravy boat. He was embarrassed; I was in awe.

Everyone was waiting for Cash Asmussen to arrive. They needed one more jockey before they could begin filming. As soon as it became obvious that Cash wasn't going to make it, I jumped into action. I begged Vince to get me into the commercial. They were going to be breaking horses from the starting gate, and I desperately needed this experience in order to ride races!

It wasn't going to be easy. The first job was convincing the man who ran the racetrack that I was old enough to have a license. (At the time of the commercial, I had not yet turned sixteen.) I had never broken out of the starting gate. In the commercial, all the horses were supposed to come out of the starting gate except for Steve's mount. The camera would focus in on Steve who was still in the gate, "busy chewing his Trident gum." Steve was on one of those New York City carriage horses. They weren't trained to run or come out of the starting gate. The old horse was supposed to just stand there as the racehorses came running out. As was the case with most commercials, many takes were necessary, so three sets of horses would be used for the commercial. Each set of horses would break from the gate twice (more than twice would be too much for these high-strung animals), giving Trident six different shots to choose from. It was a unique experience for me to not only ride three different horses, but to break from the gate six times!

Vince convinced the man in charge of the track that I was sixteen and had a license. I agreed, saying that I had experience at the starting gate (of course, I didn't elaborate that my experience was limited to close observation). The plan worked, and I got to put on my silks.

The first horse I got on was huge. The girl leading him around was quite worried about me. She wondered if I could handle Big Jake. After all, I looked like a baby and only weighed eighty-two pounds. I reassured her that very soon I would be riding races and that I would take good care of her Jake. I was thrilled to be on a new horse, one that Vince didn't train. This would test my riding skill, as well as be a chance to practice all I had learned about leaving the starting gate at Monmouth Park.

As we loaded into the gate, I whispered to the assistant starter next to me that it was my first time coming out. He told me to wrap some mane around my index finger and to leave more slack in the reins. There I was, gripping the mane of a strange big horse standing in the narrow metal stall of the huge starting gate. I looked through the iron doors in front of me to the empty racetrack ahead, waiting for the doors to open. I knew it was important that I stay straight after the break so that I didn't bother the other horses around me. I pictured an imaginary straight line down the track. Bang! The doors opened and my horse surged forward. I felt the incredible force of power beneath me as his hind end dropped down then catapulted forward. We went from a standstill to top speed within a few strides. I felt a rush like nothing before and desperately tried to stay with him. Thank God I had wrapped—embedded—my finger into his mane. I stayed forward with him as he surged ahead with the other horses.

I had a blood blister from wrapping the mane around my

finger so tightly, but by the sixth start I was much more relaxed and breaking in front of the others. Those long summer days I had spent watching start after start at Monmouth Park Racetrack were paying off.

I never did get to see the Trident commercial on television, but that was of little consequence. What was important to me was meeting Steve Cauthen and gaining the invaluable experience I needed to make my goal.

Chapter 10
Traumatic Decision

Vince decided he was going to take the racehorses to Hialeah Park, a racetrack in Florida, for the winter. He gave no consideration to Mom. He thought nothing of leaving her behind on the farm for the brutal winter months. Financially, going to Florida was a bad decision. Vince didn't have good enough horses to race at Hialeah Park, Florida's competitive winter race meeting. But when it came to racing, Vince was the expert so nobody ever questioned him.

Thinking back on this, maybe the reason Vince wanted to go to Florida was so that he could get me away, alone for the winter. Also, he could use Florida as an escape, a way to avoid the farm, the responsibilities, and Mom.

When Vince told me of his decision to go to Florida (leaving the farm, Mom, Susan, and Amy behind), he knew I would want to go. He knew I wanted to ride—no matter what. He had even been trying to convince me to quit school. I was terrified at the prospect of going to Florida and being alone with Vince all the time. But I wanted to stay with the racehorses, and Vince knew it. He told me school was not important. He said I was a good rider, and he needed me in Florida.

My immediate reaction was to protect myself. I told him that I *wouldn't* go with him unless Mom came along. If she was around, maybe then Vince wouldn't be able to get me off alone. Vince was angry at this. He didn't want Mom to go to Florida. But I wouldn't give in. I just hoped he would believe that I wouldn't go unless Mom went, too. (Riding was so important to me that I honestly don't know what decision I would have made about Florida, had he not agreed to let Mom come along.) Vince was convinced that I meant what I said. So he agreed, saying, "If your mother wants to come, then I guess I'll have to put up with her."

The next problem I faced was Mom. How could I convince her to leave the farm—the horses, the animals, the responsibilities—just to up and leave it all behind? Mom was so responsible. And what about Susan? I didn't know what she would do. She wasn't interested in the racehorses and was in her senior year of high school.

How would I convince Mom to go to Florida? It was an irrational decision, and Mom was totally unaware of my dilemma. She trusted Vince. However, my grandmother didn't. Grandma (Mom's mother) disapproved of Vince and sensed something was very wrong with letting me go alone with him. Grandma insisted that Mom go, too.

It all happened so suddenly. I don't remember leaving the farm. I don't remember saying goodbye to Jack, or the animals, or my room, or anything. I don't remember packing. I don't think I wanted to see what I was doing to my family, breaking them up by leaving my sister, Susan, behind. I felt so guilty and hated myself, so I just wouldn't allow myself to think of anything but my goal.

For years after leaving the farm I had reoccurring nightmares about it. Many a night for years afterward I would wake up in a cold sweat. Jack was still in his stall, skinny and starving to death, waiting for me to come home to feed him. The cats had many litters of kittens, which were also starving to death. The food in the kitchen was growing mold. My schoolwork was still on my desk, all dusty and unfinished. The house was awaiting our return, which never happened. In my dreams everything was still there, unchanged and the way I remembered it. Also, since leaving the farm I had this new fear of losing my things. I felt out of control, and my belongings since that time acquired an unhealthy amount of value. I became obsessed with my "stuff," clinging to it desperately and accounting for each thing one by one. My whole life seemed to be spinning out of control, with changes taking place both inside and outside of me, all based on Vince's latest whims.

We left the farm—Vince, Mom, Amy, and I—with very few of our possessions. The bare necessities (a cot, a mattress, a card table, and some clothes) were put on the horse van and shipped down with the racehorses. The four of us made the trip crammed into Vince's Volkswagen Beetle. Susan stayed behind and moved in with Grandma. The rest...blank it out.

I wouldn't look back, only ahead. I focused on what I needed to do: ride races at sixteen years old.

Chapter 11
Struggles and Frustrations

Thank God Mom came to Florida. She seemed like the only sensible person around. All I cared about was riding, and Vince was in his own world. When we first got to Miami, Mom went looking for a place for us to stay. Vince's horses were stabled at Hialeah Racetrack. As we had only one car (which sounded like it would conk out at any second), Mom searched the area nearby the track. She found a place across the street from Hialeah Racetrack, in a Spanish apartment complex. It was tiny but close—and affordable. Actually, the little apartment was perfect. If we needed anything there was a grocery store downstairs, and Mom could walk to the track if she had to. Money, as usual, was a definite problem. But Mom solved this in her typical upbeat way. She started drawing charcoal portraits of racehorses and sold them for whatever she could to pay the rent. They were pretty good, too. Eventually she experimented with pastels, painting portraits of specific horses for the grooms, exercise boys, and trainers on the backstretch. It was a good

One of Mom's pastels

thing Mom made some money to pay for food and the rent because Vince never offered to pay for anything—except dinner if we went out.

I would look for quarters around the phone booths and newspaper vending machines near the backstretch track kitchen (cafeteria). Vince was always trying to get me to go off alone with him. Sometimes we would go over to the empty grandstand to look for spare change in the Hialeah Park water fountain. Vince never seemed embarrassed when someone would wander by and stare at us as we waded through the fountain with our pants rolled up.

In the early mornings, I would get on Vince's horses. They were hard-headed, strong, and ill-mannered. They threw me many times, ran off with me on the track, and never did what I wanted them to. I didn't know it at the time, but these were definitely the toughest racehorses I would ever have to deal with. I took it in stride, though. I thought all racehorses were crazy.

One day the outrider (the person who helps catch loose horses or horses that are running off with their riders) confronted Vince. I was coming back off the track when I saw her scowl. She turned to Vince and then pointed back toward me. "Why do you let that young little boy get on those crazy horses?"

Me at Hialeah (16 yrs old)

Then there was the day I was sick with a high fever. Vince had no sympathy. "If you're ever going to make it as a jockey, you'd better be tough. Come out to the barn. You won't do any good staying in bed."

I quickly searched the bathroom medicine cabinet for something to make me feel better. I found two cold medicines, Nyquil and Contac, and took them both. Later, out on the track, the dizziness was so severe that I lost my balance and fell off. The outrider was right there watching me. I was so embarrassed. I explained to her that I really was a good rider, but that I was sick. She glared at Vince. Vince gave us an annoyed look and walked off.

"Come on," she said in an understanding way, "Let's get you back to the barn. You really shouldn't be riding when you are sick."

A few trainers near Vince's barn were noticing my determination in the face of adversity. They let me get on a few of their horses. I did really well, and the trainers were pleased. Slowly I was beginning to realize that other racehorses were actually *easy* to ride. Maybe I was ready to ride races, after all. I couldn't wait to be free, out of Vince's control and riding for other trainers.

School was still an issue. I desperately wanted to graduate. How could I ride at the track and go to school at the same time? Mom took me down to the local high school, Hialeah High. It was filled with mostly Spanish-speaking Cuban students. Most of the students looked like they were in their twenties. I looked so out of place, as if I belonged in the sixth grade. I was so small and thin, with that freckled baby face. My body wasn't developed at all. But I was thankful for my youthful appearance. I thought that if I had breasts, what happened with Vince would have been more my fault. At least, looking at my small body, I felt less guilty for what had happened. It was the only evidence I had that *maybe* it wasn't my fault, that maybe I *hadn't* done anything to ask for it.

I wasn't ready for what I was about to experience in the new school. Hialeah High was much more advanced than the high school I had attended in New Jersey. I was used to getting an A in every subject, but now I was totally lost in the math and foreign language classes. Not only was I frustrated by this, but I had to be in class by seven o'clock. The track opened at six a.m., which only gave me one hour (in the dark) to get on horses. It was not fun. I would get nowhere this way. I hated school. I hated going home, too. I had to face Mom—with Vince right there. Whenever Vince would take us out to dinner, he would have that strange lovey-dovey look on his face and stare right past Mom, directly at me. I died inside. The guilty feelings and the fear that Mom would know were so intense. But I couldn't express any of this. I stayed numb, burying all my feelings so that I was really just depressed. *I have to ride races. I have to be a jockey now. I can't take any more of this.*

I looked forward to the weekends. Without having to rush off to school, I was able to get on five or six horses in the mornings. Sometimes Vince would take me to Calder Race Course, where the races were being held (Hialeah Park's winter race meeting hadn't started yet). I didn't like being alone with him, but as long as we were at the races or some other public place, I felt I was safe. He didn't give up trying, though. One time at the barn when we were finishing up, he tried to lure me into the feed room. His advance took me quite off guard; I thought he had finally decided to leave me alone. I was angry and pushed him away. My reaction surprised us both—neither one of us expected that I would actually stand up to him.

Our tiny apartment had two rooms with a walk-through kitchen in the middle. Mom and Vince slept in the back room on a mattress on the floor, and Amy stayed on small mattress beside them. I slept on a cot in the front room. In the mornings, I would wake up to find Vince kissing me on the neck. I was paralyzed with fear at these moments. If Mom ever woke up and saw him kissing me...I would push him away and point back to the bedroom, where Mom was.

Vince always told me what a bad mother Mom was. He was extremely annoyed that she was always around. He was mad that Mom was worried about money, and he was angry that she was in Florida, making it hard for him to get me alone.

One day I was extremely upset at school. I hated not being able to follow along in class, not being able to understand what was being taught. The classes were large, so the teachers had no time to stop and explain things to "the new kid." Everything moved so fast. They spoke in Spanish a lot, only making things more difficult for me. Vince came that day to pick me up—to sneak me out of classes early. I was so frustrated. I didn't know what to do or who to turn to for help. I remember sitting in his Volkswagen with him, talking about my classes. I was in tears. Vince tried to convince me to quit school, right then and there. But I was still determined to graduate. I was a good student, wasn't I? Why did this have to be so hard? I was so frustrated, and Vince was only making it worse. I wanted to scream, to let out all my anger and frustration.

Finally, I lost control. As Vince talked, I slouched down into the bucket seat and put my feet up on the windshield. All the anger I had been suppressing was right below the surface, about to come pouring out. I braced myself against the seat and let all the anger come out, right from my guts, into my legs, and out through my sneakers. I pushed really *hard* against the windshield with my feet. I was so *angry*. The windshield cracked under the pressure. I was shocked to see the force that had come out of me, but I was glad. I was glad I had broken his windshield. After that, Vince ditched the car. He abandoned the Volkswagen somewhere, telling Mom it was "on its way out."

Not knowing what to do about school, I remembered the postcard my father had recently sent me. He had just remarried and was on his honeymoon. Maybe I should give him a call. He should be back in New Jersey by now. Dad, being a teacher, might know what to do about my school dilemma. Maybe he could tell me how to finish school without having to go back to Hialeah High. I was never going back there.

I decided to give Dad a call. I was very emotional on the phone. I told my father that I just *had* to quit school—but I still wanted very much to graduate. Dad was so sensible. He brought up another alternative, a very practical one; he suggested night school! Dad told me to check out the night school programs in the area, and he would find out what remaining credits I needed to get my diploma.

Chapter 12

At Sixteen: A Driver's License, Jockey's License, and High School Diploma

The law in Florida allowed a person to apply for a driver's license at age sixteen. I couldn't pass up this opportunity. If I could drive, I would be free. But first, I needed a car. Where could I get a car to take my driver's test? Grandma! I called her to tell her I needed a car to take my driver's test. She immediately arranged with her friends in Florida to have an old Chevy Duster delivered to our apartment.

"How is your mother ever managing with a baby and no car?" she asked.

I reassured her that things weren't as bad as they seemed. "It's okay, Grandma. We ride bikes!" (We had borrowed Bubba and Mary Sue's bikes, and Mom had a bike with a baby seat.)

Mom drove me to the motor vehicle place. I had very little experience with driving, but this didn't stop me. Even though I knocked over three cones while parallel parking, I passed.

As the man signed the papers and handed me the finished application, he asked, "You *were* aiming for those orange cones, weren't you?" Then he winked and smiled. Did that mean I got my license? They took my picture, laminated it, and handed me my ticket to freedom.

With my driver's license and a car, I could now drive to the Miami Lakes Adult Education Center to take the two classes I needed to get my diploma. After all the frustrations of Hialeah High, this felt far too easy. It seemed like I was somehow cheating my way into getting a diploma.

The guilt over this "easy way out" turned into another one of my reoccurring nightmares. Along with our abandoned farm animals, Hialeah High frequented my dreams for years to come. These dreams would always be the same: I'm still at Hialeah High trying to stick it out until the end of the school year, trying to graduate the "right" way. But always, before graduation, I leave Florida to go north with the racehorses. I am never able to finish out the year. Each year in my dream, I get a little closer to graduation day, but I never finish, never see it through, and I have to come back the following year to start all over again.

I was living with the feeling of impending doom, this terrible fear that Mom would find out about the secret. In order to put this out of my mind, I became more obsessed with riding races. I was more driven than ever to get my jockey's license. In order to get it, I had to ride in two races. Vince had promised to put me on a horse (in a race) soon.

Finally, the long-awaited day arrived. On April 28, 1979, Vince let me ride Northern Snipe in a race at Hialeah Park. I finished second!

Vince was surprised that I rode the horse so well. I had saved ground on the turn and urged Northern Snipe strongly through the stretch. This was noteworthy since the horse had run a dismal race a week prior, beaten sixteen lengths under top jockey Donald MacBeth.

My first race
Hialeah paddock (16 yrs)

My first race
Northern Snipe finishes 2nd

Some of the jockeys, trainers, and agents seemed impressed with my first race. Of course, they didn't put two and two together—that I was the little freckled-faced kid who got run off with every morning!

Leaving the races that day, I heard comments from some of the hardcore bettors.

"The girl, she looks good on a horse."

"She has a good 'seat,' especially for an apprentice. Smooth, you know—unusual for a 'bug' (apprentice) rider. I think that was her first race."

"Really? Well, I didn't bet on her. She finished second and blew my exacta. The girl saved ground. Maybe I'll bet on her next time. You sure that was her first race?" These words rang in my ears as I headed back to the apartment, pleased with myself. *Smooth for an apprentice.* That was what I wanted. After all, I had spent hours in front of my mirror, copying Steve Cauthen's style. It was imperative that I look good on a horse, because off a horse I appeared so young and innocent—and looks can be *so* deceiving.

Two days later I rode another longshot for Vince, and with my second race under my belt, I secured my official jockey's license.

Well, it was done. At sixteen, I had my driver's license, my jockey's license, and my high school diploma was on its way in the mail. I was free, and yet I wasn't. Why didn't I feel like a new person?

I had thought riding races would cure me, make me worthy; however, getting my jockey's license wasn't a cure-all. It didn't fix the bad me who was hidden deep inside. But it did make living bearable. Like taking a pain killer, riding and staying too busy to think did have a numbing effect. It was a giant distraction from reality. But deep down the problem—the real me, the bad me—was still there, buried somewhere below the surface.

We left Florida, packed into Grandma's old Chevy Duster, destination, Monmouth Park. I hated that trip. Vince made me drive most of the way. I was nervous because I had to drive at night on unfamiliar highway, with my family's life in my hands. I tried hard to stay awake. My hands were clenched tightly around the steering wheel, my eyes wide. I stared ahead at the dark highway, the white line coming at me, seemingly without end. It was exhausting. I broke out in a sweat when Vince put his hand on my leg. Mom and Amy were asleep in the back seat. *Why couldn't he just leave me alone?*

Chapter 13
My First Win

Mom, Vince, Amy, and I moved into the upstairs of a two-family house, right near Monmouth Park Racetrack. Around them, I felt numb most of the time. I liked having the privacy of my own bedroom. It became my sanctuary. I could shut out the world and control the stuff in my small bedroom. It was like the part of me where the secret was hidden could finally expand and fill the room—my room. I could let my guard down without fear of being discovered. I could be sad and depressed. I could be the real me, and not worry about it showing on my face. My bedroom door stayed closed, and I became very protective of my place of refuge. Outside my bedroom door I went into hiding again; I hid the real me beneath the happy facade of Karen the jockey. Living in the house with Mom, Vince, and Amy was extremely difficult for me. Vince ignored Mom. He was so impatient with her. I felt guilty. *It was all my fault.* I couldn't take being around the two of them, so I buried myself in thoughts of my riding career.

Grandma took the Chevy Duster back after we drove it up from Florida. Vince then got an old beat-up used car, but it didn't last long. He abandoned it less than two weeks after we had moved in. Once again, Bubba and Mary Sue's bicycles became our only means of transportation. Vince and I rode the bikes to work every morning. I felt so guilty riding next to him. Could people tell? Did they notice the way he looked at me? What did everyone think about us? At the barn, I ignored Vince. I couldn't wait to get off his last horse, so I could go to other barns and convince different trainers to use me as their jockey.

On the bicycle, away from Vince and Mom, Karen the jockey took over. She was free. I pedaled around from barn to barn, trying to get my new career started. I was willing to ride anything for anybody. All I wanted was a chance to prove myself as a race rider. I had so much confidence in myself as a rider and this covered up the horrible, self-doubting person that I was inside. It's like I was a different person on the outside. Karen the jockey was outgoing, friendly, and confident. She was very strong. Being Karen the jockey made it possible for me to survive, to exist. As long as I could be a good rider and keep up the "good me" image, I felt like I would be okay. The real me—the broken, horrible me—I learned to block out. Pretty soon the bad me became buried, nonexistent at the track. I only remembered who I really was when I saw my mother or was back in the house. Yes, Karen the jockey was taking over.

I managed to persuade Ed Rubenstein, a jockey agent, to watch me ride and consider "taking my book," the racetrack expression meaning to book my mounts or work for me. Ed was skeptical at first. He had been around the track a long time and said that he hadn't yet seen a girl who could ride well. I told Ed that before long I would be getting mounts, and he always countered with, "You'll be going back to school at the end of the summer."

I decided not to argue and to let my riding do the talking. Ed promised he would watch me ride a race.

My next race was not for Vince. A trainer who had been letting me gallop his horses decided to give me a mount when he shipped his horse to Keystone Racetrack in Pennsylvania. On May 21, 1979, I went to Keystone to ride his filly, La Prima Rose. She won and paid $31.60! I was ecstatic. This was only my third career mount, and already I had a winner! Winning was great and so was riding for another trainer—one that wasn't like Vince!

After the race the Keystone jockeys were hiding in the jocks' room, waiting to initiate me on my maiden victory. I was unaware of this tradition and caught completely off guard when they ducked out from behind the jocks' room door and doused me with buckets of water and shaving cream. I ran by them as fast as possible, hearing them hoot and holler as I headed for cover. I reached the safety of the girl jocks' room, only to be greeted with another bucket of water from Rochelle Lee!

"Good ride," she said, pointing to the replay of the race on the television above our heads. That was a compliment coming from a leading jockey at Keystone. I just had to smile.

That night Mom gave me a scrapbook. She had started filling it with pictures of me galloping Vince's horses at Hialeah and pictures of the last pony race I had won. When she gave it to me, she said, "Keep it up." I thought she meant "keep up the scrapbook," and so I added the past performances and charts of my first three races as well as the program from my winning race at Keystone Racetrack.

For years I compulsively kept up the scrapbooks. (I have over thirty of them, containing hundreds of articles, past performance, charts, and win photos.) It took a tremendous amount of time and effort to go through all the racing papers looking for articles and records of horses I had ridden, especially when I was so busy riding. It was overwhelming at times. It wasn't until many years later that I found out Mom hadn't meant the scrapbooks when she told me to, "Keep it up." She had meant the successful riding!

Chapter 14
Onward and Upward

Onward and upward. Every morning I went around the barns and introduced myself. My enthusiasm for riding came across, and people seemed to like me. Not only did I get to work more horses in the morning, but trainers were using me as their jockey, too! The horses I rode were mostly, if not all, longshots, but I was grateful for every one of them. The important thing was that people believed in me. They were giving me a chance to ride races, to prove myself. Trainers put their faith in me and wanted nothing more than an honest effort. I felt a bond, not only with the horses I rode, but with their trainers as well; we were all on the same team. I didn't let anyone down. I rode every race to win, bringing in some of the longest priced horses at the Monmouth Park meeting. If I didn't win, I rode hard for second, third, or fourth place money. I had a very high percentage of "in the money" finishes. Not only was this popular with the bettors, who learned not to leave me out of their exactas and trifectas, but more importantly, trainers knew I was riding hard for a check. To a jockey, the difference between second, third, or fourth was ten dollars, but the money to the owner and trainer was a percentage of the purse and meant a great deal more to them.

[If a purse (prize money divided among the owners of the top four horses) was $10,000, the winning owner got 60%, or $6,000, of which the jockey got 10%, or $600. At this time (1979) jockeys were paid 10% for winning only, while owners and trainers received a percentage of the purse money for finishing second, third, and fourth. Jockeys were only paid a flat fee of $55 for second, $45 for third, and $35 for just riding the race.]

By the third week of the Monmouth Park meeting, I was riding in three to four races every day. Jockey agent Ed Rubenstein liked what he saw. He was seriously considering being my agent, but kept bringing up my going back to school in the fall. Nothing could have been further from the truth. But, I just smiled at him, thinking to myself, "You'll see, Ed. In time you'll see that I'm a race rider, and that is all I ever want to be."

As a new apprentice, I received a ten-pound weight allowance. Horses I rode got to run with ten pounds less on their backs. The weight advantage compensates for an apprentice rider's lack of experience. Apprentice jockeys are nicknamed "bug riders," the word "bug" coming from the little asterisk or "bug" alongside the apprentice's name on the program. Three asterisks denote a ten-pound weight allowance (until their fifth win), two asterisks a seven-pound weight allowance (until their thirty-fifth win), and one bug stands for a five-pound allowance (for the remainder of the year starting from an apprentice's fifth win). One year from that fifth win, an apprentice becomes a journeyman, riding at equal weights with the other, more experienced jockeys. It is a good system as the weight allowance decreases with the experience of riding and winning races.

My official year as an apprentice began on July 20, 1979. After that fifth win, Ed Rubenstein decided I was serious about riding and agreed to work for me. He became my agent on a handshake and would receive the usual jockey agent's salary, 25% of the money I earned riding races.

I didn't go by Vince's barn very often. Every time I saw him it was an ugly reminder of who I really was and what I so badly wanted to forget. It brought me back to reality and made me feel riding races was just living inside of a dream. At home I stayed in my room, but I still went by his barn now and then. After all, I continued to ride races for him and won with Northern Snipe and another horse he trained at the Monmouth Park meeting.

Mom's art business had picked up at Monmouth. She would pedal her bike around the barn area with cute little Amy in the baby seat. Her work was really improving, and she was getting more money for each portrait she did. It was a good thing Mom did well with her pastels of horses because she got no encouragement from Vince. He ignored Mom, and when he did acknowledge her it was only to put her down. I don't know how she continued to put up with him.

I loved the mornings. I loved going around on my new bike (bought with the money from my first win), visiting trainers, keeping the conversation light or about horses, and escaping from the real me locked up somewhere inside. However, I couldn't recognize people until they were up close. My eyesight had been worsening since the ninth grade, but I wouldn't admit to my "weak" nearsightedness. Not wanting to offend anyone I knew at the track, especially a trainer I was riding for, I said a big hello to anyone and everyone. One morning I yelled out my big, friendly hello to someone approaching, also on a bike. As I got closer, I realized it was Mom! Quickly my smile disappeared, and I dropped my head in shame.

Mom rarely saw me smiling

"Wow. You're happy," she said, surprised. Around Mom I was always so down. That night Mom mentioned that she couldn't believe the difference in me at the track. She pointed out that at home I was so down, so quiet, while at the track I seemed so upbeat, so happy and outgoing. She said it really took her by surprise. Until she brought this up, I was actually unaware that my two personalities were outwardly noticeable. I was so used to my two roles that I didn't even think about the drastic difference in me.

A leading New Jersey trainer, James (J.J.) Crupi, noticed my determination and success with longshots. Because he was close with his family and adored his kids, I didn't feel threatened by him. When I looked up into his eyes I saw a father, a real one. He called me "Shirley Temple," which put me even more at ease around him. He saw me as a child, and that was good. That was safe. J.J. Crupi put me on my fifth winner and many more after that. He had over thirty horses in training and was instrumental in getting my career off the ground.

Winning on J.J. Crupi's Lawless Flyer - Monmouth Park 1979

One day when I was at the Crupi stable, somebody called me away to breeze (workout) a horse. I asked Mr. Crupi if he could watch my bike while I was gone. When I returned from working the horse, I saw my bike was missing. I instantly panicked. He chuckled and told me I could find it in the barn. I looked down his shed row to find my bike in a stall with a groom holding it. The front wheel was immersed in a tub of ice—as if it were a racehorse! Leave it to Mr. Crupi! He always had a sense of humor, something most trainers lacked in this serious, high-pressured business.

I enjoyed people on a surface level, on a Karen the jockey level. The conversations were kept brief and to the subject I was most comfortable with—the horses. There were so many trainers, owners, grooms, and riders to deal with every day, but I found it was my relationship with the horses that put me the most at ease. With horses I went on instinct, but with people I always had my inner wall up. I could never, ever let anyone know the real me. They knew Karen the jockey. That was enough. Hidden behind my young and innocent "Shirley Temple" face was a wary warrior, on duty at all times. Keeping a sharp eye on everyone, I sized up situations to keep Karen the jockey out of trouble. I always made sure I was *never* alone with a trainer. The shed row of the barn was safe enough, with all the other people around, but if a trainer was in his office I would always make sure someone else was in there, too—a jockey agent, an owner, one of the barn help—or I just left the barn. I didn't want to get into any bad situations, like with Vince. I wanted to ride for people because I was a good rider, period.

I really enjoyed the challenge of dealing with so many different horses every day. In the mornings I would get on five or six and then ride four or five others in races later that afternoon. Each horse was an individual with a distinct personality, a certain feel, and his own way of doing things. I tried to keep each horse happy. Most of the time this meant adjusting my riding to suit the horse's preferred running style. A horse ran best when he was allowed to run the way he liked, whether off the pace or on the lead.

Ed and I made a great team. As with most successful jockey and agent associations, we had opposite qualities. Ed was in his fifties and well respected, but he was also the typical jock's agent in that he was pushy. The joke about agents was they were like used car salesmen. Only with Ed, it wasn't a joke. He really had been a used car salesman before he came to the track! I was quite the opposite. I never pushed for a mount. I would only ask the trainers if I could help out in the mornings, hoping this would open the door to getting a mount in a race. I was the honest and enthusiastic part of the equation, while Ed was the shrewd businessman.

Chapter 15
The Two Mes

Karen's sure cute, but she can ride, too

You can usually pick out Karen Rogers in a crowd of jockeys, because the curve of her cheek is softer under the strap of her helmet, her hands are a bit frailer, and besides, how many jockeys do you know who wear Mickey Mouse socks?

The newspapers wrote articles using adjectives like "pretty" or "cute" about me, the sixteen-year-old apprentice who was winning races at Monmouth Park. Mom showed me the articles, but I stubbornly refused to believe what they wrote. I argued that I was *not* pretty. Mom would smile and look at me with a puzzled expression. She didn't understand. How could she? She didn't *know*. If she knew the truth, she would see that I was horrible and ugly.

I was in constant turmoil whenever I was around Mom. I felt unworthy of living and guilty for ruining her life. But, I would tell myself, *I am a good rider*. Because my career was my only reason for living, I rode with extreme boldness. Looking back, I know I took chances that were sometimes unwise. Nobody that valued life would have taken the chances I took in races. I made life and death split second decisions without a moment's hesitation. Boldly, I would push my horses through tiny openings that barely existed in order to win. I saved ground, no matter how tightly horses were bunched in front of me. I knew no fear, except one: the fear that Mom, or anyone, would find out the secret.

I was winning races, but the better I rode, the more I could see it really wasn't changing me. It was all just a big cover-up, a big lie that didn't change one bit who I really was. Trainers didn't really know me, and I wanted to keep it that way. I vowed never to stay in one barn too long; that way I wouldn't be accused of any wrongdoing, and nobody could get close to me. I was so glad I looked young. I connected the danger of "sex" with all trainers, but if I looked young maybe nobody would think those kinds of thoughts about me. I dreaded the day—if it ever came—that I developed a woman's body. My fear was that people would then think I was "sleeping with" trainers for mounts. My only good feelings about myself, about who I was, came from riding, from being Karen the jockey. If anyone knew the real me, what I had done and how ugly I really was, I would crumble. My image as a jockey was perfect. It couldn't crumble, or I would never survive.

Monmouth Park paddock (16 yrs old) with trainer Whitey Makowski

I didn't trust any trainer enough to be alone with them. It was odd because I trusted my agent, my father, the other male jockeys, male grooms, and exercise boys. I didn't feel threatened by them. But trainers were a threat to my very identity because I needed them to get mounts, and I didn't want to be in the position of needing anybody. In my subconscious I identified trainers with Vince, whose help I believed was necessary in order for me to become a jockey. I had never wanted to need him at all and was disgusted with myself over this fact.

It's ironic that Vince created the need in me to become a jockey in the first place and set it up so that I could only do it with his help. He had caused my low self-esteem, and then directed my life, funneling me into the "jockey" solution—all for his own self-gratification. However, he hadn't taken into account the fact that I could do well enough to not be dependent on him.

Like with the pony races, Vince's interest in me continued to be erratic and unpredictable. At times he would act like I was the only reason he wanted to live, yet at other times he was completely absent. Although he lived with us and trained in the mornings, I never saw Vince come to the races to watch me ride. I was relieved by this. I didn't expect nor want his attention. I wanted to block him out and forget he existed. I don't know what he did that whole summer with his afternoons, but I never gave it a thought. Mom was at the races every single day to see me ride. Little Amy would be with her, bottle in hand, standing by the paddock. I knew I loved Mom and Amy, but I couldn't feel it. I wouldn't let myself love them. One day they would find out who I really was, and then they would hate me. It was better not to get close.

Toward the end of the Monmouth Park summer meeting, Vince suddenly told me that I was all he lived for, and that if I didn't love him he would kill himself. This didn't make a whole lot of sense to me because I spent so little time with him. How could he be living only for me when I was never with him? I felt guilty that I always avoided him. Nevertheless, I wanted to believe, in some way, that he did love me and that he cared. I wanted to believe that everything he told me wasn't a lie, so at least I could feel better about myself. I didn't want to believe he did those horribly painful things to me because he didn't care, but because he did love me. My anger at Vince was mixed with guilt over leaving him behind—going on with my riding career without needing him or his help. Had he loved me? *Would he kill himself?* I didn't know, so I tried to be nice to him—just in case. I just wanted him to be nonexistent. In a way, I felt guilty about not caring about him; but then I thought about the way he was hurting Mom, and I would get angry at him. Always my anger turned back on me for causing the whole mess. I was *so* bad, so selfish. And nothing I could ever do would fix what I had done to my mother. I just wanted it all to go away.

The 1979 summer race meeting at Monmouth Park came to its fairy tale ending. Winning sixteen races was an achievement, considering that I had only started racing professionally four months ago. However, better things were just around the corner.

Chapter 16
Making the Leading Jockey List

Racing moved to the Meadowlands Racetrack in East Rutherford, New Jersey, for the fall meeting. I wasn't sure what Mom and Vince were doing. In a few weeks, Vince planned on bringing his horses to the Meadowlands, but I wasn't sure where we would live. Vince had been telling me that he didn't want to continue living with Mom and "putting up with her." There was only one thing to do: take care of Karen the jockey. I had horses lined up to ride right away, so I needed a car and a place to stay near the Meadowlands. Before leaving Monmouth, I bought a used Ford Maverick. When I heard about an available room for rent near the Meadowlands Racetrack, I rented it, moved in, and was suddenly living on my own.

The Meadowlands raced at night. I was riding in seven or eight races and always seemed to have a mount in the last race. Ed liked to kid me about this, calling me the "queen of the midnight handicap." I loved Ed. He made me laugh. He was always so cheerful. It was fun to watch my Ed in action, maneuvering the hesitant trainers and

Meadowlands track kitchen with Ed

wangling his way into getting mounts from guys who swore they would never use a girl.

Racing at night had its drawbacks. I hated going back to my room alone in the pitch dark. I missed Mom and felt vulnerable. Even though I always felt guilty around my mother, the safety of having her nearby was comforting. *I wish she were here.* I didn't want to be selfish, and I certainly didn't deserve her love. I wanted to be able to handle being alone, to not be a burden to her, yet secretly I wished she would suggest coming to stay with me.

Mom and Vince remained at Monmouth where the track was still open for training. When I called Mom, she must have sensed that I was lonely. With great enthusiasm, she suggested coming up and added, "I can't wait to get to the Meadowlands!" I think she was just saying that to make me feel better.

The next day, Mom and little Amy hitched a ride to the Meadowlands. She used my car to go out apartment hunting. I didn't help. I ignored the fact that she was doing anything for me, horrible me. I told myself that this was not my idea, that I had nothing to do with her deciding to come to the Meadowlands, and so I shouldn't feel guilty. So, once again I immersed myself in riding, drowning out any protesting feelings of guilt by riding more winners, validating my existence on earth.

When Mom found an apartment close to the track, we moved in. She expected Vince to move in, too. However, he explained that he was not going to live with us, but was going to stay in a tack room next to his horses at the Meadowlands. This confused Mom. Unlike me, she was totally unaware of Vince's intention to leave her; she believed everything was fine between them. I blocked all this out, lost in my dream world of riding races. Or was racing the real world and the other just a dream?

Many years later I learned Vince's response to my mother when she told him she found a place for us all to live near the Meadowlands. He said to her angrily, "No, I'm not staying with you." His reason? "You chose to go live with Karen over staying with me!" This crazy statement of Vince's had baffled Mom: we were all supposed to be together again at the Meadowlands, weren't we? Thank God I was unaware of all of this back then. I can only imagine what my reaction to Vince's statement would have been: more fuel to the already guilty fire raging inside of me. It may have pushed me over the edge. Taken literally his words meant, if I didn't exist, they would still have been together! I already blamed myself. Could I have shouldered his blaming me for their breakup, too???

By the second week of the Meadowlands meeting, I was tied for fourth leading rider. This was no easy task considering the competition. The higher purse money at the Meadowlands had attracted top jockeys from all over the country. The competition for mounts was fierce, indeed.

September 20, 1979, was my seventeenth birthday. The television show, "Good Morning America," came out to the track to film me. The camera crew followed me around all morning while I worked horses. At the end of the morning they interviewed me and Ed. That evening they came to film my races, as well.

In the first race, I rode a horse for J. J. Crupi called Forward Dancer. I had won with this horse many times, and he was one of my favorites. Forward Dancer had a tremendous will to win. On my birthday, he didn't let me down. We won by three lengths.

In the second race, the second half of the "daily double," I rode a little filly called Stolen Charm for trainer Whitey Makowski. She went off at 7-1, but ran like an odds-on favorite, winning by an awesome fourteen lengths! (A length is approximately eight feet, or the length of a horse from nose to tail.) "Good Morning America" filmed as I returned to the winner's circle. I was surprised to see a big birthday cake there waiting for me. A band played "Happy Birthday" and every

A three winner night on my 17th birthday at the Meadowlands

My agent, my biggest fan

The horse ate my birthday cake!

fan in the crowd seemed to sing along.

Later that night I won the sixth race aboard a longshot, Crown Me King. My birthday "triple" moved me up to third place in the leading jockey standings!

I was riding the crest of a wave that one only knows if one has been at the top of a leading jockey list: the flow of "live" mounts, the endless stream of winners, one right after the other. The feeling that one can do no wrong, and that no matter what happens, the horses you ride will be good enough to make it to the winner's circle again. And again.

I continued to ride with boldness, positioning my horses up close behind others. I would save ground along the inside rail, waiting for just a crack of daylight to open up between the horses directly in front of me, and then I would bull my way through. As dangerous as it was, it worked. This annoyed some of the older and wiser riders who wouldn't take the same risks. They knew this kind of boldness could cause a spill or pileup of horses.

With time, I experienced spills and their consequences; I came to understand that it was this "putting others at risk" that upset the veteran jockeys. I soon learned how to take risks without putting others in jeopardy. Even after experiencing several traumatic riding accidents later in my career, I never lost courage. As I said before, my riding was everything and I didn't really care if I lived or died. The secret was still locked inside me.

Just like at Monmouth, once in a while I would go by Vince's barn. I felt I had to. I figured I should act like I cared about him so he didn't try to kill himself. Vince would say, "I miss you so much," or "I love you." Did he really love me? How could he care, though? He still never came to the races to watch me ride.

Mom went to the races every night. She cared...about my riding, anyway. We always had hot chocolate when we got home after midnight. I could unwind as I talked about my races. Karen the jockey was learning to be outgoing with Mom now, too. Still, when the horse talk ended and I went to bed, I remembered who I really was.

Chapter 17
My First Slow Dance

Steve Cauthen was coming to the Meadowlands! The star jockey had moved to England just before I rode my first race. This would be his first visit back to ride in the United States. I couldn't wait! I was so excited at the thought of finally getting to ride with my idol.

The press was out for this momentous sports occasion. They took a quick picture of the two of us. As I stood nervously by my hero, I proudly reminded him that we had done a Trident commercial together. Did he remember? He said he did, although I don't know if he was just trying to be nice to me.

Steve Cauthen and me

After the last race there was a big party to celebrate his appearance. All the jockeys were invited. I showered and changed, wondering if I would fit in. I was on unfamiliar territory without my boots and helmet. Would Steve notice me without my jockey silks?

At the party, I was talking to someone from the press when I saw that...Steve...had come into the room. My thoughts drifted as I watched him. *I hope he noticed that I rode two winners.* Steve was talking to several people, making his way slowly over to where I was standing. I tried to be cool and casual, but my heart was beating so fast. My palms were sweating as he came over and started talking to me. All I could see was his grin. I had seen him in those pictures back on the farm and had wanted to be just like him...just like Steve...just like Steve....What was he saying? He was saying something. And smiling. Nice smile, so genuine. What?

He took my hand, and I floated away. Where was he taking me? I didn't care....

The next thing I knew we were on the dance floor. It was then that I realized I didn't know how to dance. What was I doing? I didn't expect *this*...I had never danced with anyone before. Dance? *Slow dance???* My heart was beating so fast, the music was so slow, too slow. What was I doing? Steve knew how to *dance?* I knew he could ride... I could ride...but...whoever thought about learning to dance? This is not the time to learn. I don't know how to dance and I'm dancing with Steve Cauthen!!! I'll fake it. What do I have to lose? I'm going to die of a heart attack anyway. Ugh. Why hadn't I ever *done* this before? Don't step on his feet. Concentrate. *I can't. I can't do this.*

"Um," a strange voice stammered out of me. "I've never done this before. I'm sorry. I can't. I really can't."

Steve reassured me that I was doing fine. I *was?*

He slowed down and told me not to worry, that I didn't even have to follow his steps! I was so close to him that I went numb. I thought I was going to die. I was so nervous. Steve talked to me as we moved across the floor. He spoke to me, and gradually I forgot to be nervous. I forgot that we were supposed to be dancing. I didn't notice that everyone was watching us; I was absorbed in him. No longer did I think about where to put my clumsy feet. They had already been there, and back again, to the music.

Then it was over. The dance had ended. Why did it have to end so soon? I *loved* to dance! I walked away, feeling as though I was waking up from a dream. I will never forget my first slow dance. No, not as long as I live.

Chapter 18
New York, The Big League

Ed finally stopped talking about me going back to school. I was winning races, sometimes two or three before the evening was over. Anyway, I was sort of in school: I was learning. I watched the New York jockeys, like Angel Cordero, Jr., who came to the Meadowlands to ride the stakes races. I wanted to improve, to ride as well as Angel, nicknamed "the Maestro." I still wasn't satisfied with the way I used my whip. I wanted to use it the way Angel did. He was so smooth. When he used his whip, it was like one effortless, sweeping motion. His stick, or whip, looked like an extension of his arm. It was all so natural. His whole body was in perfect rhythm with his horse. Why couldn't I do that? What was I doing wrong?

I remember the first time I met Angel. Even though I had won with Northern Snipe, Vince's owner wanted to put Angel Cordero on the tough little horse. Although I didn't know Angel personally, I decided it might not be a bad idea to tell him about his upcoming mount. I warned him that Northern Snipe could be difficult. The horse might try to bear out, but it was best to let him drift a little instead of fighting him. The greatest jockey in the world looked at me with skepticism. He must have been thinking, who was I, a seventeen-year-old girl apprentice, to tell *him* how to ride a horse? He chuckled to himself, shrugged me off, and headed out to the paddock.

I went into the girl jocks' room to watch the race on the television. At the start, the little gray horse was rank. He pulled Angel out of the saddle going into the first turn. Angel started hauling back as hard as he could to try to bring the horse under control. Angel was now standing way up in the saddle, and it was obvious that he was having trouble controlling Northern Snipe. While the rest of the horses ran ahead down the backstretch, Angel was still fighting Northern Snipe, trying to bring him in from the outside rail. Although they did finally manage to get back on course, the fiasco had cost them, and they finished far behind the others.

When Angel returned to the jocks' room he looked at me in utter amazement. He showed me his hands, which were sore from pulling on the reins, and asked me how I had handled such a difficult horse. I just smiled at him and got ready to ride the next race. I had earned his respect.

A few weeks later I told Angel that I admired his riding style, especially the way he used his whip. I mentioned that someday I wanted to be able to use a whip just like him. Angel seemed pleased to hear this, and later that night he gave me three of his very own custom made whips!

After Northern Snipe's last place finish with Angel, Vince's owner decided to take the horse away from Vince and give him to Allen Jerkens, a successful New York based trainer. The owner also wanted me to be Northern Snipe's jockey again. I wondered if maybe Angel had put in a good word for me. Or, maybe my record with the horse spoke for itself; I had never been out of the money with Northern Snipe.

Going to New York to ride Northern Snipe for Allen Jerkens would be my first chance to ride at Aqueduct. *New York, The Big League.* Finally, I had made my goal! I was a little nervous about meeting the "Hall of Fame" trainer. I wondered what he would think of me. Probably that I was too young to be any good—in New York.

In the paddock, Allen Jerkens was abrupt, to the point. "I've only had this horse for a few days. It looks like you probably know the best way to ride him." And with those brief words of wisdom, I was on my own.

When we got out onto the track, I was in awe. *This was my dream come true. This was where Steve Cauthen had ridden!* Riding by the huge grandstand in the post parade, I imagined all the trainers watching me. The best horsemen in the world would be making comments.

"Look at the girl apprentice, the one winning all those races at the Meadowlands. I wonder if she can really ride."

"Maybe in New Jersey, but this is New York, The Big Apple."

I wanted to make a good impression, the best one possible to the critical eyes upon me. I had hopes of riding in New York for the winter, when the Meadowlands closed.

Leaving the starting gate, I had a strange sense of freedom. It was like riding in an open field. Everyone gave me running room. It wasn't like in New Jersey, where all the jocks rode bunched up and you had to fight your way into position.

I let Northern Snipe settle behind three horses. As we went around the turn I noticed a big difference from the shorter, sharper turns at the Meadowlands track. The turn here was more gradual, so it didn't seem as crucial to save ground. Instead of dropping in, I stayed on the outside of horses where Northern Snipe preferred to run.

I could feel Northern Snipe taking hold of the bit as he started to make his move coming out of the turn. We charged down the stretch. *I might just win my first race in New York!* I remembered all the trainers in the grandstand and tried to stay cool and smooth. *Don't let the possibility of winning rattle you. Stay in sync...with the rhythm...of the beat...of his stride. Just ride...ride...ride...and ride.*

We almost made it and finished second by a nose.

I was getting off the scales after the race, disappointed that I hadn't won, but feeling happy with Northern Snipe's effort. I wasn't at all prepared for what happened next. Allen Jerkens came up to me, red in the face, and started hollering. At first I thought he was kidding—like J. J, Crupi would—but then I realized that he was serious! He was *very* upset with me. He yelled and blamed me for "getting his horse beat." I was shocked and cringed in horror as he criticized my riding, saying that I rode a *terrible* race.

I felt bad... *bad me*. It felt like he knew me, the real me...like I had been shot in the stomach. It hit me so hard, so deep.

Nothing like this had ever happened to me before. Never had a trainer been angry with my riding, with *me the jockey*. I was deeply hurt. Who I was, *what* I was...me the jockey...my very being had just been stripped away. With my jockey exterior torn away, I ran back into the girl jocks' room. I didn't want anyone to see me cry.

In the girl jocks' room, I wiped away my tears. I felt very alone. This place...New York...it was so big, so impersonal...so cold. Maybe I wouldn't like riding here, after all. I looked at myself crying in the mirror. The me that I had seen in the mirror on those dreadful mornings at Garden State Park Racetrack was staring back at me. The bad, weak me was showing through those tears. Suddenly, I got very angry.

"Toughen up, you!" I screamed at the image staring pathetically back at me, a tear-streaked, sad face. That's not ME. That's not ME. YOU are not ME.

"I hate *you!!*"

I turned away from the mirror, angrily vowing to *never* again let my emotions come out. Never would I cry—not here, not at the racetrack. Never while I was a jockey. *Never!*

Soon after, I got another opportunity to ride in New York. This time I would be riding for a New Jersey trainer, and I knew things would go better. My faith in my ability to ride in New York was restored when the horse, Fight at Night, won. My first New York winner even made the headlines in the sports section of *The New York Times:* "Five Winners for Pincay; Karen Rogers Scores." Next to the article was a photo finish of two horses dueling down to the wire. Was this a photo of the great jockey, Laffit Pincay, Jr., winning? Or, could it be... it *was* my horse, Fight at Night!

Chapter 19
Rookie of the Year

The New Jersey Sports Writers Association had chosen me as "Rookie of the Year." When I saw this headline in *The Daily Racing Form,* I wondered if a "rookie" was something good or something bad. It didn't *sound* good, but I figured it must have had something to do with me winning so many races. When a few people congratulated me, I figured a "rookie" was something *good.*

When I accepted my award at the New Jersey Sports Writers dinner, I expected to be honored among several other racing personalities. I was surprised when I realized that I was the only person from thoroughbred racing to receive an award! Because I didn't follow other sports, the people who were honored were unfamiliar to me. (Joe Paterno, the head football coach at Penn State, was voted 1979 "Man of the Year.") The engraved silver bowl I received was more than just an award; finally, thoroughbred racing was getting the recognition it so deserved as a sport.

FRIDAY, DECEMBER 14, 1979

Singled out for Excellence as Performer in Racing

Big M Picks Karen Rogers As '79 'Rookie of the Year'

FOOTBALL & BASKETBALL BETTING GUIDE

Latest Vegas Line

College Basketball

NBA

NHL

College Football

NFL

Silvery Moon Is Peaking

Vote for Claimer of the Year See P. 22

CAPTION: Jockey Karen Rogers was singled out for "Rookie of the Year" honors at the Meadowlands. Here she is shown celebrating her 17th birthday, back on Sept. 20, in the winner's circle after booting home both ends of the daily double. She has been acclaimed as one of the most promising apprentice riders in the nation. (Photo by Jim Raftery)

The Meadowlands was closing in a few weeks. I wanted my agent to come to New York with me, but it was not to be. "Karen, I'm going back to Keystone Racetrack, near my home in Philadelphia. But you go on to New York. You deserve a shot there. You're a good little rider. Now is the time to go, while you still have the bug. You're good enough to make it there. I know—I've been around a lot of young riders. You've got what it takes."

"But," I objected, "will a New York agent want to take on a girl apprentice? *You* almost didn't want to take me, in the beginning."

Ed laughed. "Yeah. You sure changed my mind about girl riders, though."

There was no racing for Christmas. We were going to celebrate with Susan at Grandma's farm. Mom wondered if Vince wanted to come with us, so on the way we drove through the Meadowlands stable area.

Mom waited in the car with little Amy as I went in to ask Vince. I opened the door to his room and he came over and hugged me.

"Mom wants you to come with us to Grandma's," I said, emotionless.

"No," Vince objected. "I couldn't come. You know how I feel about *your mother*." He pulled me onto his cot. I was shocked by this sudden maneuver to get me. The whole Meadowlands meeting he had left me alone. I thought he had given up all of this. I pushed him away, explaining that Mom might come in at any minute. He looked at me with a very sad face. A teardrop fell from his bloodshot eyes as he told me he loved me and had nobody to be with on Christmas. I was suddenly very angry at him for saying this, for trying to make me feel sorry for him. He could have come with us...he could have been part of our family. We *could* have been a *normal* family! We could have been, but now everything—our whole family—was messed up because of him...and me...

Suddenly, I pictured Mom and Amy in the car waiting for me and felt horribly guilty, once again. Mom is out there, waiting for me. She trusts me...

"I am going to miss you *so* much when you go to Aqueduct to ride," he said sadly. "I won't be training anymore. I am going to work on a horse farm back in Bridleton. If you don't call me every day from New York, I just won't be able to live. You have to let me know how you are doing."

Why was he suddenly so interested in me again?

He pushed me back down on the cot and started kissing me. All the sickening thoughts and feelings flooded through my mind and body. I jumped up and headed for the door.

"Gotta go now. Bye," I said, without looking back. I hurried to the car, got in, and turned to Mom. "Let's go."

"What did he say? Is he coming?"

"No."

"Did he tell you why?" Mom looked so disappointed, so confused.

I thought for a second. "He said he didn't feel well." So, I lied. I looked away from Mom, out the car window. It would hurt her so much if she ever knew how Vince *really* felt about her.

On December 31, the Meadowlands closed. I was fourth leading jockey with 56 winners for the meeting. As icing on the cake, the New Jersey Racing Writers' Association had voted me top apprentice. I led all women jockeys in the nation in purse money won for 1979. Even though I had a late start, my horses had earned a total of $584,769. I received roughly $50,000 of this, but still, it wasn't bad for a seventeen-year-old. It sure beat high school. Besides, I was getting paid to do what I loved.

Chapter 20
Turmoil

New York, New York. The big time—at last.

I was able to get Freddy Stevens, an established New York jockey agent, to work for me. I wanted so badly to make it in New York; however, even with a known agent, it was very difficult to get mounts. I was used to riding seven or eight races every night—and winning. Even though I had only been at Aqueduct for one week, things did not look good. I had heard about the lack of opportunities for women jockeys in New York. "They just don't ride women in New York." But, I wasn't a *girl* rider. I was a rider—a *jockey*, period.

With my bug year running out (one year from my fifth winner), I felt pressure to do well while I could. Vince had warned, "You have to make the most of your first year, when you have the bug. That will make or break your entire career."

I called Vince every day. I was afraid not to. As much as I loathed making the call, I couldn't risk him killing himself. So, on my way home from the races, I would stop at a little stationary store with a pay phone in the back.

"Hi-ya, kiddo." Vince's voice made the guilt pangs throb and made me tremble inside. I turned my back so that nobody in the store would recognize me.

I cupped my hand over the mouthpiece. "Hi."

Vince had that sweet sounding, I-care-so-much-about-you voice. "How'd ya do today? Win any races?" He always asked me that. I hated it. I *wasn't* winning.

"No. It's so tough here."

"Ohhh, I *know*, I *know*, kiddo. If you were down at Keystone, you would be winning a *lot*."

"I know. It bugs me. I wish I were riding more. But..."

He cut in, "I miss you."

I felt suddenly hot, guilty, and horrible. Numbness rippled over me, starting from the top of my head until it had coated my entire being, protecting me from feeling anything. The voice that came out of me was hollow, emotionless, and set apart from the rest of me. "You miss me? You...shouldn't." Karen the jockey was long gone.

"Oh, but I *do*. I miss you *so* much. I can't live without you."

I held the phone in silence, not wanting to hear anymore. How can he be living just for me? I'm miles away, and he is the furthest thing from my mind. How can he say this?

"But," I reasoned, "What about Mom? She keeps wondering what you're doing on that farm. She can't understand why you don't want to see her or Amy...or train horses...or anything."

"I just live for *you*, for your phone calls. And for when you'll come down to Keystone. Then I would train again. I'd train at Keystone Racetrack."

"But..."

"Then we could be together."

"No. I mean, what about Mom and Amy?"

"I told you, I don't care about them. I never loved your mother."

I stuffed the anger. Why did he have to put me in the middle?

I had only been in New York for two weeks, but each day without a winner felt like an eternity. The clock was ticking. Time was running out. I should be riding more, and winning. If I didn't get more opportunities to ride—soon—I'd have to leave New York. If I went to Keystone, in Pennsylvania, I'd win races again. There, connected with Ed, I would have a shot to be leading apprentice, maybe even the leading jockey!

In my despair, I called Ed. Because I hadn't ridden a winner since I came to New York, Ed suggested I come to Keystone for a day. He would line up some good mounts for me. He said, "Don't give up on New York yet. If you're ever going to break in there, the time is now, during the winter with your bug. Give it a month. You can always come down here, okay?"

Big Decision - Should I stay in New York?

"Okay," I said. "Line up some mounts."

The next time I called Vince, I told him that Ed was lining up some mounts for a day down at Keystone.

"Could we meet then?" he asked.

I hadn't expected this response from him. "I don't know. I don't even know if I'm going yet."

"But, I *have* to see you. I want you to see my new place. I live on a nice farm in an apartment right over a barn."

"I have to go. I'm running out of change for the phone."

"Call me collect next time. I couldn't live without hearing your voice. Did you get my last letter?"

I thought a minute. Which letter? He had been sending me love letters "care of the jocks' room" and I had been tearing them up and throwing them away. I hid the evidence in the bottom of the garbage pail in the girl jocks' room. I hated those letters. I hated the evidence. "Yeah, I got it. But you don't have to send me letters."

"Oh, but I *want* to. It would be so much easier if you were riding at Keystone, though. I could help you more. And it would be better for your career. You need to win. You know how important it is to win this first year with your bug."

"I'm so mixed-up. Sometimes I want to just go to Keystone. Then I think I should stay here in New York."

"Well, don't let your *mother* influence your decision. She doesn't care about you or whether you make the right decision for your career. It's very important right now that you win races. She doesn't understand anything about the racetrack—or about good business."

"What do you mean?" I asked, suddenly angry with Mom. She loved me, didn't she?

"I wouldn't steer you wrong," he continued. "I *care* about you. Not like *your mother*."

"I don't know," I said, feeling very mixed-up.

"Call me tomorrow. Tell me how things are going. Love you." He was kissing me over the phone, but I hung up before he was finished.

I drove the rest of the way home feeling lower than ever. Would Mom really want to see me fail and my career ruined?

That night I asked her what she thought about me riding permanently at Keystone.

"Well, I think you should stay here," she said confidently. "You ride so well. You belong in New York. Just give it more time. You worry too much!"

I don't know why I asked her. I didn't know whether to believe her anyway.

The very next day, I won a race at Aqueduct! Ed was right. I had to be patient. After all, I had only been in New York less than three weeks. A few days later, I rode another winner. Things were definitely looking up. But I still wasn't sure I would stay in New York. I continued to feel torn in two. What to do, what to do?

The day before I went to Keystone to ride a few races, I called

Vince.

"Can't wait to see you, kiddo," he said. "I've been counting the days." Again, he brought up riding full time at Keystone, even though I had just won two races in New York.

"I've been doing okay here. Some good trainers have promised to put me on more winners."

"You know how people make promises in New York. You can't depend on what they say, though. I know. I worked at Aqueduct for years. I know all those people. They aren't on your side. Does your mother know any of them?"

"Not really. She wants me to stay here because she says I ride well enough to make it here."

"Ha! What does *she* know? Huh? She knows *nothing* about racing. Don't believe her! Your real friends are down here—Ed and all the trainers you rode for in New Jersey. What about us?"

"Ed thinks I should stay in New York. I'm just coming to Keystone tomorrow because I hadn't won a race up here when I last talked to Ed. So he lined up some good mounts, thinking it would pick my head up. I wouldn't be coming down there except that he made those commitments already. I've been doing okay up here, as of last week."

"Your head would be picked up every day if you were at Keystone. You wouldn't have to be going through this...turmoil. Not winning races. I know. I feel so *bad* for you."

"It's not that. I don't mind not winning so much. I just want to do the right thing for my career. People say it takes more time in New York to get going. But once you're accepted here, it's much easier than other places."

"Who told you that? I'm the one on your side, kiddo. Listen, we'll meet tomorrow at the Ramada Inn. It's right on your way down here."

"I don't think I'll have time to stop. It's a long drive down to Keystone, and I have to be in the (jocks') room early. Anyway, Mom will probably come," I said.

"I'll call her. Don't worry. She won't come. I'll tell her I'm coming up there to see her. Listen, if you don't have time to stop on the way down, we'll meet for dinner on your way back. I'll buy you a real special dinner and we'll talk about what you should do."

"Uhh..."

"I miss you so much. If I can't see you, well... I just don't know what I'll do," he said.

I hated all this lying and sneaking around Mom's back. I *hated* it. I hung up the pay phone and left the stationary store, trying to block it out of my mind. Just forget what he said. But I couldn't. The more I thought about the Keystone decision, the more confused I became. I was in the middle, once again. Before I had always known what I had to do. But now, this. I had to make the *right* decision. This wasn't just any decision. This would affect my riding, my career, my whole *life*. Maybe I should go to Keystone permanently. Maybe Vince was right. Maybe Mom was just trying to trick me into staying in New York.

Chapter 21
A Narrow Escape

Mom had the directions, maps, and quarters ready for the trip to Keystone. She was all excited. "Karen, Vince called this morning!"

My heart skipped a beat. I was flush, burning red in an instant. "What...when? What did he say?"

"He is finally coming up to visit later today! He called earlier while you were still at the track. Can you believe he finally called? He said he wanted to talk to you to see how you're doing, but darn it, you weren't here. I told him how you won those two races and that you're going to Keystone to ride today. Karen, he asked about you. He's so concerned. I couldn't understand why he never came to see us at the Meadowlands, or anything. But now I know why. He was having problems with the horses and the owners. He said things are easier for him, now that he's not training. I feel bad. I didn't realize the intense pressure he was under. I just didn't understand what he was going through. He said that training really got to him. He nearly had a breakdown! But now he says he's much better off and wants to come up to visit. He sounds happy. He is living on a farm. Maybe things will come around. Maybe there is hope for us, after all."

I felt sick. I thought I would throw up. The panic, then the relief, and then the way Mom talked about Vince. She still loved him. It was just too much for me.

"Is it okay if I don't go to Keystone with you?" Mom asked, looking concerned. "Will you be all right? Do you think you'll be able to find it okay?"

"I'll be fine. I have your directions and the maps. Don't worry." I felt so guilty. Here she was feeling bad about me going alone. And I was going to meet Vince. What trickery.

"I can't believe he's coming up," she said, shaking her head in amazement. "I'm so glad he finally wants to see Amy. She's at such a cute age."

"Mom, don't you ever get mad that he hasn't cared about *you*?"

Now, why did I say that? It just came out. Sometimes I just got so angry at him...and at her, too, for letting him play games with her.

Mom was silent. Her face dropped. She looked sad. Now, why did I have to go and say that?

I made the trip to Keystone Racetrack, trying not to think about Mom or Vince.

I ended up with two winners for the day. For some reason, I had the utmost confidence in myself—as a rider. At this small track, I felt like the "big fish in a little pond." The New York rider come to Keystone.

Ed was beaming as I left the jocks' room. I hadn't let him down, and I could tell he was very proud of me.

"Keep in touch, Karen."

"I will, Ed. I think I'm going to try to stick it out in New York for a while. You were right. I could ride down here anytime. New York is a challenge. It's what I want. I know that now." The horses were the easy part, I thought.

I got in the car, dreading what would happen next. On the way home I was meeting Vince for dinner at the Ramada Inn. As I drove, the high confidence level I had at Keystone dwindled away, melting down until there was nothing left of it. Not a trace. The transition was complete. Karen the jockey had disappeared. Now, there was only me. Bad me. About to meet with Vince.

I entered the Ramada Inn, head down in shame. I found Vince in the restaurant, sitting at a cozy little table in the corner.

I *wasn't* his lover.

I was Karen the jockey, wasn't I? I held my head high, trying to beat the odds. Trying to kid myself. Again.

"Hey, there!" Vince sounded so up.

"Hi." I sounded so down.

"You won two races today, didn't you?"

"How did you know?"

He winked at me knowingly.

I sat opposite him, looking down once again.

"After we eat, I want you to come see my place at the farm. It's only fifteen minutes from here."

I couldn't look at him. He had that lovey-dovey expression. I hated that look. It made me feel so guilty. I was wrong to have met him. Very wrong. "I can't. Mom is waiting for me. She'll know if I'm late. She'll ask me what happened. I don't want to lie to her. What did you tell her about not coming up to see her, anyway? She really wanted to see you."

"Oh, your mother. *Her* again. Why are you always so worried about her? You ought to be worried about yourself and your career. You know, you really should be riding at Keystone."

"I don't know." I looked down, picking up the fork to fiddle with it.

"Sooo, kiddo, tell me how your day went. Tell me about those winners!"

Vince never seemed to notice how "down" I was. I wasn't all happy, like him. Couldn't he see that I didn't like this? All the sneaking around and lying, the secret phone calls and letters. And now, a secret meeting. It was wrong. I hated myself for going along with it. But if I didn't, Vince might kill himself, and I didn't want to be the cause of that.

Dinner was finally over. I was glad.

"I really have to go," I said matter-of-factly.

"Follow me," he said. "Just drive by, to see where I'm staying so you can picture where I am when you are reading my letters. It's only a few minutes away."

"Mom is waiting. I'm already later than I should be."

"Tell her you got stuck in traffic. Tell her anything. She'll believe it."

I walked out of the restaurant, dead set against driving to his place. I wasn't going to get in a bad spot. Vince walked right beside me.

I reached my car and unlocked the door slowly. Vince was leaning against me the whole time.

"Wait a sec," I pushed him gently away, got into the car, and shut the door. I didn't want to be too rude, but I wanted to get away from him. My car window was up. He knocked on it as I started the engine. He was pressing his lips against the window. He looked like a giant insect...a bug stuck to the window...right next to me, with only the glass between us. I felt sick and rolled down the window to get him to stop.

"Please, Karen, come see my place. Just follow me. You have your own car. Just drive by and see it. Pleeease."

"I can't."

"Then let me sit in your car for a second to say goodbye."

I hesitated. Oh, what could it hurt? He wouldn't try anything. Not here. Not now. And I was strong. Stronger than before.

I leaned over and unlocked the door to the passenger side. Vince walked around and got in the car. Immediately he leaned over and tried to kiss me, but I pushed him away.

He sat back and looked over at me. The dim light shining from the lamp posts in the parking lot cast a shadow over part of his face. He looked strange. Contorted, sad face. Definitely sad. I studied his expression, trying to read him better. A teardrop sparkled as it fell from the shadow, moving slowly down his cheek. He was crying.

"Please. Come see the farm. Come and see where I stay. I miss you."

He looked so pathetic. For an instant I felt sorry for him. Then I remembered that it was HE who had arranged his own destiny. It was HE who was living on this farm, having left Mom, the person who loved him the most. Suddenly, I wanted him out of my car. "Okay. I'll follow you," I said. "But I can't stay. It's late already, so hurry."

It was pitch black when we got to the farm where he was staying. I drove down the long driveway behind the red taillights of Vince's car. Why did I ever come here? I should just leave...turn around...now...

Finally, his car came to a stop. It was by a barn, which was all by itself at the end of the property. There was nothing here but emptiness. I wasn't safe. I wasn't staying.

I sat in the car with the radio turned up. Vince got out of his car and came over to me.

"You can't see much of the place," he explained. "It's too dark now. But you can see my apartment! Come on up. I'll show you."

I had come this far and managed to keep things on my terms. I decided I was strong enough to handle a quick look at his apartment. I didn't feel like arguing—and I didn't want him to start crying and pleading with me again. So, I followed him to the barn, up the outdoor stairway, and into his apartment.

The place was filthy. What hit me first was the smell. It smelled *exactly* like the dirty tack room he used to live in at Garden State Park. The smell triggered all the horrible memories.... I felt nauseous. The smell was too much for me. Strangely though, I was curious to see what made the familiar, sickly odor.

Vince showed me his bedroom and the kitchen. I looked around in disgust. What was that familiar smell, like in the tack room at Garden State Park? Was it dirty horse blankets? Funky shoes? The smell of a pot smoker? There were dirty dishes piled up in his sink. Everything reeked. I didn't know what caused that horrible smell, but suddenly I wanted out. Now!

I looked at my watch. "I gotta go now, Vince. I'm glad I saw your place. Mom's waiting and it's late..."

Now he looked sad again.

"Please don't go. Not yet. I'm sooo lonely. Sit next to me on the couch. I love you." He steered me toward the couch, sitting me down. Then he stood in front of me, unzipped his pants, and to my horror, pulled them down.

I jumped up and ran. *Get away, get away, out the door, out the door, down the steps, down the steps,* my heart pounded as I tried to talk myself through the escape. *Would he follow me? Would he grab me? Don't look back. Get to the car, the car, the car, my escape...*

The steps leading down from his apartment were rickety, the night pitch black. I negotiated my way down them as fast as I could without slipping. My body and mind were racing faster than my feet could handle. I tripped on a step, but caught myself. *Slow down, slow down...my car, my car, my escape....*I fell over the last step, landing on the wet grass. *Get up, run, run, run to the car, the car, the car.* I could hear Vince right behind me.

"Wait! Wait! Don't go...."

I reached the car without looking back. Groped through my pockets for the keys...*keys, keys, get in the car...no keys, open the door, open the door...get in the car....* I felt him grab me from behind. I yanked away and reached for the locked car door. Miraculously, it opened. The keys were still on the seat.

"Don't leave me," he begged.

Still stricken with terror, I jumped into the car and shut the door. I tried to come to my senses. *He let go of me! I'm in the car. I'm safe now. I'm safe.*

My heart was still pounding from the terror of the moment before. *Be calm. It's over. Put the key into the ignition, start the car, and drive away.*

"Open the window." Vince was knocking. I opened it a crack.

"I love you," he said.

"I have to go. It's late. Mom will be worried. She's waiting. See ya."

I started the car, backed it up, and sped out the driveway. All the way home I couldn't think straight. I got lost and was almost to Keystone before I realized that I had been following the directions back to that track, instead of back to Long Island.

When I finally made it home, it was very late. Mom had been worried about me. I was going to tell her that I had dinner with Ed, but was afraid she might have called him.

"You wouldn't believe what I did, Mom. I took the wrong turnoff—twice! I got sooo lost. What a waste."

"Well, next time I'll go with you. I could have come. Vince never made it up here," she said sadly. Then she changed the subject. "How did your horses run?"

With the fabricated story of why I was late filling my head, I had forgotten to tell her about the horses. "Oh, yeah. Two of them won!"

Chapter 22
A Perilous Situation

How could I ever thank Ed? His advice to be patient paid off. Not only that, Ed connected me with a winning New York trainer, Bobby Lake. At the end of the first month in New York, I won the first two races of the day, the daily double! *The New York Times* wrote, "Miss Rogers, 17, Brings in Double."

Winning the double at Aqueduct

The horses were longshots, and the gamblers were starting to take notice. "Don't discount the ten horse. Karen rides him. They run for her. She brings in those longshots."

"Don't leave Karen out of the daily double or the ninth race trifecta. She tries on everything. She gets those longshots to run, to finish in the money."

New York gamblers were a shrewd bunch. They followed every horse, every race. Nothing got by them. Nothing. And now I had gone from "the girl" to "Karen." Hmm. It was a start. The gamblers seemed to accept me, but what about convincing the trainers? That was what mattered.

On the same day that I won the daily double, there was an incident which caught the attention of the horsemen—and got me on television. I was on the lead going into the far turn when I heard a jockey screaming behind me. What was wrong? As the panicked rider moved up along the rail inside my horse, I could see the problem clearly: the jockey's reins were dangling, no longer attached to the bridle. He was helplessly out of control.

The turns on the inner track at Aqueduct are very sharp. Without a jockey being able to steer, the centrifugal force at high speed can send a horse straight to the outside rail. If he didn't gain control now, he would cut in front of all the horses and riders directly behind us and they would fall. It was an accident about to happen.

My reaction was instant. I couldn't leave the jockey helpless. No way. I was close enough to reach over and grab the bridle. I guided the horse safely through the turn. As we straightened away into the stretch, I let go. Wouldn't you know the horse kept on going straight and won the race!

This incident caught the attention of the horsemen. Top trainer Frank Wright approached me after the race. Not only did he train some good horses, he was also the host of television's "Racing from Aqueduct." Frank found it hard to believe that an apprentice rider had acted so swiftly in the face of danger—that a 17-year-old bug rider with less than a year's experience of racing—had known what was happening and taken control of the perilous situation. He asked if I would like to be his guest on the Saturday evening racing show. Would I ever! This was the very same television show I had watched every week since the day I decided to be a jockey like Steve.

On the day we taped the show, Frank asked me, "Have you done interviews like this before?"

"Yeah. I was interviewed for some television shows when I rode at the Meadowlands. I was on 'Good Morning America', 'Big Blue Marble', and some Newscasts. I know all about 'cut aways' and things like that."

Frank smiled, amused. "Well, good. This should be easy for you then. I'm going to show you winning the daily double and then show the race where you helped the other jockey. Okay?"

As we waited for the cameras to roll, Frank turned to me, abruptly changing the subject. "It is *so* difficult for a girl to get started in New York. People here just don't believe that a girl can ride. It must be very difficult for you to get good mounts."

"It's not so bad, really," I smiled, dismissing the frustrations of the last month.

The interview went by quickly. Afterward, Frank thanked me for coming on the show. "You did a fine job handling yourself in front of the cameras. You seem to do well with everything you do."

"Well, thanks for having me on," I said, heading for the door.

"Come by my barn in the morning, would you?" he said.

I stopped in my tracks. Did he say...

"I mean it," he said firmly. "Come by the barn. I've got a few horses I'd like to put you on. I'll give you a shot. If you get along with my horses, you'll ride them, okay?" His serious face broke into a smile.

Frank Wright trained some nice horses. Things were looking up, indeed.

Now that I was living and riding on Long Island, I was using a local bank near Belmont Park. I called my old bank near Monmouth Park to close out my account. However, when I called, they informed me that my account had already been closed out. All the money was gone! No way! I looked at my calendar. On the date the account was closed, I was at Aqueduct, riding four races. Someone must have forged my name! Who could have done such a dishonest thing? Vince was the last one at Monmouth. He knew I had an account at the local bank. He had access to my checkbook and knew how I signed my name. *Could it have been Vince?* No, he loved me. He cared about me. He wouldn't take my money, would he? I put it out of my head.

Chapter 23
Dead Giveaway

"Oh, Karen, did I tell you that Vince called? He said he's definitely coming up."

Mom's words cut through me like a knife.

"When?"

"He called this morning. He's been so busy, but he said he finally got some time to drive up later on today. It's such a long way."

Why was he doing this to me? He knew I didn't want to see him. Not here. Not now. I hated being in the middle, having to pretend I was the innocent daughter around Mom when I was really Vince's secret girlfriend. Vince loved me, not her. How would I handle this? How could I deal with it? I didn't want to see Mom hurt. I hated the lying, right in front of Mom's face. If she ever knew she would really, really hate me.

But she doesn't know. She thinks Vince is coming up to see all of us. I hope she doesn't figure it out. I hope he doesn't look at me with that lovey-dovey expression on his face.

Coming home from the races that afternoon, I tried not to worry. Vince wouldn't come to visit. No, he knew how much it would bother me. But as I pulled up to the apartment, I saw the New Jersey plates on the car parked outside. Vince was here.

I sat in the car for a few minutes, debating whether or not to go in. If I don't go in, if I go somewhere else for a while, Mom will suspect something. She'll wonder what's wrong. She'll wonder why I'm not excited to see Vince. She'll ask questions. Better to just go in and pretend like nothing is wrong, like I'm happy to see him. Yeah...Mom knows I never show much emotion anyway, that all I care about is my races. I wouldn't even have to hug him. I could just say hello and then go into my room. It had been so long since all of us were together. I wasn't looking forward to it. Still...I had to go in.

"Hi-ya, kiddo! Oh, it's been so long!!!" Vince hugged me. I cringed. Mom was right behind him.

"How did you do today?" Mom asked, thinking nothing of Vince's huge show of affection for me.

"Um, okay, I guess." I tried to think back to my mounts. Who did I ride, again? How did they run? Think...think... "I was second on a longshot."

"How about the other two? You were on three, right?" Mom asked, waiting for me to tell her about it. I always told her about my races. Always. But I was numb, totally and completely blank.

"They ran all right, I guess."

"We're all going out for dinner. The Tudor Inn is nice and not too far," Mom informed me with a smile. The Tudor Inn was next to the stationary store with the pay phone where I would call Vince...

"That's good," I said, trying to squeeze out of Vince's grasp.

"It's *so* good to see you. I've missed you," Vince said as he stared at me with his lovey-dovey eyes. Right in front of Mom.

"I've got to get these boots off." I ducked my head and slipped away, heading straight for my room. I couldn't get away soon enough.

"Can I see your room?" Vince asked, following right behind me.

"NO! Nobody goes in my room. It's...a mess."

"Okay...okay...you don't have to act so angry all the time" He turned to Mom and said, "Boy, I can see the races really get to her. She needs a winner."

Why did he always have to make me feel so crazy? And right in front of Mom.

I went into my room and shut the door. I wanted to cry, but all I felt was numb.

At dinner Vince sat next to me. Not next to Mom, next to *me*. Did he have to be so obvious? And he looked at me with those sick lovey-dovey eyes the whole time. Once, he even put his hand on my lap under the table, but I got up to use the bathroom.

Dinner went on forever. I was numb from fear and guilt. I couldn't look at Mom. Or Vince. I didn't want to meet those eyes. I stared down at my plate. Vince talked about me and my career. All I kept thinking over and over again was that at any moment a light bulb would go on in Mom's head. At any moment, it would hit her. She would know the truth, and then it would all be over. *She would hate me forever and ever.*

Vince just kept on staring at me, ignoring Mom and Amy. Didn't he KNOW this was a dead giveaway??? Mom could see...anyone could tell when he looked at me that way. Surely, she would know.

How could she not know???

But Mom didn't know. Vince had gotten away with it again, right under her nose. Loving me, hating her. As he said, "putting up with her in order to be with you."

After that, Vince came up more often to "see Amy." Mom was happy that he was finally showing an interest in seeing us again. I dreaded the days when he would come to New York. He always insisted on going to dinner in my car. He told me secretly that he didn't care if Mom came, that really, he would prefer it if she didn't! And Mom would take Amy and follow us to the restaurant in her car. I felt so bad for Mom. I felt so guilty. I couldn't take much more of this. I pleaded with him, "I wish you would go in Mom's car with her and Amy. Pretend you don't care about me. And, please don't look at me at dinner. Just look at Mom and Amy."

But he wouldn't listen.

Little did I know that Vince had told Mom he was going in my car so we could discuss racing and my career without Amy interrupting and wanting his attention. Many years later, Mom also told me that she was happy that Vince was interested in me and my racing because I always seemed so down.

Vince continued to be critical of Mom. He would say things like, "Your mother should get a real job. Her paintings aren't very good." I didn't understand why he was always so critical of my mother. She really was a good artist. I was proud of her artwork. Mom was commissioned by top trainers and owners to paint their horses, and everyone complimented her. They would say, "Your mother is so talented. You are so lucky she is staying with you. You are so lucky to have her for a mother."

And then I would wonder. They were on *her* side, weren't they? If they were on her side, then, like Vince said, they must be against me. Vince always told me that Mom was against me, that all her friends were against me. If this were true, there was nothing I could do about it. All I could do was hope for the best and remain Karen the jockey.

Chapter 24
Good Publicity

Frank Wright promised me a good mount. He didn't say when, but he said it was coming soon. There were promises from other trainers, as well. The difference was that now the promises were being kept.

Ever since winning the daily double and getting exposure on "Racing from Aqueduct," my business had picked up tremendously. Now, I was riding five or six races every afternoon—and bringing home winners.

On March 10, 1980, I won three races in one day. This was quite an accomplishment considering my triple was at a New York track, I was a girl jockey, and the competition for mounts was fierce. However, my goal wasn't to set records for "female" jockeys; I wanted to be a great jockey like Steve. My triple put me in tenth position on the leading jockey list. Instant, sudden success by a girl jockey was new to New York racing (two months was sudden to them, but felt like forever to me). Because this was so unusual for the "Sport of Kings," I was getting a lot of publicity.

Winning the first of three races in one day in New York

US Magazine put out a feature article about my riding career. The bold print at the top of the page read, "Move over, Steve Cauthen, this filly's on a fast track." I skimmed it, stopping to read closely the parts I liked: the part where they compared me to Steve and the part about trainer J.J. Crupi calling me "Shirley Temple." I felt a little guilty about that, as if I was deceiving everyone. Truthfully, I wasn't anything like Shirley Temple. They didn't know me—the real me. And, I still had a long way to go before I could be anything like Steve Cauthen!

Us Magazine January 22, 1980

BO DEREK PLAYS PUPIL, P. 26

KAREN ROGERS RIDES HIGH, P. 20

LYNDA CARTER GETS RELIGION, P. 22

DUSTIN HOFFMAN SCORES BIG, P. 54

FEATURES

Cornelia comes back
Cornelia Wallace is over her bitter divorce from George and now works to rehabilitate alcoholics

There's a filly in the saddle
Karen Rogers, 17, is being called the best female jockey in racing history/*by Kerrie Malloy*

A born-again Wonder Woman
Lynda Carter has a new life as a singer and a born-again Christian/*by Alan Ebert*

Sweatshirt chic's romantic look
Sweatshirts are suddenly a big hit off the track *by Didi Moore*

These kids are charming—or else
A finishing school for children opens in—where else?—Beverly Hills/*by Betty Goodwin*

First Lady Phyllis George
Can the toothsome former Miss America find happiness in the Kentucky Governor's mansion?

Wayne Rogers is back on TV as a sexy doc
"M*A*S*H's" Wayne Rogers is now making "House Calls" with Lynn Redgrave/*by Merrill Shindler*

Hollytics: Star Wars 1980
Candidates from both parties are courting Hollywood's biggest names/*by Michele Willens*

The Playboy Club's Bunny Hunt
The Playboy Club holds auditions for new Bunnies, and they come in all sizes/*by Susan M. Silver*

A little boy fights for his life
Doctors said 10-year-old Joey Hofbauer would be dead two years ago, but his parents chose alternative cancer therapy. He's still alive/*by Bonnie Johnson*

Dustin Hoffman tries to hit the perfect ball
Star of *Kramer vs. Kramer*, the season's smash movie, Hoffman nurtures his reputation as a perfectionist—and as one of the most temperamental, "difficult" actors around

A wrestler's aria
Erland van Lidth de Jeude wants to score at the Olympics —and the opera/*by Rochelle Chadakoff*

Need a wife? She can do the chores
Emma Fried's business is to be a "wife" to dozens of bachelors, couples and single women *by Nancy Trachtenberg*

The top woman cadet takes command
Linda Johansen cops a top honor at the U.S. Coast Guard Academy/*by Cherie Burns*

Seventeen Magazine published a similar article: "Is she the female Steve Cauthen?" I liked the comparison to Steve, but the article was like all the others—a lot of fairy tale, good-sounding stuff. I had to say the same thing over and over for all the different interviews. "I grew up around horses. My mother taught me how to ride." And then the worst part: "My stepfather introduced me to racing." How I hated that part. That's when I would go numb, talking through a hollow vacuum that was my voice, not me the jockey. My true feelings about my past conflicted with what I should have felt: Karen the jockey should have felt love and gratitude for Mom and Vince, but the real me just felt anger and resentment. The publicity was nice, but I didn't really believe what they wrote about me. There was nothing like riding winners to prove my self-worth.

A come-from-behind win on a muddy track!

A muddy face!

Chapter 25

Nice Catch: An Awesome Horse

Frank Wright kept his word. The "good mount" he had promised me was Nice Catch, one of the best horses in Frank's barn! I never thought I'd get a chance to ride *him*. Frank explained, "I am trying to get Nice Catch to settle so he can come from off the pace in sprint races and run well in longer races, too. I've seen how you get speed horses to relax. I've watched you control horses that are positively rank with other riders. And you're one of the best gate riders (leaving the starting gate) here in New York. You can get right out there on the lead and still get a horse to relax. You always manage to save something for the end. I've watched you 'steal' races on the front end, and that's *exactly* why I've chosen you to ride my horse!"

Ah, Frank was so smart. Why couldn't all trainers think like him?

As I warmed up Nice Catch in the post parade, I was in awe of the power he exuded. His every muscle was solid and well-defined. His neck and shoulders were massive. His muscular body was built for speed, poised to explode. This was by far the best horse I had ever ridden. I thought that maybe I would be nervous with the pressure of riding a *really* good horse, but just the opposite happened. I wasn't nervous at all! All I felt was confidence, supreme confidence in this horse. Without a doubt, I knew I could easily get used to riding "good" horses like him, if given the chance.

Nice Catch in the post parade

When we loaded into the gate, my heart did beat a little faster, though. Never mind. Just another race. Business as usual, right?

Nice Catch broke sharply and forged straight to the lead. *Easy, boy. Nice and easy.* I knew that I would have a racehorse under me, but he was something else. He was an absolute powerhouse. I took a nice long hold of the reins, relaxing my hands and arms. I could only hope that this would settle Nice Catch and let him know that I didn't want any speed from him just yet. Frank and I had discussed the possibility of sitting back off the pace and not going to the lead. But I was only to do this if I didn't have to fight him. If he would slow down on his own, it would take a lot less out of him. I waited to see if it would work.

Into the first turn we were in front, but I could feel him starting to relax. He had sensed what I wanted from him and stopped pulling on the bit. His stride shortened slightly, as he came back to me. *Good. You're doing just fine. Frank taught you well.* We weren't out of the woods yet, though. Two horses were starting to pass us. Would Nice Catch get competitive and fight to keep his lead? I didn't move my hands and hoped for the best. I could feel him grow anxious. After a few tense moments, he let them go by. *Good boy. That's right. Relax. Wait on me.*

I was very careful not to move my hands. Other than the slight pressure he was beginning to put on the bit, he was still doing okay. He was still waiting for me to give him the signal to pick up the pace.

As we neared the far turn, I could feel him growing impatient. He was tugging on the bit now, wanting to go after the leaders. *Not yet, old boy. Not yet. This race is a little longer than you are used to.*

I knew that as soon as I asked him, he would fire. *Patience, patience. We're in no hurry.* I stayed cool, my hands never moving once from the time we left the gate. But as we started into the far turn, I shortened my reins slightly, and he kicked into high gear. Nice Catch was covering ground so effortlessly. I swung to the outside of the other two and let him have his way. Ah, what a feeling! *This acceleration...riding a good horse...is so incredible.* He cruised on by the other two horses and drew off to an easy victory.

Coming back to the winner's circle, I noticed that everyone from Franks's barn was there with big smiles. The cameras snapped for the win photo. I patted Nice Catch and jumped off. Frank hugged me and beamed with pride. "Ahhh, *my* rider! What a ride!"

Trainer Frank Wright after the race

Chapter 26
Spring in New York: Riding with the Best

Not only had I made the leading jockey list after just four months in New York, I was getting more opportunities to ride quality horses. I was learning about "good" horses, and how very different they were from ordinary horses. Good horses were special. They were gifted, both physically and mentally. Talented, athletic horses always seemed to be smart, intelligent horses. They didn't run, they floated. These horses were so well balanced you couldn't feel their action as they moved over the ground: not the pushing off from behind, nor the pounding as each leg hit the ground. It was a fluid motion. I loved it when I got the chance to ride one of these horses.

With the nicer spring weather, the top racing outfits wintering in Florida or California filtered back onto the New York racing scene. The better-quality horses and trainers changed the whole mood of racing. The riding colony seemed to change overnight, as well. No longer were the "winter riders" getting the mounts. The established "name" jockeys who had gone south for the winter now replaced them: Angel Cordero, Jorge Velasquez, Jacinto Vasquez, and Eddie Maple, to name a few. These were the jockeys that trainers wanted to use. Even though it would be harder to get mounts, I looked forward to the challenge of riding with the best.

The first race I rode with all of them back made a big impact on me. *This is my big chance. I'm in the gate between two of the world's greatest riders. To my right is Angel Cordero, Jr. To my left, Jorge Velasquez. I'm psyched. I want to beat them more than anything else in the world. I want to do it right here, right now. On their turf. Not at the Meadowlands, like I've done before. No. Right here. In New York.*

Mansard, the dark bay horse with the white blaze on his face was trembling beneath me. I could feel him shake, as he anticipated the start. His neck was slightly lathered. I looked around behind the gate and saw that there were still three more horses left to load.

"Relax, boy." I patted his neck, then wiped my hand dry on my pants. "You're going to need it when it counts."

"Karoleeena!"

I looked over at Angel sitting beside me in the next stall. He looked like a bumble bee in his black and yellow silks, hunched over with his goggles down. He was smiling at me. Karoleena. He always called me that. I smiled back at him.

"You goin', baby? You got speed?" he asked, his expression changing to a more serious one.

"We'll soon find out," was all I said.

I glanced down at my colors. The black and white silks belonged to Barry K. Schwartz (of "Calvin Klein" jeans fame). I just *had* to win. I would show everyone who was back from Florida that I wasn't just a winter rider, but that I could compete with the best and win. Mansard could have had a top jockey on him, one of the many who were back in New York now, but his owner and trainer had chosen *me*. I wasn't about to let them down. The jockeys to my left and right only made me more determined to prove my point.

"Baaang." The metal doors slammed open. My horse came out first. He held onto the lead for the whole race and we won! Even

Beating Angel at Aqueduct

though the win wasn't a stakes race, it was of great importance to me. It was the first time I had beaten the best New York jockeys—not the winter jockeys—on their turf.

I was gaining the respect of the top jockeys. Willie Shoemaker, a famous jockey based in California, came to New York to ride. Angel was sitting with him, watching the rerun of my race. I was behind them and overheard the conversation.

"See that jock on the lead?" Angel asked, pointing to my horse.

"Yeah."

"Well, it's a girl."

"Nah. No way. That rider looks too good to be a girl," was Shoemaker's reply.

"Want to bet on it?" Angel asked.

"Wow," said Shoemaker. "I wish I could get *that* low on a horse. I wish I could look as good!"

Angel Cordero, Jr.

HALL OF FAME

JOCKEYS

Willie Shoemaker

These words, coming from two masters of the game—Cordero and Shoemaker—meant more to me than anything.

I was also gaining respect from the trainers. But I could never forget that I still had the bug. I thought about all the other successful apprentices who had made it in New York, only to fall by the wayside after losing their bug. Riding winners was still my best chance for continued success.

Chapter 27
The Torn Up Letter

It was just a normal day of racing. Sifting through the pile of fan mail that I received in the jocks' room, I found another one of Vince's love letters. Ugh. They were so mushy. I dreaded reading them. Vince went on in his usual way, "I am so in love with you. There are times when you take my breath away. I miss you very very much." There was an arrow pointing to his teardrop. "See the tear?" And on and on it went. I wished he would just forget about me. I tore up the letter and buried the pieces in the bottom of the little yellow garbage pail in the girl jocks' room as I had done so many times before. I still couldn't get used to his letters. Nobody could ever know. *Nobody*. If anyone ever found out I would *kill* myself.

After riding the last race, I went into the back room to take my shower. I always felt so much more alone and guilty on days when the letters came. It just made everything so *real*.

I tried to concentrate on the horses I had ridden as the water ran over my body, horrible body, horrible me. But, I was small, wasn't I? I wasn't like a woman. I was a jockey. I glanced down at my tiny frame, all ninety pounds of it. I was flat chested and looked like a little kid. I was okay, wasn't I? I turned the water off and thought I heard someone in the front room. It was probably my valet, Joe, coming to get my pile of dirty riding clothes.

"It's okay, Joe," I yelled out. "I'm in the back. You can come in. I'll wait back here." I listened for Joe's reply, holding the shower curtain tightly to the very edges. Instead of Joe, I heard my mother's voice.

"It's just me, Karen."

I opened the curtain a crack and reached for my bathrobe. I had forgotten that Mom and I were meeting after the last race and had planned on going out to dinner.

"I'll be a few more minutes," I called out to her from the shower area. I got dressed quickly and came out to meet her. She had this really weird look on her face.

"I'm about ready, Mom. I hurried..." Why was she looking at me so strangely?

At dinner Mom was unusually quiet. I hated it when she was quiet. It meant she was unhappy. Probably because of me. When we got home, I went straight to my room. I sat on the bed, trying not to think about Mom's strange silence. After a few minutes, I was relieved to hear her voice.

"Karen? Are you busy? Could you come out here for a minute?"

I left my room and found her sitting on the couch with that strange look on her face again. What was wrong?

"Karen..." Her voice sounded funny. "I saw some small pieces of a torn up letter in the garbage in the girl jocks' room. I wondered why it was torn up, and then I recognized Vince's handwriting. I picked up all the pieces and was able to tape it back together."

No!

My mind and body froze in time as she spoke. I went completely numb. Weak legs stood there underneath empty shell. My body became a void, a vacuum, unable to feel pain, unable to feel anything. My mind raced away, right out of there. I was somewhere else, somewhere safe. There stood only a weak, numb, empty shell. I wasn't there at all.

I couldn't hear Mom. Would my legs hold up, or would they collapse and fall into a heap? I should be dead now. *Now* I should be *dead.*

My body stood there, convicted. *Feel the pain! You deserve it!* But I couldn't feel the pain. I could feel nothing. Everything was very fuzzy and distant now. Was I going to faint? I couldn't hear Mom as her lips moved. I couldn't hear a word of what she was saying. There was a buzzing in my head, so loud, so loud, my ears were ringing.

My whole world had changed. It was spinning around me in a fuzzy haze. Mom was somehow different. I shouldn't be here. The bad me was exposed—defenseless. I was phasing out.

Suddenly, I heard a voice from within me. *If she blames you, you will kill yourself. Go ahead and do it.* But Mom didn't have to kill me. I was dead already.

Although I was far away in my mind, my mouth uttered these words, "Whatever you think happened with Vince—*did.* And *more.* And *worse. Far worse.*" There. I said it. Now the truth was finally out. I had ruined her life, and she had the right to kill me.

I couldn't take it anymore. The real me had finally been exposed. I went to my room, defeated. I was shell shocked. It was like living inside a nightmare, and I couldn't wake up.

Years later, Mom explained that she had told me on that night that whatever happened with Vince was NOT my fault; however, because I was in a state of shock, I didn't hear anything she said. At that time and for many years afterward, Mom didn't know how much I blamed myself.

It was nothing short of an act of God that Mom found Vince's torn up letter. I always buried the pieces of his letters in the bottom of the little yellow garbage pail in the girl jocks' room. That day, the track janitor must have come by and dumped the small yellow garbage pail into a much larger bin that he wheeled around collecting trash from all the rooms. After being dumped into the larger bin, the torn pieces of letter from the bottom of my garbage pail were now at the very top of the full, bigger bin. Instead of wheeling it right out as usual, it was left there in the girl jocks' room. I was back in the shower when Mom threw out a tissue and right there under her nose, on the very top of the full trash bin, were the torn pieces of Vince's letter. Her eyes fell on the piece with the words, "Love, Vince."

The next morning, I awoke feeling very depressed. There was this awful feeling of dread, like when you first wake up from a horrible nightmare and you don't want to move. Wait...Was last night real? No. Put it out of your head. I have to ride Nice Catch in a big stakes race today.

That afternoon, competing against the best sprinters in the nation in the $75,000 Carter Handicap, Karen the jockey was ready to ride the race of her life. My concentration was intense, so intense. I could make no mistakes. All through the race, my mind was completely absorbed in the strategy, taking in everything at once. My body carried out orders, a race riding machine. Going forty miles an hour, I was

Carter Handicap – finishing third on Nice Catch (#6)

definitely in control. There, I was focused. There, I was safe. I was riding for my life, riding as hard as I could. Nice Catch finished third in a photo finish. The race was run in 1:21, the fastest and most exciting seven furlongs I had ever ridden.

Chapter 28
Anticipating Blame

Riding was only a temporary escape. That night, Mom told me she was going to call Vince about the letter. *Horrible me. I'm still alive, and life is still going on.* Emotionless, I wondered if this was all really happening. At any moment, I was ready for Mom to blame me.

"Karen? Could you come here?" Mom was just outside my bedroom door.

I moved like a beaten soldier. Out of my room. Into the hall. Ready to face death. The firing squad. I wanted it to all be over. Mom was on the phone with Vince. Although she was standing right next to me, I didn't hear a word of what she was saying. She handed me the phone. I felt like she wanted a confession in a conspiracy, now exposed. But Vince was far away and couldn't save me. Nothing could save me now.

I heard Vince's familiar voice. I wasn't sure whose side he was on anymore. Like a robot, I said two words into the phone. "She knows."

Was he saying anything? Exposed in front of Mom, I zoned out, too scared and numb for my senses to work properly.

I had told Vince many times that if this ever happened—if Mom ever did find out—I would kill myself. He knew that. So, he would probably try to get back in touch with me later, somehow, when Mom wasn't listening. A phone call to the jocks' room, a letter...something. Something to keep me alive. He must have known how I felt. Right now, he was probably the *only* one who understood.

Mom must want to *kill* me. The only reason she hadn't was because maybe she was hoping I would do it first. Or maybe she wanted me to suffer slowly, emotionally, the payback for what I had done to her. Would she tell everyone at the track how bad I was and destroy Karen the jockey? Because now...me the jockey...that was all there was left.

Mom took the phone from me. I went back into my room. It didn't feel safe anymore. Nothing was safe anymore. As I lay there numb, I heard Mom sobbing in the next room. I had *ruined* her life.

In reality, Mom was angry with Vince and upset that he had hurt me. She wanted me to stand up to him on the phone while she was there to support me. She wanted him to stop bothering me. I was numb, heard nothing, and still assumed she blamed me. I had misinterpreted her crying; she was upset not because I had ruined her life, but because of what Vince had done to me.

Vince never acknowledged any of what happened. It didn't seem to matter to him that Mom knew and that I wanted to kill myself. No, he didn't care. There was no reaction from him. Nothing. There was never a phone call to the jocks' room, never a letter to tear up and throw away. Not one. There was no sign whatsoever that he cared anymore. There was just nothing.

After a while I stopped expecting. There was never going to be a letter or a secret phone call to let me know he understood, or that he cared how much all of this hurt me. I buried the pain of his rejection. I didn't kill myself to punish the bad me. And, I continued to function.

Around Mom, I was always afraid that the subject of Vince would come up. I anticipated the moment when she would say the words out loud, that I was guilty. As time went on and Mom didn't blame me, I felt even worse. I hated the secrecy, the hidden conspiracy. I wished she would just blame me, kill me, and get it over with once and for all. I figured that by now, Grandma and my sister Susan knew what had happened. But of course, nobody talked about it, so I wasn't sure. I couldn't bear the thought that Susan and Grandma knew, and that I was *so bad* that they wouldn't talk to me about it either. I didn't want to think that they knew and were only pretending to love me, the way I figured Mom was.

Mom felt bad for me and sensed I did not want to talk about the situation with Vince. Nobody was blaming me; they just didn't know what to say. I took their silence as a verdict of guilt.

Mom hired a lawyer in order to get a divorce from Vince and

pursue pressing charges against him for what he did to me.

"Karen, I'd like you to go to the lawyer's office with me," she said.

I became numb. I thought that if the situation with Vince was brought out into the open, I would be found guilty. "Okay, Mom." I would do whatever she wanted. I told myself I wouldn't be afraid.

The whole way to the lawyer's office I tried not to think about anything but my riding. When the lawyer introduced himself, I suddenly wished I were invisible. I felt the wall go up, my defense. I was Karen the jockey; he couldn't blame me.

We went into a private room where we sat around this big table. I felt very alone. At one point, I thought maybe they weren't going to blame me; they were talking about me being underage when it happened. But then the lawyer grew very intense and leaned toward Mom. He said, "I don't think it's a good idea to press charges against Vince—in the best interests of everyone involved. I mean, Karen is doing so well at the track. She is celebrity status. We'll lose the case, she will be blamed, and her name will be dragged through the mud."

Right, I thought. Then everyone would know that I was guilty. So what? I don't care. Maybe then I'd get what I deserved. But, what about Vince? He was off the hook. I was angry, but then my anger quickly gave way to depression. It was all my fault.

Mom was very upset on the way home. It didn't matter. I was Karen the jockey again.

I was eighth in the jockey standings at Aqueduct. Even though I was right up there with the greatest riders in the country (Angel Cordero was only five wins ahead of me), the possibility of leaving New York and going to Monmouth Park for the summer meeting weighed heavily on my mind. I loved racing with the best jockeys, but I knew it would be very difficult to get mounts here come summer when I lost the bug. My success in New York may have been due to having a weight allowance; soon, this would change. My transition from apprentice to journeyman jockey was fast approaching, and losing the bug in July in New York was about as tough as it gets. Because in August, New York racing moved upstate to Saratoga—the toughest meeting in the country for *any* rider!

Monmouth Park was opening in just a few weeks, and it was time to make this crucial decision. I spoke to my New Jersey agent, Ed, and he assured me that I would do well at Monmouth Park—with or without the bug. It was extremely difficult for me to leave New York, but after talking to Ed, I knew it was the best thing to do for my career. I could always return to New York when the top jockeys went south again for the winter.

The decision made, we rented a summer cottage near Monmouth Park. The pace was slower on the New Jersey shore. Maybe I would learn to relax and enjoy life. Maybe I would change and become normal. Maybe I had made the right decision, after all. Still, I couldn't wait to move into my new bedroom, my sanctuary, the place where I could hide the real me from the world. Maybe I would change in time. Maybe. Just not right now.

Mom didn't think my reclusive behavior was odd. She accepted it, believing that all jockeys were like me: single-mindedly dedicated to their work. She thought that was the price to pay for being a jockey. She figured that all riders were extroverts at the track, but really introverted and quiet at home, needing privacy and time to go over charts and training schedules.

Chapter 29
David: Just An Ole Country Boy

On opening day at Monmouth Park, I won the second race. It felt great. My riding had drastically improved from the previous summer here, when I began as a jockey; I was a New York rider now, and it showed.

I wasn't the only seasoned apprentice to come to Monmouth Park. David Ashcroft, the leading apprentice in Florida, was also here. My first conversation with the 17-year-old apprentice was out by the pool next to the jocks' room. I watched him dive off the low board and swim to the side. I caught him glancing over at me to see if I was watching. Now, he was headed for the high diving board. He was cute. He had blonde hair and freckles. David dove into the pool again. And again. Over and over he dove, showing off all his different moves. As

David Ashcroft

he climbed out of the pool, I called over to him."Where are you from?"

He grinned. "New Mexico."

I liked his accent. He sounded like a cowboy.

David picked up his towel and sidled over toward me. He was shivering. "Whew! That water's coooold. Wonder if they'll ever put the heat on."

I smiled and shrugged.

David sat down on the lounge chair next to me. He said, "I read about you winning all those races in New York when I was down in Florida. When I read that you were coming here, I wondered if you rode as good as they said. I watched you win the second race. You ride good for a girl."

"Thanks. I read about you, too, in the *Racing Form*. You did good in Florida. You like it there?"

"I love Florida."

My first instincts about David were good. There was nothing phony about him. I didn't feel threatened by him, nor did I feel doubtful of myself as we talked. We were both jockeys, and that was safe.

As we discussed our riding careers, I felt something more going on between us. I wasn't sure what it was, but it felt different. It didn't feel threatening or bad. My heart was going a little faster as he spoke, especially when he smiled at me. David seemed shy, and yet sure of himself at the same time. I enjoyed listening to him. We talked about our career plans. David was going back to Florida when the New Jersey tracks closed for the winter.

"Well," I said, "Hopefully, I plan to ride in New York again this winter. I love riding there."

"I hate New York," David said with a frown. Then his expression changed. He grinned, his green eyes sparkling mischievously. "No, you won't find me ridin' there 'cause I'm just an ole country boy."

And with that he stood up, rolled his eyes, and fell backward into the pool.

Mom seemed happy at Monmouth Park, but I assumed she was really depressed because of the tremendous pain I had caused her. I felt so guilty all the time, and was grateful that she didn't show any sadness or blame me. I was glad she didn't bring up the subject, but still, it didn't just go away; it was there, beneath the surface. However, I just concentrated on my horses, blocking it out of my mind. Of course, there were no phone calls or letters from Vince to remind me that it was all real.

I worked harder at the track, focused, driven, trying to prove to myself that I really was okay, that being a great jockey would somehow make me worthy of living. I was riding eight or nine races every afternoon, besides getting on five or six horses each morning. Keeping busy left no time for thoughts, no room for guilt. When I rode, all my feelings disappeared. It seemed like I could do no wrong with my riding. The horses just kept on winning and winning. I was going to have my best meeting ever. Things were looking *so* good. The possibility of a riding title entered my mind. It was not out of reach. I was the second leading jockey, just a few wins behind Donald MacBeth.

Four wins in one day at Monmouth Park

A few weeks into the meeting, I won four races—*four in one day*! The fourth win put me over the top; I was now the leading jockey at Monmouth Park! It seemed so unreal, like a dream. Only a year ago I had started my professional career, and now I was a leading jockey.

As my horses continued to win, David's horses finished second a lot. He was very frustrated. David was scowling as we headed out toward the paddock. "I'm sick of all these seconds," he said, slapping his boot with his whip. "When you gonna give me a shot, Rogers?"

I looked over at him. His face had changed. He was smiling now. David was taking my winning very well, better than some of the other jocks. He wasn't being nasty; he was just teasing me.

"Ah, David, you ride good. All those horses that are finishing second will come back and win for you. You'll have a hot streak and then everyone will want to put you on their horses. Then things will turn around. You'll see."

"If you say so," he winked as we parted, heading our separate ways in the paddock.

As if to confirm what I said, David's horse won that race. Now he had five winners to my fourteen. David approached me later that afternoon. His smile was very warm.

"Hey, you wanna see a movie or somethin' sometime?"

I liked David, but I wasn't sure I wanted to date him. I didn't want him to know the real me. And, I didn't want to deal with the sex issue. After what Vince did, I was sure that another guy would do the same thing. And, like with Vince, I wouldn't be able to stop him. Well, I just wouldn't think about it. I agreed to go to the movies with him. This would just be a date. A *normal* date like *normal* teenagers were supposed to have.

The movie was a drive-in, which I hadn't expected. I felt uneasy when we parked.

"This spot good, or do you want to get closer?" David asked.

"It's okay."

The movie started and I began to feel queasy. Why did we have to be parked here in the dark, all alone in his car? I tried not to think, to concentrate on the movie, but I couldn't. My mind was racing. What does he think of me? Can he tell I'm different? What will he do? What if he does? What should I do? What's *normal?*

The minutes dragged. Out of the corner of my eye, I saw David move. I froze. I was numb as he casually put his arm around me. I could tell he seemed awkward with this, not like Vince. Still, he was pulling me closer to him. My body was so tense. I ached all over. How do I pretend this is good?

After some awkward moments, which felt like an eternity, he turned to kiss me. I squirmed away.

"What's wrong?" he asked.

"Nothing. *Nothing!*"

He took his arm off me and leaned back to his side of the car.

"Okay," he said.

I thought that maybe he was mad at me, but couldn't really tell. Maybe it was all in my head. We watched the rest of the movie in silence. I felt so guilty. He was mad at me, wasn't he? And it was all my fault. *Why couldn't I just be normal?*

On the way home David talked a lot. I was glad he did as it meant he probably didn't hate me. He told me about his large family and his Mormon background. He had so many brothers and sisters.

When we pulled up to the cottage, he didn't try to kiss me good night. I was glad, but felt guilty again. I was thankful he didn't blame me, though.

"Thanks, David. I had fun."

"See ya tomorrow."

It was a good thing Mom and Amy lived with me. They were my built-in excuse for not inviting him in. Inside, safe with the door shut, I wondered if David still liked me.

The Monmouth Park meeting was going so well; winners were coming at an incredible clip. Things seemed to be working out with David, as well. He still liked me! He was even nicer to me now that we had been out on a date. Much to my amazement, he asked me out again. Yes, things were going so well in my life. I didn't deserve to be so happy.

David was very serious the next time we went out. He told me that having a family was very important to him. He said he wanted to settle down soon and that getting married and having kids was what life was all about. Most of his brothers and sisters were already married and had kids, he said. "The most important thing in life is finding your woman and having your kids. Family is the most important thing," he explained to me in a very matter-of-fact way.

I shuddered, and held back the anger. I was angry that I couldn't agree with him. Angry that I couldn't think like that. Angry that my family wasn't perfect like his, because I had screwed it all up. Angry that I didn't want kids of my own. Not yet, anyway, because I didn't want them to suffer, to grow up hating themselves, the way I did. And besides, I was only seventeen—and so was he! Why couldn't we just do what *we* wanted for a while? Anyway, I didn't know about him, but I was incapable of taking care of anyone besides myself. Just getting through each day *myself* was enough. The most important thing in my life—my only reason for living—was my career. Without it, I had no reason to even be alive.

"You know what the Indians say?" David asked. He was referring to the American Indian tribes near where he grew up in New Mexico.

"No, what?"

"They say that for every person born, there is the perfect mate born also, somewhere in the world."

"Do you believe that?" I asked.

"Yeah, I think so," he answered.

It was nice to hear about family values, perfect mates and all, but was it realistic?

"David, what if the person born for you is in Australia or someplace else? What if you never go to that country or ever get to meet them? Then what? Do you settle for someone else, stay alone, or search until you find them? And how do you know who is the *right* one, anyway?"

"God takes care of all that," he simply said. "You do believe in God, don't you?"

"I don't know. My family never went to church, so I don't know what to think about it." *Yeah, and Vince was an atheist. He didn't believe in God at all.* I thought back to the time when I was ten, when this subject had come up before. It was when Vince had first come around. I had told a friend in my fifth grade class that I was an atheist because that's what Vince was, and we all looked up to Vince. It seemed like the right thing to say, because Vince seemed to know about everything. I remembered how angry my friend got at me when I told her that. She believed in God, and wouldn't speak to me afterward. I didn't want the same thing to happen with David.

"You *don't* believe in God?" David asked.

"I said I don't know!"

I didn't want to talk about it anymore. I didn't want David to be right about God, because that would make Vince a liar. I didn't want to believe that Vince had lied to me about that, too.

"Let's not talk about this, okay?" I said, frustrated. "Anyway, all I care about is my riding."

David shook his head. "Is riding all you ever think about?"

I hated it when he said this to me. He didn't understand. Being a jockey was the only thing that made me okay. Couldn't he see that? David was so strong-willed. I liked this about him, but at the same time, deep down I knew that if he was right, there was definitely something wrong with me because all I could think about was riding. He could ride and want to have a social life—and a family, too! *Why couldn't I just be more like him?*

Sometimes I felt good around David, but it never lasted. Inevitably I was either angry at myself, or depressed. I was bad. I didn't deserve to have fun, or to be happy. I didn't think I could last as his "girlfriend."

Chapter 30
Tossed Like a Rag Doll

I was the luckiest person on earth. What would I ever do if I couldn't ride? I was the leading jockey, and I was going for my third win of the day. As the field entered the first turn of the race, the horses were bunched up. Bal Breeze was pulling me out of the saddle. I tried to get him back, but he wouldn't relax for me. We were in tight quarters with no place to go, but still Bal Breeze wouldn't slow down. He clipped the heels of the horse in front of us. It all happened in an instant. I was tossed upward like a rag doll. I don't remember anything else.

The track paramedics ran out to the small body lying motionless on the racetrack. Later, they told my mother that I was screaming for her, calling out as if she could rescue me from the pain. The paramedics weren't sure if I was paralyzed as they placed me carefully on the stretcher.

I don't remember any of this. I was unconscious.

I woke up in the hospital. I was in excruciating pain. "Where am I?" I mumbled. What had happened to me? *Make the pain go away, you can.* I had always been able to block pain, both mental and physical. But this time, I couldn't.

Mom was there with me, rubbing my forehead. She brushed my hair back gently with her hand. "I shouldn't have left. I left the races early...then I got the phone call..." she said.

I started to cry.

Mom looked extremely worried. Although I didn't know it, she had been told by the doctor that three of my vertebrae had been crushed. The broken vertebrae were so close (a millimeter) to my spinal cord that I was at great risk of being paralyzed until they could immobilize my back.

"You are a very lucky girl," Dr. Lehmann said, "very lucky you aren't paralyzed."

Was I lucky?

"As soon as we can," he said, "we're going to put you into a body cast. We have to be sure, though, that there are no internal injuries, no further complications. It may be a few days."

Those "few" days were the longest of my life. The doctors must have had me on some sort of potent pain killer—codeine or morphine—during those first days in the hospital, but still, the pain was intense, almost unbearable. The only thing to break up the time was the nurses coming in every few hours.

The nurses would give me a sponge bath every day, which was a horrifying experience. I hated people having their hands on me, seeing my naked body; I felt like they could tell I was different, like they would know the secret. I felt so much shame. I was afraid my body would give me away.

Mom was there with me every day. She opened all the cards and letters from fans and horsemen. I couldn't believe that so many people knew I was hurt, and that they cared—I even got flowers from owners and trainers in New York!

The nurses would make comments. "This place looks like a

greenhouse! You must have a lot of friends!"

Finally, the cast went on. It went from my neck to my hips. I was protected now; my body was finally covered. I was like a turtle, safe inside my big white shell. At last, I was no longer in pain!

Everyone in racing knew about my injury because of the tremendous amount of press:

- New York Post - "Karen Rogers hurt in Monmouth spill"
- Newark Star-Ledger - "Rogers hurt in accident at Monmouth; Karen's condition called satisfactory"
- Daily Racing Form - "Karen Rogers Hurt in Spill at Monmouth"
- New York Times - "Miss Rogers Injures 3 Vertebrae"
- The Home News - "Jockey With Stout Heart: Karen Rogers looking ahead to resuming riding career"
- Star-Ledger - "Rogers anxious to saddle up/ Will wear body cast for 3 months"
- New York Post - "Injured Karen vows to ride again"
- Bernardsville News - "Karen Rogers Injured In Spill at Monmouth"
- New York Times - "Karen Rogers's Spirit Remains Unbroken"
- The Home News - "Rogers insists she will ride again"
- ...and more.

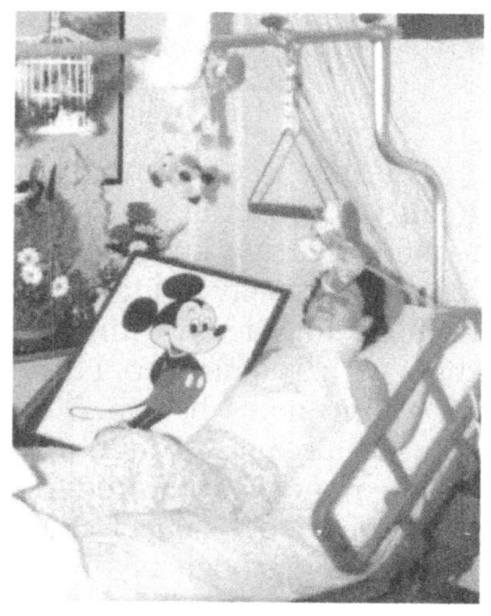

I knew I had talked to a lot of reporters, both in person and over the phone, but I hadn't realized the extent of the coverage. Maybe it was because I was a girl. Or maybe it was because I was the leading rider when I had the spill.

David came by every day, even though he was busier than ever winning races. A few of the trainers visited me and had words of encouragement.

"Take your time and come back when you're right. You know, when you're ready we'll have some good horses for you to ride."

Better words could not have been spoken.

I started physical therapy the day before I left the hospital. The doctor explained, "These exercises are designed to strengthen the muscles around your injury. They will determine your recovery, but it's up to you to do them. If you are willing to work hard, you'll make a full recovery and, hopefully, can be back riding in sixth months."

Six months??? How would I be able to go six months without riding?

I vowed right then to do all the exercises—and then some. I would do every back exercise possible. My back would be so strong that nothing like this could happen to me *ever* again! Not only that, but I would do exercises for my arms, my legs—everything. If I was strong, then nothing bad like this could ever happen to me again. I would rather die than not be able to ride.

Chapter 31
Losing My Identity

The first week home from the hospital was very difficult for me. Reality set in, and I sank into a deep depression. Without riding, I had lost my identity; I was no longer Karen the jockey. I just wanted to be left alone, to stay hidden in my room. I didn't want to see anyone, not even David. The only thing that kept me going was my exercises. I did them with a vengeance. I threw myself—all of me—into them. I always did more than I had to. More was better. More meant I would ride sooner. But more was never enough. Never enough to fill the void inside of me where Karen the jockey used to be.

Mom tried to cheer me up. "Karen, let's go over to the races. *Everyone* has been asking me how you're doing. Come on, let's go. It will do you good to get out and see some people."

"No. I can't go over there. I'm not riding. There is no *reason* to go to the races. What will people think?"

Mom looked confused. She really didn't understand how unworthy

Jane Pauley from NBC-TV
"The Today Show" autographs my cast

I felt without my riding. However, she wouldn't give up so easily.

"Come on. Let's go. You can have people autograph the cast. That can be your reason to go." She gave me a new billowy shirt to fit over the cast and hung a pen on a string around my neck.

At the races the trainers, valets, and agents came up to me with concern. "Oh, it's such a shame that you got hurt. You were doing so well!" But I just put on my old smile as if nothing was wrong. "I'll be back soon," I would say as they signed my cast. My smile always covered up the real me.

Jane Pauley from NBC-TV "The Today Show" came to the track to interview me. She added her autograph to the growing collection on my cast.

It was now covered, front and back, with signatures. Monmouth Park held a special day in my honor. They called it "Karen Rogers Day" and gave out copies of a sketch of me drawn by Peb, the artist for the *Daily Racing Form*.

Every day I did hours and hours of exercises. I did all kinds: exercises for my back, my legs, and my arms. I did each exercise over thirty times, counting as I went. Counting kept my

mind busy. Now that I didn't have riding to think about, I had to keep my mind filled up with something else. Within a week, I was doing four hours of exercises every day in my cast.

Looking back, this may have been the start of my obsessive-compulsive disorder, or OCD, which was diagnosed many years later.

In the same way that I became obsessed with my exercises—in order to ride again—I became just as preoccupied with my weight. What if I started gaining weight? I wasn't riding now. What if I got too fat to ride? If I gained weight, I might develop a chest. I still hadn't gotten my period, and I would be eighteen in the fall. If I gained weight, I would look like a "woman." That could *never* happen!

The fear of gaining weight was so strong that I would rarely eat. When Mom cooked, I would tell her that I had already eaten. The only food I allowed myself was salad with no dressing. Even though I wasn't eating and I was doing lots of exercises, I still felt overweight. Every hour I would get on the scale. *One hundred pounds!!! Ugh!!! So fat!!!* (I neglected to factor in the ten-pound body cast.) I had to get back down to my riding weight of ninety-five pounds!

Me (in body cast) and David

David came by the house every day after the races. He was winning a lot now and had moved up on the leading jockey list. I was happy for him, but the truth was I hadn't really been thinking much about him. My mind was totally absorbed in thoughts of body weight, staying thin, and doing all my exercises.

When David came over, I changed back to the role of girlfriend. I wasn't busy with my riding career, so naturally I should be spending more time with him, right?

On the fourth of July, David and I went out to the beach to watch the fireworks. He had brought along a blanket. I panicked when I saw it, but then remembered I was wearing a body cast. I was so glad for this. I felt much safer knowing the cast would be between his body and mine. Still, I knew it would only be a matter of time before sex would come up. I had hoped that maybe it could be avoided all together, that maybe my cast was a good enough excuse. I didn't really want to break up with him; I just wished he could find some other girl for that part.

Chapter 32

Obsessed with Weight and Exercises

One benefit of my spill was the timing; I still had one month left of my apprentice allowance to use when I returned to racing. According to Dr. Lehmann I wouldn't be ready to ride until late December, so when Monmouth Park ended, we moved back to New York where I would make my comeback. Without a doubt, New York trainers would want to use me again if I still had the weight allowance.

David moved from Monmouth Park to the Meadowlands for the fall meeting. He was winning lots of races there. We continued to see each other whenever possible. One day David was riding a race at Belmont, so he came to see me before he rode. We went to breakfast at the International House of Pancakes. As we sat down, it occurred to me for the first time that pancakes were very fattening. I hadn't been eating much at all. Salad, maybe a melon here and there.

I watched David consume his pancakes and eggs like it was the Last Supper. I had a cup of coffee and pushed everything around on my plate. I wondered how David could eat so much and still keep his weight down.

"David, how can you eat all that and then go ride? Doesn't it put weight on?"

He smiled. "I don't keep it down."

"What?" I asked, suddenly interested. Could I eat pancakes and still be thin?

"I go heave. Most of the jocks do it. It's easy, once you get used to it." David got up and disappeared into the bathroom. I sat there waiting for him to return, thinking about what he had said. Could it be that easy? Such a simple answer. Eat and eat...and still be thin! But...wasn't it *hard* to throw up?

I thought about all the delicious food he had eaten: pancakes, eggs, bacon, and lots of syrup. Mmmm. Even if it was hard, it would certainly be worth it.

David came back to the table in less than five minutes. Four, tops.

"How do you do it?" I asked casually. "You were so fast in there."

He smiled. "There is a little trick to it," he said and then gave me details. I took in every word he said. This was too good to be true.

"I don't heave very often," David explained, "but my horse is in light this afternoon. (He was riding a race later at Belmont). Gotta do nine (one hundred and nine). Lots of riders do it. More'n you think. Some flip all the time. All day every day. Beats starvin', for some of the big guys. They don't really have a choice, you know. But you—you're lucky, Crispy Critter (his pet name for me). You never have to worry about your weight! You're *so* light!"

Little did he know what I was thinking. And little did I know that this "casual" routine was a very dangerous one. All I knew was that if David did it—if *most* of the jocks did it—it must be okay. To David, as to most of the jockeys, heaving was just part of the job. To me though, it was the perfect answer. Maybe one day I would try this. It was a way to control my weight without ever having to starve. If I could do it, then I would be thin—and safe—forever.

The cast came off at the end of September. I was surprised to find that without the cast, I weighed only eighty-six pounds! No matter. With the cast off, I could now swim, ride a bike, and increase my exercises even more. Soon I'd be back on a horse and riding races again! But how fit was fit enough to ride after such a long absence? I wasn't sure, so I made sure. My pace quickened. I couldn't slow down. I was pumped up, busy, busy, busy with the task of getting fit.

I started adding to my exercises. I was already doing 33 of each exercise instead of the original 25 that the therapist had instructed, but now I was adding 3 more onto the end of that number. When 3 more didn't feel like enough, I increased it to 5 extras, and then 5 turned into 7. I always added an odd number of "extras," giving me the illusion or feeling that I was always doing "one more," or "one better." Soon I was up to doing 9, then 11 extras of each exercise. I would do 33, then 33 + 1 up to 33 + 11. It still didn't feel like I was doing enough, so to make sure I did 33 +11 + 1 up to 33 + 11 + 7! It was getting out of hand. The 30s eventually crept into the 50s, then 57, then 57 + 11...and so on.

After my accident, I was showing more and more signs of obsessive-compulsive disorder, also known as OCD. The compulsive obsessing on exercises, counting, food, and my busy, busy, busy mental state were all efforts to control my out of control life. I did not know my condition had an actual name until over a decade later; I just thought it was me. From researching OCD, my condition may have been caused by the blow to my head in the Monmouth Park spill, hormonal changes, stress, genetics, or chemistry changes in my brain. It could also have been triggered by the emotional trauma of Vince, which was out of my control. I became aware that I had OCD in the early 1990s, but I did not seek treatment until 1997, at which point the condition had become impossible to live with.

Mornings at the track getting ready for my comeback

On the first of December, Dr. Lehmann gave me the okay to get on horses again. It was good to be back in the saddle. New York and all the familiar faces. Recognition, respect. Most of the New York trainers seemed happy to see me. They promised to give me mounts. But those were just promises. I knew it was really up to me to show them I could ride as well as before—that I had no fear of falling, and that I could still find the winner's circle.

Two weeks later, I would ride four races at Aqueduct. Heading out into the paddock for my first race, I felt like my old self: confident, focused only on the race ahead. It was as if the past six months had never happened; it was like I had never been away.

At Monmouth Park before the spill, I was riding mostly favorites. But this was New York, and I was back on longshots. Still, my horses ran well to finish second, third, and two were fourth. All in all, except for a winner, my first day back was a success. The trainers were pleased, and my biggest worry—being fit—was no longer an issue.

The press was having a field day. All the New York papers and some of the New Jersey papers were covering my comeback. The coverage was positive.

A rose from a fan

It was good to be back in the old routine, except for one thing. Eating. The old routine was a late breakfast and dinner after the races. How did I ever eat that much when I was riding before and not get *fat?* My starvation diet of the past six months had shrunk my stomach and changed my outlook on food. Maybe I could go back to my old eating routine. Maybe... I would just have to try heaving.

I started throwing up, and it soon became a habit. Now that I was eating and heaving, food became a bigger obsession than when I had just been starving and avoiding it altogether. I felt guilty eating in front of anyone, knowing it would just end up in the toilet. The other jockeys did this in order to make the assigned weight. My "weight" dilemma was all in my head.

I was totally unaware that I had developed an "eating disorder" and unaware of the dangers of this ritual. Self-induced vomiting is extremely addicting, extremely dangerous, and is, in fact, known as the disease bulimia. I had never heard the terms eating disorder, anorexia, or bulimia. Back then, there was not the public awareness that there is now. I did not know that one out of five college girls was bulimic, nor that throwing up was an addiction that could end in death. I was not aware that I couldn't stop, even if I tried. This addiction took up lots of my time; buying, eating, and throwing up food was an endless cycle.

"Caption: "Let's ask Karen Rogers how she does it."

Chapter 33
A Brand New Relationship

Mom, Amy, and I were going to spend Christmas with my sister Susan at Grandma's farm. It would be nice to see everyone again. I invited David to come as he couldn't make it home to New Mexico for the holidays.

While sitting around the fireplace, the subject of God came up again. I remembered how David and I had talked about belief in God, and I had been uncomfortable with the subject. When Susan started talking about her "relationship" with God, I was surprised. How did she know so much about God? And more so, why?

"How do you know all this stuff?" I asked her quietly.

"I've been reading the Bible and praying," she said.

Well, if Susan believed, maybe there was something to it. I asked her to explain what she knew. For the first time in my life, I heard the story of Jesus. It was interesting. I had never heard it before. I knew the Christmas songs, but I never knew the story behind them. Susan and I had never been to church when we were growing up, so she was the only one who could identify with how little I really knew about the subject. Susan explained things very simply to me. She explained that God loved each one of us and that knowing Him was very personal. She told me she had a personal relationship with God and that He had helped her through some rough times.

I looked at Susan closely, suddenly realizing that our moving away must have affected her deeply. She must have been lonely. She looked happy now, though. She seemed at peace with things. Maybe this "relationship" with God made her happy. I asked her how I could get to know God. Her answer was simple: pray.

"How do I do that?" I asked, amazed that God would care about me.

"Talk to God. Prayer is a conversation with God," she said simply. "Start anywhere. Tell Him what's on your mind. Talk to Him like you would talk to your best friend."

I didn't have a best friend. What would I talk about? Where would I begin?

The day after Christmas I was back in the girl jocks' room. I kept thinking about what my sister had said. Was God real? Would he hear my prayers? Did He want a relationship with me? If she was right and there was a God, it was *very* important; it wasn't something I should ignore. If there was a God and He could hear my prayers, then I wanted to know.

Susan had said to pray about what was on my mind. Winning a race was on my mind as it was almost two weeks into my comeback and I had not won a race yet. Although I knew it was selfish, what better thing to pray for? Even if God wasn't real, it couldn't hurt. I turned out the light, got on my knees, and sought God. Was He listening? Could He hear my prayer? I directed my voice to Him. "God, if You are real and can hear me, please help my horse to win." Selfish prayer, but it was a start. Maybe it was a coincidence, but the horse won. Out of the eight races I rode that afternoon, I had two wins and two seconds!

Answered prayer – finally a winner!

The next day, the same thing happened. I said a prayer, only this time I focused more on finding God. Was He there? Would He listen? I wasn't sure, but I didn't feel as alone as when I had prayed the day before. Maybe He was listening. Would He get angry at me for praying for the same thing? Was I abusing prayer? Was that possible? Susan said you couldn't pray too much—that God liked it when you prayed. Still I didn't want to push it. I was sure He had better things to do than to make my horse win.

When the horse won, I didn't feel so alone winning a race. I sensed very strongly that someone was there with me, a Presence.

Chapter 34
Belonging

David won the leading jockey title at the very competitive Meadowlands meeting. At the end of December he went back down to Florida to ride. I wanted to stay in New York. We remained friends, but went our separate ways.

Even though I had only ridden for six months out of the year (1980), again I ended up as the leading female jockey in the country. Now, I was back riding and winning, but soon I would lose the bug. Would I continue to get good mounts in New York after I became a journeyman???

I need not have worried. I underestimated the loyalty of the trainers who used me, a female jockey. On my first day as an official journeyman, I rode five horses at Aqueduct. My first winner came three days later on a horse trained by Bobby Lake. Now that I had won without the bug in New York, it didn't seem to be the big deal that Vince had always made it out to be; I remembered his words that had created so much anxiety in me. "Come to Keystone where you are sure to ride winners. You must make the most of your bug year. This is the most crucial time of your career."

Over the years, Vince's words had become my thoughts, my fears. I didn't realize the tremendous influence he had on the way I felt about racing, about my mother, and about myself. Even though I hadn't spoken to him since Mom found the letter, his opinions powerfully affected my thoughts and feelings and played an instrumental role in the course my life would take.

My prayers for winners continued. Whenever I had a really good shot to win or the race was especially important to me, I would pray. During this time, the significance of my prayers was only linked to my horses. It seemed selfish, and I carried some guilt about this; however, Susan said that prayer would develop a relationship with God and that this relationship would grow. She told me that if I prayed *believing* God could hear my prayers and *believing* He would answer—that was what mattered. It was all a matter of my faith.

Oddly enough, this was true. Every time I prayed *believing* my prayers would be answered, they were. And every time I prayed with doubts—doubts that God was listening and sometimes doubts that He even existed—my horses didn't run well. While the prayers themselves were insignificant, something else really important was going on: my faith was growing.

My relationship with the jockeys was growing as well. The New York riders were accepting me as one of them. One day Angel and I were getting on the scale before a race. He looked at me with concern. "It's not fair that you have to spend the day all alone in that room (the girl jocks' room). You should be able to come in our rec room where we play ping pong, cards, and pool."

"I don't mind, Angel. Really. I like it back there. I like being alone." I got on the scale and the valet handed me my saddle. After the clerk of scales nodded, I handed the saddle back and stepped off the scale. "Really, Angel. All I care about it getting to ride. I'm fine."

But he insisted. "Listen, baby, why can't you come in with us? Eat at the counter and play ping pong."

"That's okay, Angel. I don't want to put anyone out. I'm fine, really."

"I'm going to talk to the guys. We'll have a vote. I'm sure it will be fine with them." Angel winked as he took his whip from the valet and we headed out to ride the next race. There was no stopping Angel when he set his mind to doing something. He was very much a leader with the other jockeys.

The next day he approached me. "Karoleena, I have some good news. We took a vote and the majority voted you can come in the rec room. Isn't that good?" he smiled.

I wasn't sure. "Thanks, Angel."

Even though I had permission to join the other jockeys, I was reluctant to invade their space.

Angel approached me a few days later. "Karoleena, why aren't you coming in with us between races? You're allowed in." He looked concerned.

"I don't want the other riders mad at me."

Angel laughed. "Come on, baby. Nobody would be mad at you. We voted, remember?"

With encouragement from Angel, I started spending time between races in the jocks' room. My afternoons were really fun. They were the best times I ever had. I played backgammon with Jacinto Vasquez, bumper pool with Angel, and ping pong with Jerry Bailey. I belonged. I wasn't alone anymore. I looked forward to my afternoons, as much now for the company as for riding races. Some days I rode seven or eight races, but I preferred to ride less and spend more time in the jocks' room!

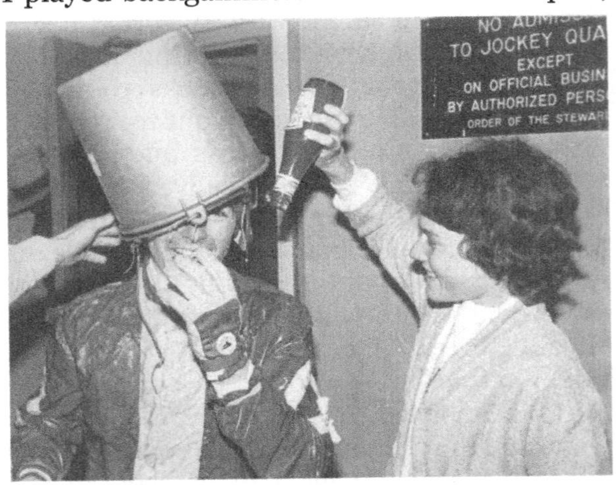

Initiating apprentice jockey
John Santagata after his first win

Chapter 35
Interesting Encounters

I continued to be written up in the newspapers and magazines: *People, Teen, Spur, Family Circle* and other publications. Because of this, some well-known people stopped by the girl jocks' room to meet me. I wasn't familiar with most of them, as I didn't watch television or follow the news. However, when Larry Hagman, the star of TV's "Dallas" (Who Shot J.R?), introduced himself, I remembered him from my early childhood when he starred in the TV series, "I Dream of Jeannie." I met sports figures like George Steinbrenner and entertainers Sandy Duncan, Cab Calloway, and Jack Klugman. Sandy Duncan gave me free tickets to her Broadway show, "Peter Pan." Jack Klugman, who was starring in television's "Quincy" at the time but whom I recognized from his earlier T.V. series, "The Odd Couple," was a real racing enthusiast, not unlike the character he played, Oscar Madison! Jack Klugman owned some horses and even had a Kentucky Derby contender the previous year, a horse called Jacklin Klugman. When he spoke to me about racing, his eyes sparkled with excitement. I could tell he really loved the game.

One morning Frank Wright arranged for me to meet George C. Scott at his barn. Because of my childhood love of dolphins, I recognized the actor immediately from his starring role in the film, "The Day of the Dolphin." (Susan and I were dolphin fanatics, obsessed with Flipper. I thought back to my early childhood, before Vince, when Susan and I watched every episode of Flipper, taping the dolphin sounds and thinking we could learn their language.) I asked the actor what it was like to work with dolphins, and so our conversation centered around these intelligent mammals. I left the barn, never realizing the reason I was to meet him: Frank told me later that he wanted to train horses for George C. Scott, and I was supposed to enthusiastically promote horse racing! Oh, well.

Another fun person I met was Mickey Rooney, who starred in the Broadway musical, *Sugar Babies*. As a racing fan and follower of my career, he invited me into his dressing room during the intermission. Clad in his bathrobe and poring over the *Racing Form,* he couldn't wait to hear about the horses I was riding the next day!

Chapter 36
Near-Death Experience

I was living my dream. I had finished among the top ten leading jockeys in New York for the Aqueduct meeting. Belmont Park opened for the spring and within a few weeks I was the third leading rider and had the highest win percentage at the meeting! I was doing extremely well considering that all the best jockeys were once again back in New York, and I had just recently transitioned to journeyman rider. I was so lucky.

Kuja Happa, a sleek thoroughbred mare owned by the renowned fashion designer "C.Z." Guest, was shipping in from Maryland for a stakes race at Belmont. Her regular jockey got stuck in traffic and couldn't make the race. I was asked to ride her at the last minute and donned the unfamiliar silks. On my way out to the paddock, one of the valets said to me, "Hey, little rider, this might be your first stakes win!"

I hadn't won a stakes race yet, and was excited at the prospect.

We broke from the gate in good order, and I could tell Kuja Happa loved the going. However, after rounding the first turn, all the horses had passed us. This worried me a little, but I didn't try to rush her. I wanted to keep her happy and let her settle where she was comfortable. After three quarters of a mile we were still in last place. It was time to try something else. I thought that maybe she didn't like horses around her and that was why she had sucked herself back. I wheeled her to the outside and as soon as I did, I knew I had pressed the magic button. She accelerated, taking off like a jet on a runway. She blew by the pack and caught the lone horse out in front. It was a photo finish.

After the wire, I wasn't sure if we had won or not. Angel Cordero, Jr. had been in front on the rail aboard Gemrock, a nice Dubai Stables filly. He hadn't seen me coming because I was so far out in the middle of the course. Angel looked surprised and a little upset as we pulled up.

"Do you think I won?" I asked him.

"Yeah. Congratulations, baby. Your first one?"

I nodded and felt a sudden rush. I was numb with both joy and disbelief. I had not only won my first stakes race, but beaten one of the top stables in the country, Dubai Stables.

In another week, the Saratoga race meeting would start. I couldn't wait. The jockeys, valets, owners, and trainers were all excited to head

My first stakes win (#2) - nosing Angel out at the wire

upstate for the month of August. It would be a refreshing change and the closest thing to a vacation that most of us would get for a while. Mom was also enthusiastic. At Saratoga, there would be a lot more opportunities to display her horse portraits and get new business.

Opening day at Saratoga. The grandstand mirrored a festival with colorful vending booths selling everything under the sun: popcorn, hot dogs, T-shirts, hats, racetrack paraphernalia, paintings, pictures, lemonade made with real lemons, and Häagen-Dazs ice cream. A live band was playing near the outdoor betting windows. I couldn't believe the crowd. Saratoga, for the month of August, was definitely *the* place to be.

All the activity got my adrenalin flowing. Having heard so much about this legendary place from the jockeys, valets, and trainers, I wanted to go everywhere and see everything. I didn't want to miss out on any of the action: the parties after the races, the polo matches, the softball games, and the places to go dancing. It was exciting and even though it would be difficult to get mounts at this premier race meeting, I was glad to be in the middle of all the action. I decided to enjoy myself and not get upset if I didn't ride every day. I was a proven journeyman rider in New York now, so some of the pressure was off. I would lighten up and take advantage of the social scene. I wanted so badly to feel good about myself as a rider *and* as a person.

On the first Saturday of the meeting, I was riding a horse called Wiggle Waggle in the second race. Heading into the turn, a new apprentice rider started to cut me off. He knew I was there, yet he kept coming in. With two horses inside of me, I had no place to go. My horse clipped his heels as he cut me off. I was going down.

The next thing I remember...

I was floating up slowly, watching my body in the room below. Boy, was my body small. It looked so little lying there on the gurney, wearing all white. I had on my white riding pants and a white t-shirt; my racing silks had been taken off. I looked so tiny and frail lying there with my arm contorted and twisted up over my head. I continued to drift up toward the corner of the room. Two doctors were leaning over me, cutting my t-shirt. God, I never knew I was so small!

I looked over toward the far side of the room. There were some nurses around a big old oak desk, but they didn't seem concerned with my being there on the gurney.

Wait a minute. Where am I going? Up! Up and...out? I must be dying! Am I leaving the room? I am floating up. No, I can't die yet! Wait! I can't leave my mother like this. I have to tell her I'm sorry—I have to say goodbye. I have to tell her that I love her and that I am so sorry for ruining her marriage, her life. I feel it so strongly. That's all I care about right now. Nothing else matters. Nothing! I have to tell her how I feel. That's all I have to do—and then I can go.

I was moving upward more slowly now. Looking down, I suddenly felt sad. I looked so young, so helpless. What a shame. I was too young to die. I would go...except for Mom. I had to make things right with her. Maybe if I stayed focused on my body below, I wouldn't leave.

Everyone was smaller, farther away now. My body below was the size of a pencil. I could feel behind me where (I thought) the ceiling and wall of the racetrack first aid room touched. Something was stopping me, because now I was just hovering, suspended high up.

I wanted to turn around. I wanted to see what was behind me, but somehow I knew that if I turned around—even for a second—I would go. This was my last chance. Although I really wanted to turn around, I thought it might be final. Don't give in! Don't turn around! I felt I couldn't take my eyes off my body down on the gurney below for one second, lest I turn and go. Concentrate! Focus! I can go another time. Don't give in. Don't even think about turning. If I do, I won't ever get back!

I fought the urge to turn around. I had no time to spare. I had to get back to tell Mom. That's all that mattered. That's all that ever really mattered. I know that now. When I get back, I will tell her. Right away! Because I might not get a second chance! Focus!

When I became semi-conscious (I was in an ambulance, but didn't know it), I was confused. My eyes were closed, but I heard my mother speaking. She was right next to me. "Am I going to die?" I heard myself ask her. Then I felt my tears. Had I said goodbye? Had I said it or just thought it? I still couldn't open my eyes.

I was in and out of consciousness. I heard Angel Cordero talking. He had come to see me in the hospital, but then everything faded out.

I woke up, finally, in the ICU (intensive care unit). I had lived through yet another bad spill. Fully awake for about half an hour, I was trying to piece together the day before and the events leading up to the spill. It happened in the second race on only the fourth day of the Saratoga meeting. What bad luck! What bad timing! I was aboard Wiggle Waggle. I remembered the apprentice rider cutting me off going into the turn. Then what happened?

I was sore from head to toe. My right shoulder had been dislocated. My mouth was cut. My back hurt. My knee hurt. My shoulder ached, and my head was throbbing. I was told they did a CT scan on my brain, and that everything came out clean. However, because I had suffered a major concussion, they were keeping me for observation.

I had no recollection of my near-death (out-of-body) experience. Not yet. When Mom came into the intensive care unit, the first thing I thought when I saw her was that she hadn't been there for me, that she hadn't been there at all.

"Where have you been?" I asked her, feeling abandoned, betrayed.

Mom explained that she had been right there with me all along—at the races, in the ambulance, and at the hospital all through the night. She had been in and out of the ICU all morning, waiting for me to regain consciousness.

Suddenly, with her there, a feeling of deep sadness came over me. I didn't know why at first, but then I remembered: *I had wanted to say goodbye to her!* Tears flooded down my face as I recalled thinking that I would never see her again. I hugged her and cried. Mom was happy to hug me. We never hugged. But she didn't understand why I was suddenly so emotional.

"I was going to die," I said, a little confused. "Did I say goodbye to you?" I knew I had said it in my mind, but had I actually said it, and when?

"I was with you in the ambulance on the way from the track to the hospital," Mom explained, "and you asked me if you were going to die. Of course, I told you that you would be fine, that you had just dislocated your shoulder."

I still didn't recall my out-of-body experience. I just had the feeling that I knew I was never going to see my mother again. I was still somewhat confused and emotional. The emotion came from a very deep part within me that hadn't felt anything for a long, long time.

Suddenly, the memory became clear: I had floated up out of my body, knowing I was going to die and never see Mom again. The sad, sad feeling came flooding back now full force, and I knew I was being given a second chance. Mom couldn't know why I was being so emotional. I couldn't explain what I didn't understand. I hugged her again and told her that I loved her. Uneasy with this sudden flow of emotion, I had to get back in control.

For some reason, the intense feelings that had surfaced during my near-death experience—the extreme importance of apologizing to my mother for ruining her life and the magnitude of leaving her behind with those words unsaid—were quickly buried once again. Back in my body, success (winning races) and material things (food and my weight obsession) became the focus of my attention as before. The eternal and meaningful things, brought forth in my profound and unusual experience, slipped back beneath the layers.

The Saturday of my spill was the day of the Whitney Handicap, a big day in racing. Thank God I fell at Saratoga on a day when 29,000 racing fans filled the stands. Because the crowd was so large, Dr. Fritz, a track veterinarian, had decided to watch the races from the backstretch, where it wasn't so crowded. Dr. Fritz happened to be positioned by the half mile pole to watch the second race. He had seen my spill, watching in horror as I lay there motionless on the track. Dr. Fritz later recalled what had happened.

He explained to me, "The ambulance was slow to reach you, and your face was buried in the sand. You were unconscious. I knew if someone didn't get to you soon, you would suffocate. I ran over and picked your head up—very carefully. Your face was a mess and you weren't breathing well. I undid your chin strap—if it weren't for that helmet, I don't think you would have survived. I held your head up until the ambulance arrived."

Had it not been for the quick thinking of this track veterinarian, I might have died right there on the track.

The spill left me with not only a dislocated shoulder, but another broken vertebra. Because of the back injury, it would be *another* six long months before I could ride again. The good news was that this time I wore a brace and not a body cast.

I got lots of encouragement from trainers, owners, jockeys, and fans. Although this didn't ease the pain, it did make me smile. I got a "Get Well" telegram from Governor Hugh Carey, and the people at the track were so friendly and positive.

This time while I was injured, I knew my identity as Karen the jockey was secure. I *knew* I would come back to riding races because I had done it before. This was only a temporary setback. Instead of withdrawing and just obsessing on "getting fit and strong," I took advantage of experiences outside of racing.

Meeting tennis star Billie Jean King

While still at Saratoga, I was invited to a tennis tournament where I met the well-known tennis player, Billie Jean King. In addition, I was nominated for the Women's Sports Foundation pro sportswoman's award and attended their dinner at the Waldorf-Astoria. I met Peggy Fleming of figure skating fame, champion gymnast Cathy Rigby, and tennis star Chris Evert Lloyd, who ended up winning the award. Even though social events were nice, they didn't compare to riding races. That was where I really belonged.

Six months later when I made my comeback, Howard Cosell's ABC Sports television crew was in the paddock to film it. I was invited to be a guest on the popular television shows, "Late Night with David Letterman" and "The Donahue Show." *Us* magazine called me "Little Miss Comeback," and I even made the "Peanuts" cartoon strip featuring famous women in sports!

Cosmopolitan magazine did an exclusive on "women jockeys." Looking at all the "women jockey" photos, I was bothered to be included among them. They looked like real women. I was nineteen, and my chest was starting to grow. Even though I still looked very young, I guess I was becoming a *woman* jockey—not a girl jockey. I didn't like this fact, but I accepted it. Unlike when I first started my career and was establishing myself as a capable jockey, I could handle the transition now. I no longer had to prove to anyone—especially myself—that I wouldn't "have sex with trainers for mounts." The guilt from what happened with Vince was so deep-seated that I was still trying to convince myself that I hadn't committed a crime.

Some of the jockeys noticed that my body was changing. I wanted them to view me as just another rider, but I didn't feel threatened at this point because I knew they respected me as a rider and as a *person.* They were always nice to me before, but now some of them were asking me out! Whether they were serious or not, I'll never know

Angel Cordero, me, and Jerry Bailey in the jocks' room

because I continued to kid with them and made a joke of it. They were like brothers or fathers to me. One day Angel Cordero asked me if I had implants! I was shocked that he thought anyone could possibly *want* these things. As my body changed and the hormones kicked in, something else happened: I started to notice men.

At home around Mom, I acted very upbeat. I shared stories of the jocks' room and about the horses I rode. She didn't think anything was wrong because she didn't know how much the past had affected me. Beneath my cheery surface was great fear that she blamed me and guilt that I had ruined her life. As much as I was sorry, I wouldn't bring it up. It just festered underneath all the layers.

Logically and outwardly, it seemed to me that Mom loved me. Yet I knew (believed as the truth) that she did not love me. With Vince's negative words buried in my subconscious, I was a prisoner of his sordid lies. Until I could remember, go back in time and separate the truth from the lies, there was no sorting out my feelings. I felt crazy. I found no peace in who I really was, especially when I was around Mom.

Chapter 37
Milestones

Things couldn't be better. When I won the Top Flight Handicap aboard Nelson Bunker Hunt's Adept, I became the first female jockey to win a $100,000 Grade 1 stakes race in New York. Not only was this a milestone for me, but it was a breakthrough for New York Racing as well. At this time, women just didn't win big stakes races in New York.

Since I was having such a good year, my agent Freddy suggested we stop by Dubai Stables, one of the most prestigious outfits in horse racing. The American division of the Dubai racing and breeding operaton was run by Ramon Garcia. A successful trainer in Argentina, he had won the prestigious Gran Premio Nacional (Argentine Derby) in the 1940s before moving to the United States to train and oversee Dubai Stables. His son Pablo was now the trainer for the forty Dubai horses stabled at Belmont Park. Over the years, Dubai Stables had bred and raced many, many winners. Big winners. Stakes horses, and lots of them. With my agent encouraging me, I got my foot in the door and worked some of the Dubai horses in the mornings. I only hoped Pablo Garcia had noticed my recent success in stakes races and would put me on a horse in a race. After all, I had beaten Dubai Stables Gemrock, with Angel Cordero riding, when I won with Kuja Happa.

One day Freddy told me that Pablo Garcia had given me a mount in a race. The horse, Iroquois, was one of the cheaper horses in his stable, but it was a start. I went by the Dubai barn to find out more.

When Pablo spotted me coming, he waved me into his office. "Come on in," he said. Pablo had an air of importance about him. In his mid-thirties, he was tall with dark hair and dark eyes. He was very handsome. The trainer went inside and settled down behind his big desk. I sat down in the chair opposite, and he continued. "Listen, this is my own horse. Tell you what. If you hit the board (finish first, second, or third), I'll take you to dinner."

Was he serious? I could brush off his comment as I had with so many other trainers, or I could let myself think of the possibility...

I left the barn smiling. Pablo was attractive. He wasn't like other trainers. He was different. He was *mysterious*. Everyone knew he owned a racing yacht. Whenever I overheard him talking, it was never about the top horses he trained. It was about his gun collection or his racing yacht.

Even though I had promised myself never to go out with a trainer, things were different now. I was a proven jockey that had never dated trainers for mounts.

I told Mom about Pablo and what he had said. She knew that some jockeys and other trainers had been asking me out, but that I wasn't interested in them. I wanted her opinion and approval. Mom listened to me and smiled as if she had been waiting a long time to hear this.

She offered her best advice. "Let Pablo know you are interested. If you don't 'hit the board' with Iroquois, tell him you really tried and were disappointed because you really wanted to go to dinner with him. Say it seriously so he knows you mean it and aren't just kidding around. Then leave it up to him."

But did I mean it? Now that I had proven my ability as a rider, it might be okay to go out with a trainer. It was time to take a chance. Besides, Pablo wasn't like other trainers. He wasn't like Vince. He was different. I went over the list of differences in my head:

- *He was a successful trainer—unlike Vince*
- *He was wealthy—unlike Vince*
- *He raced yachts and had interests other than horses—unlike Vince.*

Yes. I would take this chance.

Iroquois failed to hit the board. Coming back to unsaddle after the race, I felt my heart pounding. Should I say it? Should I? No. But I may never get the chance again. Oh, go on. Be brave. Take the plunge. Nothing may even come of it. You can always still back out.

I summoned up all my courage as I dismounted. Pablo was standing there as I pulled off my saddle. I wasn't brave enough to look at him. "I really tried to hit the board," I said, speaking the words quickly.

Pablo leaned into me and said, “It’s okay. I’ll still take you to dinner.”

“Okay, see ya.” Uncomfortable, I quickly headed for the scale, heart pounding, mind racing.

A month went by. Nothing came up again about our “dinner.” I took a new “wait and see” attitude. Whatever will be, will be. I went on with business as usual.

Racing moved to Saratoga, once again. This was the land of opportunity—dating opportunities, that is. I went by Pablo’s barn every day, intrigued with this new game of “when will he ask me out?” I didn’t have to wait much longer.

One morning Pablo asked me out to breakfast. It was not unusual at Saratoga to see trainers and jockeys having breakfast together. Everyone was seen mingling here during the magical month of August.

Good, I thought. This is safe. I’ll get to know him better. It takes the pressure off a “dinner date.”

Pablo was fifteen years older than me and a lot more experienced. He had probably sensed my uneasiness at the mention of dinner a month earlier and knew that going to breakfast here was a lot less intimidating for me.

Pablo arranged for us to meet at his barn at 9:30 A.M. That was earlier than when I normally quit my morning rounds. “This way,” he said, “we can get a head start on the breakfast crowd.”

I rushed around all that morning, seeing the trainers I rode for, my mind somewhere else completely. I wanted to get done early so I could go home and take a shower. My hair always got flattened down from wearing my helmet all morning, and I wanted it to look nice for our first date.

I briefly filled Mom in. The much anticipated “date” had finally arrived! I dressed back into my same morning attire of jeans, boots, and a sweater so that Pablo wouldn’t know I had gone home and showered. Then I raced back to the track to arrive at his barn looking casual, nonchalant.

Nestled in the heart of Saratoga Springs, Mother Goldsmith’s was a favorite breakfast café of the racing crowd. The line to get into the place went all the way out the door and down the sidewalk. I was taken by surprise when Pablo ignored the long line and went right in. I followed him, feeling a bit guilty. We were met inside by the restaurant owner, who impressively whisked Pablo right over to an empty table. I squeezed by some racetrack people who were waiting their turn to be seated, and met Pablo at the table.

Over breakfast we talked about me, mostly. Or rather, I talked and Pablo listened. I told him about how I got started in the pony races, the trainers I would be riding for at the meeting, and mostly just racing stuff. My conversation was light and upbeat. I was enthusiastic, typical Karen the jockey. Pablo listened attentively.

We finished breakfast, and he drove me back to the track in his big dark blue Cadillac. It felt weird to be sitting next to him in the car I had so often searched for at the track, trying to "bump into him" over the past month.

When we arrived at his barn, I thanked Pablo and got out of his car. Was that *it?*

"We'll have to do this again sometime," he said and smiled a rare Pablo smile.

Every morning I went by the Dubai barn. My morning rounds got shorter and shorter as I spent more time at Pablo's barn. He had picked out a few horses that I could ride in races, so it wasn't like I didn't have an excuse to be there. I think people were noticing. Anyway, it wasn't like we were hiding the fact that we had gone to breakfast. The whole world seemed to know your business at Saratoga, especially if you were seen at Mother Goldsmith's.

We went to breakfast a few more times before he finally asked me to dinner. The day of our dinner date, my mind was on Pablo. It was all I could think about as I put on my silks to ride the fifth race. I wasn't as interested in joking around or playing ping pong with the other jockeys.

On my way out to the paddock, one of Pablo's exercise boys ran up to me. "Pablo can't make it tonight. He sent me to tell you he has to have dinner with his owner," he said, out of breath. I tried not to get upset over the news. After all, it was business. Pablo would ask me out again, I hoped. I reached the paddock, back in control of my emotions. Dead set now on bringing home a winner.

Chapter 38
Taking the Plunge

The next morning at the barn Pablo apologized for canceling our dinner date. He didn't bring up going out to dinner, but he did mention that the house he was renting at Saratoga had a pool and that I could use it any time.

"You and your mother," he corrected himself. Then he added, "I noticed you're not riding every day. Maybe on a day when you don't have any mounts, you and your mother could come by and use it." He casually handed me his address and phone number. "I don't have to be there for you to use the pool. I'll just leave the gate unlocked."

"Sure. Maybe. I like to swim to stay fit. Thanks."

Eagerly I checked the papers in the mornings, noticing that Pablo ran horses almost every day at Saratoga. Hmm. I waited until his name wasn't among the entries...and mine wasn't either. Then, before thinking too long about what I was doing, I picked up the phone and dialed his number.

No answer. I dialed again.

"Hello?" said a sleepy voice.

"Oh, sorry. I guess I woke you up. I'll call back another time." I flushed a hot burning red. What a jerk I am. What awful timing I have. Of course, I thought, looking at my watch. It was eleven in the morning, when most trainers took naps!

"No, wait," he said. "Who is this?"

"It's Karen. Uh, I was just calling to see if you, umm, if the pool is, well, never mind. I didn't want to wake you up." My temples were pounding now. All the blood had rushed to my head, making my body weak.

"No, it's okay. Look, you can use the pool. I'll be here. I'll let you in. I'll just be reading in the den. I had to get up anyway. Did I ever give you directions?"

I wrote the directions down numbly, unsure if I should be going at all. But, sure enough, a few minutes later I found myself in the car, heading towards Ballston Spa, where Pablo stayed.

Before reaching his place, I slowed the car down. I didn't want to arrive too early. He needed time to wake up, and I didn't want to seem anxious. I turned on the car radio, feeling very up. "You make me feel like dancin'..." filled the car, the song blaring through the speakers. I sang along, becoming the singer of the song as I stepped harder on the gas, smiling.

I pulled into the driveway of a large, typically suburban, two story white house. As I got out of the car, I felt the confidence drain out of me. I left it back in the car with the song I was singing.

I looked at the front door to the house. The formidable front door. Door to the unknown. I made it the rest of the way. Knocked. Maybe he won't answer. Maybe I have the wrong house. Maybe, I'll just go on back home...

The door swung open. I was startled by Pablo's silhouette emerging from the darkened house. For a minute, I was afraid of him. Until he spoke, opening the screen door and stepping into the sunlight. "Ahh, it's a beautiful day. Come on in."

I stepped gingerly into the house, careful not to slip in my rarely-if-ever-used heels. He led the way down the dark hallway, through the kitchen, and into the den. It was cold in the house. Very cold.

He waved toward the couch. "Have a seat. Relax."

I sat awkwardly on the sofa and Pablo sat down in a comfortable looking chair in the corner.

"Gee, it's kind of cold in here," I said without thinking.

He nodded. "Yeah, I like it that way. Always have liked the cold. I hate the hot weather. Makes me uncomfortable."

"So, where's the pool?" I asked.

Pablo got up and pulled aside a curtain that revealed a sliding glass door. I walked over and looked out from the cold dark den, squinting from the bright sunlight outside. "Do you use the pool much?"

"No, hardly ever. I don't like to swim. But you go ahead. There's the bathroom," he nodded toward a door. "You can change into your suit in there. I won't bother you. I'll just be in here, reading."

To prove his point, he went over, sat down in his chair, and picked up his book. Reaching over, he lit a pipe, put on a pair of glasses, and settled back more comfortably into the chair, probably right where he was before I interrupted him at the front door.

I swam in the cold water, wondering why I had come. Did Pablo even like me? Was he watching me secretly from inside the darkened den? I decided to swim laps. The water was very cold, and I had told Pablo that I needed to swim to stay fit since I wasn't riding every day. I had better look like I was swimming, just in case he was watching.

After fifteen minutes, I got out and dried off. I went back in through the sliding door and was hit by the sudden draft of cold air from the dark air conditioned house. As my eyes adjusted, I shivered. Pablo spoke from his chair. "How was your swim?"

"Fine. Great. It was really nice of you to let me use the pool." I was freezing and suddenly very uncomfortable standing there in my bathing suit. I wrapped the towel around me, covering my body. He noticed.

"You look good in a bathing suit," he said with an interested half smile, then went back to reading his book, absorbed.

I went into the bathroom, changed out of my suit, and feeling much more comfortable in my clothes, reappeared. "Well, I guess I'll be going."

"Are you riding any races tomorrow?" he asked, looking up from his book.

"Yeah. I'm riding two. One for Dick DeStasio and one for Ben Wiley."

"Ben Wiley? Why would you want to ride for him? He does drugs, you know."

"Really? I didn't know that."

"Oh yeah. Everyone at the track knows that. He's bad news."

"I don't want to be around someone who does drugs. You think I shouldn't ride for him?"

Pablo looked at me with compassion. "You can do what you want, but everyone knows about him."

What a caring guy, I thought. "What do you think I should do?"

Pablo looked pensive. He puffed on his pipe. Little puffs, one right after another. "Well, you really have no choice," he explained with authority. I admired him more than ever at that moment. He continued very seriously, "If you ride for him, you will be guilty by association." He stopped and looked at me, waiting for a reaction.

"Well, then, I guess I won't go by his barn anymore."

Pablo looked very satisfied that he was able to help me. He knew from our breakfast conversations how much I cared what people thought of me.

I was so happy as I drove away from Ballston Spa. Pablo was so smart! I had been so blind, and he had made me see!

"How are things going with Pablo?" Mom asked.

"I think I'm in love," I said wistfully, stars in my eyes.

"Oh, I'm so happy for you," she said, hugging me.

When I went by Pablo's barn the next morning, I watched him walk around the barn with authority, the Boss. I felt a new connection to him. He noticed me watching him and nodded. I was so lucky. Nobody is as smart as Pablo, I thought, happy that he had acknowledged my presence.

Chapter 39
So Romantic

I wasted no time in taking Pablo's advice; I had my career to think about. When I told Pablo that I hadn't been by the Wiley barn, he was so proud of me. He said he would take me out "to a real nice restaurant for dinner." I trusted Pablo. I could handle a dinner date with him now, and he probably sensed this. He was so in touch with my feelings!

The day we planned to go to dinner, it poured rain. I was riding a race for Pablo, and he met me by the jocks' room with a big umbrella. We walked out to the Saratoga paddock together, he and I, me and him, under the big umbrella.

After the races, I went home and changed. As we had been doing for breakfast, we met at his barn and went together in his car. I felt so important when I was with him.

It was still pouring rain when we got to the restaurant. Pablo opened the car door for me. He reached for my hand, helped me out of the car, and escorted me in under the big umbrella.

The restaurant, The Wishing Well, was a very popular place and was very crowded. Right away I spotted people that I knew from the track. However, I was proud to be with Pablo. It didn't bother me to be seen with a trainer, the way I thought it would.

Dinner was...romantic. I was glowing inside. Everything was perfect. The food, the company, the conversation. Pablo was drinking "Chivas Regal on the rocks," a brown liquid in a short fat glass. I finished my second drink, what was left of a screwdriver, the only "cocktail" I had heard of (drinking age in NY was 19 at this time). I was feeling pretty good now and wondered what would happen next.

"What do you say we have coffee back at my house? I make a mean cup of coffee," Pablo said as he put his platinum American Express card on the table next to the check.

"Well, that would be all right, I guess," I said without thinking. I was mesmerized now. I knew I would go back to his house.

What am I doing? I thought, looking down at the table, trying to break the trance. *Do I really want to go back to his house at night?*

The waiter came back with the check, setting it down in front of Pablo. I watched as Pablo signed his name, a confident, well-mastered slash.

We left the restaurant and headed for his place in the big blue Cadillac. I felt great, carefree. I wasn't going to worry. I could trust His Majesty.

We drank the coffee, Pablo from his chair in the corner, me across from him on the couch. The coffee woke me up, out of my dreamy state. This was a trainer I rode for. I could be making a big mistake. I must be more careful.

When we were finished, he cleared our cups away. Then, when he returned from the kitchen, bingo, he slipped right in next to me.

"Well, how did you like it?" he asked.

"Like what?" I asked him, feeling uneasy now.

"Why, the coffee, of course." He smiled. Rare smile, knowing smile.

"Oh, yeah. The coffee. It was great. Really good. You were right," I said. I fixed my eyes on the television, trying to seem at ease. Maybe nothing would happen. Out of the corner of my eye, I saw him move his hand over to my leg. Oh, no.

"What are we watching?" I asked, moving my leg away from him a little. Just enough. Not too much. I didn't want him to think I didn't like him.

"Oh, I don't know, some cable movie, I guess. I don't get cable at my house in Oyster Bay. But here, they get everything. I've rented this house three years, now. Yes, let me think. This will be the fourth year. I like it. It's kind of big for just me, but I like it. It's comfortable."

He was distracted now. Good. Keep it going. "What are the people like who own it?" I asked him.

"They are a nice family with young kids. They didn't want to rent to racetrackers, but one of the guys from the (yacht) club knew them and made the connection for me. They like sailing, too, and go out on Lake George, not far from here. Sometimes I go up to Lake George. I would have rented a place up there, but it's a little too far from the track."

This was the most I had ever heard him talk about himself. I waited for him to continue, but instead he put his arm around me. I froze. There was a long, awkward silence. The only sound was the television. He pulled me closer to him. My body was frozen, breakable. I wouldn't bend if he pulled me any closer, I would just break. I tried to go with the flow and conform to a new position closer to him. With concentration and a big effort, maybe I could relax.

There. That wasn't so bad. His arm, strong arm, was pulling my shoulders around to face him. I looked down, but his hand lifted my chin up to a kiss. Right on my frozen lips. I watched his face so close to mine, kissing me. He started to unbutton my shirt. I was grateful to have so many buttons on my shirt. Thousands of tiny little buttons. I watched his hands. Big hands on tiny buttons. My shirt fell to the floor. He pulled me next to him, lying down now on the couch. I faced the television and away from him. His arms were around me...

Wait a minute. What's happening here? What am I doing here with my shirt over there, on the floor? I slid out from under his arms. *Gently, don't get him angry.* I got off the couch and picked up my shirt. I held it over me and looked down at the floor. "I've got to go now," I said, feeling very unsure of myself. "I've really got to get going." There. That sounded much better. Much more sure.

"So soon? Come on, stay the night." he said, casually.

What? Was he *joking?* I couldn't stay overnight! I couldn't even last two minutes on the couch! Think fast. *Think fast.* "I've got to go because of my car. My car is at the track by your barn, remember? You met me there before we went to dinner," I said, figuring he would understand what that meant. People would *know.*

"So? It'll be all right. It will be safe there," he reassured me.

"No, someone will *see* it there." I said, looking for him to understand my sudden dilemma.

He continued to looked confused.

"It's late," I went on, explaining, "What will they think?" Whew. I was on a roll.

He got up sadly. "Okay, then. I'll take you back to your car. But next time, I'll have you meet me here at the house."

I lay awake most of the night, thinking. I replayed the evening over and over in my mind, giving it a new ending each time. First, I stayed. We were happy. Then I left, and he was mad. Then I stayed and he threw me out, never wanting to see me again. Then I stayed and decided I didn't like him after all. Finally, I was so confused that I fell asleep.

I awoke with a start. Yes, I was home. Was last night *real?*

Chapter 40
My Knight in Shining Armor

I floated through work in a dream world. It was hard keeping my feet on the ground. All I could think about was the next time...the next time. How would the script go? How would the story end? The story, forget the story, we're talking the first chapter.

We ended up back at Pablo's house, once again, for his delightful cup of coffee. My car was in his driveway this time.

Take Two:

We finished our coffee. I knew what might happen next, but didn't want to admit it. It was bad enough my car was here; we both knew what we were thinking.

When Pablo started unbuttoning my shirt, I stared over at the television.

"You are a bad girl," came from within me. No, I'm not, I whispered back faintly. This is normal. Pablo is a grown man and expects to do grown man things. Be brave.

I could see the television sharply because my contact lenses were in. My contacts! A great excuse to leave. He was on top of me. I was detached, somewhere else.

"What's wrong?" Pablo said as he moved off of me, next to me.

"Huh?" I asked, still focused on the T.V.

"I mean, what's wrong? You're so distant. Like you're not here. Not with me, at all."

"Oh, yeah? Really? Is there something wrong? With me?" I looked at him now, wondering what the problem was, why he hadn't gone through with anything. Why he hadn't "done it" to me.

"Are you uncomfortable?" he asked me.

Not any more than I should be, given the situation, I thought. Was I supposed to feel comfortable?

"I'm just...not used to doing this, that's all." I confessed. "Am I doing something wrong?" I really wanted to know. I was actually the most comfortable with him than I thought I ever could be with anyone. I was messing everything up. Suddenly, a wave of sadness came over me. I felt very, very sad. "Maybe I should go home," I said distantly, almost like it was a question. I was confused. Is this supposed to be what happens next? It's all so unromantic. And it's all my fault.

"No, don't go. Stay. I won't do anything. I promise." He sounded so believable. So caring. My knight in shining armor. But I was not a princess. I was ugly, damaged goods. I didn't deserve him. I didn't *need* anyone. I was doing fine just the way I was before I met him. I wanted to go home, wanted to never see his caring face again. A face that reminded me of what a failure I was, of what I could have had, but didn't deserve.

"I can't stay." I stuffed back my tears. "My contacts are still in. I wear contacts, you know. I've never told anyone that before. It makes me feel weak. But I'm not weak, I just have weak eyes..."

"I wear contacts, too, you know. It's not such a bad thing," he said with a little smile.

Maybe not. Maybe not. But I was a bad thing. I must leave and forget about him, this wonderful understanding man.

"I need to go home so I can take them out and put them in the case. I don't have a case with me. I can't stay," I said with finality.

"You can use one of my cases," he said. "Please stay.

"Oh, no. I've really got to go," I lied. "I have a special solution for the lenses."

"All right, then. You can go. But next time bring your solution along. You never know when it might come in handy."

I felt lonelier than ever leaving Ballston Spa that night. All wasn't lost though. Pablo hadn't given up on me. Not by a longshot.

Take Three:

Saratoga. One week later. I was surprised when Pablo asked me out for dinner again. Again, my car was at his house, but this time I had my contact solution with me.

For the first time, I didn't detach. For the first time, I allowed myself to feel. And the feelings, the emotions were like a flood. It happened so naturally. I was part of him. He was part of me. I trusted him. I let go of the fear, and felt something wonderful. It took me far away from everything. I was lost in this new feeling, this new emotion, this feeling so real, so unreal, it made me cry. Real tears. Flowing out of me like a river. This new emotion must have a name. I gave it one...Love.

"What's wrong, honey?" Pablo leaned back and looked at me, wiping the wonderful tears from my face. Warm tears. Love tears. Tender man, tender Pablo. He loves me so much.

"Nothing. Nothing. Is there something wrong?" I asked, not believing anything in the world could possibly be wrong. Not now, not ever, next to him.

"You're crying. Why are you crying?" he asked me gently.

"Because I'm so happy." I laughed a little through my sniffling nose, hugging him, loving him. My heart had melted into mush, and I was now putty in his hands.

Chapter 41
The Subject of Drugs

Before leaving Saratoga, one of the trainers approached me. "You know, Pablo is a drug addict."

What??? He was talking about the one I loved!!! How could he say such a thing??? I was very upset, and of course, I didn't believe him. Although I knew it couldn't be true, I couldn't get those ugly words out of my head: Pablo is a drug addict. Where was this horrible accusation coming from? Was there any truth to it? I had to find out. I would just ask Pablo. I could trust him. He would tell me the truth.

The next day, I went to Pablo's house, unsure of myself. *Bury your doubts. Keep an open mind.*

"What's the matter?" Pablo asked, immediately sensing something was wrong.

I looked down. He was so perceptive. I had to tell him now. I couldn't seem to hide anything from this man of higher intelligence.

Just tell him. Blurt it out. Be direct. Just hope he doesn't get angry. "I heard from someone that you do drugs." There. I said it. Now it was done.

"Who said that? Someone on the racetrack?" he asked, not sounding at all surprised. Rather, like he expected it, coming from the racetrack.

"Yeah. But I can't tell you who," I said, not wanting to get the trainer in trouble.

"Well, there was a time," he started, "when I did do drugs." He paused, thinking back to his past. "A long time ago, when I first came on the track. I was young and rebellious. I got a rather bad reputation for it."

I waited for him to continue, to explain.

"I guess they'll never forget. The racetrack is full of knockers. They never give you a break. I used to ride a motorcycle, too. I was a real bad dude, but that was a long time ago, before I trained for Dubai. I don't do drugs any more. No, no more. Hate the stuff. Hate anyone associated with drugs." He frowned. "I don't really want to talk about it, but if you want me to, I will."

I looked at him, trying to size up what he had just said. It sounded about right. He probably did have a reputation from the past, but I just thought it was because he had guns, had a racing yacht, and was sort of a rebel. I had never thought about drugs entering into the picture. But, everyone had skeletons in their closet. Nobody is perfect. Everyone has a past. So, it didn't burst my bubble. He's okay now, so what was the big deal? He's being honest with me. He's admitting the problems from his past. And they are in the past, obviously. He works hard, he is successful, and he doesn't hang around with anyone. My doubts were satisfied.

"Okay," I said, trying to soften the blow. "We don't have to talk about it anymore if it bothers you." Poor Pablo. Nobody wanted to love him because he used to be a rebel. I would love him, though. I really would. I would prove to the world that he was a changed man, a good man. A smart man. Then he would get the respect he deserved.

Pablo looked away, distant. After a pause, he focused back on me. He looked me right in the eye, as if he was going to let me in on a big secret.

I leaned towards him, listening closely to his every word.

"You know, the racetrack, they are all jealous. Jealous of my position with Dubai. Jealous of my success. They hate anyone who is more successful than they are, and they will say anything to bring me down. But I don't listen to their talk. You ought to do the same," he advised.

I nodded. He was so sure of these things. He knew about the racetrack. Pablo knew about everything.

He went on, "Whoever it was that said those things about me was very, very jealous, of course. Probably doesn't even know me. Not that it was ever any secret," Pablo explained. "It just was in the past and I didn't think it was necessary to tell you about it, before now."

The subject of drugs didn't come up again; at least, not for what seemed like a long time.

Chapter 42
Cinderella

Back at Belmont. The trees are greener. The birds sing sweeter. Pablo's barn attracts me like a magnet. I was spending more and more time there and less and less time at other trainers' barns. Our "breakfasts" continued on into Belmont, cutting short my morning work hours. We would go off, just the two of us, pressed together in the front seat of his big blue Cadillac. Our song, "Islands in the Stream," would play on the car radio. It felt as though nothing could separate us.

It was my birthday, and Pablo promised to make it special. He made all the arrangements. The limousine was scheduled to pick me up at my house. We would ride into New York City and have dinner at a fine restaurant called Le Cirque. Pablo told me it was a very fashionable place to eat, one of the best. Then it was on to see the hit show on Broadway, *Cats*. The evening would end with a romantic night—our first actual night spent together—at the Waldorf-Astoria Hotel. What style. What grace. I looked forward to the night with great anticipation. I was being treated like a princess, a queen. A Royal Highness. Part of His Majesty's Secret Service.

Clothes. I needed clothes! What would I wear? Quick, Mom, help me look the part!

Although I felt guilty about it, I still needed my mother. The real me, the bad me, the one who had allowed my mother's husband to do those terrible, sexual things to me, deserved nothing. I didn't deserve my mother's love. But now, maybe I had found someone who could really love me—Pablo. I had never wanted to date a horse trainer, like my stepfather, but Pablo was nothing like Vince, was he?

Shopping. I hated it. I had no time to shop for clothes, but Mom was game and suggested we head out to the mall. Department stores made me feel hot, tired, and ill. There was no air in the tiny changing cubicle. Mom handed me another blouse under the swinging door. I tried it on. Backwards! Darn. I'd never get it right. I think I rush too much. Throw it on the pile. The pile was growing. I'd need another room to hold all these clothes. How many stores had we been to? Five? Or was it six? I'd lost count, with all the rushing around. In and out of stores. Shoe stores, discount stores, dress shops, accessory stores, wholesalers...It was exhausting. All the colors had to be "basic" so that every blouse, skirt, and pair of slacks were interchangeable, making new and more beautiful outfits for a new and more beautiful princess. I looked at the pile of clothes on the floor. Beautiful clothes with beautiful colors. They should be on a hanger, at least. Exhausted, I longed to just throw on my boots and jeans, leave the stores behind, and be done with it all. Ah, well, the price of a successful relationship!

The night of my birthday, I kept looking out my bedroom window. Where was this limousine? I went back into the bathroom. "Mom, does my hair look okay?" I fluffed up my curls with a special pick I used. It was shaped like a pitchfork. Mucking out my hair. Fluffing it up for the occasion.

Through the mirror, I saw her appear in the doorway behind me. "Yes. It looks fine," she reassured me for the hundredth time. "I wish I had hair like yours," she said stepping into the bathroom, looking wistfully into the mirror at my hair. I looked at our reflection, both of us standing there, alike, yet different. My hair all full like an Afro, her hair flattened down and starting to gray. Mother and daughter. I felt like Cinderella. Where is my glass slipper? Prince Charming will soon arrive. I must be ready for the ball.

Mom looked at me in my new clothes. We both laughed. I had undergone the impossible, a true transformation.

"Happy birthday." Mom gave me a big hug and laughed happily, proudly.

Pablo had planned everything to the minute. He arrived right on time in the long black limousine. I was ready. I went outside to meet him, careful not to slip in my new heels. Pablo was waiting outside the limousine. He looked absolutely dashing in his three piece suit.

Mom stood just outside the front door, watching. As Pablo opened the door to the limo for me, Mom called out. "Wait! You two look so nice. Let me get a picture." She disappeared back into the house to get her camera. We stood there in the fading afternoon sunlight, hugging, so happy to be together.

Mom reappeared, her face hidden behind the camera. She pointed it at us and focused.

Click, click.

"Okay. Now you two can go. Have a good time," Mom said, smiling, happy for me.

Pablo helped me into the limo and then settled down beside me. The driver put the car in motion. Onward, James!

New York City, here we come. Bright Lights, Big City. Big town. Big man.

The gentleman standing just inside the entrance to Le Cirque ran his finger down the names in his book. "Reservations for two? Garcia? Let's see. Yes. Right here." He left his post and led us to our table.

The restaurant was small, but crowded. Comfortably packed. Elegantly and fashionably stuffed. The tables were set at angles in order to fit them all in. Everyone appeared quite content to rub elbows, happy with the scene.

Yes, this is *the place* to be. Step right up.

"What do you feel like having, honey? What looks good?" Pablo asked me from across our tiny little table.

I had been staring at the white menu, trying to decipher the "French Code." The elegantly scripted green letters formed into words I remembered from my eighth grade French class. But I only recognized some of the words. "Poisson." That was fish. I liked fish. I think I would order the poisson.

"I think I'll have the fish," I offered.

"Why don't we find out what the specials are before you decide?" Pablo suggested. "Maybe they'll have a special you'll like. You know, the maître d'e will often suggest the best thing to order. He knows the chef and what goes on in the kitchen. He'll know what's fresh. We'll hear what he has to say." Pablo looked so sure of this. He knew about these things. Pablo knew about everything.

"Okay," I said, happy he was helping me make a decision, the *right* decision.

The maître d'e came over to our table. He reached toward the ice bucket that was in a stand beside our table. Using a white cloth napkin, he gently took out the champagne bottle that Pablo had so carefully ordered when we had first sat down. "Dom Perignon. The best bottle you have," Pablo had said. Now the man with the mustache, holding out the champagne bottle, waited.

Pablo lifted his glass. I watched as a small amount of champagne was poured into Pablo's glass. *Why didn't he fill the glass?* The mustached man waited now, watching Pablo closely. I started to lift my glass, but decided against it. Not yet. They weren't finished with their mysterious ritual.

Pablo touched the glass to his lips. Sipped slowly from the goblet. Closed his eyes. *What were they doing?* Pablo opened his eyes and nodded his head up and down, satisfied.

The little Frenchman proceeded to fill Pablo's glass with sparkling, bubbly champagne. It looked like ginger ale. Very important ginger ale. I watched, totally absorbed, curious. He stopped pouring, suspended the bottle in the air, and looked over at me. "Madame?"

That was me. I knew that much French. I lifted my glass. He filled it very slowly and carefully. Must be careful with "the Madame's champagne," I thought. He was very good at this. I set my glass back on the table.

"The specials for this evening are...." Rambling on and on with his French accent, he lost me somewhere. It all sounded important. One special ran into the other. I got confused. What was that with the mushrooms? The stuffed what? I looked at Pablo. He could tell I was confused.

"Could you repeat the seafood specials, please?" Pablo requested. "She is interested in the seafood."

Yes, that's right. The poissons, the fish.

The maître d'e started again, repeating his memorized sing song of seafood specials without skipping a beat. I tried to absorb the words and picture each one. Each poisson. I was lost again. The man was quiet. They were waiting.

"I'm not sure. You go first," I said, looking at Pablo.

"What do you recommend?" Pablo asked the maître d'e. "Which of the seafood dishes do you recommend?"

"Oh, sir, the red snapper is quite good. A favorite of the chef. It's fresh, just came in today," he said, beaming with approval. Beaming because Pablo had so wisely asked for his opinion.

"She would like the red snapper, then. With the white wine sauce. Does that sound okay, honey?" Pablo asked me.

Red snapper? I didn't want to eat anything red. Or a snapping turtle, for that matter. The pressure was on, though. They were waiting.

"Sure. The snapping thing sounds fine." I said, swallowing. God, how would I eat it? Well, I won't have to worry about heaving tonight. I won't eat it. If I have to eat it, I'll just throw it up. Fine. No problem. I was *lucky* I was a heaver.

I reached for my champagne, drinking it down fast, like soda. As a heaver, I was always somewhat dehydrated and thirsty. The maître d'e looked over, surprised to see my glass was already empty. Pablo's glass was hardly touched. Oops. I wasn't supposed to do that. The Frenchman picked up the bottle to refill my glass as Pablo ordered something. I felt conspicuous, out of place. Only my fancy clothes made me blend in.

I was relieved when dinner was finally over. The red snapper turned out to be a type of fish that was actually quite delicious. It didn't even taste fishy! I told myself to remember to have it again someday. (I must start building a menu of new food!) And the chocolate "soufflé" that Pablo ordered for dessert was also really good. We had to order it special, before our meal, so that it could be ready when we were finished with our main course. I hadn't known what to expect for the dessert. It wasn't at all like the spinach "soufflé" that Vince used to make. I was glad to find out it was more like hot chocolate pudding, runny hot chocolate pudding that hadn't quite set on the inside, with a crust on top. Oh, and I can't forget to mention the birthday candle stuck in my soufflé. It came accompanied with a song, sung by the chef himself. "Happy birthday to you..."

I will never forget my birthday dinner at Le Cirque. Only the most important people go there, Pablo told me.

The Broadway show, *Cats,* was uneventful and boring. It was just a bunch of men and women dressed like cats. They had whiskers, little ears, and big tails. They meowed and came down the aisle to mingle with the audience. I guess I just didn't get why it was so popular. Pablo admitted he was disappointed with the show, too. We agreed to stick it out until the curtain of the first half of the show. Pablo said he didn't want to get up in the middle of a scene. Wasn't he considerate?

We left the Winter Garden Theatre, Pablo holding my hand as we made our way through the crowd. We got in our waiting limousine and headed off into the evening moonlight. Destination: Waldorf-Astoria.

Our "suite" at the Waldorf was posh—exquisite—to say the least. When I walked through the door, I expected to see a fancy hotel room with a bed. Instead, I backed up and explained to Pablo that we were in the wrong place. This was surely someone's apartment. He smiled with the satisfaction of having surprised me. Surprise, try shock! It looked like the first floor of a furnished mansion. There was a living room, a kitchen, a dining room table with *six* chairs, and of course, a bedroom. Everything looked very expensive, antique, and breakable. I touched the furniture gingerly, in awe. How could anyone rent a place like this for *one* night? It seemed impossible. I tried to look more casual, now that it was sinking in. We were staying here!

"Nice place. Real nice," I said, sitting down on the printed material drawn tightly over the antique couch. The arms and legs of the couch were made of dark wood, carved into the shape of claws. I got up off the stiff couch and went in to check out the bedroom. Ah, this was much more modern and comfortable.

"Pablo, look at..." I started to say as I turned to leave the bedroom. Pablo was directly behind me and I bumped into him. He kissed me hard on the lips, stopping my sentence, sending it reeling back into my brain, brain turning to mush, brain forgetting everything.

He ended the kiss too soon. "Happy birthday, honey."

I watched him move over towards the dresser, removing his rings as he went. Next, he took his pocket watch out of his jacket and set it down carefully on the dresser. I studied him closely. He took off his jacket and tie and hung them on a chair. *What a man! What a handsome, handsome man.*

Pablo looked much more comfortable now. He walked out of the bedroom and back into the living room. "Let's see what's on cable. Nice to get cable here." He flicked on the television, pulled a chair over, and sat down. I took up a place on the couch. The movie *War Games* was on HBO. We watched Matthew Broderick hack into a supercomputer and almost start a nuclear war.

"Television," Pablo said sadly, shaking his head. "Isn't real life here at the Waldorf-Astoria much more interesting?" he asked as if stating a fact. Then, he swept me up and carried me off to the bedroom.

Chapter 43
Little Did I Know

One day, out of the blue, Pablo asked me, "Honey, have you seen my pocket watch? It's been missing since I had it with me on your birthday when we went into the city." He looked at me expectantly.

"No, why? Should I have seen it?" I asked. I didn't remember seeing it anywhere since that night. I knew he loved his pocket watch. He had talked about it quite a bit, how much money it was worth. Whenever we got dressed up and went to a nice place to eat, he would bring his pocket watch. Now, he had lost his treasure and seemed quite upset.

"You don't remember putting it anywhere?" he asked me suspiciously.

"No. I never touched it. Don't worry. It'll turn up," I reassured him. "That's what my mother always tells me when I can't find something."

He turned and left me alone in the den.

Little did I know the significance of the missing pocket watch.

I told Pablo everything. About the people I rode for. My likes. My dislikes. Every night now he was picking me up at my house and taking me to dinner, whisking me off to some intimate restaurant where we would share our thoughts. And then we would go back to his house in Oyster Bay, together. We were so close now. So close, almost like one.

At Belmont Park, Pablo was the second leading trainer. Angel rode most of his winners. Dubai horses, mostly top stakes horses, had earned over two million dollars so far this year, and the stable was ranked third in the nation. This was big money. Big pressure. Big, big Pablo.

Out of the forty-five horses that Pablo trained, he continued to pick out a few that I could ride. They didn't have much chance, and I was beginning to think I would never win a race for him. It made me look bad that I wasn't winning for this prestigious stable. I was a capable, winning New York jockey. Why wasn't Pablo giving me better horses to ride?

Little did I know that Pablo was methodically starting to tear down Karen the jockey.

One afternoon between races Angel Cordero and I were playing bumper pool in the jocks' room. Angel paused, made his shot, and missed. He looked up at me curiously. "Why don't you ride more races for Pablo? I know you two are going out." He seemed truly baffled.

I took my shot. The little white ball bounced off the bumper and headed towards the corner of the table, right where I didn't want to be. Rats! "Oh, I ride for him some. You ride the good horses. That's okay. I don't even care if I ride races for him," I lied. In a way, I meant it. And in a way, I didn't. I didn't want people to think that I was going out with Pablo for his good stable of horses; that was very important to me. In fact, by not riding the good ones it proved to me and to others that I wasn't "sleeping with him for mounts." Of course I wasn't! That was all that mattered. Still, it would have been nice if Pablo had shown more faith in my riding ability. I was as capable a jockey as Angel, and Angel knew it.

That night, I brought up my conversation with Angel. "Pablo, Angel thinks I should be riding more races for you," I said casually.

Pablo spoke after a thoughtful pause. "Angel really wants to ride all of my horses. Don't you trust him. Don't believe everything he says," Pablo advised.

A few days later, I got the first real chance to win for Pablo. Imminent, a gray filly, was one of the favorites in the race. She was a very temperamental filly, and for this reason, Pablo said he had chosen me as her jockey.

"Don't touch her mane. If you do, she'll wig out. Talk to her. You two will get along just fine," Pablo told me in the paddock.

In the post parade, I said a quiet prayer. "Please, God, let me win a race for Pablo. Just this once. *Please.*" I looked up into the sky, hoping that God was listening. I felt a little guilty because I hadn't been talking to God lately. After all, I had a new best friend in Pablo!

To my amazement and relief, Imminent won. Finally, I had won a race for Pablo! Now maybe he would let me ride some of his better horses.

Angel congratulated me back in the jocks' room. "Good ride. I told Pablo to put you on her. I told him you would suit her better than me. She's funny to ride. You can't touch her mane. I don't like her." He winked at me. Was he telling me the truth? Pablo's words of warning rang in my head. *Don't trust Angel. Don't believe everything he says.*

"Thanks, Angel." I didn't know if Angel was trying to take credit for putting me on a winner, or if he had actually told Pablo to put me on the temperamental filly. Angel *had* gotten me mounts before. He really did like the way I rode.

That night, I asked my Pablo. "Did Angel ask you to put me on Imminent? Did he tell you he didn't want to ride her?" I asked, seeking the truth.

"Why do you say that?" Pablo asked.

"Oh," I explained. "Because Angel told me he didn't want to ride her. He said he told you that I would suit her better." This made sense because how else would Pablo have known about Imminent being sensitive about her mane unless her previous rider (Angel) had told him about it? It wasn't the first time Angel had gotten me a mount that he didn't want to ride.

"Angel wanted to ride her, honey. I wanted you to ride her, though. Remember what I told you? Don't listen to him. Just listen to me." He shook his head sadly, disappointed in me. How could I have questioned him? Didn't I love him? Didn't he want what was best for me? Didn't he know about everything? I didn't want him to be sad. I didn't want to let him down. I knew he wouldn't lie to me. I would listen to him from now on. He loved me. He really did.

Little did I know that Pablo was methodically discrediting anyone I knew and respected.

Not long after Imminent won, I won with Egotist, a well-bred colt that Pablo also trained. Pablo had high hopes for the promising speedball. Soon after I rode one of Pablo's best stakes horses, Jetson, in a sprint race on the dirt. It wasn't the horse's best distance or preferred surface (he liked longer races on the grass), but he ran well to finish second for me. Things were looking up, and I hoped that Pablo had finally realized that I was a capable jockey, good enough to handle his most expensive charges. However, when Jetson ran in his next race, the prestigious Manhattan Handicap (it was his ideal race at 1 ¼ mile on the grass), I was disappointed to see that Pablo had replaced me with Angel Cordero. Usually when a horse runs well for a jockey, the trainer keeps the same jockey on the horse. I watched from the sidelines as Jetson won and Pablo gave Angel a high five in the winner's circle. I tried to convince myself that it didn't matter that I was taken off the horse because Pablo loved me, and that was what counted.

One day Pablo said it was high time for us to take a little vacation. He asked me not to commit to riding any horses the following week so we could go to Paradise Island in the Bahamas. With the exception of my injuries, I had never taken time off from racing. How could I justify this to the trainers I was riding for? I was torn. I wanted to be with Pablo and please him, but my career had always come first. I would definitely lose mounts by going away and maybe even get some trainers mad at me. Still, Pablo really wanted to go. Reluctantly, I told my agent not to book any mounts the week of the trip, and Pablo went ahead and made our travel arrangements.

I was thinking about the trip as I entered Pablo's office by the barn. He was sitting at his big desk. "Hi, honey. How's your morning been going?"

I sat down in the familiar folding chair, across from him.

"Come sit over here, with me." He put his arms out toward me.

I went around the desk and sat on his lap. We hugged. We kissed. We looked into each other's eyes. *God, I love him.*

There was a knock on the door. We both looked up and laughed.

Caught again! And we didn't even care! Let the whole world know how much we loved each other!

It was Frankie, Angel Cordero's agent.

"Come on in, Frank," Pablo yelled.

The door opened, and Frank peeked in. He smiled sheepishly. "Hi, you two." It wasn't often that people on the racetrack displayed such affection.

"What's up?" Pablo asked him, leaning forward to put his cigarette out in the ash tray on the desk. I moved to get off his lap. "No, stay put, honey," he said, shifting his weight and setting me on his other leg.

"Umm. Do you have a rider for that race tomorrow?" Frank asked.

"Yeah, I'm all set. Thanks," Pablo said from his usual position of authority. All the agents wanted their jockeys to ride for Dubai Stables.

"Okay. Just thought I'd ask." Frankie started back out the door. "Have a nice day," he added as he left us.

I watched him leave, then turned back to look at Pablo. Ah, alone again, at last! I gave him a big hug and a kiss.

Pablo leaned back, away from me. "Uh, honey, there is something I have to tell you."

I didn't like the way that sounded and got up off his lap. "What?" I asked, not quite sure of myself.

"Come, sit back down." He reached for me and pulled me back onto his lap, where I perched half on, half off. Suddenly, I was unsure of everything.

"About our trip," he said, "I've heard some people talking." He leaned over to pick up a pack of his Marlboros.

"What do you mean?" I asked. "I know I really shouldn't be taking off. But my mounts weren't really that great and you said..." Pablo held up his hand, stopping me.

"People are saying, uh, they are insinuating, that you are going to get...well, you know how the racetrack is." He paused for effect.

"Get what? What are they saying?" My mind was racing now. "What do they think I am getting?"

"Going to get an...No, I can't tell you. It would hurt you too much.

I know how you worry about what people think." He moved me off his lap and got up to get his lighter.

"What? *What* do they think? What are they saying? Tell me. I must know or I won't go. That's all. I just won't go to the Bahamas unless you tell me what they're saying." Now he *had* to tell me. I felt hot and flustered inside. I was mad, upset. What were "they" saying about me?

"Oh, all right. But I told you about the racetrack. How everyone is jealous. You can't worry about what some people might think," he said, lighting his cigarette now.

"WHAT do they think?" I asked again, raising my voice. I was beginning to get really upset. Karen the jockey felt unsure, exposed. I looked down at my boots and touched my helmet.

Pablo looked at me, inhaling on his cigarette. I waited for him to speak. He set the cigarette down in the ashtray and exhaled. "Well, honey, they say you and I are going there—to the islands—to get you an abortion."

"What? Me? An abortion? That's *crazy!* How could they think that about me?" Not only were my feelings hurt, but I was shocked at the idea. Getting pregnant had never occurred to me, maybe because I was young and naïve.

"Yeah, I don't know who started the rumor," Pablo said, as if the whole world, the entire racetrack was talking about it.

"Well, I just won't go, then." I said firmly. "*That* will show them. Where did they ever get that idea, anyway?" I said, truly wondering. "I'm not going," I said with finality. "That's all there is to it."

Pablo nodded in agreement. He wasn't even upset! He understood me so well!

Later on that day I thought about the "rumor." It didn't make sense. I had only just told my agent about our trip. How could anyone possibly have known about it? I asked Pablo, "How did you hear about this rumor?"

Pablo thought for a minute. "Your agent told me about it. He was afraid for your business. Disgusted, you know."

"Yeah, but how did the rumor start? Who did you tell about our trip? The only person I told was my agent."

Pablo looked thoughtful. "You know the racetrack. They want to bring everyone down."

I was getting so disheartened. From all the things Pablo told me, I was really disappointed in the one place I had come to love and trust, the one place that had made me someone and saved me from myself, the racetrack. After that, the only barn I wanted to go to was Pablo's. He was the only one I could trust anymore. He was the only one who believed in me.

As much as I tried to forget, I was still bothered by what Pablo called the "widespread rumor." I decided to ask a trainer who knew everyone at the racetrack. I could trust him.

"They are saying *what*?" he asked me in disbelief. It was the first he had heard anything about an abortion rumor. Maybe it wasn't so widespread, after all. Maybe I shouldn't tell anyone else. No sense discrediting a rumor if it wasn't even a rumor.

The trainer saw that I was upset. "Don't listen to whoever is saying that. They're in a pit. They just want to drag you down into the pit with them. Just keep doing your thing and don't let it bother you."

I left his barn feeling pretty good. *Just keep doing your thing. Don't let it bother you.* Now that was good advice.

The following week, I had another issue that I needed Pablo to help me understand. "Pablo, do you know what?"

"What, honey?"

"Bob Lake has been asking me to exercise a lot of horses for him recently. He never asked me before. I always just rode his horses in races. I wonder why he wants me now, almost every morning. I can't say no to him because he's been so good to me over the years. He's put me on so many winners."

"Don't you see?" Pablo asked cynically.

"See what? All I know is I would rather be here at Belmont, working horses for you."

"Don't you see? You just said so yourself. You would rather be here, with me. He is jealous. Bob Lake is jealous of you spending time at my barn, and he wants to take you away. He is jealous of you riding for Dubai Stables. Now you're riding and winning for someone other than him. He wishes he trained for Dubai Stables, but since he can't he doesn't want you riding for Dubai, either."

Could this be true? Bobby Lake wasn't like that. He was always rooting for me to win races. He wanted me to do well. The better I did, the easier it was for him to convince his owners to use me. But Pablo knew about people. He knew about everything. *Why did Bob Lake suddenly want me at his barn every morning?* There was only one way to find out. Ask Bob Lake himself.

"Bob, why do you need me so much, lately?" I asked him on my way to the track on one of his horses.

He walked beside me as we headed towards the racetrack. "I've been having trouble with my new exercise boy. Billy Klinke, the jock I was trying to help out, left for Finger Lakes to ride. I use you on the good horses, and I guess he got discouraged. So, he left me. My new boy is no good at working (breezing) horses. He has no sense of how fast he is going. I need somebody desperately. Do you know of an exercise boy or girl that can do a good job working horses? It's so hard to get good help over here at Aqueduct." He shook his head and stopped to joke with the Pinkerton guard.

Bob Lake and me in the paddock at Aqueduct

I clucked to my horse and went onto the track, satisfied with his answer. I didn't mind working horses for him. It was just that I missed being around Pablo.

When I explained to Pablo that we were wrong to think that Bob didn't want me at Pablo's barn, he disagreed. I tried to explain what Bob had said to me. "He just needs me now. That's all. This will pass when he gets a new exercise boy," I said with relief.

"Don't be so sure." The skepticism and contempt that Pablo felt toward "racetrackers" came through, once again. "Over all the years you've ridden for Bob Lake, he's always managed to find an exercise boy, hasn't he? I'm sure he's not looking very hard." He raised his eyebrows, leaving me to figure out the rest. Pablo would continue to make me see the light.

Little did I know that Pablo was methodically changing my perception of the trainers I knew and trusted.

Chapter 44
Pablo, A Top Secret Mercenary???

One night while Pablo and I were out for dinner, I told him about my belief in God. I knew that my love for Pablo was growing very strong, and I didn't want God to be left out. "No matter what," I said emphatically, "God will always come first in my life, before any other relationship." I wanted this to be true, but wasn't sure that if I had to choose between Pablo and God, that I would make the right choice. I only prayed that Pablo was on board.

Immediately, Pablo pulled out his wallet. He opened it and carefully took out a big beautiful gold cross with Jesus nailed to it. He handed it over so I could get a closer look. Each detail was intricately etched into the crucifix. I noticed the face of Jesus as He suffered. I couldn't believe that Pablo carried a cross, or rather, a crucifix! A great big beautiful crucifix! And all this time I thought...

Pablo watched my expression of awe and approval. Then he said, "I carry it wherever I go. Ever since I was almost killed, I carry it with me."

I looked at him curiously. "When were you almost killed?"

Pablo hesitated. He gently took the crucifix from my hand and put it back into his wallet. Then he looked away.

"What happened? Or, don't you want to talk about it?" This was a big deal, to almost be killed! I didn't want to upset him. He would tell me someday, I thought.

"It was when I was almost shot. When I was a mercenary. Everyone around me was killed, but somehow I survived. God was looking out for me," Pablo said wistfully.

"What's a mercenary?" I asked, picturing those people who went to other countries to talk about God and Jesus. I knew those people traveled to poor countries and risked their lives to spread the gospel, but I didn't know people shot at them!

"A mercenary is...well, like a soldier, sort of," Pablo said.

"I thought it was someone who preached about God," I said, waiting for him to explain more.

Pablo's serious expression broke for a moment. He laughed. "Mercenary, not missionary."

"So what is a mercenary, again?" I asked, wanting to hear him finish telling me about almost getting killed.

"A soldier, sort of, you could say. A paid soldier." Pablo looked at me, and then looked away.

"So what war was it? I mean, when you almost got killed?" I was trying to figure it out. It was probably Vietnam.

"Well, it was a guerrilla war," he answered. "It's kind of hard to explain. I'll tell you more about it someday. Not right now, though."

"It wasn't Vietnam, then?" I asked, still curious.

"No. I didn't fight in Vietnam" Pablo said, shaking his head.

"Lucky for me," I said, smiling. Then I thought about it some more. "Why didn't you fight in Vietnam?"

"I got out of the draft," he replied.

"How?" I asked.

"Well, they don't take drug addicts, so I put marks on my arms, tracks, you know. They thought I was a junkie and threw me out. I thought it was pretty clever, at the time," he said.

I was shocked. Who would have ever thought to do that? What a smart thing to do! Pablo was so clever. Never in a million years would I have thought to do something like that! He was so smart to get out of Vietnam. I had heard it was a terrible war.

"That was really smart. How did you ever think of that?" I asked him.

Pablo smiled, pleased that I had approved. Then he said smugly, "That's why I get the big bucks."

I wanted him to tell me more war stories. "Tell me more about the war you fought in."

He was on a roll, now that I had shown interest in his stories.

"Well, as a mercenary, I would get hired to go into little countries to fight. A bunch of us would go into a country that was fighting their government for power, planning to overthrow their present government. They would hire us to do their fighting," he said, trying to make it sound as simple as possible.

"Why do they need to hire people? And what country are you talking about?" My curiosity roused, I had to learn more. Pablo was so *interesting.*

Pablo glanced around to see if anyone was listening. Then, he leaned over and whispered, "They hire guys like me—from America—because we have better weapons and are highly trained. Our government doesn't acknowledge that we exist. It would embarrass them. As long as we keep it quiet, that Americans are involved in other countries' wars for money, they don't mind. But they try to act ignorant about the whole thing. Meanwhile, they sell us the weapons. It's all top secret you know." He leaned back to his side of the table.

"How do they know to call you? The other countries, I mean. It is another country that hires you, right?" I asked, trying to get it all straight.

"They know we do a good job. We have a reputation. We're sort of on a list," Pablo said quietly.

"Who is 'we'?" I asked, wondering who else was involved in these top secret missions.

"Just some other guys. They are all really good fighters, too. But, no names. We use code names, anyway," Pablo said, narrowing his eyes.

"Do you still fight in these wars?" I asked, a little worried now.

"No. I was younger then. They still call me now and again. But I turn them down. No cause worth fighting for anymore. And the money isn't an issue, now that I train for Dubai. I'm happy, right where I'm at...*now.*" He reached down and squeezed my hand. I was *so* lucky to have him.

Pablo had invented many exciting stories about himself based on books he had read and movies he had watched.

Chapter 45
Karen the Jockey Gets the Axe

As one of the leading trainers in New York, Pablo continued to win races. In the first week of November, I won two races for him (as well as winning for other trainers). I had been dating Pablo for three months, and this brought my total wins for Dubai Stables up to four. Four wins was a drop in the bucket compared to Pablo's total number of wins, but that was okay—I was doing what I loved for someone I loved—and doing it well. I was on top of the world, and it was only the beginning. Egotist, the Dubai colt I had won with, was entered in a stakes race and was training super for it. Winter was almost here, and the top jockeys would soon be going to Florida or California. I assumed that would mean I would be Pablo's main jockey. Things were definitely looking up. As winter racing approached, even the slower horses I had ridden for Pablo would now be able to win. I was glad I hadn't said anything about not riding his good ones, which were going to a farm in Florida for a winter rest.

It seemed that lately, the happier I was, the more uneasy Pablo became. There was definitely something wrong. It wasn't long before I found out what it was.

We were at the Sea Cove Diner, our favorite place to eat a casual dinner, when he broke the news to me.

"Honey," Pablo said, sounding more serious than usual. "I have something to tell you. I hope you won't be too upset."

Bad news was on the way. I looked down at the menu.

Pablo continued. "I'm very upset over what I have to tell you. In fact, I don't know what to do. I'm in a real tough spot." He reached over and shook my arm. "Honey, are you listening?"

"Yeah."

"My father doesn't like you riding the horses. He said so in the beginning, but now he's really on my case."

Karen the jockey disappeared and Karen the girlfriend took over. As his girlfriend, I had convinced myself that riding for him did not matter. I wasn't dating him in order to ride his horses. Somewhere deep down inside me there was this protective wall I had built. It was made so that I could separate my career, my pride in riding, from my relationship with him—just in case. Now, I needed that wall. Karen the jockey hid behind it, listening.

"My father never chose the riders before, and I'm not about to let him now. Even if it means losing Dubai, I must take a stand. If he tells me which jockeys to use, I should just quit."

"Well, what are you going to do?" asked Karen the girlfriend, not Karen the jockey who was about to get the axe. She was hiding behind the wall, remember?

"I don't know," Pablo replied. "It's like this. I could quit Dubai. I don't want to work for them under these conditions," Pablo said. He looked at me, waiting. What did he want me to say? *Karen the jockey, come out from behind that wall and defend yourself! You have the right! You are a good rider!*

"Oh, don't quit, Pablo. You have a great job with Dubai Stables. All those good horses to train," said Karen the girlfriend. "And if it's about me riding the horses, don't worry. I'm fine," I said. Half of me was fine, the girlfriend part. Numb, but fine. The other half, Karen the jockey, was in hiding. *Come out, come out, wherever you are! Last call! Where are you? Aren't you going to defend yourself???*

Behind the wall, and that is where I am going to stay, said Karen the jockey. *You take over, girlfriend. You seem so sure of yourself. If it's so important that you prove you love him no matter what, then go ahead. You said it yourself anyway: you don't want to look like you're sleeping with him for mounts. I'll just stay here hidden and watch you lose all those good horses I worked so hard to ride. And I rode them well, too. But never mind me. You go ahead. I know you have your principles and I'm not going to argue with that.*

Pablo shook me out of myself. He said, "I'm really going to quit this time. I don't need Dubai. And besides, honey, all those horses you rode in races for me are now ready to win." He stopped, waiting for my reply. The reply he knew would come from his loving, faithful girlfriend.

"No, you don't quit. Not over this. Not over me. I'll show your father I don't care if I ride races for you or not. And I don't, really." Karen the jockey had totally disappeared. "If anyone should quit, it should be me," I said. "But I'll be fine. I have plenty of other business, and besides, I was spending most of my mornings at your barn. Now I'll have time to see other trainers." *Did I have any business left? Anybody left that I cared to ride for?* I had let most of my other outfits go in an effort to be with Pablo and in order to get on his horses every morning. I had put all my eggs in one basket. *Quick! Who else was I riding for? Who else?* "You know, Pablo, it really doesn't matter. It will be better this way. Now, everybody will know I don't go out with you because of the stupid horses," I said.

Karen the jockey reappeared. *So now the horses are stupid? What else are you going to say to put me down? Pretending I don't exist is pretty easy for you. You're his GIRLFRIEND. I'll just stay here hidden behind my wall. But don't come looking for me now. No, not now. You've said enough to put me down. I rest my case.*

"No, honey," Pablo said sadly. "It isn't fair. It isn't fair to you."

"It's okay. Really. Your job is important. Just do what you have to do, and don't worry about me. I'm fine, *really*." I felt fine, too. I felt better than fine. Karen the jockey was hidden so well now that she had disappeared. She no longer existed in my mind or my feelings. I had forgotten about her now. I felt suddenly free. Free to be just Pablo's girlfriend. There would be no dual role now, no arguments within myself. I was fine. I was just Pablo's girlfriend and I loved him so much! I was glad. I was *happy* this happened!

I was so convincing, to both Pablo and myself.

"Oh, I'm sooo glad, honey. I was so worried you wouldn't take this too well. I know how much your riding means to you." He reached over to hold my hand, but I had withdrawn it earlier in the conversation. If I could have withdrawn my whole body I would have, and in a way, I already had.

My hand was conspicuously missing, resting on my lap. Resting in a sweaty grip. I pulled it out from its hiding place and put it to use, picking up my menu again.

I changed the subject. "So, what're you gonna order?" *Did I care about what he ordered? Of course I did. Remember? Remember how much you care about your sweetheart?*

At the track, I tried not to think about the Dubai mounts I had suddenly lost and the trainers I had abandoned to be at Pablo's barn every morning. I hoped that I could rekindle business from my old supporters; however, my heart was no longer in my work.

Chapter 46
Why?

Pablo was about to take the test for his captain's license. "I'm going to miss you when I'm away," he said, with a worried look on his face.

"What do you mean?" I wondered. Miss me?

"Yes, I have to go to the Coast Guard Regional Exam Center for the test. I'm taking the time off from the barn and staying there for three days."

Three days without Pablo??? How would I make it through *three days?*

In those three days, I watched the horses I had been riding for Pablo win without me. From the sidelines, I watched Sequoia enter the winner's circle with the one jockey I did not like.

Pablo called me that night. "Hi, honey. How was your day?"

"Sequoia won."

"I know, honey. I feel so bad. And especially with Jimmy riding her. I know you and he have had your differences. I didn't want to put him on her. It was my darn father. If there was *any* jock I didn't want to ride her, it was him. I know it hurt you badly enough to watch her win, without that," Pablo said, sounding upset.

"Oh, that's okay. If it wasn't him, it would've been some other rider. It doesn't matter, really," I said, holding back the tears. "So, how is the test going?"

"I think I'm doing all right. It's really tough, though. Tomorrow it will be even harder. I'm going to get a good night's sleep now, so I'll be ready. I miss you. I'll be back in a few days," he said, sounding more chipper. Then he hung up.

I held the phone, not wanting to hang it up. Karen the girlfriend wanted his voice to stay with me, to comfort me all through the night.

Karen the jockey hung up the phone. She was sad. She had a bad day at the track. Oh well, tomorrow is another day.

Tomorrow was another day, and another one of my old Dubai mounts won. I left the girl jocks' room after watching the race. In the hallway, on the way to the jocks' room, I bumped into a jockey agent. "Why weren't you on that one?" he asked. Everyone could see from the *Daily Racing Form* that I had ridden Pablo's horse in his last race.

Good question. "It's a long story," I said, hurrying past him. The jockeys were coming back, all muddy from the race. On second thought, I think I'll go back to the girl jocks' room. I don't want to see the winning jockey's happy face. Was there any place left on the racetrack where I felt like I belonged? I didn't belong at Pablo's barn. And I didn't belong in the barn area or at the races, where trainers, jockeys, and agents were questioning me as to why I wasn't riding for Pablo anymore.

With me no longer riding for him, the jockey agents surrounded Pablo like vultures. Nobody (including me) seemed to be able to figure out why I had been taken off his horses. It was no secret we were dating. "If anyone should be using you," the trainers would say, "it should be Pablo." I think they thought Pablo knew something they didn't—like maybe I was sick or something. Or maybe it was that abortion rumor. Or maybe, it was simpler than that. Maybe they just thought, *if Pablo isn't using her, why should we?*

I was getting more and more depressed, answering trainers' stupid questions each morning and agents' stupid questions at the races each afternoon. I didn't want to face anyone and have to explain myself. What was there to explain anyway? At first I had convinced myself that it would be a good thing not to ride for Pablo. I thought it would prove to other trainers that I wasn't dating him for his horses. However, it was turning out to be just the opposite. Everyone now wondered what was wrong with me. Things were not looking good.

One morning when I was at Aqueduct, trainer Bobby Lake commented, "Not riding for Dubai Stables any more, huh? Figured that would happen." Now, what did he mean by that? I let it go, not wanting to talk about it anymore.

To add insult to injury, Frank Wright took me off Adept. I was upset, to say the least. I had ridden her in her last ten starts and won two stakes races with her, including the Grade 1 Top Flight Handicap. "K. Rogers" was next to her name all the way down the past performances in the *Daily Racing Form*. Why now...why *this*?

Pablo had the answer. He had the answer for everything. "Frank Wright is upset that you are dating me. He is jealous. It ruins his reputation, the story he has been spreading about you," Pablo said smugly.

"What?" I was lost in thought, thoughts of Adept running without me. Depressing thoughts, all of them. The only thing that was keeping me going was the fact that Pablo loved me. It was all I had left in the world.

"Don't you know what Frank Wright has been saying all this time?" Pablo asked me seriously.

"No. I mean, yeah. Frank has been my greatest supporter. He had me on his television show and used me when I first came to New York. He even put me on his best stakes horses, Nice Catch and Adept. He is my biggest fan and encouraged other trainers to give me a chance on their good horses. I just don't understand this." I shook my head, more disappointed than upset that Frank had replaced me on Adept.

Pablo narrowed his eyes suspiciously. "Don't you know what he's *really* been saying?"

"No. What?" Maybe he had the answer to this one. I certainly didn't. But I didn't expect in a million years to hear what he told me.

"Frank Wright had been telling everybody that you are his girlfriend. That you two...you know."

"*What?* He *what?* No. It couldn't be. No way. That's *impossible*."

Pablo watched me closely. Watched my expression as the news hit me and I went from shock to disbelief to disappointment to utter despair. Was there nothing left of Karen the jockey? Had it really come to *this*? I looked at Pablo to see if maybe he was joking. No...he was leaning back, sure of himself, watching me fall apart.

I shook my head, no.

He nodded his head up and down slowly as this news sunk into my head. "It's true, honey. And now he is upset because everybody knows about you and me. It ruins his story." Pablo smiled.

"No way," I countered, very upset now. Pablo knew this would upset me. He knew just how fragile I was about people thinking I would sleep with a trainer for mounts. "There is just no way," I argued in disbelief. "Frank is sixty-five years old. He could be my *grandfather*! Nobody would believe it. Besides, Frank is my *friend*." Suddenly, being taken off Adept no longer mattered. It was a small matter compared to *this*.

"He put you on his stakes horses. Come on, Karen. Why do you think he did that?" Pablo looked so cynical.

I answered him weakly. "Because...I'm a good rider?"

Pablo shook his head sadly, knowingly. His silence said it all.

Could this be possible—even true? Pablo knew these things. He did have a point. Maybe Frank *had* put me on his good horses to make it look like... *No!* It couldn't be.

I needed Pablo more now than ever. He was all I had left to live for.

Pablo would continue his lies until he completely destroyed Karen the jockey.

Chapter 47
You Still Love Me?

Once again, Pablo and I were having dinner at the Sea Cove Diner. I was having one of my favorite meals, Greek salad. I had been making a big effort not to heave my dinners. Pablo was sharp, and I was afraid that he would pick up on me going off to the bathroom after I finished every meal. Greek salad was perfect. It wasn't fattening, and it didn't fill me up to the point where I felt the "urge to purge." Throwing up was a big part of my daily life now. I knew it was bad, but I told myself that I was a jockey and lots of jocks heaved.

"You like that Greek salad," Pablo commented, noticing that I had been ordering it quite a bit.

Guilty, I looked at him. Did he know? "Yeah," I said, trying not to panic. "I like salad. It's not fattening."

"Wouldn't you like something else to eat, though? You must still be hungry." He looked around for our waiter in case I decided to order something else.

"No, I'm okay. Really. I ate a big lunch," I lied.

"Just the check, then," Pablo said as the waiter appeared. Then he leaned back and lit a cigarette. He had a very concerned look on his face.

Uh, oh. My brain raced. He knows. He knows I throw up. He figured it out. I *knew* he would. I should have ordered something else and held it down, just this one time.

Pablo set his cigarette down in the ash tray. "Karen, your mother told me something. Something I don't think was her place to tell me, but she told me anyhow."

What? Mom didn't know I threw up. Nobody knew. Phew! Maybe he didn't figure it out, after all. Or maybe Mom had figured it out after all this time.

Pablo continued, "She told me what your step-father did..."

His voice trailed off. I wasn't listening. *No. No. It couldn't be true. She wouldn't. She didn't. How could she?* I went weak. Hot flashes. I was going to faint. *No, no, this couldn't be happening. He must hate me now. How could she do this to me? How could Mom destroy the only good thing I had left...He wouldn't want to see me again, not ever. Now he knew I was bad, damaged goods. Dirty, horrible me. How could she?* I resigned myself. She had won. He would leave me now, and guess what? I deserved it. I had ruined Mom's life by taking Vince away, and now she was ruining my life by taking Pablo from me. All right. That was fair. We're even. I lose. Goodbye, sweet Pablo. It was nice while it lasted.

"Honey, are you listening? You seem so distant, so far away." Pablo looked at me with concern. Not hate. Not disgust. Concern.

"I can't believe she told you." The words fell out of my numb mouth. Surrender to defeat.

"I know. She shouldn't have told me. But she did. And I wanted to tell you she told me. I don't think it was her place. If you wanted me to know, it should have come from you," he said.

God, I can't believe this is happening. Not this. Not *this*. The Deep Dark Secret from my past. Why did Mom want to ruin everything for me? I know why. I always knew why. Because I *deserved* it, that's why.

"Well, I guess you won't want to see me anymore." I looked down, resigned to the fact that I had lost my Pablo forever.

"*What?* You must be joking." He leaned over the table and touched my hand. My hand that was holding my head, covering my face. Head down. Tears falling, rolling down my arm.

Pablo shook my arm gently, noticing my little river of tears. He tried to pull my hand away from my face so I would look at him.

"What's wrong? Of course I still want to see you, honey. I love you. I feel bad for you. I feel terrible that this had to happen to you when you were young. I love you. Why are you so upset?" He gave up trying to get me to move my hand away from my face.

I couldn't speak. History was stuck in my throat. Couldn't talk. Mind buzzing. Humming. Hum a nice tune. Go away, thoughts.

"Come on, honey. Talk to me. Tell me why you are so upset."

I could see Pablo's arm through my bleary, teary eyes, as I peeked out from under my wet, sticky hand. He was still with me. He hadn't left. I wiped my nose and attempted a word. "You...don't hate me?" There. I got it out.

"No, of course not. It wasn't your fault. Quite the opposite. Didn't anybody ever tell you that?" he asked.

"Why do you say it's not my fault? Of course it is," I said, wanting to hear him say it again, say it really wasn't my fault. I wanted to believe it so much. Wanted to hear it again, to believe what he said was true.

"You were young and he took advantage of you. It wasn't your fault. Didn't anyone ever tell you that? How could you think...ooh, honey." Pablo got up. I watched him from under my arm as he slid out from his side of the booth. I felt him sit down beside me.

"You still love me?" I asked him, a little rainbow starting to form, peeking out through the clouds in my head.

"Of course. More than ever." He hugged me.

I could see, now, a little better. Blinked the remainder of tears out of my eyes. There, pull yourself together. See, he still loves you. He's not going anywhere.

Pablo pulled me close to him. "Come on, honey. Let's go home."

It was hard for me to believe that maybe what happened with Vince wasn't my fault; however, what mattered the most to me now was that Pablo knew the secret and he still loved me.

Because I was still living at home and sharing racing stories with Mom, she had noticed a negative change in my attitude toward my career and my growing dependency on Pablo for my happiness. Mom's intentions were good in telling Pablo what had happened to me with Vince. She saw how totally devastated I was after Pablo took me off all his horses; in fact, I told her I didn't want to live anymore. She thought if anyone could help me, Pablo could. I always defended Pablo so Mom thought he would do what was best for me if he understood more about my past.

Chapter 48
Should I Quit?

I was still riding and winning for Bobby Lake and, despite what Pablo said, I still had a few mounts for Frank Wright. I didn't know what to think anymore. What did they really think of me? Were they jealous, like Pablo said? They didn't act like it. Frank had taken me off Adept, but he blamed Adept's owner for making the change. I was riding other horses for Frank, so maybe he was telling the truth. If what Pablo was saying had been true, why was Frank still putting me on horses?

One night I was telling Pablo about a horse I had ridden in a race that day. Pablo stopped me. "There is more to life than just horses. The reason I never dated girls from the racetrack was because I don't like to take the horses home with me, if you know what I mean," he said. Well, he was a smart guy and knew about other things. Horses had been my whole world; I guess it was time to learn about other things, and who better to teach me than my very own Pablo?

Pablo was happy to share what he knew. He loved the old movies, especially war films and true stories. "You can learn a lot from history," he said. "History repeats itself and that is why it is so fascinating. Take Hitler, for example." Pablo told me he owned every book ever written on the Nazi leader. "I studied his way of thinking,"

Pablo explained. "The interesting thing about Hitler is how he got so much control over the people. In order to gain so much power, he had to be leading a desperate people. The Germans were desperate and had nothing when he rose to power. They looked to their new leader for all the answers. That's the trick to taking over lives—start when someone has nothing. Nothing to lose, nothing to hold onto, except you."

Egotist, the horse I had won on for Pablo, won his next race with Angel as his new jockey. I had never before been taken off a horse after winning with it; I had reached a new low in my career. The list of Pablo's horses that won after I was fired from riding for him grew. In fact, all the horses I had ridden for him were now put in races where they *could* win. And they did. I tried not to let it get to me. I *did* try.

I was thinking more and more about quitting riding all together. I was getting sour on the whole racetrack scene. Instead, I just wanted to be with Pablo. I was so *lucky* to have him. He would teach me about the important things in life—things outside of horses and the racetrack.

"Everyone who works at the track is a lowlife, an idiot," Pablo informed me. "My job is easy. I just delegate the work to my two assistant trainers and my help. My job," he laughed, "is telling everyone *else* to do the work!" Then he looked at me with seriousness. "Yes, the key to success is getting everyone else to do things for you."

I began to feel stupid and ashamed of how hard I worked, making my rounds in the mornings, doing favors for trainers by working their horses for free. Sometimes I didn't even ride those horses in races. This was nothing new to me, but now I was really bothered by it. I suddenly felt like one of "those idiots" that Pablo was talking about. Nothing had changed about my job; I was just looking at it differently now. Pablo was certainly opening my eyes to the truth!

As a leading female jockey, I had been invited to Europe and Japan several times to ride races. I had also been asked to do other interesting things outside of racing. Because the horses and trainers I rode for in New York were always a priority to me, I had mostly turned down these invitations. However, this time when I was asked to participate in the "Superstars," I thought differently about it. Because I was considering ending my career as a jockey, it made sense to take advantage of this opportunity.

The "Superstars" was a televised event held annually for star athletes from all different sports. The competition would be held in Miami Beach, Florida. It might be fun, and I might not get another chance like this again. Thinking Pablo would be excited to go and stay in a nice hotel, I asked him what he thought.

"That sounds really stupid," he sneered. "I've seen that thing on television."

"Well, I thought you and I could go. It might be something different to do. It's not about horses or racing or anything," I reminded him. "And we would stay in a really nice suite in the Fontainebleau Hotel."

Pablo paused, thinking. "No, I can't go. I have too much work to do at the barn. But you go, honey, if it's that important to you."

It wasn't that important to me. *He* was important to me.

"Well, I just thought it might be fun," I said, trying not to sound disappointed.

The next day in the jocks' room, I asked Angel about it. He said he had competed in the Superstars twice before and encouraged me to do it. I didn't tell Pablo right away, but I decided to go. I could bring someone with me at no cost and since Pablo wasn't interested, I asked Mom to come. She was thrilled to go. It was first class all the way, from the plane tickets to the hotel. But still, I missed my Pablo.

In the Superstars competition, I was much smaller than the other female athletes. Consequently, I did poorly in the events (cycling, swimming, bowling, running, golf, and basketball). However, I had a great time and got to know lots of nice people. I met and competed with renowned tennis player Martina Navratilova, medal Olympic winning speed skater Beth Heiden, and many other successful athletes.

Lynn Swann, of NFL Pittsburgh Steelers fame, and Cathy Rigby, the well-known medal-winning gymnast, were commentators for the ABC Sports Superstars. Lynn Swann was intrigued with horse racing and asked me lots of questions about the sport. I even got him up on

Sitting with tennis star Martina Navratilova

Right: Cathy Rigby, star gymnast and commentator for the Superstars

Above: Lynn Swann, NFL football star and commentator

Making Lynn Swann into a jockey

a chair into a riding position and showed him how to use a whip. He had a great sense of humor, and we laughed a lot. The trip was a nice change from all the turmoil I was experiencing at the track.

The best thing to happen on the trip was that Mom and I got along great. Without Pablo (or Vince) to twist her words and actions, it seemed like she loved me.

When I got back from Florida, I couldn't wait to see Pablo's reaction to the ABC telecast of the Superstars. But he hadn't even watched it. I hid my disappointment.

I continued to be depressed about my riding. All I could think about was Pablo: Pablo vs. riding. Riding vs. Pablo. One day I made a trip to Maryland to ride a stakes race for a New York trainer. At the airport after the race, I called Pablo. His voice was sweet music to my ears.

He sounded cheerful. "Hi, honey. Where are you? How did you make out?"

Hearing him made me smile. Karen the girlfriend was happy now.

"I'm still in Maryland. The plane is delayed. I miss you, though." My moods were going up and down like a roller coaster. Should I quit riding??? Riding vs. Pablo. Pablo vs. riding.

"Oh, guess what, honey?" Pablo's voice came across the receiver clearly. But he was miles and miles away.

"What?" I said excited. *What? What did my sweetie have to tell me?*

Now his voice sounded sad. "Aw, honey, your filly won the stakes race in New York today."

There was a long pause.

Pablo repeated, "Adept won. Honey, are you there? Are you still on?"

Am I still on? No. I just died. Karen the jockey is dead. Please revive her. "Uh, yeah, I'm still here. I knew she'd win," said a hollow voice from the grave. "But I don't care, anymore." Maybe if I said I didn't care, I wouldn't.

Pablo corrected me. "Of course you do, honey. Of course you still care."

Chapter 49
Racing With My Shadow

I've been putting off the inevitable. Every day I say I'm going to quit riding. Every day. I have been dating Pablo for seven months, and I guess it's time to put riding behind me. *God, if this is what You want me to do, then let me just do it today.*

I was highly emotional. *This was it. I would do it.*

Maybe this was what God wanted for me. I didn't seem to know anything anymore. Adept had won. My business was slow. I was fired from Dubai. *Well, this is it, boys. My last race.* My God, it's *Northern Snipe!*

Here I was, reunited with Northern Snipe, the horse I had ridden in my very first race for Vince in April of 1979. Now, in 1984, I was back on him again. He had changed hands many times, and was now trained by Debbie Casson. Things had come full circle. *My first career mount, and now my last.*

I thought back to those times at Hialeah when I lived in fear of Mom finding out about the secret. A lot had happened since then. I had been through the extremes of a jockey's career: the good year as an apprentice and the difficult transition to journeyman. I had been through, literally, all the ups and downs that came with it: spills and injuries, comebacks, struggling for mounts, and being a leading rider. I had lived through the most difficult time of all, when Mom found out about Vince from the letter. And then I had met Pablo. Yes, it had been a long road.

Through it all things had changed, yet they remained the same. The long and winding road had led me right back to the same place I had started—riding Northern Snipe. I wondered where the road had taken him before it brought him back to be reunited with me. He, too, had changed, yet remained the same. Now he was a snowy white instead of an iron gray—but he still liked to run on the outside.

I whispered to Northern Snipe, "Let's win this one, boy, for old times' sake."

Northern Snipe made his typical big run, barreling down the homestretch. *Come on, boy, COME ON!* We got up to win by a nose.

Pulling him up, I felt the tears flood my eyes. *This was it. This was really it.* I patted Northern Snipe and turned him around to gallop back to the winner's circle. *Feel him gallop beneath you. Feel it for the last time. Farewell, sweet career! It's been nice.*

My face was wet from the tears as I pulled my saddle off for the last time. I was resigned to it now. Nobody but God knew that I was ending my career. Not my agent, not the trainer, not anybody.

"Reuinited"
Northern Snipe, the horse I rode in my very first race, wins for me in my "last" race. As an older horse, he is much lighter gray, almost white.
(Gray horses are born black and lighten with age.)

Debbie Casson, the trainer of Northern Snipe, looked at me as we walked back to the jocks' room for the *last* time.

"What's wrong?" she asked. She didn't understand. How could she? She didn't know I was quitting. I shook my head without explanation and hurried back to the girl jocks' room.

I had not cried since riding Northern Snipe in my very first race in New York, when trainer Allen Jerkens had yelled at me, and this strange sense of history repeating itself seemed somehow worthy of noting. The horse, the tears, the first, the last....

How could I have known that this was just the beginning of things going full circle? It was the beginning, though, the start of strange twists of fate weaving through my life like a theme, weaving a web which would eventually entangle me and take me back to my ultimate destiny... my past. I wasn't free. My riding had been a painted picture of freedom. Painted pictures on prison walls. This prison cell with no way out, would eventually reveal itself for what it was. Until that time, though, I would race ahead. Race into what I believed was a way out. Painted pictures, prison walls, tangled web. But the web was not yet complete. I was the prisoner...yes, and me the jockey, too. Held captive. Yet, I was unaware of this. I was too busy racing full speed ahead.

Racing with my shadow.

For the shadow of my past had never left me. It had kept pace throughout, as shadows do. I hadn't left it behind, like I had figured. It was still right there where it had been all along. It lingered, moving ahead when I did, slowing when I slowed.

My life had yet to go full circle. My past would track me down. There was no escaping. There was no way out.

Chapter 50

Now What?

I awoke with a start. I was sweating. I had another nightmare. In the dream, I was still alive after our plane crashed into the ocean. There were some survivors. I looked around at the wreckage and bodies strewn about. I could hear moaning. Wait a minute. That was me moaning. There was a small sailboat approaching. It was Pablo! He could see me, now, as he approached. *Come get me, Pablo. Come save me!* He could sail us out of there, but he could only fit a few people in his small boat. He could come back for the rest of us.

The water was cold. My back hurt, and my legs. As he approached, I saw him point away from me, toward other survivors. *Go on, then, take the others. I can wait. I'll make it. I'm strong...and if I don't...well...it won't really matter.* I held onto a piece of wreckage, still drifting, floating. I watched as Pablo sailed away with some of the survivors. My hands were slipping off the broken wreckage. I was doomed to a cold death as I dropped beneath the surface into the black, murky water below. Groping in the dark waters, I lost all sense of direction. Up was down. Down was up. I swam a little, going farther down instead of back toward the surface. I would never make it. I had gone too far down. I stopped swimming. Rested. Breathed in the water, getting used to the sensation of drowning.

Even though I was awake now, the feeling of dying was still so real, so vivid. I was so cold, so depressed. I hated sleeping. All I did was dream about death. Was today my last day of riding? Yes. That wasn't a dream. That was real.

I lay in bed going over my decision again. Riding had been my whole life. I had been into racing since the age of eleven. Now, at twenty-one, I had decided to quit. Or retire. Say it any way you want, it still meant the same thing: the end of my life as I knew it. I got out of bed, hoping I could face the day.

Last night I had a bad dream, but this morning I am living one. I'm tormenting myself. It's ten o'clock in the morning. I told my agent I wasn't riding today, but I didn't tell him why. Not yet. Not until I'm sure I can go through with it, sure I can really quit. Karen the jockey was dying, yet still fighting to stay alive.

I was confused and split apart, not realizing how much Pablo had torn down Karen the jockey. No matter what I did as a jockey, he put it down in some way. He criticized the people I rode for, the horses I rode, and the racetrack in general. I didn't realize the huge influence Pablo had on me in making this decision to quit. He made me "see" that riding was a waste of time.

I looked forward to Pablo picking me up for dinner later. After the races yesterday, I had told him of my decision to quit riding. He had approved wholeheartedly, telling me this was what he had wanted, but that it had to be my decision. Tonight he was taking me to Manero's Steak House as a sort of celebration.

Now I just had to get through the day, this first day without riding. My horses would run without me. This will probably be the hardest day of my life. I wonder if I'll be able to stay away.

I will never ride again, and I might as well start accepting this fate.

Pablo came to get me—what was left of me. We drove off toward the steak house. My depression was only lifting slightly because I was with Pablo.

We sat down in a booth in the corner. I would tell Pablo how empty I felt, not having ridden today. Maybe he could fill my void.

"It was really hard for me today, Pablo," I said sadly.

"I know, honey. It must be hard. But you're doing the right thing. You were riding so many bad horses. I had a feeling you were going to get hurt again. Now is the time to stop riding," he said with a warning look on his face. Warning me to not even think about going back. Oh, well, order something good on the menu. Get fat. Who cares? This will be good. Now maybe I'll stop heaving, too. An added bonus to my decision.

Pablo pushed the menu aside. "What do you say we just have the Chateaubriand for two? You love that. It's such a tender cut of meat." He looked at me, inquiring. Yeah, that sounded good. Great.

"Okay. And let's get the fried onion rings to go with it. They're so greasy and delicious," I added, getting into it. I loved to eat. But, wait. I thought I might stop heaving, too. Ahh, who cares? This is a celebration. I had a tough enough day. I deserve to eat and eat and eat. And flip. So what? I really don't want to get fat. I may eventually go back to riding.

"Where is our waiter? You can never find them when you need them," Pablo said, looking around the room. The guy that had served our drinks appeared from behind the swinging doors that led to the kitchen. I wondered if there were ever collisions from those swinging doors. I wondered what it would be like to be a waitress. Would it be difficult? Maybe I would be one, now. I needed a new job. But I probably couldn't be a waitress. I'd lose my patience, drop the tray, mix up the order, or mess up somehow.

"Honey, do you want another drink? I'll take a Chivas on the rocks, and she'll have another screwdriver," he explained to the waiter. "And then we'd like the Chateau Briand for two. Medium rare, just pink in the middle." He always said that. Just pink in the middle.

"And the onion rings," I reminded him.

"And, of course, the onion rings," he repeated to the waiter. "Lots of them." He looked at me and smiled. A rare Pablo smile. He loved me so much. What would I do without him? I'm never going to find out, I decided.

On the second day of my retirement, I bought a new car, a Ford Thunderbird. I thought this would make me feel better, like a new person. But, it didn't change anything.

On the third day of my retirement, reality set in. I seemed okay after Pablo picked me up in the late afternoons because I spent the evenings with him, but doing nothing all day at home was starting to get to me. What was I going to do with my life? I began to worry. All I could think of, besides checking the racing results, was *what am I going to do now?* I had to have something to do. What would people think? Oh, yeah, I just retired from riding to do nothing, to just sit around and watch the world go by. Watch my horses win. Yeah, I just thought it was the thing to do??!!

I started my day in a new way. When Pablo dropped me off at my house on his way to the barn in the early mornings, I used to put on my boots, go to the track, and work horses. Now, I went straight to the kitchen and found whatever leftovers Mom and Amy had for dinner the night before. I didn't care what I found, or if it had been left out all night. The important thing was to stuff it down and then throw it up before Mom and Amy woke up. I had said I would stop heaving, but now I ate and threw up around the clock until Pablo picked me up for dinner. Eat, throw up, shop to replace the food, cook it, eat it, repeat. What a productive person I had become!

I was miserable. I hated myself. I hated my life.

Pablo was no help. The only thing he served as was a barrier between me, food, and the bathroom. At least when I was with him, I didn't throw up. Well, not until he fell asleep, which was usually around eight p.m. He was always so tired. I knew he got up very early, around five a.m. (he let me sleep until six, when we would leave his house), but he always took a nap in the afternoon before he came to get me again. Still, I couldn't understand why he was always so tired. He always went to bed early, leaving me alone with my horrible self. Useless, bad, good-for-nothing me. And my good-for-nothing thoughts. At night, I had my death dreams. I hated drowning. Those were the worst. And falling dreams. And the dreams where Pablo was Vince and Vince was Pablo. I never saw Pablo's face in my dreams. It was always Vince's face, but I knew it was Pablo. I couldn't just lie there awake in the bed, so off I'd go, down to his kitchen to eat.

As I was trying, sadly, to "finish" my scrapbooks, I noticed I had still won a lot of races for the year. At least I had gone out in style. Nobody could ever say that I "had to quit" or that I wasn't doing well. So many jockeys were forced into retirement because they just weren't getting any mounts. Not the case with me, I thought proudly. I quit on my own terms. I had gone out a winner. But did that make me a winner or a quitter? I wasn't sure. I always referred to my quitting as quitting. Maybe that said something of what I thought about myself. Later on, my quitting was labeled "retirement," making me sound so old.

My walk with God was fairly new, and I didn't know the Bible. Therefore, I didn't know where to really look for answers and looked for "signs" in events and even read my "stars" in the newspaper every day. Maybe they would tell me something about my future. I wanted desperately for Pablo to ask me to marry him. Then I could be something. I could be a wife.

But until then, what would I do with my life? Quick, turn to the "help wanted" ads in the middle of the paper. There it is. Jobs, jobs, jobs. Now what would I be talented at?

DRIVERS. CLERK/TYPIST. BOOKKEEPER. RECEPTIONIST.

Hmm. I don't know...

IMMEDIATE.

That looks good. Immediate what?

There were lots of IMMEDIATES. IMMEDIATE—FOOD SERVICE SUPERVISOR. Food. I could definitely handle food. Then I read the small print.

FOOD SERVICE SUPERVISOR
For 200 Bed Nursing Home in Queens.
Nursing Home experience essential.

Experience in a nursing home? Nah, that wasn't for me, anyway. Let's see what else is IMMEDIATE.

IMPORT CLERK.

What could an import clerk do? I read on.

Growing service co. JFK location. Exp & good typing required. Must be fluent in Spanish/English. Excel growth oppty.

Well, I had no exp (experience, I assume) and definitely was not fluent in Spanish. I took French in school, a lot of good it did me now. Well, I just wasn't meant for this job. I'll keep looking. Maybe in the restaurant section. Why is it I'm always so preoccupied with food? If I'm not eating it, buying it, cooking it, or heaving it, I'm reading about it!

WENDY'S HAMBURGERS
NEEDS
people with ability to lead, motivate,
make decisions & think independently.
If this is you, we need your abilities
to continue our successful growth.

Right. Could you see me working at Wendy's? With one of those little outfits and a hat? I'm not getting anywhere with these "help wanted" ads. Maybe I'm looking in the wrong place. Maybe I'll just go down to Wendy's, get a hamburger, some fries, a milkshake, and think about this "second career" stuff later.

I jumped in my new Thunderbird and headed toward the Wendy's across the street from Belmont Park. I went directly into the drive-thru entrance out of habit. I felt guilty about eating and didn't want anyone to see me order so much food.

"Welcome to Wendy's. One moment please," the voice came out of the speaker as I pulled up to the big colorful menu. I pictured what it would be like to work inside: wearing my Wendy's outfit and talking so calmly to the customers while the other employees were frantically throwing burgers and fries at me to put in a bag and hand out the window. No, I think I preferred being on the other end, right here where I was, ordering and eating the food. The sweet voice came back over the speaker as I waited, more patiently now. "Yes, may I take your order?"

God, please forgive me for doing this again. I promise I'll stop this merry-go-round of eating and heaving, but not right now. The pictures of juicy burgers on the menu looked too good to resist. Oh, the heck with it, I thought, ordering everything good on the menu. She'll never know I'm not taking these "lunches" back to the other "four" people at my job!

Now that I had my fill of Wendy's, I was back to pondering what I should do with my life. The craving to splurge on food was gone, for a while. It would be back, though, soon enough. My stomach was now empty and it would take about an hour for the hunger to set me in motion, once again, sending me on my food rampage, my hunt for some new deli delight. Yeah, maybe I'd go to a deli next. Maybe get something Italian, like baked ziti, if they had it. Or lasagna would be okay, too.

I suddenly wondered if it was even *possible* to stop throwing up. I had tried to stop. A few times I had stopped for almost an entire day. But I always felt so bloated and fat that by evening I couldn't stand the feeling anymore. I wondered if it was the eating or the heaving that had me so "addicted." I couldn't use my riding as an excuse any longer. At any rate, I didn't want to think about it anymore. It was too scary to think I could never stop, never be "normal" again. Besides, I had enough scary things to keep my mind occupied. Like, what was I going to do with my life?

After going through some more want ads, I decided to give up on the idea of finding a fulfilling job. There was nothing even close to riding. I missed it. I missed the horses. And, even though I would never have admitted it to Pablo, I missed the people, too. As bad as he said they were, they had to be better than just being with myself, in this condition. I was depressed. I needed to get back to doing something active. Aside from the food missions, I was spending all my time in the seclusion of my room. Except when I was with Pablo. He was the only thing worth living for. I wished Pablo would have asked me to go to work for him. That way, I could be around him. Yes, that's the only thing I wanted. To be with him. What a great thing it would be if I could just work for him for a while. Just until I knew what I was doing.

When I was with Pablo, I dropped hints that I wanted to work for him. "You know, Pablo, I need to keep busy. I need to be around the horses, like at your barn. Wasn't it great when I was riding for you and spending time at your barn? Do you need someone light to breeze (work) the horses? Someone good?" I figured he would get the hint with that. But he never seemed to get the idea.

"No, my help situation at the barn is fine," he said.

I was beginning to wish I had never quit riding. I stayed hidden from the world. I wished Pablo would marry me.

I told Mom how depressed I was. How the only thing that mattered in my life was Pablo and how I wished I could be working for him. I told her that I couldn't understand why he didn't want me around the barn and that I didn't know if we would even get married. I told her that my life was totally useless and that I didn't want to live anymore.

I went outside, frazzled over the things I had just said, the things that had been staring me in the face, but now, having been said, they were more tangible and terribly real. I was in a horrible state of mind—suicidal—and decided I would finally do something about it. Maybe do something bad, but at least I would do *something*. I had to get away from my situation. I couldn't stand not knowing who I was or where I was going.

I got into my new Thunderbird and started the engine. As I sat there deciding what I would do, Mom came out of the house. She looked *really* worried. My car radio was turned all the way up to blast out my thoughts. Mom knocked on the car window. She looked pale and very upset. I didn't want to upset her. I could be upset enough for both of us.

I turned off the car and got out. I give up.

Mom put her arm around me. We went back into the house, and the phone rang. Mom answered it. "Hello....Yes, she's right here." Smiling, she handed me the phone. For me?

"Hello?"

It was Pablo. I was relieved to hear his voice. It brought me somewhat back to the feeling of wanting to live again. "Hi, honey. Guess what? One of my help just quit and I need another exercise rider. Would you want to help me out?" he asked, plain and simple.

Would I??? What timing!!! "Oh, yeah. That would be great," I said, trying to sound calm. My enthusiasm was bubbling just below the surface. Mom was beaming, too. Wait a minute. How did she know? She was probably just happy to see me happy—finally.

"When can I start?" I asked. I hoped soon. Please, make it soon, God.

"Tomorrow, if you want," came the sweet, sweet reply. Oh, YEEESSSS! Where were my exercise boots? And my helmet? Maybe I'll just try them on *right now*, for starters.

"Tomorrow will be great. You'll pick me up later?" I asked. He always picked me up later.

"Yeah, I'll see you around four. Bye," he said. Oh, goodbye my *sweet*, loving savior. I hung up the phone and ran up the stairs. I dug through my closet. Bingo. My boots. I put them on and felt better already. I could hear Mom coming up the steps.

"Guess what, Mom? You'll never believe what happened!" I waited for her to ask me what great thing had brought me out of the black hole.

Mom was smiling. "You look so happy. What happened? What did Pablo say?"

"He wants me to go *work* for him. Just like I wanted! Can you *believe* it? And I was ready to just take off. Lucky thing I didn't. I'm so happy."

The first horse Pablo put me on was a flighty filly, just off the farm. It was her first day at the track. I was jogging her around the barn when she stopped suddenly, scared by a pigeon that flew up in front of her. My pinkie jammed down into her neck and was dislocated. I couldn't do anything right....

The next day I hoped that Pablo would put me on one of the older horses to breeze. Jockeys were good at workouts or breezing horses and rarely just jogged or galloped them. However, instead of giving me the job I was good at, Pablo put me on the same skittish filly and had me take her to the track.

Pablo obviously wanted to discourage me by putting me back on the same problem filly.

I was jogging the filly around the turn when she wheeled suddenly and I went flying off. I sat on the sandy track, totally disgusted with myself. *No wonder I quit riding. I'm totally useless. Face it. You've just got to quit.*

Tears were welling up in my eyes. My throat felt like it was going to explode. I started walking off the track, waving everyone away who asked me "how I was." *Oh, yeah, I'm fine. I can't even jog a racehorse, anymore.*

Pablo was waiting for me by the gap to the track. Waiting in his big blue Cadillac. Someone had caught the filly. He opened the window to his car. "Come on. Get in." He sounded disgusted. He was probably fed up with me, too. Sorry he ever hired me.

I got into his car, feeling very, very low. I couldn't even look at Pablo. "I'm quitting," I said, looking down at the dirt covering my boots. "I can't even gallop anymore."

Pablo seemed happy with this. "Okay, honey. It's probably better this way. You know, it wasn't my idea anyway, you working for me at the barn. Your mother suggested it," he pointed out.

I was shocked. *It wasn't his idea?*

He looked at my expression of shock and continued. "Your mother begged me to put you to work, but I knew it wouldn't work out."

Mom *begged* him??? I only wanted to work for him if *he* wanted me to.

"It's better this way," he said with finality.

What was left for me? *Face it, all you really want is to be with Pablo. You want to be his wife. Or you just don't want to be, period.*

Chapter 51
I'll Just Have to Marry You

I couldn't go on like this anymore. I decided it was time to find out about my future with Pablo. Were we going to "have a life" together? I needed a life. Isn't that what all women wanted in the end, to get married? I'll just bring up marriage, plain and simple. That's all there is to it. I can handle rejection. Sure, why not? My life as it stands now can't get much worse.

I decided to practice on Mom. "Mom, listen to what I'm going to say to Pablo. Ready? 'I need to know where our relationship is going. I hate just being a girlfriend. It wasn't so bad when I was a jockey, but now I need a more meaningful purpose to my life.' How does that sound?" I asked Mom, hopefully.

Mom shook her head. "I don't think so. Why don't you let him bring it up? I think it would be better if it came from him."

"I can't wait for that. He may never bring it up. I can't stand my life as it is. I don't know what to do." I let out a sigh. Life was so difficult.

Mom opened the yellow pages. "Let's get something going. If you do something, maybe Pablo will get jealous of your time away from him and ask you to marry him. Sound good?" she looked at me knowingly.

Mom made a good point. Pablo was jealous of my time. He hated it when I talked to other people, or did anything without him. The way it was now, I was always available to him—at his beck and call—an exclusive at-your-service girlfriend. Maybe Mom was onto something. Maybe it was a good plan. Maybe there was a light at the end of my dark tunnel. I was willing to try anything, at this point anyway.

"Okay. What do you think I'd be good at?" I asked. That was the real question. The real-fast-becoming-old question. "What do you think I should do?" I asked her impatiently.

Mom closed the yellow pages. "You know so much about racing. Why don't you do something at the track? Monmouth Park is opening soon, and I heard that they are looking for someone to host their racing show on cable television. If you do that, Pablo will miss you. If he doesn't want you to go away, he will have to marry you to give you a reason to stay. You know the old expression, 'You don't know what you've got 'til it's gone.'"

Yes! And I would be the "it" that was gonna be gone! That was the plan, anyway.

Mom added one more word of advice, "Make sure you go. Commit yourself to the summer there. Make him know he *has* to marry you to win your time."

I knew this was something I had to do. When I broke the news to Pablo about taking a job at Monmouth Park, he wasn't happy. "Whatever made you decide to want to do that?" he said critically.

"I just need something different to do. I need to get out of my situation," I said, trying to convince myself that I was going to do it. I thought about Mom's advice: commit yourself to going. *I'm going? Yes, I'm going. I must go now. I must follow through. Don't let him talk you out of it. But I don't really want to go. But, I must. I MUST!*

I continued on, trying my hardest to be believable. "There is a job opening to host their racing show for cable television. I want to do that." There. I said it.

"Television? Why, honey, you don't have any experience with that sort of thing," Pablo said, leaning back to get a better look at me—as if I were crazy to think I could do such a thing.

Hurt by Pablo's lack of confidence in me, I countered, "Yes, I do. I've been on lots of television shows. Granted, I was always the one being interviewed, but I'm comfortable in front of a camera and I know racing."

"That's good, honey. But are you *sure* you want to do this sort of thing?" he asked, shaking his head doubtfully.

No, I'm not sure. In fact, I'm pretty sure it's NOT what I want. But I DO want you to marry me. Please, please ask me.

I got up the courage to say it. "Well, I have to do something. It would be different if we were married. If I was your wife, then I would have to stay with you and be, well, your wife. But as your girlfriend, I have to find work." There. Whew. I said it fast, without looking at Pablo.

"Okay, honey. If that's *really* what you want," he said skeptically. I don't think he believed I would really go.

When I contacted Monmouth Park about the job, they were thrilled. After all, I had been an attraction there before, as the leading jockey. They hired me as the television commentator for their nightly racing show, and I offered to host a daily "question and answer" session for the bettors by the paddock before the races.

Finally, I had a valid reason for my sudden "retirement." Now I could tell the news reporters that I had retired from racing to take a position at Monmouth Park. Immediately, Howard Cosell wanted to have me back on his show, *SportsBeat,* to talk about my recent decision. I wasn't sure what I would say about it, but agreed to appear on his show anyway.

Howard Cosell sent a limousine to pick me up and take me into the city. The interview went smoothly until the end, when the colorful sports commentator threw me a curveball. He asked, "I'm sure we'll see you back riding again real soon, won't we?"

This caught me off guard. I was supposed to be *retiring*. Didn't that mean I was done with riding for good? I thought for a second and then came back with "Well, I've learned to never say never, but it looks like I won't be."

He turned away from me, looked into the camera, and finished with, "Yes, and I'm sure we *will* see you back."

As the time approached for me to leave for Monmouth Park, all I could think about was how much I would miss Pablo. But I knew I had to be strong—that going away from him was only temporary. I had to do this. Anyway, I could call him every day from New Jersey. Since I stopped riding, my self-esteem was at an all-time low. The only time I seemed to feel good at all was around him. Before my riding was my reason to live. Now, it was only Pablo.

Down at Monmouth Park the job was going well, and I received lots of compliments. But I didn't care. I just wanted to be back with Pablo, who never did watch my cable show or see my live question and answer sessions at the track. He rarely came down to visit, preferring instead for me to drive back to see him. It was a two hour trip each way, so I didn't want to put this added burden on him. After all, it was my decision to go to Monmouth! One day, he brought up how inconvenient the whole situation had become. He wanted me to quit the job, but I told him I couldn't because I had made a commitment.

"Well, honey, if that's the way it has to be, I'll just have to marry you then!"

I almost choked. *Really???*

"Really? Would you? Will we? Should we?" I couldn't believe the plan had worked! Pablo gave me a long "I love you so much I want you to be my wife" kiss. I was left dizzy, delirious with love. Drunken with happiness. Prince Charming has just won the princess. Or had she just won the prince?

The next time I saw Pablo, he surprised me with an engagement ring. I couldn't believe my good fortune. I had just been promoted! I was going to be a wife, and the best one there ever was!

Chapter 52
Answered Prayer

When we first dated, Pablo seemed to have a lot more energy. Now he was tired all the time. Something just wasn't right. I worried, but tried not to show it. I had this terribly ominous feeling, like something bad was going to happen to one of us. Shortly after we were engaged, we had agreed that we couldn't live without each other—that we *wouldn't* live without each other. It was like a death pact.

On one of my trips from Monmouth to see Pablo, I told him about my strong premonition. As I explained how I felt, I realized that I was shaking. I was that frightened. Pablo tried to comfort me, but it was no use.

"I'm afraid I'm going to lose you," I said, my eyes tearing up.

"Don't worry, honey. I'm fine," he said, trying to reassure me.

Maybe it would be me then. That would make things easier, I thought.

I drove back to Monmouth, but the feeling didn't go away. It lingered and only grew stronger.

The following week when I made another trip, the foreboding feeling was back with a vengeance. It was coming down on me full force—an overwhelming cloud of gloom and doom. Why? Why was this happening? When I reached Pablo's house, I was fraught with fear. Somehow, he did not look like himself. His eyes were dull and he had no expression. *Everything will be all right,* I kept saying to myself over and over, trying to push away the ominous, threatening future as we raced head on into it.

"What's wrong, honey?" he asked, looking very concerned.

"Last week I didn't know if something really bad was going to happen to you or to me," I explained. "But I think it is going to be you. You are my whole life. I feel so *helpless!*"

I was frazzled. Instead of watching television with Pablo, I went upstairs to lie down. Exhausted from worry, I dozed off. I don't know how long I was asleep when I was awakened by Pablo. He was standing by the bed—pale, shaking, and sweating profusely. Paralyzed with fear, I didn't know what to do. He was having trouble breathing and couldn't talk. *My God, he is going to die!*

Pablo headed out of the bedroom. I jumped up quickly and followed him down the stairs and to the front door. I was terrified. Adrenlin coursed through my body as I followed him out to the car. He went to the driver's side. *Where did he plan to go?*

"You can't drive," I said pushing him aside. *He won't make it.* "Where do you want me to take you?" I asked, frantic, but trying to remain calm. He pushed me away, waving his hand. *He doesn't have much time. God, help me. What do I do?*

I felt totally helpless as he got in behind the wheel and started the car. I ran to the passenger side and jumped in. I didn't know where he was trying to go, but I was going with him. He was leaning over the steering wheel, gasping for air, sweat pouring off his face. As I closed the door, the car sped off down the driveway. I was scared.

"Where are we going? You shouldn't be driving! Let me drive. Come on," I begged. My mind was racing. I just couldn't make it without him. *Don't die. Please, don't die, Pablo.*

He was getting worse, leaning forward and back again in his seat, gasping for air. "No..." he managed. "I know...where the hospital is. You don't...I'll..."

I stopped him. "Don't talk—keep driving. You can do it. I know you'll be okay." I was shouting now, trying to convince us both that he would be okay.

I was sure he was delirious and just driving recklessly down the back wooded roads. *There is no hospital out here!* I was convinced of it now as we sped through several red lights. At that point, I thought we were both going to die in a car wreck. "Let me drive!" Now I was fighting him for control of the wheel.

He pushed my arm off the wheel, making another sharp left and I fell back, catching a sudden glimpse of a sign off the road. A blue H! There *was* a hospital nearby! He made two sharp turns and drove the car right up to the EMERGENCY door and got out.

I jumped out and ran to the first person I saw—an ambulance driver parked by the entrance. I knocked frantically on his window. "HELP ME! HELP ME!" The driver started to roll down his window and looked confused. Pablo had disappeared into the building. There was no time to explain. I turned and ran through the emergency room doors, following the direction Pablo had taken.

Pablo was nowhere in sight. I was in shock, I think. *Where was Pablo?* I ran over to two women behind the counter.

"Where is my...fiancé? He is very sick! I don't know where he went!"

The two women looked at the room to their left, so I ran that way. I spotted Pablo on a table in the room. I was shaking. *Don't die. Don't leave me. Not now. Please, don't die!*

There was a doctor and two nurses standing over Pablo. I pushed them aside. He was unconscious. I slipped to the floor, too weak to stand. I was going to faint. *Be strong. Be strong!* I sat and put my head between my legs so I wouldn't faint. *Don't faint now. Not now. Be strong!* I felt a hand on my shoulder.

It was the nurse. "Come on. You can't be in here. You look white as a ghost." She pulled me to my feet.

"No. I'm *not* leaving him!"

"We all have to leave," the nurse said kindly, gently.

"Why?" I begged. "What's going on?"

"His blood pressure is dropping so low that he will die unless we find out what is causing it. The doctor can't figure out what is wrong. We must do something to get his blood pressure back up right away. Every second is vital." She helped me out the door.

I walked into the waiting room and sat down. Now I knew why I had been so upset these past weeks. Here I was, alone, waiting to hear the fate of Pablo. And my fate, too. Not only couldn't I live without him, there was the death pact. If he died, I promised to die, too. And vice versa. We planned to have a double coffin so we could still "be together," even in death. It had sounded so romantic at the time. But now, with him dying, I didn't know if I could go through with it. I knew I couldn't live without him, but suicide was...an act against God. God made me for a reason. I didn't know what the reason was, but surely it wasn't just to die. Maybe God had used Pablo to get me to quit riding races. God probably knew that was the *only* way I would quit! I drew strength from knowing that I was lovable—to Pablo at least—as a person, not just as a jockey. Pablo had given me that reassurance, that love that I desperately needed to accept myself. But, without him, I didn't think I could go on.

I closed my eyes right there in the waiting room and prayed to God. I spoke to Him out loud, giving Him my full attention. "Okay, God. So, you used Pablo to get me to quit riding, and it worked. Now are You just going to let him die, so I can go on and do whatever it is that You have in mind for me? But, I will be no good for Your plan if he dies! *I will be a useless basket case*. If you want *me* to live, then please let *Pablo* live. Then, I promise that no matter what it is—I will do Your will. I'll do whatever it is—even if it means leaving Pablo and doing whatever it is without him. Yes, with *or without* him. Only, please, just let him live."

There, I said it. I had just made the biggest promise I would ever make in my life. And I meant it, too, with all my heart. I had made a deal with God. God could have my life to do with as He pleased if only He would spare Pablo. That seemed fair. It was my life for Pablo's.

I opened my eyes. My palms were sweaty. I was exhausted, but at peace. I was sure that God had heard every word of my intense prayer, and I felt His presence right there with me in the waiting room. Immediately after my heartfelt-said-with-every-ounce-of-power-and-strength-within-me prayer, a weight came off my chest. My burden became light. I *knew* for certain that God had heard me, and I *knew* that He had answered my prayer. *Pablo would live.* And now I would have to keep the most difficult vow I had ever made. Would I have to live without Pablo? Right now, it didn't matter. What mattered now was that Pablo *would* live. And yes, I would live, too. Live to see what God had planned for me....with or without Pablo....with or without him...

I looked around the waiting room, where people were staring at me strangely. I hadn't noticed them before; I hadn't been aware of anything but pleading with God for Pablo's life. *Pablo was going to live!*

As I basked in the glorious peace surrounding me, the nurse came to get me. I was smiling. I think this surprised her. I knew the news would be good.

"Your fiancé seems to be all right, now. The strangest thing happened. One minute he was about to die," she said, shaking her head in disbelief, "and then all of a sudden—like magic—his pulse shot back to normal, like nothing had ever happened to him at all! We just don't understand it. The doctor is totally baffled by this wonderful turn of events. He still doesn't understand how quickly and for no obvious reason, he came back from the dead. He shouldn't be alive, you know."

I know. And I knew. I knew the moment God answered my prayer was the moment Pablo's blood pressure was restored to normal. It coincided with the story the nurse told me.

The doctor let me in to see Pablo. He looked much better than he had an hour ago.

"God, I'm so glad to see you. I thought...well, you know." I gave him a big hug.

"Yeah, we all thought..." piped in the doctor. "You know, it was amazing, Pablo, the way you just came back to normal so suddenly. You went from being dead to, well, as if nothing had ever happened to you. I'm not really sure why you got sick, and I'm even less sure of why you got better." The doctor looked at me, and then at Pablo. He just shook his head quizzically. "Well, we're going to keep you a few days anyway and run some tests. You can't get out of here so easily."

Although Pablo said he felt fine, he stayed for testing. I stayed that night with him. I didn't want to miss being with him. Not for one second. I sat in a chair by his bed, refusing to leave his side. The nurses finally stopped asking me to leave, breaking their visitation rules. Eventually, as the night wore on, I curled up next to Pablo in the hospital bed. I squeezed as close as I could to him, thinking that I never wanted to leave his side again. I never wanted to be without him. I wanted to forget that crucial part of my prayer and promise to God. I never wanted to do anything without my Pablo. *Thank You for sparing Pablo, God. Thank You so much. Please let it be Your will that we always be together.*

Chapter 53
Identity Crisis

Monmouth Park ended. Now that Pablo and I were engaged, instead of going back home, I spent most of my time at his house. Soon Pablo would marry me, and I would be someone again: Mrs. Karen Garcia. Karen the jockey was already dead. Replacing me now would be someone new and better: Karen the wife.

When I stopped by to see Mom and Amy, I was shocked to find my room, my sanctuary, had been changed. Not that it should have mattered. I was getting married soon and moving out anyway. But all my things were gone. I had told Mom specifically *not* to touch or move anything in my room. Couldn't I at least have my old room for some sense of identity and comfort? At least until I was officially dead and Mrs. Karen Garcia, the married wonder wife, appeared?

I ran back downstairs. "Mom, *where* is all my stuff? What happened to my bedroom?" I was close to tears. How could she have done this to me?

"I meant to tell you. Amy and I slept in your bedroom all summer because you were at Monmouth and your room had the only air conditioner. It was *so* hot," she explained, thinking nothing of it.

"Why did you move all my stuff? I asked you specifically *not* to do that!" I tried to sound reasonable, but couldn't contain my anger. Her explanation was logical, but I felt betrayed. Didn't I matter at all? My stuff was the last thing I felt I could control. It was the last vestige of who I was.

Mom looked at me, baffled that I was so upset. "Well, I put your things in boxes. I didn't throw anything away. It's all there, only in boxes. I didn't think...it was *so* hot. I'm sorry." She looked like she was genuinely sorry, like she didn't mean to turn my world upside down.

I went from anger to disappointment. Finally, I accepted that this tragedy wasn't fatal. After all, she didn't throw anything away. That was my worst fear. For someone to throw away something of mine...anything...was out of my control. Just like my whole life.

Obsessing over my "stuff" being moved or touched was one of many symptoms I had from my undiagnosed OCD, or obsessive-compulsive disorder. My mother had no idea how much I suffered from this overwhelming condition, and I just thought it was crazy me.

Now that I was staying with Pablo, I would get up early with him. While he went to the barn, I would straighten up his house. Then I would do my exercises—just in case I ever rode again. You never know, and it didn't hurt to stay in shape. I hid the fact that I did my exercises from Pablo because I felt I was accomplishing something, and I didn't think he would approve. When Pablo came home in the morning around nine-thirty, I would have breakfast made for him. After breakfast, Pablo would take his nap. I would go to the deli and get food to eat and throw up before he woke up from his nap. The rest of the day Pablo and I sat around watching television. He was always "too tired" to do anything else.

Pablo said he didn't want me around the barn in the morning. Consequently, I never asked to go. But if he had a horse in an important stakes race, he would ask me to come with him. Then we would both get dressed up. Pablo always wore his captain's sunglasses. He bought me a pair just like them, and we would both go to the races looking like twins: matching colored outfits and sunglasses. We must have looked a sight. I mentioned to Pablo that I felt very out of place, which I did. No longer Karen the jockey, not quite his wife yet, and without a real job, I was very insecure at the track. I felt I had no reason to even be at the races, but Pablo argued that was nonsense and that I was "with him." So I became a "with Pablo." Somehow, I had a hard time believing people could like me, now that I was no longer Karen the jockey. I told Pablo how hard it was for me to sound chipper, to give people at the races my old friendly "hello" when I saw them. I just felt so out of place.

Pablo told me what to do. "Don't say hello to anybody. Wait for them to say hello to you first. Then you'll see who your friends are." In my role as a "with Pablo," I followed his advice. Whenever I saw a trainer I used to ride for, I would look down, hoping to become invisible. If I couldn't greet them, I didn't want them to see me. If they saw me and they didn't say hello, it would only reinforce the fact that they really didn't care about me—now that I wasn't Karen the jockey.

It soon became apparent to me that Pablo was right: nobody really cared enough to say hello. They had only returned my greetings in the past out of politeness. Pablo told me I was too nice and that it wasn't necessary to say hello now that I wasn't riding and getting business from them.

Looking back on this time, I think people at the track sensed the wall I had put up. I was withdrawn, hiding behind Pablo and my sunglasses, wanting to be invisible. I was fearful of what they were thinking about me, and they probably sensed that I didn't want to interact.

Going to the races was just awful. I stuck to Pablo's side and kept my head down. The only one who loved me or cared about me anymore was Pablo. Sometimes I longed to be in my boots and jeans, out of my dress clothes and "with Pablo" role and saying hello to my old friends. But, as Pablo pointed out, it wasn't the thing to do anymore—they weren't really my friends. See how nobody approached me anymore?

I became very depressed and dreaded going to the races. I always wore sunglasses and avoided meeting anyone's eyes. I wanted to hide from the world. I had no reason to even be at the track. Pablo belonged. I didn't. Maybe if I stuck by his side so closely, people wouldn't even notice me. I would be just be his appendage.

Aside from the brief visits to the races, we didn't go anywhere. We just stayed in the house. The only thing in my life was Pablo. Why bother with the rest of the world? Nobody liked me now, anyway. What was there left to like? I was no longer the confident jockey. My energy was spent trying to please Pablo when he was around. When he was sleeping (which he did a lot) or at the track, I would eat and throw up. After four in the afternoon, I would drink with Pablo. We drank until he went to bed, and then I drank some more. Usually at night he would pass out early, and I felt rejected and alone. The house was both my sanctuary and my prison. I was safe with someone who loved me and hidden from the eyes of a harsh, judgmental world, yet I was a prisoner of my self-destructive behavior.

Pablo constantly reminded me how much he "loved" me, explaining that our love for each other was like no other. He always told me how "happy" we were. I heard it so often that I really and truly believed we were the *happiest* couple in the world. Happy, happy, happy. That was my new definition of seclusion and togetherness. We were *so* happy.

I hoped our life would improve once we got married and became a "Mr. and Mrs." I hoped that Pablo would feel better and have more energy. I imagined that once we were officially married, we would go more places and do lots more things. We would get a group of new friends, like other married couples. If this didn't happen, well, as long as I had my Pablo, I would be happy—even if we did just sit around and get old together. With Pablo watching television in his chair while I cooked, we would be like Archie and Edith Bunker on the television show "All in the Family." We would just be average ordinary married people. I could settle for that. However, there was one issue that was still in the back of my mind. I wondered what it was that God had planned for me to do. There had to be something more...something meaningful. The fact that God had given me the courage to quit riding and then let Pablo live that night at the hospital, I didn't think He would want me to waste my life away in a house. But, then again, I would be with Pablo. *Maybe I was just meant to be with him.* Maybe he was the one who would do something special in this world and I would be (as his wife) the one to support and encourage him. They say that behind every great man is a great woman. Pablo was certainly *smart* enough to be great, but he was always so tired. Well, time would tell.

Pablo was always ready for bed by eight o'clock. Even if I got excited about the possibility of going out, the worry of Pablo "feeling tired" or "feeling bad" had me in a constant state of depression. Would he ever feel better? I began to feel ill myself. Maybe it was sympathy pain. Or maybe it was from drinking so much. Every day went on the same way. I really looked forward to getting married, when everything would be different. At night, my dreams became increasingly riddled with the ghost of my past...the Vince/Pablo man. Pablo was Vince. Vince was Pablo.

Since the incident with Pablo at the hospital, something continued to gnaw at me. I wondered what God had planned for us...or for me. I finally decided to share these thoughts with Pablo.

"Pablo, you know when you almost died at the hospital? How it was so weird that you just all of a sudden got back to normal, and the doctor never could figure out what was wrong with you?"

"Yes, honey. That was strange. I've thought about it a lot. I was very lucky." He puffed on a cigarette, reflecting.

"Well," I continued, "you know how I could sense something was going to happen to one of us? And then that night..." I shuddered, thinking about that awful night. How scared, desperate, and alone I had felt...until I prayed. "Well, while you were in there, possibly dying, I said a prayer to God. Not just a regular prayer. It was a big, meaningful prayer. I said it with all my heart, and I meant every word I said."

Pablo looked at me curiously.

"I made a promise to God that if He kept you alive, I would do whatever it was He had planned for me, with or without you." There. I said it.

"What do you mean, honey? Do what? What is it you have to do?"

Pablo asked, truly baffled by my statement.

I thought a minute. "I don't know yet. All I know is that it is something. Maybe not important to the outside world, but important to God—for His plan for me. You know how I quit riding? How I had the feeling that I had to quit? Well, it's as if I was meant to do something. Not just waste my life away..." Oops. That didn't sound too good. *Waste my life away.*

"You're not 'wasting your life away', honey. You're with me. You are going to be my wife. That's important." He waited to see my response.

I was confused. "Well, it was just sort of strange the way I prayed that I would be strong enough. I would just have to be strong enough to go on *without you*—even if you lived. And then you did live, so it just made me wonder if I would have to do something apart from you."

Pablo hugged me. "It was God that brought me back. For whatever purpose, I don't know. If you say He was answering your prayer, I believe you. But that doesn't mean you have to be away from me. We love each other. We were meant to be together. You were meant to be my wife. That is what God wants for you, I'm sure."

"It just doesn't seem like I make any difference to anything—except maybe to you. I don't know." I shook my head. I knew there was something missing in my life, but I couldn't explain it because I didn't know what it was.

"You do make a difference, honey. To me. And you will be an example to other people by being a good wife. People at the track can see how much we love each other, and they are envious. They want to find someone, too. Maybe we give them hope. You being my wife will be a good example of true love, an example for them to follow."

That made perfect sense. Yeah. We would be an example of true love and commitment in a world full of lonely, uncommitted people. There were a lot of lonely people at the track. I was satisfied with Pablo's explanation for the time being. However, I wasn't a good wife yet. I wasn't even a wife.

Chapter 54
Ask Not, Be Not, Do Not

The Dubai horses continued to do well at the track. Pablo had some of the best horses in the country. They were stakes caliber and Breeders' Cup nominees. He trained the top 3-year-old colt, 3-year-old filly, best turf horse, sprinter, 2-year-old colt, filly, etc. It was incredible. Most trainers never got the opportunity to train even one good stakes horses, while Pablo had access to so many.

One of the horses was entered in a prestigious million dollar stakes race at Hollywood Park in California. I was excited when Pablo made plans for us to go. I really looked forward to seeing California. Pablo promised to take me to see the famous Rodeo Drive.

The day finally arrived. However, we went straight from the airport in Los Angeles to the hotel room. This was my first time in California, and Pablo had promised we would see the sites. But, as usual, looking forward to something was always better than when we did it—if we did it.

"When can we go to Rodeo Drive?" I asked, hoping for a miracle, that Pablo would "find" some hidden source of energy.

"I'm not feeling too well, honey. Why don't we just stay here in the hotel? We'll go before we leave, I promise. I just...haven't been feeling well. Maybe the pressure of the race is getting to me. How about a little room service?"

I hid my disappointment. Needless to say, we never left the room. The following day when it was time to go to the races, I was definitely ready. Not that I enjoyed the races, or worrying about Pablo, but I looked forward to getting out. However, this turned out to be a disappointment as well. We got stuck in traffic, and in order to make it to the race on time, I had to drop off Pablo and park the car myself. I had no pass to get in, no money on me, and consequently missed the race. At least Pablo got there in time to saddle the horse and watch him finish third.

We never did get to sightsee, remaining in the hotel room until we left for the airport the following day. I told myself it didn't matter; I didn't like California much anyway. Well, Pablo didn't like California, so I figured I didn't either. So much for California. Goodbye wonderful Rodeo Drive, restaurants, and California beaches. I wondered if I—we—would ever come back to "experience" the west coast again.

The consistent broken promises were conditioning me to expect nothing. We *were* going to that party. We *were* going to play golf... My hopes, dreams, and expectations invariably crumbled away into nothingness. So I would not be disappointed, I adjusted; I expected nothing. Subtly and slowly, with the kindest, most sincere repetition of apologies, I was trained to be a docile, contented creature. I was Pablo's appendage. His want nothing, do nothing, expect nothing wife-to-be. I would be Mrs. Ask Not, Be Not, Do Not Garcia.

Home after our California trip, I went to put Pablo's empty suitcase away. I checked the suitcase to see if Pablo forgot to unpack anything. Maybe I would find a lone sock, his lighter, or some other thing that he would be looking for later. I opened the suitcase, unzipped the side pocket, and saw two small plastic bottles. They were odd-looking. What could they possibly be for? There was sediment on the bottom. They were only two inches tall, made of white plastic, rectangular in shape, and had white childproof caps. I had never seen anything like them. Hmm. I also found an empty Tropicana grapefruit bottle. What on earth was that doing in there?

Puzzled, I replaced the empty bottles where I had found them. I felt a little guilty, like I was spying or something. I didn't feel like I should ask Pablo about the bottles. Maybe they were some private hang-up. He still didn't know about my throwing up. I had a secret. Maybe he had one, too. I zipped up the pockets and put the suitcase away.

Pablo was the leading trainer at Belmont Park in both money won and number of wins, yet he depended on his two capable assistant trainers to do everything. On many afternoons, Pablo didn't bother to go to the races to watch his horses run. On those afternoons while Pablo slept, my job was to dial "stretch call" to hear the finish of the race so I could tell Pablo how his horse had run. My other job, and the highlight of my afternoon, was making Pablo's coffee and watching him wake up from his nap.

Whenever I questioned my purpose in life, I just remembered Pablo's words of wisdom. *You are doing something important, honey. You are going to be my wife, and we will be an example for everyone at the racetrack, an example of people who are really in love.* At the time he told me this, I had my doubts (surely God had some greater purpose for me), but as time went on, this became my truth. Pablo was my only purpose. He was who defined me. And he was all I had to cling to and believe in. He was my whole purpose of existence. And this was very dangerous. Had I forgotten God?

Even though I put all my faith in our future (and the great example we would set for the world), Pablo continued to be tired and depressed. Even as his horses continued to win, Pablo was apathetic. He didn't even buy any win pictures to hang in the house. I would read about his horses winning big races in the newspapers, and wonder why Pablo didn't save any of the articles. I had stopped my scrapbooks. They were dated up to my "retirement" and then put away to gather dust. I was almost ashamed of them and who I had once been, the hardworking jockey. I wanted to be Mrs. Karen Garcia. I *was* Mrs. Karen Garcia—just not officially, yet.

Chapter 55
Wedding Preparation

Before we got married, Pablo "prepared" me for how my mother would "react" to my new life.

"I just want to tell you," he warned. "Your mother will probably rearrange everything in the house after you move out—like when you came back from Monmouth and your mom and Amy had actually moved into your room!" Pablo looked at me cynically. "Now, you'll be out for good, and your mother will be so happy! Wait and see what she'll do to your old room. She might even use it for her own bedroom," he said smugly.

Pablo was consistently taking what information he knew about my relationship with my mother, and twisting it so it appeared that she was "against" me.

"Your mother is jealous that we are getting married. She is so jealous of you," Pablo remarked.

"Do you think so?" I asked. That had never occurred to me. I thought she was *happy* that I was marrying Pablo.

"I know she is. I never told you how she always flirted with me when I came to pick you up. I had to send Amy upstairs to get you. Your mother wouldn't call you down from your room. She just wanted all my attention. One day I sat there for fifteen minutes listening to her go on and on. Sometimes she talked about you, trying to get me to dislike you. Once she even tried to kiss me."

Why hadn't he told me this before? Mom really didn't want Pablo and I together, did she?

"Honey?" Pablo could see I was upset.

"What?" My head was down, guilty, ashamed. My anger at Mom turned back on myself, as usual. Then it went from anger to helplessness, to defeat, and finally to depression. I was filled with shame and despair. Would Pablo still want to marry me? I had *told* him many times that I was afraid Mom would take away any man I really loved—the way I felt I had taken Vince away from her. Maybe Pablo would want to marry Mom now. *I just knew this would happen.*

With the information I had given him, Pablo knew just how to manipulate my feelings. His fabricated story about Mom flirting with him stirred up the old emotional chaos. Because I believed I had taken away Vince's love from Mom, I felt I didn't deserve to be loved. Who did Pablo love? Who did Vince love? Who did Mom love? It was all so tangled together. I felt these emotions now as strongly as when I was young, but as of yet, I hadn't made the connection of Pablo to Vince, and couldn't put my feelings into words.

"Honey, are you okay?" Pablo touched my shoulder. I wanted to cry, but couldn't. The tears from this ancient feeling of mine had long since forgotten how to fall. I didn't look at Pablo. I couldn't. I felt so rejected. Did he still love me?

Pablo said with reassurance, "You know I only love *you*, honey. I love only you." Pablo hugged me. I loved him so much. And he loved me, not Mom. Yes. He was the *only* person in the world who understood me and loved me.

When I was young, it felt like Vince was the only one who "understood" me and "loved" me. Now, with Pablo, the familiar feeling of being understood was comforting, especially when it involved Mom "not loving" me. I didn't connect Pablo to Vince consciously, so Pablo didn't have to do much to convince me that Mom didn't love me—what I had believed for so long. Although I didn't realize it yet, my "truth" was based on Vince's lie, "Your mother doesn't love you," words buried in my subconscious. I had suppressed anger at my mother for "not loving me," even though I felt I didn't deserved her love. My unexpressed anger inevitably led to depression. And always the question remained, the raging battle inside of me, tearing me apart: Did she love me or didn't she? No matter what the answer, one side of me could never be convinced. I was a seeker of the truth, and this was one truth that I could not make sense out of because it was based on a lie.

My vivid dreams increased in strength and number as our wedding date got closer. In one dream my sister Susan was at the altar next to Vince, or maybe it was Pablo (the Vince/Pablo man). They were getting married. I was sad. It was supposed to be me! I stared at their backs as they said their wedding vows. Suddenly, I knew it was Pablo that she was marrying. Oh well, I don't deserve him anyway. As I looked closer, Susan became Mom. It was Mom and Pablo getting married! *I deserve this*. I don't deserve to marry anyone I love.

I awoke feeling very sad. So sad. So depressed. Was I really getting married next week? Or was it just a dream? A bad dream or a good one? What was real, anyway? This just couldn't have a happy ending.

One afternoon, Pablo said out of the blue, "I have a prenuptial agreement for you to sign." I had read about "prenuptial agreements." I was shocked. The *only* purpose of a prenuptial agreement was for a divorce! I resented the fact that Pablo wanted one. It made our marriage seem cold, calculated, and financial. And worse yet, it made it sound like our marriage could fail!

"But, we'll never get divorced. I'd *die* first, and so would you," I said, believing this with all my heart. I couldn't live without him! The whole idea of a prenuptial agreement devastated me. It burst my bubble. It rocked my world. He was my Prince Charming, My True Love! Marriage was "til death do us part," wasn't it?

"Oh, honey," Pablo said soothingly, trying to ease the blow. "This is only to protect you and your property. You don't want your mother to be worried about your house, do you? The agreement says that what was yours before the marriage will remain yours. We'll never use it."

"I still don't think it's necessary," I argued. This document was a threat to my very life. My existence without him was...nonexistence.

"Just sign it, honey. But you'll need to sign it in front of a notary. You can do that, can't you?"

Why was he being so persistent?

"I don't know. I don't like the idea. No, I *hate* the idea." This was one of the few things we had ever disagreed on.

"We'll never use it," he said again, giving me a hug.

"Oh, all right," I said, caving to the pressure. "If you say we'll never need it, I guess it can't hurt." Couldn't I enjoy the thought of forever holy matrimony? The wedding was only a week away. Did he have to be so unromantic?

As the only son of the Garcias, Pablo knew he would come into millions of dollars when his elderly parents died.

I made the last few wedding preparations. Thinking about the wedding was good. It was going to happen. It just *had* to happen. Still, I was worried. What if Pablo was sick? He avoided people and parties. What if Pablo didn't feel like going to the wedding? I had invited lots of guests—family, trainers, jockeys, and people from the track. Maybe a big wedding was a mistake. I shouldn't be putting him through this. Well, it will be all right. Just this once. It was the *only* thing I had asked for.

"Pablo, are you sure you are okay with the wedding plans?" I just had to be sure. I mean, this would be the beginning of our "example" with me being his wife. I had to make sure it went right. I wanted everyone to see that we were *happy*. We were happy, weren't we? Of course, we were. Pablo said we were the happiest, luckiest couple in the whole world.

"Yes, honey. Everything will be fine. Remember, weddings are for the bride. It's your day." He hugged me for reassurance.

If wedding days were for the bride, was the whole rest of the marriage for the groom? I supposed so. Well, then, I would make it the best marriage Pablo could ever want!

"You won't be tired or sick, will you?" Maybe I shouldn't have asked such an honest question. He was *always* sick and tired! Still, I had to know before I was let down in a big way. "I mean, if you don't think you'll be up for it with all those people, uh... let me know now." I tried to sound kind and understanding. I loved him so much. Maybe we should just get married in a courthouse.

"Of course I'll be fine. I love you. It's the only thing you've ever wanted, asked for, and looked forward to. I won't let you down."

Those words meant *everything* to me. I hugged him tightly and then kissed him. "I love you soooo much." My Pablo. My honey. My sweetheart!

"I love you, too," he said with reassurance.

Remarkably, the wedding went off without a hitch. My nightmares about Pablo not showing up were finally put to rest. We were married at The Lake Club in front of more than two hundred guests, mostly family and racetrack friends. The ceremony was beautiful. As Pablo later said, "It was like God was right there. Just as we said our vows, the sun peeked through the clouds and shined directly on us. It was like the heavens opened up."

Yes, the wedding was a success. Pablo and I were officially married. Now I had nothing left to look forward to.

There I was, the Final Product. Mrs. Karen Garcia.

It was supposed to be The Beginning...

But it felt more like The End.

We spent our wedding night at the nearby Hilton. It was late when we got to the room. Pablo was taking off his rings and said, "Honey, have you seen my pocket watch? It's been missing since I took you to the Waldorf on your birthday."

"No, Pablo. I haven't."

"Are you sure? Maybe you should check through your things."

"I'm sure, Pablo. Why do you ask?"

"Oh, it's just my favorite piece of jewelry, and I've been missing it. Like tonight. I miss not having it." He got into bed and fell right to sleep.

Wasn't your wedding night supposed to be romantic? Or was that just a myth? I guess most couples went through this, falling asleep before the romantic part. Maybe they shouldn't serve liquor at weddings. Or maybe I hadn't had enough to drink, I thought, listening to the harmonious sound of wedding bliss silence.

Chapter 56
Unlovable

"Now that we're married, don't call your mother. Wait and see how long it takes *her* to call *you*. Then you'll see how much she cares. I'll bet she never calls. She doesn't care about you. Do what I said. Don't call her. We'll see then!"

No family. No friends. No career. No job. No life. But I had my Prince. I had my Pablo. I wonder how long he'll live? Dying wouldn't be so bad, really. I'm ready.

We had been married a few months. I was getting used to the numbing routine. My stuff remained in boxes in Pablo's guest room. There it remained, unpacked.

I continued to worship the ground he walked on. And I read one part in the Bible over and over.

> "For the husband is the head of the wife, as Christ also is the head of the church, He Himself *being* the Savior of the body. But as the church is subject to Christ, so also the wives *ought to be* to their husbands in everything."
> – Ephesians 5:23-24 (NASB)

Mom didn't call. I guess she didn't want to disturb my new life. She knew how protective Pablo was of me. But I didn't take it that way. I took it the way Pablo told me to take it: that she didn't love me.

Again, Vince's words, etched in my subconscious mind as the truth, continued to haunt me. "Your mother doesn't love you. She doesn't care about you."

As time went on, Pablo discouraged me from calling or visiting my mother. "I'd be happy if you *never* went to your mother's again. That's the way I like to keep it with my parents. See them as little as possible."

Pablo sounded like he had the whole Plan of Life worked out. The best way to live. Parentless. Familyless. He would say, "*You're* my family."

Pablo knew me. I had told him everything—past, present, and future. Well, except my throwing up. Feeling guilty about keeping it from him before we were married, I had told him, "I do something very bad." And you know what he had said?

"So do I."

Then I said, "No, but mine is really bad."

And Pablo said, "No, mine is worse."

Now that we were married, I thought it was time to share our mutual vices. I revealed the fact that I threw up, expecting Pablo to be shocked, reject me, or have some strong reaction. Rather, he seemed to just accept it.

"Do you still love me?" I asked, wondering.

"Of course I do, honey."

I expected him to share what he was hiding, but he remained silent so I didn't ask. I was glad that now he knew all my secrets—and loved me anyway.

Married life was going to be great, wasn't it? Sex every night with no guilt. Pablo loved me.

I reached over to him. No response. I kissed him. He turned away from me. What was wrong? Was I doing something wrong? I kissed him again.

"Honey, don't you think you could give it a break?" Pablo mumbled.

Huh? What did he mean?

"I can't keep this up," he said with his back still toward me.

Did he mean sex?

"What? What do you mean?" I asked, a bad feeling starting to come over me, creeping into my very core. The bad me was waking up from her long slumber. The Guilty One.

"You always want to...well, let's not so much...you know," Pablo said, sounding irritated that he had to explain. He hated talking about sex. In fact, he told me that we were *never* to discuss it.

"Do I want to too much?" I asked, suddenly feeling very guilty, very confused, and very shocked over this rude awakening. There *was* something wrong with me! I knew it. I never should have liked it, never should have wanted to do it. I wished Pablo had told me this before!

"Yeah," Pablo answered, still facing the other way in the bed. "Let's not so much."

Okay! Okay! I won't ever touch him again, if that's the way he feels! I must be really bad. From now on, I'll let him make the first move.

I was always more comfortable making the first move. It felt less like I was being forced into anything and it kept the horrible Vince flashbacks to a minimum.

As I lay in bed, I wondered. Had I been forcing Pablo into something that he hated? Was I acting like Vince???

As the weeks went by, and Pablo didn't make a move, I began to hate my body. I hated the fact that it made me have feelings toward him. Why did I have to have a body?

Pablo loves my legs—at least he used to. One day in the shower I took the razor and cut my legs so that they bled. *Good! That will stop him from ever wanting me. Now I'll be unlovable. Then I'll have a reason why he doesn't want me anymore.*

The legs weren't enough for me, though. I continued to draw blood from whatever guilty body part I owned. *There. Now I am really bad.*

Pablo never noticed. He continued to turn his back on me in bed. I couldn't take lying there awake, rejected, unwanted, and alone while Pablo slept beside me. I decided to do something about my dilemma. I had a plan to avoid the pain of rejection.

The next night, I put my plan into action. As usual, Pablo turned off the television at 8:00 pm and said, "Let's go up, honey."

I thought about how Pablo would go right off to sleep, or read a little and then the inevitable deep slumber.

"I'll be right up," I said. Pablo stood there waiting for me to come with him.

"In a sec," I said nonchalantly. He shrugged, turned, and disappeared into the hallway. I heard him going up the stairs.

I went to the bottle of vodka, took the cap off, and swallowed it down as fast as I could. I didn't know how much it would take to reach oblivion, but that was my goal. I would drink it all if I could be oblivious when my head hit the pillow.

The straight vodka stung going down, and I felt slightly guilty. I held my breath and kept swallowing. I shuddered as my insides burned. Would that do it? Nah. I wanted to be *sure*. Has it hit me yet? I put the cap back on the bottle and hurried up the stairs. My head was starting to numb. It felt like it was floating off my body. Yes, this is pretty painless. I don't care if Pablo is sleeping. I don't care what happens now.

When I woke up in the morning, I was dizzy and felt sick. What was wrong with me? Then I remembered the vodka. What had happened after that? I didn't remember. Had we been intimate? If so, it wasn't my fault. It was the vodka. I continued to drink myself into oblivion every night after that. I didn't know what we did or didn't do, but I had solved my problem.

Chapter 57
Kept in the Dark

One morning Andy, Pablo's accountant, called while Pablo was at the barn. "You know, Karen, I wish Pablo kept records. I wish you would talk to him about it. He had a very good year, and I need more documentation for write-offs. I'm trying to get him a tax shelter as well."

"Really? I thought he already had one of those," I answered. Pablo had told me that was why he could never access his money.

"Where does all that money go?" Andy asked. "Where are all those 'cash' checks going?" He sounded so cynical, as if I was part of some conspiracy.

"Cash checks?" I asked. I had never discussed money with Pablo. I didn't want to be nosey, and I figured he was making good money. Pablo gave me a check every month to deposit in a separate account in a different bank. I used that money for food and household expenses. We didn't have other expenses because Pablo drove the Dubai company car (an Audi), and we lived rent-free in the smaller house on Pablo's parents' estate.

"It's going to cost him *a lot* of money. You really don't know about this?" he asked skeptically.

"No. Why should I? He probably just keeps bad records."

"Well, see what you can do about it," the accountant retorted.

"Okay. I'll talk to him," I said. I couldn't understand why Andy was getting so bent out of shape over a few cash checks. "But I doubt if it will do any good. I don't try to change Pablo. I love him just the way he is."

"Well, good luck with that," he said and hung up the phone.

Now, what did he mean by that?

The accountant never explained that Pablo's checks made out to cash totaled hundreds of thousands of dollars. I didn't know anything about Pablo's finances. I only knew what he told me. I was kept away from the track people, his parents, and his barn, where I might actually talk to someone. I didn't think this was odd because Pablo had convinced me that everyone was so bad. Except for Pablo, of course. He was so good.

It was a big day of racing at Aqueduct. Pablo won a million dollar race that afternoon. In the winner's circle, the NBC television cameras focused on Pablo and me. I took the opportunity to be "a loving, supporting wife" in front of the whole world. I hugged and kissed him. I could have cared less about the race. I was more interested in being the "good example" Pablo had told me that I would be. I was there by his side, giving him emotional support, instead of where I could have been—in the saddle. Wasn't my new role *wonderful?*

The horse that won the big race also won the very prestigious Eclipse Award, the Emmy or Grammy Award of thoroughbred racing. This was the top prize, the ultimate trophy in all of horse racing.

Pablo and I never made it to the Eclipse Awards Dinner. We

weren't there to accept this highest honor in racing, this once in a lifetime achievement award. I was unaware that we had missed the awards ceremony until I read about it later in the *Daily News*.

"Pablo, didn't your horse win an Eclipse Award?" I asked. Maybe I was mistaken? Pablo never talked about the horses.

"Yes, honey," Pablo answered with indifference. It was almost as if he had to think about it first to remember. Yawn. Ho hum, like it bored him to have to think about it.

"Why didn't we go?" I asked. "The dinner was last week, I think."

"Oh? Was it?" Pablo stopped a minute to think. "That's right, it was. The tickets were too expensive, or something. I forget exactly why. I'd have been too tired anyway. Those things are always late at night, and they drag on and on."

"Will you get the trophy?" I asked. I had only seen a photo of it once, in the *Daily Racing Form* when Steve Cauthen had won it. "I wonder how big it is," I said out loud, almost to myself. The trophy was a statue of the great racehorse, Eclipse. It would have been so important to me had I won it. It would have meant winning the title for leading rider in the nation. Wow. That would mean winning *a lot* of races.

"My father has it up at his house. It's smaller than you would think," Pablo said as if he were glad that it was small.

So, he had seen it. Huh.

Pablo seemed to back off racing more and more. I sensed that even though he had a great year (earning over 2.5 million dollars for Dubai Stables), he was unhappy. One day he mentioned starting a charter service for luxery yachts and other ideas for possible business ventures.

"If you don't want to train horses, that's fine with me," I said with encouragement. "I only want you to be happy." I needed Pablo to be more enthusiastic about life, so that I could be, too. I was hoping to get pregnant, and that would make things better. However, the home pregnancy tests I took were always negative. I felt so inadequate, so unworthy.

Everything Pablo did influenced me.

His world was my world.

His love of sailing was my love for him sailing.

His lack of interest in horses and racing was my lack of interest in horses and racing.

His lack of motivation was my lack of motivation.

His tiredness was my tiredness.

His opinions and views became mine.

Wanting to please Pablo, to keep him loving me was all there was. Pablo was my world, my life. We never argued. Why would we? He was always right. I never questioned him. If anything was wrong, it was because of me. My greatest fear was that Pablo wouldn't love me anymore—and that he would abandon me.

Pablo talked more and more about "quitting Dubai," leaving the successful racing outfit and starting some other business. I was so proud of him. After all, it was hard to walk away from a job that offered so much money and was pretty easy, from what I could see. I was pleased that my Pablo was putting principles before money. I always knew he was special.

Change was definitely in the air. Things are going to be different. Better. I can feel it. I think I can, I think I can.

"Pablo, if you don't want to start some other business right away, maybe you should just train horses for other people. You might enjoy it more. I know how you hate working under your father."

What Pablo hadn't told me was that Dubai Stables was considering liquidating their American racing division. If this happened, Pablo knew he would be out of a job.

I looked forward to a change, any change. A different lifestyle gave me hope. If Pablo quit his job, maybe he would be motivated to start something new, something he could take pride in. I looked forward with anticipation to our new life. In fact, I couldn't wait.

But nothing changed. Nothing happened. Sure, we talked about what Pablo would do. I would say, "So, what do you think you want to do? Maybe become a full time captain?" I knew he enjoyed being out on the water, and this would be a painless way for him to make a living.

"It would take all the fun out of sailing," he had said dully.

"How about if we move into the woods, or maybe a little farm somewhere and start over. We should have enough money to do that," I suggested, remembering him mentioning us doing that at one time.

He just nodded pensively. He did a lot of that. I was the talker, he was the thinker.

Pablo's next idea was to buy the local bowling alley and transform it into a gun range/gun shop. Then he talked of buying a marina somewhere and running a charter business out of it. If it made Pablo happy, I was all for it. He even said that if we had a marina, I could run a little restaurant by the docks and cook all the things he taught me to cook so well. This sounded exciting. If I ran a restaurant, I would get to see other people! So, we drove past some of the marinas nearby and discussed the possibilities. As usual, nothing ever happened or panned out.

Even though our life remained unchanged, I had hope. It was as though Pablo and I were living in a fantasy/dream world. Still, it was better to live in a dream world than to have no hope at all. For once, I was excited. With the right idea he would come to life, and I could too! All he had to do was make the decision, and then we could get the ball rolling and act on it. I continued to pour out ideas, and he continued to nod pensively.

I was ready, but nothing happened. So, I continued to eat and throw up. I continued to cut myself, and I continued to drink myself into oblivion each night.

Chapter 58
Getting Help

When my sister Susan was visiting my mother, they happened to see a TV show on bulimia. Learning the telltale signs of the disorder, they suspected that I might be suffering from it. They called me up, and I readily admitted the truth. It didn't matter to me now that they knew; I had moved out and didn't have to hide it from Mom anymore. I told them I couldn't stop, and they encouraged me to get help.

Of course, I checked with Pablo first. I was apprehensive about getting help, but he seemed supportive. With Pablo's approval, I found a psychologist, Dr. William Davis, who specialized in eating disorders.

Before my appointment, Pablo enlightened me. "Psychologists only know what you tell them. Their job is to listen. I know these things because I studied psychology in school. At one time, I thought I might want to be a psychologist. If this doctor is focusing on the wrong things, I will straighten him out. Just tell me what he says. Don't you worry," he continued, easing my fear, "I want you to be able to get as much out of this as possible. He isn't going to be cheap, you know!"

So, off I went to see Dr. Davis. Pablo wanted to sleep so he could be fresh when I came home to tell him all about the experience.

I liked Dr. Davis. When he asked about my childhood, I was very matter-of-fact. It was as if I was talking about somebody else, and I was completely disconnected from my past. I just repeated the things Pablo had told me about my mother and my past.

At this time, I remembered that Vince had sexually abused me. However, I was unaware that I had suffered mental and emotional abuse as a result of his behavior. I had blocked out the earlier memories with Vince, when he told me that he was my "secret boyfriend." I didn't remember that I wanted Vince's attention or approval at all when I was younger. I had blocked all this out to protect myself from my own belief that it really was my fault, and that I really was to blame because I had wanted Vince's attention. These most painful memories were all buried far too deep in my subconscious to access and could not be retrieved until much later when I hit rock bottom—when I finally cried out to God for help.

Sometimes with Dr. Davis, I felt like Karen the jockey. I had a sense of humor and self-assurance. It was during one of these upbeat visits that I decided to bring in my scrapbooks to prove to Dr. Davis that I really was okay. Then I would go home to Pablo and get all depressed again.

One day Dr. Davis asked about my relationship with Pablo. I became very protective and defensive. "We're not supposed to talk about Pablo. He says he is my best psychologist—better than you. If you blame him for anything, I just won't come back here."

Dr. Davis asked, "What makes him a psychologist? Did he go to school for it?"

I rushed to Pablo's defense. Although I didn't have proof that Pablo studied it, his knowledge made it apparent to me. "Of course. He is really smart, you know."

"Hmm," Dr. Davis uttered, and then complied with my wishes and changed the subject away from Pablo.

I continued to throw up. Although I knew Pablo and I were happy, I was depressed. My weight was the only thing in my life I was able to control. I didn't want to be fat; I wanted Pablo to love me, and he often said he hated fat women. I needed Pablo to love me because that was all I had.

Pablo's mother couldn't wait for us to have children, and frankly, neither could I. She generously paid a contractor to put a forty-thousand-dollar addition onto the small house we were living in on their estate. Mrs. Garcia bought a new Cadillac and wanted to give us her older model. Mr. Garcia, on the other hand, felt Pablo had it too easy, and wanted him to pay for their older Cadillac.

As for me, I really didn't want their car. I had my Thunderbird, which I loved. The Thunderbird was all mine and still something I could control. It had become my sanctuary in times of trouble, whether parked in the driveway or on its way to see Dr. Davis. Even though Pablo drove the Audi, which he loved, he wanted the Cadillac, too.

"My parents said we can't have three cars," Pablo explained. "If one of the cars has to go, it should be your Thunderbird."

"I don't want their car, Pablo. I like my Thunderbird." I wasn't about to give up my car for their car.

"But, honey, what if we have kids?"

Kids? What? Huh?

Pablo watched me perk up. "Yeah, that's right. Your Thunderbird is two-door. The back seats are tiny. The Cadillac is big and has four doors. There is plenty of rooms for kids and all their stuff."

He was right. The Cadillac was a *family* car. I looked out at my loyal Thunderbird, waiting for me in the driveway. It had to go.

"Pablo?"

"Yes, honey?"

"If we have kids, one of us will have to be around for them."

"What do you mean? I want us to be able to go away. We'll get a babysitter. *We* will always come first. No kid will change my life," Pablo said.

This shocked me. Still, it wasn't what I had meant.

"No, Pablo, I mean, the dying thing. If you die first, I can't kill myself. That double coffin idea. Who would raise our child? One of us has to stay around." It was the only thing to do.

"No way. If you die, I'm going with you," he said. Just like that.

"But you can't, Pablo. You must promise me that if I die, you won't. So if you die, I won't. It's not right. Somebody has to take care of a child."

"I couldn't live without you, honey. A kid would be better off without me if I didn't have you," he argued.

No. That wasn't the way it was supposed to be. He must promise to stay, or I'd better not ever die.

"If I did die, Pablo, you have to promise me you would raise our kid. Because if you die first, that's what I'm going to do. I have to. It's what a mother is supposed to do. A mother has to be there for her child. Like Mom. She was always there for us. She hardly ever got a babysitter..." I thought back to my early childhood and how happy I was then. I wanted my child to grow up like that: happy, carefree, just like the days before I was nine—before Vince. I was going to stick around to make sure nobody messed with my kid.

"Your mother did exactly what she wanted to do, just like we will," Pablo stated defiantly.

I decided to keep my decision to stay alive to myself. I just better not die before he did or before the child grew up.

Chapter 59
Heroin???

"I'm going up to take my nap now. I'm tired. Why am I always so tired?" he asked. He always asked this. *Why am I so tired? Why am I so tired?* I didn't know why he was so tired!

"Pablo, maybe you should see a doctor and get a check-up," I suggested.

"Oh, no. That's not necessary," he said, shaking his head. "I know what it is." Instead of going upstairs, he sat back down in his chair, picked up the remote for the television, and flicked it on.

"You *know* why?"

"I had hepatitis when I was younger," Pablo explained.

"What's that?"

"It's when you have damage done to your liver. Some people die from it. I was lucky though."

"How did you get it?" I asked, truly curious. He had never mentioned anything about this before.

"Bad clams. You can get it from eating bad clams. Years ago there were a lot of bad clams on Long Island, and I ate a bunch of them. I was sick for quite a while and had to stay in bed."

"Does it still bother you? Could you die from it?" I asked, worried about my diseased husband.

"I just have to be careful. I shouldn't drink. Well, one or two scotches every night isn't so bad. But that's all I should have," he said.

We shouldn't be having drinks before dinner, I thought. No wonder he always got so tired after dinner.

"And I should eat good food," he said. "But I taught you how to cook good food for us." He smiled to reassure me.

"What else should I know about this hepatitis?"

"I should quit smoking cigarettes," Pablo said purposefully. "But I could still smoke my pipe," he added.

"Is the hepatitis why your color is yellowish?"

"Probably. If I get it again, I could die. My liver is only functioning at half its normal capacity. The damage that was done is permanent. Maybe I'll quit smoking."

"Really? It's hard to quit. Mom tried and couldn't," I said.

"Your mother is weak. I could quit if I wanted. I quit heroin. I can quit cigarettes," he said.

"*What?*" I was aghast. "You took *heroin?* That's a really bad drug!" I tried not to sound too shocked because he was supposed to be drug-free now. Still...I hadn't known that he had taken *heroin*. Wasn't that just the worst drug on the planet? Wasn't it so addicting that nobody ever got off it? Didn't people stick needles in their arms just to get it? I didn't want to judge him on his history, but still...*heroin*??? The very word was creepy, the thought sent chills up my spine.

"Yeah, I quit that on my own. Went up to a cabin in the woods and locked myself in for days. That's how I beat it. You sweat and feel like you're going to die. But I did it—on my own!"

I tried to feel proud of him. I mean, he had quit *heroin*. But the very idea that he was on heroin, sticking needles in his arm...it just made me sick.

"I didn't know you had taken heroin." I could feel the color draining out of my face. I thought I might faint just thinking about it. "How long did you take it?"

"I told you I had a bad reputation. I experimented with every drug on the face of the earth. Heroin, pot, pills, LSD, uppers, and downers. It's a good thing they didn't have crack back then, or I'd have been dead by now. Yeah, I took it all. I thought I was tough."

"So you just stopped? By yourself?" I asked. All the information was sinking in and now I was amazed that he had stopped. I didn't think *anyone* could stop heroin.

"After a friend died of an overdose, it hit me. We weren't invincible. I decided I would 'cut down.' But then, that wasn't enough. I had to get out of the drug environment. I had to stop drugs altogether. Get away from the people involved with it."

"What people?" I asked. He had never discussed this part of his past before, and I could tell it was painful for him. Still, I wanted to know more about it, and he was talking now. I wanted to learn more details about his painful past.

"The people I did drugs with, sold drugs with. Sold drugs to and got drugs from. We were all in it. I ran drugs. They used to call me 'Rider.' I rode a motorcycle and would bring the drugs over the Canadian-U.S. border," he boasted.

"Really?"

"I used to fake out the cops, take all the back roads. I had this motorcycle and a fast, souped-up car I had built. Sometimes I would run the stuff over the border, and then, to make sure the cops didn't catch me, I would hand it to one of my contacts on a certain stretch of highway, right after the bend. I'd hand it off from my motorcycle to their car doing eighty miles an hour."

My eyes grew wide. Wow. He did have some exciting drug past.

"Or other times I would get in my fast car—it could outrun any cop—and cross the border in it. Then I would hide the car in a garage, change to my regular car, and drive away. If I kept changing routes, cars, and motorcycles, they wouldn't catch on."

"Did you ever get caught?" I asked.

"Once it was a close call. There were four of us cutting up the drugs. The cops were onto us and had staked us out. That day I was practicing a getaway, pretending a cop was after me. Little did I know, one was actually following me. I was doing ninety, reached the garage, and changed cars as usual. I thought nothing of it until the next day when I found out the other three guys were caught right after we made the pick-up. Unbelievable, huh? Lucky for me. I'd have been in jail and had a record. Yeah, God looked out for me. I don't know how I ever got away with it, but it would just be a matter of time before I would get caught if I continued. So I quit the whole thing. Dealing *and* doing the drugs."

"So, you were never caught?"

"They knew I was dealing, but they couldn't prove it. One day I was on my way back with the drugs, and there was a roadblock. I thought it was for me, so I stepped on the gas and went right through it. They chased me for a while, but, as I said before, my car was super-fast."

Of course, I never doubted the fact that Pablo was telling me the truth. As I said before, Pablo watched a lot of movies.

"Didn't they get your license plate number?" I asked, doubting the getaway.

"Yes, and they took my driver's license away. But that was all, thank God. It turned out the roadblock was just a routine thing, but I couldn't chance them searching my car with the drugs on me. Because I went through the barrier and ran from them, they revoked my license. That's why I still don't have my driver's license."

"I always wondered why you used your gun permit when someone asked you for your I.D. I never knew your driver's license was suspended...forever?

"No. For five years or something. I don't remember," he said as if it were no big deal to be driving without a license.

"What happens if you get stopped without a license? Why don't you get one now?" I asked, concerned. I didn't want him going to jail. Not now!

"Why?" Pablo laughed again. "Why should I?"

"In case you get stopped. Just in case," I added.

"What can they do to me?" He laughed cynically. "If I don't have a driver's license, what are they going to do? Take it away?"

He had it all figured out! He was so smart.

Chapter 60

Taboo Subjects

Even though I wasn't supposed to, I told Dr. Davis about Pablo's being tired all the time. Dr. Davis said it wasn't normal and urged me to get Pablo to see a doctor. After much persistence on my part, Pablo finally agreed to go.

At my next appointment with Dr. Davis, he asked me how the doctor visit with Pablo had gone.

"Oh, fine. Pablo told me the doctor said he has low blood pressure and that he has to stop smoking," I said.

Dr. Davis looked pensive. Then he changed the subject back to me.

On the way home, I pulled over by a pizza parlor. What the heck. One or two slices of pizza wouldn't hurt. No big deal, right?

I ate the pizza, threw up in the bathroom there, and hated myself for it. Right then I knew how Pablo must have felt, trying to stop smoking, yet not being able to. Suddenly, I had a brainstorm. Since we both cared more for each other than for ourselves, we could use this to our advantage! *I would stop heaving if Pablo would stop smoking!* If I threw up, he could have a cigarette. I was less likely to throw up if I pictured him lighting up because of me. In the same way, if Pablo smoked a cigarette, I would be allowed to throw up. This might just work! We had to be honest with each other though—no sneaking or lying, or the plan wouldn't work.

I hurried home. I couldn't wait to propose my new "deal" to Pablo.

Because he hadn't had much success either, Pablo agreed to my new idea. As an added incentive, we took a trip to the tobacco shop and he bought a brand new Dunhill pipe. It cost over one hundred dollars, but if it helped him quit the cigarettes, it was well worth the expense.

Things went well for a few days. It was really, really hard for me. On the fourth morning, I caved to my addiction. Right away, as part of our agreement, I called Pablo at the barn.

"Pablo, I'm so sorry. I did it. That means you can, too. But you don't *have* to. Please don't. I don't want you to smoke. It's been four days. They say it gets harder to stop smoking if you have a cigarette."

"I'd love to have a cigarette, honey, but I won't. Just try a little harder. I won't have a cigarette. I keep my pipe with me instead," he reassured me.

"Really?" I felt so relieved. I was glad that Pablo was giving me another chance.

"Really. I promise I won't smoke." Pablo said. "Now, just try again. It's okay. One of us was bound to break down sooner or later. I'm just glad it wasn't me!"

Wasn't he wonderful? So forgiving. I wouldn't let him down again. No, sir! I would do better next time.

I was working on my twelfth day of not throwing up, one day at a time. I definitely felt better about myself. Well, not great, but better. I still felt fat. My biggest fear was that my weight would continue to go up until I reached two hundred pounds. In the past, whenever I stopped throwing up, I would gain seven pounds in water weight alone. If that continued...

Much to my relief, my weight started to level off. It actually went back down again. I was 107 and could live with that. No heavier though, or Pablo would hate his "big fat woman."

Pablo said he hadn't had a cigarette in over two weeks. Although I smelled smoke on him, I figured it was from his pipe. Now that he had quit smoking, I was sure I would see a difference in him. Yet, his color didn't seem to get any better and he was still tired. I had heard it took seven years after quitting cigarettes for the lungs to completely heal and for new cells to regenerate. Seven years! Would he be tired for *seven* more years?

At my last appointment, Dr. Davis had asked me if Pablo had any blood tests taken at the doctor. Before I went to see Dr. Davis, I needed to find out.

"Pablo, when you were at the doctor's, did he take any tests, like blood tests?" I asked nonchalantly.

"No. What would be the point?" he asked.

"Oh, in case you had something wrong. Maybe they could tell from the tests." I hoped he wouldn't realize I had been telling Dr. Davis about him.

Pablo poked his pipe tool into his favorite Dunhill and dug at the tobacco. He had so much smoking paraphernalia: all kinds of pipes, pipe tools, tobacco pouches, and glass containers with different mixes of different brands.

"I already know I'm anemic from that bout of hepatitis," Pablo explained. "The doctor knows it, too. There was no point in testing me. I just need to eat right."

It was Pablo's nap time, and time for my appointment with Dr. Davis. "I'm going to Dr. Davis now. I'll see you when I get back," I said and turned to leave the den.

"Honey?"

"Yeah?"

"Maybe next time you go to Dr. Davis, I'll come along. He seems to be getting away from the important topics. He knows about our deal, about me not smoking and you not throwing up, right?"

"Yeah, I told him," I said, feeling defensive. "I had to. He's an eating disorder doctor. All his menus for me never worked. I *had* to tell him what finally worked for me."

"Well, I think he should be concentrating more on your mother. If you want, I'll go with you next time and steer him in the right direction—if it's okay with you."

I stood there, silent, thinking.

"Honey? I think it would be a good idea."

Pablo was on "my side," right? He couldn't ruin my good relationship with Dr. Davis. Only Mom could do that. Yeah, maybe it would be a good idea for Pablo to talk to Dr. Davis. Then he would know how wonderful Pablo is. "Okay, I'll ask. I mean, I'll tell him. See you when I get back." I went back over and gave Pablo a kiss before I left.

I wondered what I would talk to Dr. Davis about this time. I couldn't discuss the sex issue with him because it involved Pablo. I still drank a ton before bed and nights were a total blank. (I think they call them "blackouts" when you don't remember things from drinking too much.) I wasn't allowed to talk to Pablo about sex, and I wasn't allowed to talk to Dr. Davis about Pablo. But maybe I could discuss sex to Dr. Davis without mentioning Pablo. After all, it was my problem. Why shouldn't I bring it up? I would just tread lightly. I trusted Dr. Davis. I needed him. He was my only connection to the outside world.

I gazed down at the soft, white, familiar cushions of the office couch where I sat. "I'm sort of having a problem dealing with...you know."

"With what?" Dr. Davis wanted me to say it: making love. I *hated* that term. It was Mom's term. It was her term for the repulsive act that Vince had done to me.

Years later Mom told me that the word "sex" was taboo in her day; therefore, the only term she knew for sex was making love.

"Sex. Having sex." There. I said it. It was a much better term for what Pablo and I did together. I slowly lifted my head and looked out the window. Two birds were in the tree. They never felt guilty about it. Why did humans make everything so complicated?

"Don't you think that's kind of a cold term for something so special? You love Pablo so much that I don't understand why..."

I cut him off. "Because I *hate* the other words for it."

"Why?"

"I don't know. I just do." I fixed my eyes on the happy birds, flitting around each other in the tree. The sun was shining so brightly and the tree was in full bloom. It was July, a happy month. Why couldn't I just be *happy?*

"Okay. So use your word. What's the problem, then? Is Pablo too tired?"

"No. He is fine. It's *me* that's the problem. He says I want to...you know... too much." I kept my eyes fixed on the window. I wouldn't look at Dr. Davis.

He laughed. I looked at him. Why was he laughing at me?

"What? What's so funny?" I asked.

"I'm sure you don't want to be intimate with him too much. You're a woman. You love your husband. That's a natural feeling. It's a natural thing to want to do." He sounded more serious now.

"No. It's *bad.* I know it is." I looked down at the couch again and wanted to sink into it. I could just disappear right into the soft, billowy, white couch.

"Why do you think it's bad? Because of what happened to you with your stepfather? That happened *to you.* This is different. You are a grown woman, an adult. You are married. You are having *normal* feelings."

I wanted to believe him. I did believe that, for a while. Until Pablo told me that I wanted...ugh. I was *horrible!*

"Karen? What's happened? Don't you make love...uh, have sex with him?"

"I don't know. I mean, yes. I think so, but I can't seem to remember or don't want to remember. I get really drunk and have no memory of anything, you know?" I looked directly at the doctor. I wanted him to know, to *understand* what I meant.

"I get the feeling you aren't communicating well with Pablo about this. Do you talk to him about how you're feeling?" Dr. Davis looked genuinely concerned.

"No. We're not supposed to talk about it. He told me we were never to talk about sex. I shouldn't even be telling you this." I looked down again, feeling guilty. I noticed a black mark on one sneaker and the other one was untied—just like my life. Only my life looked so picture perfect on the outside. But on the inside, it felt so black, so untied. *What was wrong with me???*

"Well, that's not good. You should talk to him about it. Maybe he is the problem. You seem to be having normal feelings and he seems to be having trouble with this."

No, No! I was the problem. I was always the problem. "You don't understand. Pablo is wonderful. *He* is normal. He doesn't have *anything* wrong with him. It's me." I was getting frustrated and upset. Why didn't anything make sense? Why didn't Dr. Davis blame me? I was the problem. Couldn't he see that?

"Then why is he, like you say, always so tired?" he pointed out.

I looked at Dr. Davis. Yes, Pablo was always so tired, wasn't he? And I didn't know why. But that had nothing to do with this! "We can't talk about him. He wouldn't like it. And besides, he is my best psychologist."

"Yes, I know. You've said that before. Yes, and you won't come to see me anymore if I talk about Pablo. Leave him out of everything. Your life with him is fine. Then, where is the problem with this issue? You seem fine to me," he said.

"No, I'm not. Pablo wants to come here with me next week. He says you are getting off track. We're supposed to be talking about my mother."

"I look forward to meeting him."

I felt better now. Soon Dr. Davis would talk to Pablo and then he would know that I was the problem and that Pablo was right. Pablo was always right. I couldn't wait for Dr. Davis to finally see this and understand. However, Pablo never did come with me to meet Dr. Davis because it was during his naptime.

Chapter 61
Deception

I hadn't thrown up in three months, and Pablo had stopped smoking. I was so proud of him. Surely, there was hope for our future. We had conquered our problems, for the most part. Then why was I so unhappy? Why did I feel like my life was in a downward spiral? Pablo was coming home later from the barn each morning, taking longer naps, and spending longer periods of time sailing. He seemed to be avoiding me. Something was wrong. Very wrong. I could feel it.

One morning, Pablo's friend from the club, Pete, came to the door. He had been trying to reach Pablo to cancel their sailing plans for that afternoon.

"Oh, here. Give these to Pablo," he added, handing me a carton of Marlboro cigarettes. "He left them at the club a few days ago."

"Those can't be his. He doesn't smoke."

"Yes. These are his. He smokes all the time."

"Recently? You have seen him smoke recently?"

"Yes. Why?"

"Never mind." I took the carton of cigarettes. "Thank you. I'll give him the message about not meeting you this afternoon."

My blood was boiling. *So that's why he was acting so strange...avoiding me...taking longer naps. Staying away, and going off sailing more.* How had I missed this? Because I *trusted* him, that's why. We were supposed to be *honest* about our deal! My mind raced. That was why he bought the pipe—to cover up the cigarette smell. He probably never stopped smoking at all! I felt so low. The lowest of *the low. Pablo was a liar. Liar, liar, hearts on fire.* My mind went back in time...

...I was riding my pony, Flower, down our dirt road. Mom and Vince were up ahead of me on their horses. Mom had not smoked in almost a year. I didn't know that she had started up smoking again—with Vince. Suddenly, I spotted the white cigarette in her hand as she waved it around, talking to Vince. There they were, smoking their cigarettes TOGETHER. I was livid. It was "their little secret," kind of like Vince and I had "our little secret." I felt betrayed. I hated them both at that moment. It felt as if Vince was cheating on me with Mom...

The sudden flashback made me feel sick and depressed. Now, I had the very same feeling of betrayal. Only it was *Pablo* cheating on me.

When Pablo got home from the barn, I couldn't contain my anger. I showed him the carton of cigarettes. "Why did you have to *lie* to me, Pablo? Why couldn't you have just been honest, like we agreed? I was honest with you! I *can't* believe you've been lying to me all this time." I was devastated.

"Well, honey, I did stop smoking for a little while. Then, you were doing so good with not throwing up. I just couldn't tell you."

"We were *supposed* to be *honest*. Remember? I told you when I screwed up, and you were supposed to do the same!" I felt like crying. "Go ahead and smoke, then. I don't care."

As I watched him light up his hateful Marlboros, I had the same flashback of Vince smoking with Mom. I felt so betrayed. Pablo *didn't* love me. I couldn't stand to watch him smoke and went upstairs. What else was he lying about? I opened his nightstand drawer and found more cigarettes, stashed in the back. They were hidden everywhere. Why hadn't I seen them before? Because I had never looked. I had trusted him. Even if I had looked, I would have assumed they were from before he quit. I never imagined that he could lie to me. Why had I ever made this deal in the first place? Dr. Davis had told me it was a bad idea. I just didn't know how much it would hurt.

I went into the bathroom and forced myself to throw up. My body was out of the habit, so it took some effort to get it going again. I hated Pablo. I hated myself. *This is what I deserve.*

I wondered what else could go wrong. I just wanted to end it all. Would Pablo be willing to keep our deal and die with me? Probably not. He wouldn't keep that deal, either. Well, if I had to live, I would have to get used to him smoking again. Logically, smoking wasn't a direct attack on me. Yet, it felt like a betrayal. I had never felt this way about his smoking before, but that was before he tried to quit—before all the deception and the lies.

I went back downstairs. "Pablo, what else have you lied to me about?"

He looked at me.

"Come on. I want to know. And I want to know now. Because if you are keeping any other secrets from me, I will hate you for it. Telling me is much better than lying. It's the deception that I hate. I can accept anything bad that you do, as long as you don't lie to me about it."

"Well, there is something," Pablo said meekly.

Good. I wanted to know. Nothing was worse than secrecy. Nothing. Suddenly, I felt more forgiving.

Pablo flicked his ash into the ash tray. Then he crushed the whole cigarette. "You know when you always said you did something bad, and I said I did something worse?"

"Yeah, and I finally told you about my throwing up. And, by the way, I just went upstairs and threw up. I don't care, either. I don't even feel bad about it." I wanted to be *bad* like Pablo. I needed to be *worse* than him, so he could regain his place above me.

Pablo didn't react to my saying I threw up again. He was trying to get the courage to tell me something.

"Well, this is really hard," he said. "I don't know if I can tell you. I was going to tell you before. I was going to tell you before we were married...but...I couldn't. You see, I had planned on stopping by then...and I'm doing the best I can. I still plan to stop, but I haven't yet."

"Stop *what*?" I asked, dying of curiosity.

Pablo got up out of his chair. "Let's go for a drive." He headed for the front door and I followed.

"It's okay if you don't want to tell me yet, Pablo. At least I know you're trying. Take your time." I love him. Poor thing.

We got into the car and pulled out of the driveway. Pablo was beginning to sweat. *That's odd. Pablo never sweats. Except that time when he almost died...*

"Honey, I'm going to tell you now. It's just that I hadn't planned on telling you, but you say a secret is worse." He looked over at me, sweat running off his brow. I was worried now. Maybe this *was* a big deal.

"I'm telling you because...it's life threatening. I could die trying to stop, but I'm going to try anyway."

I was shocked. He could *die*? What? What was going on here?

"Pablo, this is serious. You could die? You never told me this before. You could die?" *Must be calm, must be calm or else he'll never tell me.* "Uh, that's okay, though. Just tell me when you're ready. But I think I should know since you could die from it."

"Well, it's more that I could die from not having it. That's what I'm trying to do. Cut down. But it could kill me."

"Then don't! Don't!" I didn't know what I was saying but I blurted it out anyway. I didn't want him to *die!*

"It's all right, honey." He put his hand on my leg. Sweaty hand, sweaty Pablo. Oh, I loved him so much. *I forgive him for everything. I love him. I love him. I love him for telling me this....*I didn't want him to die and *leave* me. I couldn't live without my Pablo.

"Well, I might as well tell you then. It's this medicine I have to take. I have to have it or else I'll die."

"Then have it! Have it! I don't want you to die! What's wrong with medicine? It's okay. I'm not mad." I was confused, shocked, and filled with fear. I didn't know what I was dealing with, but as long as he was alive, I could live with it, I thought.

"You aren't mad, then?" he asked, appearing immensely relieved.

"No! No!" I hugged him as he steered the car around a bend, heading down the back roads of Oyster Bay. "I love you. I'm on *your* side. We'll do whatever we have to do. It will be okay. You can have your medicine. Just tell me how to get it so you won't die."

"No, honey. I have to stop taking it. I've been cutting down now for a few months, but it's the last bit that is the worst."

I didn't understand what he was trying to say, but I wasn't going to press him. He was being honest, and whatever it took, I would be there for him.

I leaned over and kissed his sweaty cheek. "I love you soo much."

I went through the next few days trying not to ask questions. Pablo had told me "no questions." He said he would explain more about the medicine as he felt comfortable. But I wasn't allowed to ask for details. However, I couldn't stand the worrying any more. He was sweating a lot lately. I couldn't take not knowing what was going on with him.

"Pablo, do you think you could explain it a little more to me? If you are in a life-threatening situation, I really should know. I'm really worried about you."

He hesitated. "I told you, honey. I already told you more than I wanted to. Trust me. I know what I'm doing."

It didn't make me feel any better. I stopped throwing up again. Suddenly, life was a little more precious as I stared death, or rather, Pablo, in the face every day.

Chapter 62
Pablo's Big Secret

A few days later I was hit with more bad news. "Dubai Stables is liquidating their American division," Pablo said. "I'll be out of a job." Nothing shocked me anymore. Nothing.

"How do you know?" I asked. "Is it definite? The Dubai horses are doing so well and winning big races."

"I knew this was coming," Pablo explained, shaking his head. "I could just sense it."

"You could? Since when? Maybe this is good, Pablo. You hated working for your father anyway. This will force us to make a change."

"But the timing isn't right." Pablo shook his head.

"Why? You said you wanted to do something else. This will be a *good* thing. Don't you think?" I was worried. What was wrong? It must have something to do with the "medicine."

"I should be off the medicine by now. It may take me a while longer than I thought. Dubai Stables is selling out in less than a month."

"What does that mean?" I asked, confused. All this was so sudden—although Pablo said he "knew it was coming."

"That means money will be tight," Pablo said, looking concerned.

"That's okay. I can spend less. We don't spend much, anyway."

"I know, honey. You don't spend much. Have you saved any money from when you rode?"

Hmm. That was my emergency money. I didn't want to spend that. I earned it. And I would never earn it again. It would have to be a real emergency for me to spend that. And anyway, Pablo should have quite a bit saved from all those good years he had. No, I wouldn't have to touch my savings. Not yet, anyway.

"No, Pablo, I don't have much saved. I put my money into my house."

"Well, I hope it doesn't have to come to selling that. But, of course, it is your money, and you're certainly not getting anything out of it with your mother living there. She doesn't pay you rent, does she?"

"No. But it's her house, too. She helped buy it."

"But it *is* in your name, right?" Pablo asked, looking desperate and worried.

"Yes," I answered reluctantly. "But I wouldn't sell it because Mom and Amy live there. It wouldn't be..."

"Then you can do whatever you want," he said confidently.

I looked away. I'd use my savings *first*.

"With Dubai selling out," Pablo explained, "they will take their Audi back from us. We'll get a Jeep Cherokee for a second car. Since I don't have a driver's license, the Jeep and the loan will have to be in your name."

Later that afternoon while Pablo slept, I couldn't stop thinking. What is to become of us? But, this is for the best—if Pablo doesn't die. I have to find out more about his "medicine."

When Pablo woke from his nap, I eased into my questions. "Pablo, how long have you known that Dubai was going to sell out?"

"Oh, several months, I guess. I sensed it, that's all."

"Is that why we went looking for marinas to buy?"

"No. I wanted to quit Dubai anyway. I would have sooner, but the money was so good."

"Why is money so important now? It never was before, to us."

"My medicine is expensive," he said quietly.

And no money, no medicine, I thought. And no medicine, no Pablo.

"How much does it cost?" I asked.

"No questions. I'll tell you if it gets bad."

My life was in turmoil. I was worried. Everything was changing. Before, I had looked forward to change: having a baby, moving away, that sort of change. I always loved Pablo, but hated our do-nothing life. Now, though, our "old life" didn't look so bad. At least some things were certain. Pablo was always tired. Dubai always had horses to race. Even bad certainty was good. At least then I could count on some stability in my life.

Now suddenly, our future looked so uncertain. I didn't even know if Pablo was going to live very long. I had always sensed this before, but now I knew it. He was really sick. Still, I wasn't losing hope. Things were going to get better, weren't they?

I was in such a worried state all the time. My body and mind were starting to go numb. Questions were not to be asked. Pablo would give me information as he found it necessary. It only hurt to think. Mustn't think. Mustn't think. Just get by. Do the laundry. Cook the dinner. Ignore the signs. Ignore the feelings. Go numb. You can do it. You've done it before.

Pablo told me that nobody knew about his medicine. *Nobody*. And it had to stay that way.

"Why?" I asked him.

"Because if my father ever found out, I would lose my job."

"You already lost Dubai. And besides, I'm sure your parents would be understanding about you taking medicine," I said. I wanted someone else to know. I felt so alone and helpless in all this. I was helpless to help Pablo.

"No way," Pablo said vehemently. "My father is thinking of buying some of the Dubai horses for me to keep training. He can't know about this."

"Why do you want to work for him, anyway? Why would you want to train for him?" I asked. None of this made any sense. If anything, Pablo liked working for Dubai Stables, but didn't like the fact that his father was involved.

"My father wants to buy ten or twelve horses out of the Dubai sale. I talked to him about it. He wants me to train for him. He wants me to take these horses to Hialeah in Florida this winter."

Oh, so now we were moving, too. "What does your father think of Dubai selling all their horses? Isn't he upset?" If I couldn't understand the medicine, maybe I could understand what was going on with the horses.

"The old man knew it was coming. Sure, he's a little bothered. He did so well for them. But he says he's ready for semi-retirement."

"I still don't understand why you would want to train for your father. Isn't he the *last* person you'd want to work for?"

"It's just for now. Just this winter. It's a transitional thing. It's not forever." Pablo sounded frazzled. I was asking a lot of questions again.

"And *nobody* can know about your medicine?" I asked. "Lots of people take medicine. Diabetics, people with allergies. It's nothing to be ashamed of. What worries me, though, is that you have to have it. I don't really understand what it's for." There. I had wanted to ask that one.

"Honey, nobody can know. People talk. I don't need anything against me now. I'm going to need new owners to train for. The old man would just love to see me get out of the business. He always says that he is the only one who will ever give me horses to train. But I can get other owners."

"I know you can, Pablo. You just don't get out to meet them. You've been so used to training privately for Dubai Stables that you are out of practice. But you had other owners when you first started training, right? You can do it again if training horses is what you really want to do. Is it?"

"For now. Just for now," Pablo answered, sounding tired and defeated. I think I was exhausting him with all my questions. But I wasn't through yet.

"Can you just explain a little more about the medicine?" He had been avoiding this subject as if it didn't exist. But it was *real.* Sometimes I liked to pretend that he had never told me about his medicine, and that things were as they used to be. I didn't like living like this. "It's just that not knowing has me scared," I added, trying to sound sympathetic, not judgmental. "I promise I won't ask again. And I won't judge you. My lips are sealed." I pretended to zip my lips.

"Okay. Just give me a minute." Pablo took a deep breath.

I waited.

"The medicine was made so that I won't want to take drugs. It keeps me from wanting to take drugs again."

"I thought you hated drugs and didn't ever want to take them again."

"Just a minute," Pablo said, sounding a little irritated. I had better keep quiet.

After a few minutes, he continued. "That's true. I don't want to take drugs. And I haven't. But a long time ago, I had this craving to take drugs again. I had stopped. But I had this urge again." He paused to light up a Marlboro. He inhaled it deeply. "Well, I found myself driving by the road where I used to get my drugs. And I said to myself, 'Pablo, you better do something about this. If you take drugs again, it will be a sure disaster.' I had heard about this new medicine. If you took it, you didn't crave heroin, or any other drugs." Pablo leaned back in his chair. "So, after thinking about it for only a minute—I had to act before I got the drugs again—I wheeled the car around and went to a doctor. He prescribed the medicine, and I've been taking it ever since."

Pablo leaned forward. Then he continued. "What I didn't know, though, was that this medicine is more addicting than heroin. The doctor tried to talk me out of taking it, but I was desperate. I had to do something. And I've been paying ever since."

"It's more addicting than *heroin?*" I asked, completely aghast. How awful! He would take this medicine forever and ever!

"Yes. I have to have it or I will die."

"Well then, you have to have it. We'll just always have to have it." Like a diabetic, I thought.

"No, honey. I've been trying to get off it for quite some time now. The medicine is affecting me. I don't have any energy. Years ago when I took it, I felt normal. Now, it seems like the past thirteen years of taking it has caught up with me. It's like my system is rebelling against it.

"And besides, it causes me constant worry—whether or not I can get it or if I will have enough of it. It never bothered me before I met you, but I want us to have a future together. I want to live a long time."

"What would happen if you couldn't get it? Hasn't that ever happened? It must have happened before." Thirteen *years?*

"It did happen, once. I was in a car accident outside the gate at Belmont. They rushed me to a hospital. I get the medicine in the mornings at the barn. My exercise boy, Tony, gets it for me. Anyway, I was in some hospital, barely conscious. There was no way I could get in touch with Tony. I was sweating and feeling awful. Not only was my face all cut up, but I needed my medicine. They were doing emergency plastic surgery on my face. Tony found out about the accident and went to every hospital in the area looking for me. He finally found me—just in the nick of time."

"Tony knows you will die without it? Isn't that a lot to ask of somebody? I mean, your *life* depends on him!"

Pablo nodded. "That's why I always do so much for him. I try to take good care of Tony. I gave him a job at the barn. I give him money and help him out whenever I can."

"Why does he do it, Pablo? I couldn't take that kind of pressure. Especially if I wasn't family." I shook my head. I wouldn't have wanted to be in Tony's shoes.

"I told you, he's good. He's loyal. He thinks a lot of me."

"So nobody knows about this but him and you?"

Pablo smiled. "And now, you. I told Tony you know now. He's glad. He always thought you should know. He likes you. And now, if there is an emergency, he can deal through you—if something happens to me."

"You get it at the barn, right? Every morning?"

"Yeah, but I've been trying to get a three day supply and take it home. It's complicated. I'm trying to cut down and it can be difficult. I sweat a lot. And I get anxious, then depressed. It's hard to explain. Tony is helping me cut down. Now, he measures it out in bottles and regulates it for me."

"And he gets nothing for doing all this for you?" It sounded a little suspicious to me. "No money?" That, at least, would make *sense*.

"No. He only charges me what it costs him."

"Where does he get it? Why don't you just get it from a doctor?"

"Tony gets it from a hospital where they treat drug addicts. Some of them don't need the medicine anymore, so they sell it on the side. That's where Tony buys it. He has to collect it from a lot of different guys to get enough for me because I need more than what the doctor prescribes."

"You take a lot? Show me. What does it look like?" Now, I was pushing it.

"It looks like orange drink. I have some for tomorrow morning. Wait a minute." Pablo got out of his chair and left the room.

I waited. I was getting the creeps. I was going to see his "secret medicine." The Big Secret. The one nobody knew about except the three of us.

Pablo came back in the room and held up an apple juice bottle with orange liquid in it. "See? That's all. Looks harmless, but it's not. Don't ever touch it, okay honey?"

I nodded. It looked like orange drink. So that was why all those empty juice and soda bottles were in the hall closet with his guns and bow and arrows. I thought he stored gun solution in them. "Is that what it comes in? Bottles like that?"

"No. It comes in tiny containers the size of those little mini paint containers that come with model kits. A normal dose of this medicine is very small, two tablespoons or so. A half of one of those tiny paint jars. But I'm on a higher dose, so Tony measures it out and gives it to me in bigger soda bottles. I keep all the measured out rations separated. That way I know I'll stay on an even keel and still be cutting down.

I had seen a Gerber baby food jar in the garbage once. I had wondered about that, but never asked.

"Pablo, did you ever get it in a baby food jar?"

He laughed. "You'd be surprised at some of the weird jars Tony puts it in."

Those odd shaped little bottles in the bottom of the suitcase must have been from the medicine, too! "Sometimes do you get the tiny bottles that it comes in?"

"Yeah, but only if the measuring is very precise. Okay, honey. Have I told you enough now?"

"I guess so." He started to leave the room, holding carefully to his apple juice bottle filled with his precious Source of Life.

Now that I knew, I wished that I didn't. I saw it. It was real. This was no joke. His life depended on that orange liquid. I didn't like the feeling. Not one little bit.

Every day after that, I thought about it. Did he have enough? Pablo told me not to ask any more questions, that he and Tony had it under control and that in a few months, if he kept "cutting down" at the rate he was going, he would soon be "off it." Then I could ask all the questions I wanted. But, he explained, now was the hardest. The "last little bit" was the hardest to get off, he explained.

The reality of it all was hitting me. I felt so alone and anxious. In a few months, we'd be going to Florida, and then I'd really be alone. I wouldn't be able to see Dr. Davis. I had to tell someone about what I was going through. If Dr. Davis promised not to tell a soul, I would share Pablo's secret with him. Pablo would kill me if he knew. But I needed someone to help me cope. I could trust Dr. Davis. He would tell me what to do.

The medicine. The medicine. It was all I could think about lately.

When I told Dr. Davis about Pablo and the medicine, he was very understanding. I explained that Pablo had to take the medicine so that he wouldn't want to take drugs, mostly heroin.

"It sounds like methadone to me," Dr. Davis said. He pulled a big red medical book off the shelf. He flipped through it looking for something.

Methadone. I had never heard of it before.

Dr. Davis stopped turning the pages. He was reading intently.

"What have you found out?" I asked, anxious to know more about this "methadone."

"Methadone. It can be taken in pill or liquid form," Dr. Davis read from the big book. "Sounds like that's it."

Methadone, medicine. What's the difference?

At this time, I didn't realize that methadone was just another addictive "drug" similar to heroin, and not really "medicine."

"Now things make much more sense," Dr. Davis said. "Now do you see, Karen, that everything is not always your fault? Pablo has his set of problems, too."

"I guess he's not perfect. He lied about not smoking. And he was addicted to some horrible medicine called methadone and never told me about it. Now he's losing his job and we're moving to Florida." There. I said it. It felt good to get it all out.

"Thank God I'm not pregnant," I continued. "Maybe it's because of the medicine. He told me he takes a lot of it. At least now I know why he is always so tired."

I was exhausted just thinking about it all. For a do-nothing life, things were happening a little too rapidly. Nothing was as it had seemed before. But I was adjusting, or at least trying to. I still had my Pablo. Not exactly the Pablo I thought I had, but it was still him. As long as I had him, I could deal with anything. After all, Pablo was my life, my only reason for living. And as sick as he may have been, I was hanging on to him for (my) dear life.

Pablo was awake when I got home from my appointment. Since Dubai was taking their Audi back, Pablo suggested we go look at Jeep Cherokees.

As we headed for the dealership, I asked casually, "It's called methadone, right?" I had yet to understand the severity of the drug, and still considered it his "medicine."

Pablo looked at me. "Who told you that? Who have you been talking to?"

Oh, God. I was in it now.

"Nobody. I just figured it out, that's all." I looked away, out the car window. I couldn't let him see my face. I couldn't lie very well. The highway stretched outside my window. Millions of people were out there driving back and forth in their cars every day. How many of them felt like me right now?

"Honey, who told you? Who did you tell?"

"You're going to *kill* me, right? Because you told me not to tell anyone. Well, I did. But don't worry. You won't be discovered." I looked right at Pablo. He looked very, very upset. "You're going to kill me, but I don't care. I might as well be dead, living like this," I mumbled. What was coming over me?

"Why? Why... *Who*?" Pablo looked like he might die, right there behind the wheel. Then we would veer off the road and hopefully get killed in a car crash. No. With my luck, I would survive to suffer. Maybe I'd be maimed for life. But what if we hit some poor innocent soul?

"Oh, don't worry," I said sarcastically. "I had to tell somebody, for *my* sake. I can't stand all the secrecy. And the worry. And the unknown. I told Dr. Davis because I needed someone to talk to. Is that okay?"

Pablo drove on in silence. A few miles and possible crash sites later, he spoke. "Yeah, it's okay. I guess this has been hard on you. Telling Dr. Davis was okay. Just don't tell anyone else, okay?"

I didn't want to look at him. The roadside was much more pleasant. There were trees and friendly road signs. Creedmoor, the mental institute was off this exit. I wonder if they are any more insane in there than I am out here. No, I'm still sane. I think.

On the morning of the Dubai Stables horse sale, Pablo and I flew to Kentucky. Millions of dollars in horseflesh went through the Kentucky sales pavilion. We watched the horses go in and out of the ring. Some of the names of horses I recognized from the articles I had read. Many of the horses I had never heard of before. I wondered if Pablo knew them all, or if he even cared.

Pablo's father picked out ten horses that he liked for Pablo to train in Florida. The Garcias would let us stay rent free in one of their three condominiums, part of a gated community in Palm Springs North, near Miami. I never could understand why Pablo resented his parents.

I dreaded the thought of going to Florida. Everything was slipping away, out of control. Still, I would be with Pablo. It would be okay.

Pablo tried to sound chipper. "My parents say the condos are really nice. Everything we need is within walking distance. We'll only need one car. We'll just take the new Jeep because we can fit more in it."

"That's good." *But, what about the medicine?*

Pablo seemed to have read my mind. "I've worked out how to get my medicine from Tony. He's going to send it to me twice a week by Federal Express. It's had me worried for a while now. I've never had to leave New York before." He seemed to have thought of everything.

He continued, "I thought that, well, I hoped that I would be 'off' it by now. But no need to worry. Tony will just have to work a little harder to get it more often. Everything will be fine. I'll have it delivered right to the condo, now that you know."

"Pablo, what would you have done if I didn't know?"

"Oh, I'd have had it sent to a post office box. But it would have been a real hassle."

Yeah, more lying and sneaking around is what he meant.

"It's much easier now that you know," Pablo said, smiling.

I guess it would be. Wasn't it nice having such an understanding, forgiving wife?

My world had gotten very small, all-consumed with Pablo and his medicine. I was going headlong down a very dangerous road and about to take the ride of my life.

Chapter 63
"The Package"

The day arrived when we were to fly to Florida. Pablo was making sure all the last minute important details were in order.

"I set up an account with Federal Express," Pablo explained. "It's all set with Tony, except for one thing. He can't get the package until tomorrow. My father's ten horses already left Belmont and will be in Florida by tonight, but we can't leave without the package."

"Why don't you go ahead and fly down so you can be there for the horses," I suggested, "and I'll wait for the package tomorrow from Tony. (Pablo's new term for the medicine "en route" was "the package.") Then I can just take another flight and bring it down to you."

"Oh, honey. You would do that?"

"Of course. I'd do anything for you."

"Well, let's wait and see. Maybe I'll just wait the extra day so we can fly down together," he said.

"Don't you trust me with your medicine, Pablo?" Maybe the idea of not having it with him scared him.

"What do you mean? Of course I do. I'd just rather be with you, that's all. I want to be with you when we go down. I'll make the arrangements with the travel agent right now and change our flight." Pablo was able to purchase two first class airline tickets, LaGuardia to Miami, leaving in the morning at eleven. Of course, it was always first class with Pablo. While we would fly in style, driving the Jeep to Florida would be left to Tony. Pablo had also paid Pete and some of the guys to sail his boat down for him.

In the morning, we waited by the phone for Tony to call to say he had the package. We would meet him at the barn, and then he would take us to the airport. We waited. And waited. Finally, the phone rang.

Pablo jumped into action. "Hello? Tony? You got it? Great! We'll be at the barn in half an hour. I hope we can still make our flight. You cut it close!" He hung up the phone. "Okay, honey. Let's go!"

Our plane was scheduled to leave in two hours. There were no other commercial flights from New York to Miami until the following day, and a huge snowstorm was in the forecast. If Tony got to the barn in the next hour, we would be lucky to make our flight. Pablo, however, had to take that chance. He *had* to wait for Tony and his life support package.

Back then, airline security was not as strict. They did not check luggage for liquids.

We arrived at the barn before Tony. And we waited. Hurry up and wait. It was all we seemed to be doing lately. The medicine was running our lives.

Pablo kept watching out his office window, waiting for Tony's familiar car to drive up. It had already started to snow. I looked out the window at the tiny flakes coming down steadily. It was the kind of snow that lasts and lasts. And it was sticking.

Finally, Pablo spotted Tony's car. It had just turned the corner at the end of the barn. Pablo sighed with relief and stopped pacing.

The whole idea of Pablo's medicine was still sinking in. I didn't really want to know more about it. After all, one can only take so much shock to the system.

On the way to the airport, Pablo had Tony open the package. Tony had put the orange mixture, Pablo's "liquid life," into two glass spaghetti sauce jars. Pablo was livid. "I *told* you to use *plastic* containers! If that glass breaks, I'll be in big trouble."

So many life-threatening possibilities. Would it never end?

We made the flight. I felt like I had been through the mill. All Pablo's worrying was rubbing off on me. I was constantly afraid for him. Did he have enough medicine? Did he take too much? Too little? Pablo insisted on calling it his medicine as if methadone was a dirty word.

When we reached Florida, I asked Pablo what would have happened if the glass jars had broken.

"Honey, you'd better be ready to take a quick flight back to New York for me. It just may happen. And if this Federal Express doesn't come on time..."

"Okay, Pablo. Don't worry."

When we arrived at the Garcias' condos, I was surprised to find they were located on an exclusive golf course. Pablo and I were given the condo above his parents. Their help (housecleaner/cook) lived in the third Garcia condo, next door. Mr. and Mrs. Garcia played golf every day. They had no idea what was going on in the condo above them.

Twice a week, the package would be delivered. On those days, Pablo would come home early from the barn. Then we would sit in the living room and wait for the Federal Express truck to come.

I watched Pablo closely. He looked like he might die at any moment. Sometimes he said he couldn't even talk, that he was in too much pain. So, I watched Pablo sweat and listened for the truck. I would go to the window and pull back the curtain. Where was the white truck with the purple and orange lettering? I hated that truck. And yet, I wanted it to come so the watching and waiting would be over.

Sometimes we would wait like this from eight o'clock in the morning until four in the afternoon. It was a nightmare. I pictured Pablo dying. We had arrangements for me to fly back to New York at a moment's notice to get another package in order to save him.

When the package arrived, Pablo would open it with apprehension, and then absolute delight. He was like a kid at Christmas. Had Tony sent enough? Oh, yes, *yes!*

And then I would watch Pablo measure it out so very carefully, from the two-liter plastic soda bottles into smaller soda bottles. To Pablo, it was liquid gold. Can't spill a drop! I wasn't allowed to touch it. In fact, I was privileged that Pablo allowed me to watch him measure it out. He didn't like me watching his little love affair with the stuff, but I was curious. Did it make him feel *that* good? Pablo insisted that all it did was make him "normal" again. Never, never was I allowed to touch it. If it spilled, well, we knew what would happen to Pablo.

Chapter 64
The Depth of Our Dysfunction

Pablo promised that he would be "off" the methadone (always "medicine" to Pablo) soon. He figured it would take two more months of agonizingly "cutting down." As usual, I watched him closely. Now was the dangerous part, the hard part, according to Pablo. Pablo didn't like that I watched him so closely. He didn't like when I questioned or doubted him. Early in our relationship, my eyes were closed because I had trusted him implicitly. Now my eyes were open, and I questioned him about everything. I wanted to believe him like before, but I couldn't help investigating his stories...and catching him in more and more lies.

It was hard for me to tell if Pablo was really cutting down because he tried to hide the measuring from me. He claimed he was cutting down and pouring some of the bottles down the drain. However, I found those bottles with medicine hidden in odd places.

When I questioned Pablo with the evidence, he denied it, saying they were "extras" in case he ran low. But that didn't make sense because he told me the medicine went bad in a few days. I was getting more and more angry, desperate, and depressed. Why couldn't I just make Pablo *tell me the truth?* Being mad at Pablo just didn't work for me; it was easier just to be mad at myself. At least I was comfortable and in control that way. It wasn't Pablo's fault for lying to me—it was my fault for doubting him, questioning him, and discovering his lies!

And so as the days wore on, I began to drink more and more. I argued with Pablo. I didn't know if I loved him or hated him. Things were going from bad to worse. I just didn't care anymore.

I wanted to call Mom and tell her things weren't going so well. Even though Pablo said she didn't love me and never called me, I still felt that deep down maybe she would be supportive.

"Your mother would just love to see your marriage fail! Yeah, she would just *eat this up,*" he said smugly. He was so sure that Mom wanted to see me fail and that it would make her the happiest person on earth. So, I didn't call her.

Of course, whenever I saw Mr. or Mrs. Garcia, I smiled. I think they could sense something was wrong. They may have heard us arguing from their condo below. But they never could have guessed the depth of our dysfunction. Pablo was very good at deceiving them. He had been doing it for a long time. However, I think they could tell something was wrong with me. I wasn't so good at hiding my emotions.

Every time I bugged Pablo about the methadone, he changed the subject to Mom. He reminded me that *she* was the source of my depression and anger. He suggested, "Why don't you type up a letter to your mother? You can tell her how you feel about the past. You don't have to send it to her. Just write it. Maybe it will make you feel better."

So, to please him, I typed up a letter to Mom. Pablo gave me suggestions and egged me on. It made me angry, but at least I wasn't attacking Pablo. It was a great diversion from our sick situation.

I bounced between my angry mixed-up feelings for my lying, loving husband and my equally mixed-up feelings over myself and my mother. I started to cut myself more and continued to throw up. Add to this the drinking, and I was quite a mess. But I felt better knowing that I was the bad one, not Pablo.

Dr. Davis had given me his home number so I could call him from Florida. It was unusual for a psychologist to do this, but after finding out about the methadone and how alone I really was, he felt it might be necessary for me to call him if I was desperate. After all, Pablo had done such a good job separating me from my family. When I called Dr. Davis, he said he felt helpless and that I should get a doctor nearby. I was slipping away from reality, lost in the insanity of our crazy life. But I didn't care. I was going down with the ship. Down, down, down with my Pablo.

One afternoon, Pablo sat silently in front of the television, sweating and waiting for the Fed Ex truck. Things were not getting any better. I wanted to show Pablo just how much I was hurting, so I sat on the couch in my shorts with a knife. I started working on my legs, sawing them up. The more blood, the more pain, the better. The blood was staining the white shag carpet of the Garcias' condo, but I didn't care. Pablo only shook his head in disgust. I made him get out of his chair and led him to the unflushed toilet, so he could see that I was still throwing up. I wanted my pain to be visible, tangible.

Once in a while I remembered to pray. Sinner that I am, I wondered how God could ever save me. What was I worth saving for, anyway? I had forgotten about my meaningful prayer three years ago when God had saved Pablo's life at the hospital. If Pablo had died that night at the hospital, I never would have found out about his medicine or his lies. Had Pablo died at that time, I would have held him up on his God-like pedestal forever, or at least until I died.

I was starting to lose my faith. Not so much my faith in God, but my faith that God would care about me anymore. There was a flicker of something though. It wasn't hope. It was more curiosity. What *was* God all about? He felt so far away. It was like there was some dark force at work all around me. Things were getting darker with each passing day. There wasn't much fight left in me, and I was caving in to the darkness. When I opened my Bible to fight the bad thoughts and feelings, it was out of sheer desperation. I would pray, "I know you're there, God, but I don't see how you could ever want to help someone like me." He felt so very, very far away.

Pablo had the Jeep again. He was gone a lot lately. I don't think he could stand to come home and see the state I was in: bloody, angry, drinking, and throwing up. I decided that on this day I would do something positive. I would go to the library and find out more about this methadone, this stuff that was ruining my life. With no car, I walked. At the library, I went to the card catalog to look it up: methadone. Here goes.

I quickly found out from reading all I could that methadone was a horrible, horrible *drug*. It was invented in World War II in Germany. A synthetic opioid, it was invented by Hitler's people so that the German soldiers could have it instead of heroin, morphine, or opium, which were unavailable during the war. I learned that like other opioids, methadone numbed emotions. I wondered how many German soldiers it had numbed. The more I read, the angrier I got and the more betrayed I felt.

I read that one could die from an overdose of methadone, that it slowed the heartbeat, and that it had other bad side effects. I also discovered that it was impossible to get off methadone without medical supervision. Suddenly, I was filled with fear. But Pablo was different. He'll be okay. He did it before. He got off heroin, didn't he? Or maybe he didn't. Maybe he just went from heroin to methadone. Hmm. Oh, would the lies and deception never end??? Well, I had wanted answers. Now I had them.

My skin crawled as I read everything I could find on this awful "drug." Yes, it was a *drug*. The full effect was starting to hit me. I was married to the worst kind of drug addict, the worst kind of junkie. According to these books, there was no hope for these kinds of addicts. Opiates, opiate derivatives, or synthetic opiates (methadone) were the absolute worst kind of drugs. They were the most powerfully addicting and if Pablo was to ever get off this drug, he needed medical help. Even that wouldn't guarantee success. He could die or most likely go back on the drug again. Well, at least in this, Pablo was telling the truth: it was dangerous, it was deadly, and coming off it might kill him.

But staying on it was surely killing us both.

I wanted the information to be wrong. But in my heart, I knew it was right. I felt as if a razor blade was tearing me apart. I didn't want to live with a drug addict, yet I couldn't live without Pablo. There was only one thing to do: get numb, like him. But first, I had to confront him.

When Pablo came home, I threw the library books at him. "You're on *drugs!* Methadone is synthetic heroin, and you're on a dose that's twenty times higher than the people treated at a clinic! This is no better than *heroin!*"

Pablo looked sheepish. He didn't know how to deal with me anymore. Whether he was honest or dishonest, it no longer mattered. I was angry and going insane. I wished I hadn't gone to the library. Then I thought about what the books said about drugs and sex. It explained that drugs were more important to the addict than sex! He loved that stuff more than me!

I hated myself. I was hurting too much and couldn't stand it any longer. I went into the kitchen. I kept thinking that when Pablo took the methadone, it was like having sex without me! I reached for the vodka, the strongest kind I could find: Absolut. I grabbed it and went back to Pablo in the living room. "See this? Well I'm going to drink the whole thing. You can have your 'medicine' and I'll have mine. Since I'm not allowed to take your stuff because you will die without it, I'll take mine. I'll get numb, like you. Watch me. Just watch!"

I think I wanted him to stop me, or at least to care. Or maybe I wanted him to promise to stop taking his drugs. The books said the only way to stop opiates was to stop cold. And he was stopping by himself by "cutting down???" Had he told me the truth about anything??? I was so angry. I hated Pablo and I hated myself. I guzzled the bottle of Absolut until it was half empty. Pablo watched. I knew this should have made me sick to my stomach, but it didn't. I wasn't about to make myself throw up, either. I wanted to be numb. I wanted to just *die*.

When I woke up later, I didn't know how long I had been out of it. I didn't know anything anymore. Except that things just kept getting worse. Pablo was gone. I guessed he left when I took the vodka or passed out. He came home late that night with tacos from Taco Bell. He loved Taco Bell.

"They should have Taco Bell in New York," he said. "It's even better than Burger King."

I felt too sick to eat. If I ate, I'd throw up. Not the usual way I threw up. I'd throw up in a sick way that I couldn't control. It would be the kind of retching where your stomach muscles contracted and forced you to vomit.

Pablo ate the tacos himself and watched television.

I wasn't a properly functioning "with Pablo" anymore. I was having an identity crisis. Pablo was my identity, and I was losing the man I thought he was. Before I had been like a remote control doll with Pablo holding the remote. Now the remote was lost. My thinking was far from rational; the old way of trusting and believing Pablo didn't work anymore because now I knew that he was a liar. I didn't like what we had become, but I didn't know who else I could be anymore. I would either have to make myself numb, go completely insane, or just die.

While all this was going on, I discovered Elvis. I watched a movie about his life and then went out and bought tapes of his music. I bought everything I could get my hands on. His songs were so appropriate. Like "Suspicious Minds." My suspicions were killing me, I felt trapped, yet I loved him too much to leave. I listened to Elvis and cried a lot.

Pablo bought me a Casio keyboard, a "toy" or distraction for miserable me. He also bought himself a guitar. He thought maybe we could have our own little band. Was this supposed to make things better? Actually, it made things worse. Watching him play songs from the sixties made me realize that he was just a druggie from the hippie era. I hated that guitar. Pablo was regressing to "better" days. I felt jealous and left out.

Pablo was acting more and more irrational. But I was adjusting. Aside from when I caught him in lies and hated myself for it, I was trying to be patient and understanding. With my extreme anger and mood swings, Pablo didn't know how to deal with me anymore.

One day Pablo decided that we should buy a bigger sailboat. He said we could get away to the South Seas and maybe even sail around the world together. So, we went looking at big, luxurious sailboats in Ft. Lauderdale. We found two or three that he really liked. Pablo said it would be tough to get the $150,000 to buy one, so he suggested that I sell my house to get the money.

Looking back, Pablo was probably using the idea of getting a bigger sailboat to get me to sell my house. Little did I know he had run out of money. If I had sold my house, then he could have canceled the boat idea and used the money for his drugs.

Once in a while, we went to the races. I stuck close to Pablo, feeling more apart from the world than ever before. I felt trapped inside our secret. On this particular day, Gotham, the horse Pablo owned in partnership with his father, was in a race. The horse was easily worth $100,000, but Pablo ran him for a claiming price of $30,000. When the horse was claimed (bought) for $30,000 out of the race, Pablo seemed relieved. "Well, at least now I'll have some money in my account."

Was money a problem now, too? I couldn't conceive of it. "Pablo, how much is your 'medicine' costing?" I figured it was around fifty dollars a package.

Pablo looked at me seriously. "You really don't want to know."

"Yes, I do."

"It costs a thousand dollars a day. But since I've been cutting down, it's less."

I thought about it and let it sink in. Yes, that *was* a lot of money.

"I'm glad the horse was claimed," Pablo said, sounding relieved. "He's worth more, but the money will come in handy."

"Doesn't your father own half the horse? Shouldn't he get part of the money?" I asked.

"The old man will never see it. He doesn't need it."

"Then what's the point of him sharing ownership, if you don't pay him his half?" I asked. His father was not a stupid man.

"He'll never miss it."

As we left the races, Pablo said once again, that he had quit smoking. However, a few days later I found a pack hidden in the Jeep. I told him I didn't care if he smoked, that it was better to smoke than to lie to me and say he had quit. He insisted that he wasn't lying.

As I was compelled to do lately, I wanted to see if he was telling me the truth. While he took his nap, I went out to the Jeep and counted the cigarettes in the hidden pack. There were twelve. The next morning, the pack contained five cigarettes! I couldn't help it. I had to confront him.

"Pablo, you smoked, didn't you?"

Of course, he denied it.

"I *hate* it when you lie to me!" I said angrily.

"I didn't smoke, honey. Really."

"I *know* you smoked because some the cigarettes you hid in the Jeep are missing."

"Okay, then. I did have some cigarettes. But I didn't smoke them."

"What did you do with them?" I asked.

"I chewed them up."

Was he *for real?*

"Pablo, nobody chews up cigarettes." I laughed. "Come on, admit it. You smoked them, right?" This was really getting out of hand.

Couldn't he be honest with me about *anything?*

"No. I chewed them up. I started to light one. Then I changed my mind."

"So you chewed it up?"

"Right."

"And what about the other six cigarettes?"

"I chewed them up, too."

Okay! I didn't really believe him. But who could make up something like that? He should have said he gave them away, or lit them and threw them out. But, *chewed them up???*

Now Pablo knew that I knew where the cigarettes were hidden. So, he left the five cigarettes right where I had discovered them. I checked on them every day. There were still five cigarettes. After a few peaceful days with Pablo, I wondered if I was being tricked again. While he slept, I took a fine line marker and put a small dot at the end of each of the five cigarettes.

The next day I couldn't wait for Pablo to take his nap so I could check my results. I went out to the Jeep. There were those same five little harmless, non-smoked cigarettes. I pulled one out. No blue dot! None of the cigarettes bore their mark! Pablo had smoked them all and replaced them with new ones! Oh, how I hated him and his lies. He knew just how to fool me. Was *everything* a lie? Had he *ever* loved me?

I ran back up into the apartment, yanking out his methadone bottles from all their hiding places: under the cabinet, over the closet, in his jacket pocket. I got them all and put them in the refrigerator.

I heard Pablo coming out of the bedroom, going straight for the cabinet. Oh, so now he was taking the medicine after his naps, too? Well, well. Old "one-a-day" Pablo had added to his dosage. Seems he had many, many secrets. Ha! He was looking for his medicine. HA! HA!

Pablo came into the kitchen, glaring at me. "Honey, you took my medicine. Where did you put it?"

"I poured it out," I said casually, enjoying the look of horror on his face. He looked like he was going to die. "No, I'm only kidding," I said. "I wouldn't do that to *you,* my wonderful, *honest* husband. No,

I didn't pour them out. I THREW them out."

Pablo went right to the garbage, rustling through it. "Come on. This isn't funny," he said after failing to find any of his orange potion.

"No. Actually, I drank it. Now I can be just like *you.*"

Pablo grabbed me.

"No, I hid it. Try to find it." This was going to be fun.

Pablo became frantic, searching everywhere—except for the most obvious place for liquids that supposedly "went bad."

Pablo looked like a ghost. He had entered Panicsville. He was covered with white fright.

Oh, dear, oh dear. What have we done with our medicine?

Pablo stopped searching and came into the kitchen. He looked at me helplessly. I couldn't let the suffering continue, so I started to hum a little children's tune. *Oh where, oh where, has my medicine gone? Oh where, oh where, could it be?* As I hummed, I opened the fridge.

Pablo dove in and abducted one of his bottles. Then he disappeared into the bedroom to have his little love affair with it.

I waited for him to come out. He came back into the kitchen to count all his blessed little bottles, making sure his little children were all safe and accounted for.

"Pablo, why don't we just keep them in the fridge? Maybe they won't go bad that way. And they look much less secretive in here. They almost look...harmless. Like orange drink."

"Maybe. I don't know." Pablo looked much better now. Much more like Pablo.

"Have you had any cigarettes today? I haven't asked you in a few days." *But, oh, did I ever check the Jeep and fall straight into your trap!*

"No, honey. I haven't had one. As a matter of fact, I haven't smoked in a few days. I'm proud of myself."

"Are you sure? Absolutely and positively sure? Because I don't care if you did. But I *will* be angry if you are lying."

"I didn't smoke."

"Really? Look at me and swear."

Pablo looked right at me with a dead serious expression. "I swear I didn't smoke."

"Swear to God, not to me. And shame on you if you lie to God."

"I would *never* do that," he said and pulled out his crucifix. "See, honey? I swear to God I didn't smoke."

"LIAR! I CAN'T BELIEVE YOU JUST DID THAT! YOU WOULD EVEN LIE TO GOD!"

"Honey, calm down. My parents are downstairs. They can hear us."

I didn't care. "I *know* you lie."

"Honey, calm down. I didn't lie. Why do you think I am lying?"

I didn't want to give away my secrets to him anymore. I wouldn't tell him about the marked cigarettes. "I just know, that's why. I know more than you think!" I wanted to end it all. So I opened the refrigerator and took out one of his precious bottles and uncapped it. Pablo watched, horrified.

"How much do I have to take for it to kill me?" I asked calmly.

Pablo said, "Three swallows would do it."

Should I? Three swallows. So now I knew.

Pablo watched, waiting.

I recapped the bottle.

"No. This is yours. I'll use my medicine," I said, mocking him. Then I went to the liquor cabinet and took out all the liquor: Pablo's scotch, my vodka, Pablo's cognac, and some gin the Garcias had stocked in the cabinet before we had arrived. I poured it out into little cups, measuring it first, just like Pablo did with his medicine. Then I drank it down. Each measured cup. All the liquor. Everything I could find, I measured out and drank methodically while Pablo watched.

Then I said, "Pills? Did you say you took pills in your drug days? Well, then I want to be JUST LIKE YOU."

I went into the bathroom and took out the bottle of Excedrin PMs that Pablo had introduced me to. One or two before bed would promise a good night's sleep, and I wanted to sleep *forever*. I took the top off the bottle and put a huge handful of pills in my mouth. I swallowed them all. Then I took another handful of the blue tablets. Then another. And another. *There. If I don't die now, I don't know what I'll do for an encore.*

I staggered into the bedroom. Pablo followed me.

"Come on honey, throw them up. Throw up the pills. I know you can if you want."

"No. I don't want to."

I don't remember anything after that. I must have passed out. Eventually, though, I did wake up. *Would this never end???*

I don't know how long I was out cold. Hours, days, I didn't know and didn't care. Pablo was home when I woke up. I wanted to show him that I could be bad, too. I wanted to show him that I was worse, but lately it was getting really difficult. After reading the books at the library a few weeks earlier I had said to Pablo, "You know when we used to have that argument about who was worse? Well, you won. You *are* worse." Now, it seemed I was trying to win back the argument. If only I could be worse, then maybe I could gain back some respect for him and put him back up on his pedestal. If I wasn't worse than Pablo, I was better off dead. But I wasn't dead.

Late that night, as awful as I felt, I decided what I would do. I would leave. I couldn't take it anymore. I didn't know where I would go or what I would do, but staying with Pablo was killing me. I was doing all this to *show* him what he was doing to us. I wanted my actions to have some kind of effect on him and make him change. But I didn't seem to have any effect on him. He continued to live his lies and take his drugs. Nothing I did mattered.

I packed everything that was mine.

"Honey, what are you doing?" Pablo sat up in bed.

"I'm leaving you, Pablo. I mean it. Staying with you is killing me." I continued to pack. I didn't want to think about leaving. I just wanted to do it—get out of this evil place.

Most of my stuff was packed in the Jeep. It was one o'clock in the morning and pitch black out. Good. The Garcias won't see me leave.

Pablo got out of bed. He hadn't taken me seriously at first. He knew I couldn't live without him. Now, he was worried that maybe I meant it.

I made my last trip for bathroom stuff. I separated Pablo's things from mine, packing them up in a duffel bag. I was taking every little thing that belonged to me. Pablo could see that I wasn't kidding. I really was leaving him.

Pablo followed me to the door. "Don't leave me." He reached over and hugged me. "I can't live without you," he said, sounding genuinely sad, like a little child. He pulled me back and kissed me again and again. "Please don't go. I *need* you."

It sounded like he meant it. No games this time.

"Really, you mean that? Staying here like this is killing me. I have to go, for my sake." I looked at the door, caught between here and there. If I didn't just go, he would melt me, trap me with his love, make me into a "with Pablo" again. Momentarily, I had my independence. For the first time, with this plan, I was thinking clearly. My mind was set, but deep down I wished he wanted me back. I wished it could be like before. "Really? You need me?" How could I leave my husband in his time of need?

A tear rolled down his cheek. Yes, a tear.

"Pablo, I've never seen you cry." I thought it was impossible for him to cry on the medicine. He must love me! He must!

"See honey? That's how much I love you. I couldn't bear life without you."

"Okay. Okay." The teardrop had done it. The tear was evidence that he loved me and not the medicine.

I unpacked my bags and stayed.

"Pablo, what did you think when I drank all that liquor and swallowed all those pills?"

"I thought I was going to lose you. I thought you were going to die."

"What did you do then?"

Pablo touched my head, caressing my hair, "I prayed to God that you would live."

"You did?" I was impressed. God had answered Pablo's prayers.

"Yes, honey. And I knew He would save you."

I was so happy. Pablo loved me. He really did. He had prayed for me!

Logically, Pablo should have rushed me to a hospital. Months later I asked others what they would have done in his situation and they had replied, "Taken you to a hospital to have your stomach pumped." But in Florida I wasn't thinking logically. In my desperation to see Pablo the way I had in the beginning, I was blind.

The Vince/Pablo dreams were worse than ever in Florida. Both men were still the same person in my dreams. Now, I couldn't decide which was worse—my nightmares or my reality.

Subconsciously, Pablo and Vince were beginning to merge into one. The lies and deceit felt the same. Their words were exactly the same: "You are everything to me," and, "I can't live without you." But this was a lie. My emotions from way down deep were stirring and groaning. The repressed pain of Vince's betrayal was surfacing with twice the intensity. I didn't realize that the pain of Pablo's lies was directly related to the pain of Vince's lies because I had no memory of Vince's lies!!! Long ago, out of guilt and in order to survive, I had buried them in a very deep place, blocked and hidden from my conscious memory. Now, with these familiar feelings, Pablo was Vince, back to haunt me, to lie to me, to desert me in my hour of need (when Mom found the letter). All my anger and hurt came up out of me like an erupting volcano, spewing forth pain and old feelings that had never seen the light of day. If it weren't for the pain of my buried, unresolved past, I may have been able to act more rationally and see Pablo's problem for what it was—drug addiction—and not as a direct attack on me. But because it felt like the past, my reactions were extreme. I couldn't bear another rejection. Emotionally, the betrayal was intertwined; it felt one and the same.

Pablo and I were in bed. I couldn't stand the reality I was living, but I couldn't stand the reality of my dreams, either. Asleep or awake, it was all a nightmare. I was drunk and had the courage to say the words to Pablo that I had been thinking for days.

"Finish me off," I said to Pablo.

I had sworn to Vince that if Mom ever found out the secret, I would kill myself. I wanted Vince to know how much pain the secret was causing me. When Mom found Vince's letter, I thought for sure Vince would care and call me. I thought he would rescue me from killing myself. He never did. So I had repressed my suicidal feelings, stuffed the pain of Vince's betrayal, and gone on with my life, my riding. Now, with Pablo's betrayal, I could stuff the pain no longer. I would do what I should have done years ago. But I needed help. I couldn't do it alone. The pain that Vince had caused I now wanted Pablo to end—to "finish me off."

"What, honey?"

"Finish me off. I can't do it. I don't have the guts."

"Huh?"

"You know. Just do it. It must be done. Choke me. Kill me. Do whatever it takes. I just can't live like this anymore."

Pablo leaned over me.

"Just *do* it!" I urged, taking his hands and putting them around my neck. "Go ahead, now. Choke me. Finish me off."

Pablo tightened his grip and started choking me. It felt good. I would just nod off into painless oblivion. Suddenly, I gasped for air. My body didn't like what was happening and wasn't going along with my wishes. This was going to hurt.

I struggled a little, and then tried to accept my fate. I was choking and gagging as Pablo tightened his grip and forced me down hard. My back hurt. I gave up and relaxed my body. My fate was sealed.

Why, then, did Pablo let go of me? Now, why did he do that?

I breathed in the precious air. "Pablo, you hurt my back."

"I'm sorry, honey."

My throat and back hurt. But physical pain was much more tolerable than emotional pain. For now, it distracted me. Just for now. I would fall asleep concentrating on the physical pain. It was the closest thing to counting sheep, and much better. The sheep always took the form of Vince's face. I couldn't let my mind drift off my pain for one second.

Pablo seemed more comatose than usual. I think he was taking higher doses of the methadone, or something. I didn't quite understand the effect it had on him, or should have had on him, if at all. Pablo said it made him feel "normal," whatever that was. Normal for Pablo or normal for normal?

I had asked him, "That's the only effect? "

"Well, it does take away your emotions. That's why it's so incredible that I can feel so much love for you." (Remember the tear?)

Yes, according to Pablo, his love for me was so strong that it could overcome the numbing effects of methadone.

Things were so out of control. I remembered God and said a prayer asking Him to help me. Two minutes later I discovered a thin red book on a shelf in the condo. I had never noticed it before. Simply written, each short chapter quoted a different passage from the Bible and then explained the message. I couldn't imagine a timelier discovery. It was definitely a miracle. To me, it was a light in the evil day. Surely, God was reaching out to me when I remembered to cry out to Him.

I didn't want to sleep in the bedroom with Pablo anymore. Most nights I spent on the couch, reading the red book. It made me feel safe. The living room felt like the safest part of the condo. The bedroom felt especially evil. I would kiss Pablo good night and leave him there in the bedroom. I didn't have bad dreams when I slept on the couch. Or maybe it was because I was reading the red book about God.

Each winter, my grandmother stayed in Pompano Beach at her apartment. It was only an hour away from us. One day I went for a boat ride on the waterway with her and her friends. It was a nice change of pace from the insanity I was living. It felt strange to be "normal" and sane around her and her friends. At one point when we were alone, I told my grandmother that things weren't going so well with Pablo and that he had a secret drug addiction. I knew I needed support, but Pablo discouraged me from telling Mom. Even though Grandma didn't understand, she promised not to tell my mother. However, she did tell my sister, Susan. Out of deep concern, my sister started sending me long encouraging letters with Bible verses in them. It really did help. Just when it seemed like I couldn't take it anymore, one of her letters would arrive. She also called me.

"Hi, Kar." She sounded so close, yet so far away. Everyone was so far away. Nobody understood. You had to live through this to understand how it felt. "I've been so worried about you," she said. "I've been praying for you ever since I heard from Grandma. I pray with a believer at school. We pray for you and Pablo, but mostly for you. What can I do? Do you want me to come down?"

I couldn't believe she was offering to come down! What a great sister! But, I couldn't have her do that—not without Pablo's approval. She would have to know about the drugs, and as it was she knew too much already.

"Mom can't know about this," I explained. "Promise me you won't tell her. Pablo says she would just love to find out I had a failing marriage."

"I don't think that's true. But, if that's the way you feel about it, I promise not to say anything. I can come down any time—at a moment's notice. Just let me know, okay?"

I told Pablo about Susan's offer.

"Your sister has serious problems," he said, shaking his head. "She would just complicate things and make matters worse."

What problems? My sister was just trying to help, to be there for me.

Pablo didn't want me to be around anyone who might knock some sense into me, especially a caring family member. And Susan or my mother would have been just that.

Susan continued to stay in touch by phone and letters. An instrument of God, she kept me from falling too far. The verses she sent were just what I needed in my darkest hours. Like the verse about God not allowing me to endure more than I could handle, and providing a way of escape.

"No temptation has overtaken you but such as is common to man; and God is faithful, who will not allow you to be tempted beyond what you are able, but with the temptation will provide the way of escape also, so that you will be able to endure it." – 1 Corinthians 10:13 (NASB)

My faith at this time was still shaky, at best. Thank God He is true to His word and didn't allow me to endure more than what I could bear. It sure seemed close, though. God, in His mercy, kept sending me lifelines to barely keep my head above water. He really did love me. Only after all this was over could I appreciate this verse:

"And not only this, but we also exult in our tribulations, knowing that tribulation brings about perseverance; and perseverance, proven character; and proven character, hope; and hope does not disappoint, because the love of God has been poured out within our hearts through the Holy Spirit who was given to us." – Romans 5:3-5 (NASB)

I felt as if I was being tossed around in a giant storm. There was no stability left in my life; I had lost every good thing I knew. Even my old life with Pablo was gone. We were in a different state, but it felt like we were in a different universe, the twilight zone.

One day when I was really angry with Pablo, he took the Jeep and didn't come back. I stayed up all night, worrying. I was worried sick about him and promised myself that if he came back, I would be nicer to him. Suddenly, it hit me. He *has* to come home to take his methadone! I raced around the apartment, looking in all the hiding places. (Pablo still insisted on hiding the bottles and not keeping them in the refrigerator.) *All the bottles were gone!* He was gone for good! He had *left* me! My mind was racing. What if he took *all* the methadone and killed himself? That is what I would have done if I were him. Yes, that was what he was doing. I was sure of it. And it was all my fault. I had pushed him so much, pushed him right over the edge.

In a panic, I dialed Dr. Davis. It was very late.

"Hello?" The voice sounded sleepy.

"Dr. Davis? Oh, I'm so sorry to wake you. But this is an emergency. Pablo is gone. He left yesterday, and I think he's gone and killed himself."

"What makes you think that?" he sounded more alert now.

"Because he took all his methadone with him. He has never been gone for the whole night before. He always came home."

"Relax, Karen. He probably went some place to get away. To think. He is in a pretty bad situation, you know."

"I know. That's what makes me think he killed himself. That's what I would do."

"But Pablo is not you. You and Pablo think differently. He is not the suicidal type, I don't think. I think you should wait a while before you panic. Call him at work. He wouldn't miss work, would he?"

"No. But he would if he was *dead*."

"You're overreacting. Call him at work in the morning. I'm sure he'll show up there. Call me later at my office. And Karen, will you promise me you won't do anything to yourself? This isn't your fault, you know."

"It is my fault."

"No, it isn't. Pablo got himself in this thing. And nothing you do will change what he has planned. So do me a favor. Go back to bed. Call Pablo at the track in the morning and then call me. And don't do anything else, okay? I've tried to be there for you. Now you've got to do this for me. Okay? Karen?"

"Okay. I will, for you. Thanks...for everything."

"I'll talk to you later. I'm sure Pablo will be at work, and you will be feeling much better. Bye, now."

Dr. Davis was so sensible. Was he right about Pablo? That, unlike me, he wouldn't have thought about suicide? I couldn't comprehend it. Pablo and I were the same, weren't we?

I went in the living room and prayed. I read the little red book and waited for the sun to rise. Just after dawn, I dialed the barn. Then I held my breath.

"Hello?" Someone picked up!

"Is Pablo there?" I asked, hoping, praying. *Please, let him be there!*

"Uh, yeah. Hold on a sec."

He's alive!!! I couldn't wait to hear his voice.

As I waited, the anger started welling up in me. Why did he do this to me? Why? He knew I would worry.

"Hello?" It was Pablo, sounding completely normal. Not dead. Not even close. It was business as usual, for him. It was as if I didn't even exist. Thank God for Dr. Davis. He had been right. Pablo *didn't* think like me. He didn't even care what I thought or how I felt!

"Oh, Pablo! Where have you been? I've been so worried." I honestly didn't know how I felt anymore. The relief had fast given way to anger. But I had promised myself I would behave if he was all right.

"Could you call me later? I've got to go out to the track with a set," he said, sounding annoyed with me. Of course. It was always my fault.

"Okay." I wanted to be nice. I didn't want him to leave again. I don't think I could have taken it. Later on, I called Dr. Davis to give him the good news and to apologize for my late night phone call. It had seemed like an emergency to me at the time.

"That's okay. Keep me informed," he said.

Pablo came home that morning. Late, but at least he came home. I asked him where he had been.

"I went to Ft. Lauderdale to look at some more sailboats."

"Did you see any nice ones?" I asked, feeling as if I had just been slapped in the face. I liked looking at boats, and he had gone and left me out!

"Yes. I saw two beautiful boats."

"Can I go back with you and see them?"

"I'm not sure if they are still there at the dock. It was a one shot deal. They may have sailed out again. That was why I just had to go yesterday." *Why hadn't he told me? Why hadn't he taken me along??? Because I was horrible and selfish, that's why.*

Trying hard to be nicer, I suggested we go see a movie. *Dirty Dancing,* which was playing nearby, was supposed to be good. Much to my surprise, Pablo agreed to go. While watching the movie, I became immersed in the love story, in the never-never land of happy endings. The couple in the movie reminded me of Pablo and me when we first dated. It could be like that again, couldn't it? We could make it work. All this wasn't real anyway, was it? The methadone was no big deal. It just wasn't. I was overreacting to everything, wasn't I? Things were going to be normal and sane again, just like in the movie. I held onto the feeling as we left the theater. Hold onto that good feeling. Hold on.

"Don't you feel good, Pablo? Wasn't that movie great??!!" I pretended Pablo was Patrick Swayze as I walked beside him.

"It was okay, but a little unrealistic. Nobody would just go off like that at the end. I mean, the guy was a loser and just because he fell for that young girl didn't mean he was going to get his life together."

I know. I know. Pablo had told me this a thousand times. Movies are so unrealistic. And so predictable. And he could write a better script. Well, why didn't he then? And make it our life. I was ready for a new script. So ready. "But, Pablo, it had a happy ending. They were in love. They were going to stay together and make it work."

"It was just a movie. Don't you see that? This is real life. Here. You and me." *And don't forget the methadone, Pablo. It's part of your movie, your script.*

That night I stayed in the bed with Pablo. Finally, I fell asleep. I dreamed about the Vince/Pablo man and wanted to die. In the dream, I felt loved and hated at the same time. The Vince/Pablo man said, "I can't live without you....I never loved your mother....I live only for you." In the dream, I was watching from afar. Vince/Pablo's face was contorted as his hands went over my body. I watched his dirty hands touch my dirty body. Dirty hands, dirty body. Vince's face, Vince's words. Lies. But it was really Pablo. Then I woke up. It was morning.

I looked over at Pablo in the bed. Pablo loved me, didn't he? I could trust him, couldn't I? *He* could touch me. *He* wouldn't hurt me. No. Pablo didn't love me anymore, either. I felt sick to my stomach. I wondered if when Vince did those things to me, saying he loved me, if I would have felt differently with a more mature body.

"Do it to me, Pablo." I said, waking him up. I needed to know.

"Do what?"

"You know."

We hadn't been intimate in ages. However, when he got close to me, I felt no love for him and became cold. I felt violated. I hated it. But I deserved this, didn't I? Was this love or hate? It was like with Vince. The familiar feeling put me into such a depressed state that I started to cry. Why had I gone and done that?

"What's wrong with you?" Pablo asked me as I cried.

"I wanted to see what it was like now, as an adult, when I didn't want to do it. I always did it with you when I was in love with you, when I wanted you."

I hadn't meant to offend Pablo, just to put the pieces together and figure out if I would have liked it back then if I had been physically mature. Well, now I had my answer. I wouldn't have.

Pablo glared at me. "So now you've done it—what you've always wanted to do. You've made me into *Vince*."

"No, Pablo. I swear. I didn't *want* that. I just wanted to see if I could like the physical part, without the love."

Pablo stormed out of the bedroom. He was *really* angry with me. I hadn't meant to hurt him, had I? He really hates me now, and it's all my fault. But, it's easier to take that way. Now I can go ahead and kill myself.

Had I turned Pablo into Vince, subconsciously? Had I made the transformation complete? Pablo seemed to think so. With the completion of turning Pablo into Vince, I now had the resolve to kill myself, the way I had always told Vince I would. My next action seemed to confirm that maybe I was, without consciously knowing it, reenacting the past. Now all it needed was the right ending.

How could I kill myself? What would work? I went through the condo, looking for something to use to choke myself. Finally, I found a piece of rope in the closet. I brought it to Pablo in the living room. "I'm going to choke myself, Pablo." I went back into the bedroom and pulled the rope around my neck, tighter and tighter. But I wasn't dying.

Pablo came into the bedroom. "You're not doing it right," he said. "Here, let me have it." He loosened the rope and took it back off my head. Then he tied a knot in it. He instructed me on how to use the knot and where to place it on my throat so that it would choke me.

"And you can't do it like that," he explained. "You have to hang from something." He took the rope into the bathroom. I followed. "Use the shower head. Tie it and put the knot on your throat." He handed me the rope. He had looped the end into a perfect noose. Then he left me in the bathroom and shut the door behind him.

I climbed into the tub and tied the rope to the shower head. I put the noose around my neck and bent my knees so that I would be short enough to hang. The rope pulled down. It stretched and tightened around my neck. Blood was pounding in my head. I was seeing spots and starting to pass out. Dizziness...spots...

Bang! I hit my head on the hard tub. My throat hurt. The rope was still around my neck. How long had I been....I looked up at the shower head. It was all bent down out of shape. A piece had broken off the end, causing the rope to slip off.

I sat up in the cold tub and rubbed my head. I was going to have a lump where my head hit so hard. Suddenly, I thought about Pablo. I wondered where he was and what he was thinking.

Still dizzy, I got out of the tub slowly and went to the bathroom door. I remembered Pablo shutting it behind him. I went into the living room, but he wasn't there.

"Pablo? Pablo!"

Maybe he is in the kitchen?

No.

Where had he gone? Had he left me? Oh, no, not again. Well, it was my fault. I had been acting bad again.

I ran outside, looking for the Jeep. It was gone.

I hated myself. I hated my life. Why did the shower nozzle have to break loose? There must be some reason. *There must.*

I took up the methadone search, once again. If he was leaving for a while, his stash would be gone.

It was.

He had probably gone off to kill himself, thinking I was dead and we could be together. Oh, God. This was all my fault. He would be dead now, and I was still alive. Couldn't I do *anything* right?

I waited, hoping that maybe Pablo would change his mind and come home. I waited for two hours. Then a thought crossed my mind. Maybe he went to look at the boats, like before! It was worth a try. If he went to look at boats, maybe I could catch him *before* he killed himself. But how would I get to Ft. Lauderdale? It was only a hunch, but still.

I called a cab and was off to Ft. Lauderdale. When we got close to the docks, I spotted our black Jeep in the parking lot. Pablo was here! He was alive! I paid the cab driver and headed over to the Jeep to do a little detective work.

The Jeep was locked. I looked in the window and saw a pack of Marlboro cigarettes on the seat. Right away I got angry. *Don't be mad. Don't be bad. Not now. I must find Pablo and stop him from doing anything to himself.* I peered through all the windows as I walked around the Jeep. I wondered where he had hidden his methadone bottles. From what I could see, there was no sign of them.

Next, I headed off to find Pablo. I tried the boat sales office, but the door was locked. He was probably off looking at another sailboat. I decided to leave Pablo a note (so he wouldn't leave without me) and walk around the docks until he got back. I found a pen and paper at a motel office next door. Then I left the note on the windshield of the Jeep.

Feeling alone and unwanted, I walked around the docks for about an hour. Heading back, I spotted Pablo and the boat salesman coming out of the office. I wanted to be happy to see him, but didn't know how to feel anymore.

"What are *you* doing here?" Pablo asked when he saw me.

"I came to find you. I figured you would be here, like the last time you left."

"How did you get here?" he asked me. I wondered if he had thought I was still hanging from the shower, dead.

"I have my secrets, too, you know." I was insanely jealous of his new thing—leaving me out of his life.

"I looked at some nice sailboats," he said casually.

"Can I go back and see them with you?"

Pablo started to unlock the Jeep and saw my note. He read the note and then let it drop to the ground. I watched it fly away. A strong ocean breeze sent it soaring into the air, and then it disappeared underneath the bridge. It reappeared again and settled a few feet from the waterway.

"Get in," he said.

I went around to the other side of the Jeep and got in. I noticed that the guilty pack of cigarettes was now mysteriously gone. Of course. Pablo would have hidden it.

"Pablo, did you think I was dead?" I asked, breaking the silence on the ride home.

"No. I fixed the knot so it couldn't choke you." He looked ahead, not even glancing my way.

"You...I thought you fixed it so it *would* choke me." Maybe he did love me, after all.

I pulled out the ash tray and pointed to the cigarette ashes. "Have you been smoking, Pablo?"

"No. They're old." He was probably lying.

Pablo pulled off the road.

"Where are we going, Pablo?"

"I checked into the Marriott this morning. I have to get my stuff."

So that's where the methadone was! I waited in the car while he checked back out of the hotel. Then we continued on to Palm Springs North. We were complete now, one big happy family: Pablo, the methadone...and me.

Looking back on this, I question why Pablo had checked into a hotel that morning, leaving me hanging in the shower. Was the motel check-in and being with the boat salesman his alibi for when the police found me dead in the shower? Why did Pablo seem to want me dead? Was it because he couldn't get away with lying to me anymore? Was it because he had lost control over me, with all my drinking and suicide attempts? Or was it simply because if I were dead, he would inherit my house and sell it for his precious drugs?

When we got back, Pablo sat in front of the television. Nothing seemed to faze him. I wondered how much of the methadone he had been taking lately, and what effect it had on him. Suddenly, it hit me. We can't sail around the world in a sailboat! Federal Express had to bring Pablo his package twice a week!

"Pablo, you know getting a bigger sailboat is stupid. We can't sail to the South Seas like you want. I know *Shogun* is your favorite movie, but you can't be like Richard Chamberlain. Federal Express won't drop your package off in the middle of the ocean. First thing's first. You have to get off the medicine."

Pablo didn't take his eyes off the television. "I know. You're right."

Reality was finally hitting me. Pablo wasn't going anywhere, and neither was I. By five o'clock I decided what I would do. I was already on my way to getting drunk. I didn't care anymore. I didn't care about anything. We had no future. We had no life. Yes, I knew what I would do. I would take his methadone. Why not? If he wasn't going to get off it, then at least this would make me like him, finally. It was the only answer left. It was the only way to share in his total conspiracy, his way of life. Then his problem would be my problem, too.

"Pablo?"

"Huh?"

"How much methadone do you have? Enough to last a while? Any extra?"

"Yeah. I've been cutting down, so I have extra that I should throw away."

"Can I take it, then?"

"NO! Never, *ever* take the methadone. It's extremely dangerous. I told you that!"

I left him in the den and went to the refrigerator. I had seen him unload it into the fridge when we got home from Ft. Lauderdale. I opened the refrigerator door and took out a bottle.

Pablo was right behind me. "What are you doing?"

"I'm just...looking at it. I wonder what it's like to take. It looks harmless enough. How much did you say it would take to kill me?

"About a normal dose. Three tablespoons. Maybe less." Pablo took the bottle from my hand and returned it to the refrigerator.

"You just don't want to share it, that's all. You want it ALL to yourself. You and your methadone. You'll never get off it, so I might as well be like you and take it, too."

"No. I'll get off it," Pablo argued.

"When?"

"As soon as...as..."

I quickly grabbed the bottle, uncapped it, and put it in my mouth. I was sick of listening to his lies. I wanted to try it, to be like him, and to get to him.

"Honey, spit it out," Pablo said vehemently, turning sheet white. I had a mouthful and hadn't yet gotten the courage to swallow it.

"Spit it out! This isn't funny."

I had my cheeks puffed out, so he knew it was still in my mouth. Now Pablo grabbed my cheeks, trying to make me spit it out.

NO! *I would do it.* Gulp. *There.* "There, Pablo. Now I've done it."

"Heave. Go heave. Throw it up! Do it! Now!"

"Why? You think it will *kill* me?" I laughed. I wondered if it would kill me. I only took one big swallow. I didn't think it would be enough to do it. We'll see, though. "I don't feel anything," I said, smiling at him.

Pablo was angry, very angry. "I can't believe you took it." He shook his head and left me standing there. He went back into the living room. Was he leaving me to die? Again? I followed him into the living room.

"Now I can be a drug addict—just like you," I said with a smile.

Pablo shook his head in disbelief. He had finally lost total control of me. Now the drug was starting to take effect, taking control of me where he couldn't. I was lying on the floor.

"Pablo, Pablo, my back is broken!!" I felt like I did in the hospital when my back was broken from the Monmouth Park spill. I lay there, paralyzed.

Pablo looked down at me from his perch on the chair. "You just think it's broken. It isn't. Trust me."

"It is. I know it. I know what it feels like."

"You are just feeling the effects of the drug. They probably gave you morphine when you broke your back and that's what you are feeling. The sensation of morphine is probably like methadone."

Could he be right? I now felt *exactly* the way I did when I was in the hospital down at Monmouth. I couldn't move then. I had broken three vertebrae and they hadn't put me in the body cast yet. They were afraid to move me. This was *just* the way it had felt. "Are you sure?" I asked.

"Sure. You just never knew you were on morphine then."

"Then I *can* move? My back is okay?"

"Yeah. Go ahead. Get up."

I moved slowly onto my side. I rolled ever so slowly, the way they had turned me in the hospital to prevent pneumonia from setting in.

Hmm. There was no pain...yet. Maybe Pablo was right. This was all just a sensation. Wasn't this strange??!!

Finally, I sat up. Pablo was right! My back was fine.

I took up my usual place on the couch. "This is nothing, Pablo. The methadone isn't killing me," I said, smiling again.

Pablo shook his head, thoroughly disgusted with me. "I'm going to read," he said, getting up and heading for the bedroom. I followed him. I felt great! I got into the bed next to Pablo and talked about everything under the sun. I was in such a good mood! I felt no emotional pain and had the answers to the world's problems; *nothing* could bother me now!

I don't know how long I talked that night. Like in the hospital when I broke my back, I wasn't aware of time. I didn't think the drug had much effect on me, but I did get sick to my stomach.

"Why am I so sick, Pablo?"

"Because you took the medicine."

"No, it can't be that. I only took a tiny amount!"

I ran back into the bathroom. It actually felt good to retch. Now Pablo could see me physically suffering. This was good. It was better to physically retch than to feel emotional pain.

In the morning, Pablo wouldn't talk to me.

"Oh, it wasn't so bad, Pablo. I liked it. Come on, let me have more."

"You were sick all night, and you say it *wasn't so bad???*"

"It didn't *make* me sick. I was sick anyway. You're just saying that so I won't take any more of your precious medicine. You want to keep it all to yourself!" He was just saying that it made me sick, wasn't he? That tiny little bit couldn't have had that much of an effect on me. At least, I didn't think so at the time. Pablo was just lying again, same as usual. "Anyway, it didn't have any effect on me," I said.

"The hell it didn't. You wouldn't shut up for hours."

"Really?" I didn't remember talking that much. Well, maybe. Then I was too sick to talk. But it couldn't have been because of that tiny amount of orange liquid. Was I becoming addicted? So fast? Or was it just in my mind?

Pablo looked at me. Maybe he was sad that I was becoming like him and that I wouldn't listen to him anymore. Now I had all the answers, just like him.

Pablo finally spoke. "Look at what I've done to you." He shook his head sadly. "I'm leaving. I can't stand what I'm doing to you. I can't trust you here with the medicine anymore."

He took all of the methadone out of the refrigerator. I was sorry to see it go. Then, with all of the methadone, including his hidden "extra" bottles, he left me. "I'll call you," he said as he went out the door.

I watched him go. Maybe it was better this way.

I didn't worry about Pablo this time. I was worried about myself. If

I didn't get it together, Pablo never would. I had to be strong and behave better so I could help him. I hadn't been doing a very good job of that. I had thought that I could scare him into action, but I had only been making things worse.

So there I was, alone.

What should I do?

The apartment was a mess, but I didn't care. My life with Pablo was the real mess, the important one, the one that needed to be cleaned up.

I knew I needed help. I needed someone to talk to, someone that understood what I was going through. I needed a new direction, and not a destructive one.

I opened up the yellow pages and started with A. When I got to "alcoholism," an ad caught my eye:

THERE IS HOPE...THERE IS HELP!
AN AFFORDABLE ALTERNATIVE PROGRAM
FOR THE CHEMICALLY DEPENDENT

Hmm. It was a start. I called the number, which turned out to be Alcoholics Anonymous, or AA. The woman who answered asked me where I lived. I gave her the address, but explained that I had no car.

"Well, you are in luck. There are no meetings within thirty miles of you, but a new group started about a month ago and they are quite possibly within walking distance." She gave me the number and wished me luck. God was looking out for me, once again. Whenever I sought help, He was there.

When I called the number, a man named Bill answered and informed me that I was less than a mile away and that they were having a meeting in just one hour! "Why don't you come down here right away?" he asked, encouraging me. "You can talk to me before the meeting starts."

"Okay. I'll be walking, though. It might take some time."

"I'll come and pick you up then."

Wasn't he nice? I hoped he was as nice in person as he was on the phone. Still, I declined the offer. "Thank you. That is so nice of you, but I prefer to walk. I'll see you soon." I hung up the phone, hoping that I would find some direction and some positive answers for my dilemma.

Chapter 65
Left Out

I headed along the highway, walking with a little spring in my step. I thought positive thoughts. *This is going to be good. God is sending me here, maybe for answers.*

I spotted the mini shopping mall where the "meeting" was supposed to be. There was a Pizza Hut. Mmm. And a food mart. And another pizza place. Food. Forget the food.

I kept walking, looking in all the store windows. I passed a laundry mat and a liquor store. I slowed my pace and considered turning back. No! I *have* to go through with this. Finally, I came to a glass store front with a curtain concealing the inside. I gathered all my courage and went in. There were lots of chairs in an empty, carpeted room. A man had his back to me and was pouring himself a cup of freshly brewed coffee. It smelled good.

He turned around and smiled. "Hello. Are you Karen?"

"Yes. You are Bill?"

"That's right. Like some coffee? It's fresh. I just made it." He poured me a cup of coffee and explained a little about AA. "This afternoon is a women's meeting. I'll introduce you to the girls, and I think you'll be quite comfortable. So, tell me, what brought you here?" Bill asked kindly.

"It's a long story." I briefly told Bill about Pablo, the drugs, and all the craziness. "I just don't know what to do."

"Sounds like your husband should go to NA."

"What's that?" I asked.

"Narcotics Anonymous."

"But I like it here. I think he would, too." I thought about bringing Pablo here to meet Bill. Bill would tell him what to do. "Does it make any difference if he goes to NA or AA?" I asked.

"Well, if he has a drug problem, he will relate better to the people who took the same drug. Alcohol is a drug, but it's different from other drugs. But, as we say in the program, a drug is a drug is a drug."

"Pablo went somewhere. But when he comes back, I think I'll bring him here. Can you talk to him?"

"Sure. Now, here come a few of the ladies. Sit down and make yourself at home. I'm sure you'll make some new friends!"

The women in the group were nice and seemed concerned about my situation. They kept telling me that I needed to focus on myself and not on Pablo. I couldn't comprehend this. Maybe they just didn't understand my situation. Pablo and I were in this together. We were like one. Couldn't they see?

I spent the entire day with the people at AA. There was a meeting in the evening, and when it was over someone gave me a ride home. Pablo had not returned, and did not come back that night.

Dr. Davis called me in the morning. He said Pablo had called him and told him to call me. "Pablo didn't want to call you because of your suicidal tendencies whenever you are with him or talk to him," Dr. Davis explained.

"Where is he?" I asked Dr. Davis.

"He just told me to tell you he was safe and that he would be back soon. He was afraid to call you because you might do something to yourself."

Why was Pablo suddenly interested in my welfare? He had never wanted to talk to Dr. Davis before. Why now? Although what Pablo said about my suicidal tendencies was true, was he now contacting Dr. Davis to free himself from any blame should I end up dead?

"Oh. Well, if he calls you again," I said, "tell him to come home. I want to take him to a place I went, AA. They were really nice and understanding there. Maybe they could help Pablo."

"Are you all right, then?"

"Yes. I'm fine. Just call me if Pablo calls you again. I can't wait to take him to this place. But don't tell him about it. He may not want to go. He hates to be around other people, and I wouldn't want to scare him off. He only trusts me."

"Take care, Karen. And call me if you need to."

"I won't need to. Things are going to be better."

I felt better having been around other people and not just Pablo. I felt more normal. I wanted Pablo to feel good, to feel normal, too. To pass the time, I spent another afternoon at AA. Walking home later, I wondered if Pablo would come to a meeting with me. When the condo came into sight, I spotted the Jeep parked outside. Pablo was home! I ran the rest of the way.

"Pablo!"

Pablo came out of the kitchen, dragging his feet.

"Oh, I'm so glad you came back!" I said, going over and giving him a hug. He looked like he was just getting up from his nap. He had a cup of coffee in his hand. "Guess what?" I asked cheerfully, following him to his chair.

"Let me wake up first," he said, sitting down.

"How long have you been here? Did you take a nap?"

"I came back an hour ago. I wondered where you were. Where were you?"

"That's what I want to tell you about." I leaned over and kissed him.

"Boy, you're in a good mood. What happened to you?"

"I went to this place and met some nice people."

Pablo glared at me. Then his look softened. "Where did you go, honey? Tell me about it."

"I want to take you there. I want to show you."

"The truck should have been here by now."

"What?" Suddenly, it occurred to me that it was Monday, Federal Express day. One of them, anyway.

"I hope the package comes soon," he said, distracted.

"Pablo, I thought you had extra bottles. I was worried before that you might try to kill yourself, but Dr. Davis said you..." I stopped myself. I didn't want Pablo to think Dr. Davis knew about him or that we talked about him.

"Dr. Davis said what?"

"Uh, he said you were fine, that you called him to say you were fine."

"Yeah, I did."

"So I wasn't worried about you killing yourself. I was worried the first time you left, though, when you didn't call me. I was worried you would overdose on the methadone."

"Well, I almost did overdose." Pablo looked at me, waiting for a reaction.

"You *what?* You *did* try to kill yourself?"

"I took all the medicine I had. All of it. I could see what I was doing to you—to us—and I hated it. So I took all the extra."

"To try to kill yourself?"

Pablo nodded.

Dr. Davis was wrong, then. Pablo *was* the suicidal type. I knew it. I just knew Pablo thought like me.

The Federal Express truck finally showed up. But Pablo was visibly upset. I guess he didn't get the amount that he was expecting. Or, maybe now that he had taken so much, he was back on a higher dose. It was time to end all this. I just had to get Pablo to a meeting.

"Pablo, come with me to meet the people I told you about."

"Where? Who are they?"

"They know about these things. They can help us. And they are anonymous. They don't care who you are. They just want to help. You have to meet Bill. I told him about you."

"You told *who what*?"

"Come with me. Bill is really nice."

I wouldn't tell Pablo anymore. I had raised his suspicious curiosity. This, for Pablo, was a chance to play detective, like in all those movies he watched. Besides, I thought, now he would come with me—to find out who else "knew."

We got to the meeting before it started. Bill talked to Pablo. Pablo was so congenial, Mr. Friendly. And so receptive to it all. I was very surprised. I wondered what Pablo was thinking. What was he up to?

I overheard Bill telling Pablo that he had been in a hospital to detox from alcohol. Bill explained that it had gotten that bad and he couldn't do it on his own. "It's nothing to be ashamed about," Bill explained to Pablo. "As long as I attend my meetings, I can stay sober. It's been three years now. I'm a new man."

As the meeting began, Pablo and I sat in the circle. I was so proud of him. My new friends could see now that I wasn't lying about my situation: my husband really did have a drug problem and I wasn't crazy.

As Pablo shared, everyone had their full attention on him, Mr. Wonderful. He said he wanted to be like all of them. "I want what you have," Pablo said.

Isn't he amazing, they commented, whispering to each other. Bill and all the others were awestruck by my Pablo.

One of the leaders smiled and said to the group, "Wow. Pablo is so willing to admit he has a problem. I wish I could have been like that when I first came into the rooms (AA)."

Everyone quickly agreed. Pablo held the floor. Everyone focused on him, Mr. Mesmerize. I couldn't believe what was happening. He was supposed to be the one who was driving me crazy, the one who wouldn't admit that the drug had any real effect on him, the one who could get off it without any help except mine...and now, here he was turning to complete strangers! They were *my* friends. Now he was even saying that he couldn't stop on his own! I listened, dumbfounded, not believing that this was the same Pablo that I knew.

"...and that is why I've decided to go into a hospital," Pablo stated firmly.

What???!!!

Pablo continued, "Because of Bill, here, I'm convinced that is what I need to do."

I heard everyone oohing and ahhing, commenting on how wonderful that was, how great Pablo was: Mr. Admit He Needs Help! HA! A hospital? Who was he fooling? He told me more times than I could count how he could get off the stuff any time if he really wanted to. That if I just left it to him and Tony, he would do it. That if I didn't ask questions and supported him and loved him, everything would be fine! But now it felt as if he was sticking a knife into my gut. I felt so betrayed. Pablo was confiding in total strangers and not in me!!! Why couldn't he have discussed this with me before he so boldly *announced* it to the room? And now, I looked like a total jerk.

"You are so lucky to be married to him," one of the women said with a smile. "He understands his problem and is willing to get help." At this point, I was numb. Angry. In a state of total shock and disbelief.

Yeah, after all those years on drugs! Don't you people understand how much torture I've been going through? Trying to get him to stop taking it? Trying to get him to be truthful to me, his wife??? This was no "quick admission" to his problem. *Something is wrong here. Pablo is up to something, and I'm being left in the dark.*

We left the meeting with everyone patting Pablo on the back. "We'll come visit you every day in the hospital," they said. "We'll be your support group."

I was so mixed-up. I wanted him to get help, but not like this. I wanted to be a part of helping him. Besides, I didn't think he needed to go into a hospital. If he did, why didn't he tell me first—at least before announcing it to the group??!!

I didn't know if I could stand Pablo going into a hospital and leaving me. He didn't really mean all those things he said at the meeting, did he?

We got into the Jeep in silence. Pablo was very distant. I tried to be understanding and supportive, like the people at the meeting, but at the same time I felt betrayed.

"Pablo, are you really going to go into a hospital?"

"Yes."

"But why? You said you could get off it yourself. Like with the heroin."

I wondered now if he had made that story up. Maybe he never got off heroin himself...the story of how he went to the cabin in the woods. Maybe that was just another lie.

"I may die if I continue cutting down like this," Pablo said. "I need to be monitored by a hospital."

"Okay, Pablo." I didn't want him to die. And the library books had said that the methadone addict shouldn't try to get off the drug without medical supervision.

Okay, okay. I can take this. I didn't expect this, but I can deal— if we work together. I'm part of this thing now, too. I was as dependent on Pablo as he was dependent on the drug. I expected that *we* would get help. If he got better, then I would get better, too.

Suddenly, it hit me. If Pablo got off the drug, what would he be like? Would he be the same Pablo that I knew? Or would he be completely different? Would he still love me? Or would he love his new AA friends? Would he need me, or just throw me away?

He did love me, didn't he? He couldn't live without me, could he? He wouldn't desert me. No. Not my Pablo. He loved me. He really did. He didn't just say it. He meant it, didn't he?

I was paralyzed with fear. Fear of the unknown. Fear that I would be thrown away, unloved. Somehow, it felt all too familiar.

Still unaware that it was the unbearable pain of the lies from my past—the ultimate betrayal of Vince and his "love" for me—that was surfacing, I was becoming more and more desperate. I knew I would not be able to bear the pain if Pablo rejected me, too. If he really didn't love me, I just couldn't live anymore. All during my relationship with Pablo, I had no idea that my past emotional abuse was so deeply connected to my feelings, my "love" for Pablo. My emotions and reactions to his behavior were obviously misplaced, but I didn't know this. This was my normal. It wasn't until much later that I made the connection to my past, which eventually revealed the truth and set me free.

Pablo decided that he would check into a hospital the following week. Mount Sinai Hospital in South Miami Beach was highly recommended by some of the people at the AA meetings, so that was where he decided to go. A normal detox program meant twenty-eight days as an inpatient. I didn't believe he would actually go through with it, but went along with him to meet a doctor there to set it all up.

We drove south toward the hospital. If Pablo did go through with it, I wanted desperately to be with him. Why couldn't I go into a hospital, too? I wanted to be around people and not so alone. But Pablo would not hear of it.

"You can't go into the hospital. I need you on the outside to take care of things."

So, if he did go through with it, I would have to be strong...alone.

At Mount Sinai Hospital, Pablo met privately with a doctor. I waited outside, in the waiting room. After forty minutes they both came out, laughing and shaking hands. Pablo suddenly had so many friends. I felt so left out.

The doctor looked at me sadly. "This *is* a family disease," he said, shaking his head at poor, pathetic me. Did it show that much that I needed Pablo? How could he tell? "You have problems, my dear," the doctor said. "But first, we must take care of Pablo, right?" He smiled at Pablo and frowned at me.

What was going on?

We drove home in silence. I felt like I was being left out and pushed away. Pablo was very distant. I didn't know what he was thinking. Probably that he didn't need to go into the hospital after all. Maybe that doctor could just monitor him.

"I'm checking in tomorrow," Pablo finally said.

What??? "But I thought you said next week...and...what am I going to do?" It felt like Pablo had just severed one of my main arteries. The life drained out of me. How would I cope? He was leaving me alone, apart, cast out of his life.

"Don't tell my parents," he said firmly.

"What about the horses, Pablo? What about me?"

"I can't tell my parents. They will try to talk me out of it and make light of it. I know them. I must check in before they find out."

"What am I supposed to do?"

"Cover for me until they have to know."

"Why can't you tell them, Pablo? I'm sure they'll understand." And, besides, I needed support on this one.

"No!" Pablo said vehemently. "They can't find out until I'm in. Then they can't bother me. In the detox, nobody can bother you for four days. No phone calls. Nothing."

"What about me? How will I know what's going on? How will I know if you are alive or dead from detoxing?" Suddenly, a thought crossed my mind. Pablo had said he had to cut down slowly, not all at once. "They're still going to give it to you, right? Cut you down slowly, right?"

"I don't know how they are going to do it," he lied.

Pablo was getting his things together. He packed a small bag. I still couldn't believe what was happening. I didn't really think he would go through with it. How could he?

"Don't pay any bills," Pablo said with authority.

"What? Why would I pay any bills? I never pay any bills."

"When my old man finds out, he'll try to get you to do things. So don't pay any bills, okay?"

I didn't understand why he was bringing this up, but agreed to do as he wanted. "Okay."

"And don't take the money out of the horsemen's account, the money from Gotham (the horse that was claimed at the races for $30,000)."

"Why would I do that?" I asked, confused and feeling more lost than ever. How would I cope without my Pablo?

"Just don't take the money out—under *any* circumstances."

"Okay, Pablo."

"This is going to be very hard on me. I'm going to tell Jim (the assistant trainer) that I've gone away for a few days. Then after those few days, you can break the news to my parents. My old man will tell Jim what to do with the horses after that."

I still didn't believe he would do it. Not really. He wouldn't leave me.

"Pablo, is it my fault you couldn't get off the drug the way you wanted?" I felt like I had failed in being a good wife. I had driven him to this. He just couldn't stand me anymore. I couldn't help him get off the drug. I had just made things worse. I had acted so angry. I was such a failure. His going to the hospital was proof that I had failed—proof that he didn't need me.

Pablo didn't answer my question. I guess that meant it *was* my fault. He just didn't want to say it and get me upset again.

"Pablo, what if I go stay with my grandmother for a while?"

"You must stay here. I may need you. You got that?"

"Yeah."

I was trying to be good, trying to not get upset, trying to be the wonderful, supportive wife that Pablo needed. I went over his wishes in my head:

1) Don't tell his parents for two days
2) Don't pay any bills
3) Don't take any money out of the horsemen's account
4) Don't stay with my grandmother

I had my instructions, four things I must remember *not* to do. That should take care of Pablo's problems. But now, what about me?

Although I was unaware of it, Pablo had run out of money for his drugs and was deeply in debt. He had timed his hospital stay perfectly for his own benefit. Pablo had not paid any of the track bills for the three months we had been in Florida. (This added up to thousands of dollars in feed, vet, shipping, and blacksmith bills, plus the employees' paychecks.) While his father was paying Pablo to cover these costs, his father's checks had obviously gone to Pablo's thousand-dollar-a-day methadone purchases.

We headed off to Mount Sinai Hospital. I didn't really believe he would go through with it. No, not Pablo. He would never check into a hospital and let someone else control his life. It just wasn't like him. I was sure he was just making the effort for me. When we got there, he would chat with the doctor and then happily agree to come back a few times a week so the doctor could monitor his "cutting down." That's all. Yes, then we would be going right back home again, together. Anyway, just look at the size of the bag he packed! It was so small. No way did he have enough stuff to last for twenty-eight days! Ha. Who was he kidding? I knew him better than that! Besides, it was already March 30th. The horses were supposed to ship back to New York next week! Now, how could that happen if Pablo were really planning on staying down here in the hospital for another month? I decided to go along with the charade—if it made Pablo feel better.

We drove over the causeway. The water below was a beautiful, crystal clear aqua blue. If this were a different situation, Pablo and I could go walk on that beach. We could wade in the water. It looked so inviting. So pure, so clean, so fresh. I took my eyes off the water, which was putting me in a tranquil mood. I could see the hospital looming ahead. The sign on the top of the massive building read Mount Sinai Medical Center.

We went into the building and rode the elevator up to the third floor. Pablo got out and headed for the desk. I followed sheepishly behind him. I didn't feel like he wanted me anymore. Pablo and the doctor he had met with yesterday had totally left me out of any conversations. I wondered what Pablo had told him about me. I had the feeling the doctor didn't like me.

I felt even more left out when Pablo leaned over the desk and was very friendly with the woman in charge of admittance.

"You can leave your bag here," the admittance lady said smiling broadly, "while you see Miss Peterson." She pointed down the hall. "Room 309."

"Thanks," Pablo said, lifting his small bag onto the desk. Then he turned as if I wasn't even there and headed down the hall. I followed. He didn't even wait for me to catch up.

Pablo turned the corner and stopped in front of one of the doors. It opened. Then, before I could follow, it was shut in my face. Room 309.

I knocked. A young woman cracked the door. "Can I help you? I'm busy right now."

"I'm with Pablo. He's my husband."

She shut the door again. Then it opened. "I'm sorry. I have to talk to him alone first. Then you can come in." The door was shut again.

I waited. I wanted to cry. Was he really going to go through with this?

Pablo's new doctor appeared from around the corner. I quickly looked down at the floor, knowing he didn't like me.

"Excuse me," he said.

I looked up, realizing he was talking to me.

"Oh." I moved aside as he opened the door. Then he disappeared into the conspiracy room.

About ten minutes later, the doctor came back out. "You can go in now." He swung the door open wide. There was Pablo, sitting on one side of a desk, the young woman on the other. Pablo was smiling.

I went in, feeling very out of place. The room was tiny and the desk took up nearly all the space. There was no place for me to sit, so Pablo motioned for me to sit on his lap. I did.

Miss Peterson asked Pablo a variety of questions. I started feeling awful, knowing I was about to be abandoned.

Miss Peterson looked up from her notebook and addressed me for the first time. "Pablo is going to be with us for a while. Isn't that good?"

"I don't know," I said, trying to digest all that was happening. My insides were turning upside down, screaming, *No! It isn't good! He's leaving me. I can't live without him! He needs me—not this stupid hospital. He can't leave me! He doesn't need you, he needs me!*

She went back to her notebook and questioned Pablo. "Will it be smoking or non-smoking?"

"Smoking," Pablo answered, driving the knife just a little harder into my guts.

"But...he can't," I objected. "Pablo *quit* smoking. He will start up again if he goes in the smoking section. It makes no sense. He quit already, and it will be so hard for him to quit again. If he smokes even one cigarette..." My voice trailed off as I realized that I must have sounded like a whining worrywart. But she didn't understand the smoking and...

The knife plunged deeper yet.

"Oh, come now. Let's just take one thing at a time. Right, Pablo? It's more important that he get treatment for what he came in for. It will be smoking then, right Pablo?"

"Yes, smoking. Definitely."

She made a check mark in her notebook.

I felt like they were both against me now. I didn't want to live anymore. Not without Pablo. And now, he hated me anyway. He was leaving me for his cigarettes.

I whispered to him, "Finish me off." He had taken me so far down. I just couldn't take it anymore. I was just so tired of all the pain. I whispered intensely into his ear, "Do it! Choke me. Kill me. Just finish me off. Right now!"

Pablo put his hands around my neck while Miss Peterson continued to write in her notebook. She was unaware that Pablo's hands were choking me. I went limp in his arms, right there on his lap. I didn't struggle. I just didn't care anymore. In fact, I held my breath to help things along. Let me die already, please.

Pablo released his grip. He couldn't kill me right there in front of Miss Peterson! But all I felt was anger at him for not finishing the job, for leaving me alive to suffer so much pain.

"Why did you let go?" I screamed at him.

Miss Peterson looked up from her notebook, completely surprised by my outburst. "What's going on?" she asked sternly, reaching for her phone.

"Pablo wouldn't do it. He wouldn't finish me off," I explained miserably.

Pablo looked at her with surprise and shrugged.

"I hate all this!" I yelled, taking the keys to the Jeep and stabbing them into my leg. I just couldn't take it anymore!

"I'm going to call for help," Miss Peterson said, looking very distraught by this sudden turn of events.

Good! Now they can lock me up with Pablo and he won't leave me!!!

"Take me with you!" I pleaded.

"You can't stay with him. You are making him crazy," she said to me. Now she was talking on the phone, asking for "Code White."

"But I want to stay with him. He can't leave me like this—and he won't finish me off!"

Pablo pushed me off his lap. I stabbed the keys into my leg again.

All of a sudden two large men burst through the door and grabbed me.

"What are you doing?" I asked, frightened.

Pablo backed away from me. Miss Peterson looked relieved that her "Code White" men had arrived. The two of them shoved me quickly out the door and lifted me up onto a waiting gurney. Before I even knew what was happening, they tied me down.

"What are you doing? Pablo! PABLO! HELP ME! STOP THEM!"

Where was Pablo??? He would rescue me! He would tell them to stop, that I was just upset with him. "PABLO! PABLO!"

Once again, I was reliving the rejection of Vince. Why hadn't Vince saved me from killing myself after Mom discovered the secret? Vince never called me to see how I was doing. He never cared. He just deserted me. But Pablo wouldn't desert me, would he? Pablo cared. He loved me, didn't he?

The two men wheeled me away. It was no use struggling. I couldn't move at all. Where was Pablo? Why wasn't he stopping them? Why wasn't he *doing* anything? He would rescue me if I just remained calm. This was all a misunderstanding. I was just upset. I didn't want Pablo to desert me.

But the gurney continued to whiz down the hall and into an elevator.

"What are you going to do with me?" I asked as the elevator went down. "I came in here to have my husband admitted!" It was no use. They treated me as if I didn't exist. I was just another crazy patient. Well, maybe I was. But only around Pablo.

The elevator stopped. They wheeled out my gurney and parked me in the hall. A nurse came over to me and asked for my name. I wouldn't talk. I didn't want to get in any deeper. And I was angry.

"Oh, come on now. Give us your name."

What did it matter? I was mad now. I wasn't staying here. Everybody in the hospital was against me.

The nurse asked me again, "Your name? We have to put this wristband on you."

I didn't want to talk to anyone. If they wanted to treat me like an animal, I would be an animal. Animals don't talk. You go figure it out, lady. If you're so smart, why don't you know that I'm Pablo's wife, who came here to have *him* admitted?

They admitted me under the name "Jane Doe." I even had the wristband to prove it!

A few hours later, my gurney was wheeled out of the hallway and into one of about eight cubicles with a curtain around it. (I could tell by looking at the ceiling.) I heard people moaning and someone calling out for the nurse. I guessed that I was in the emergency room of the hospital.

After a few hours, I was bored to tears. My arms were aching from not being able to move. I wondered what Pablo was doing. Why hadn't he gotten me out of here yet? Why hadn't he straightened this mess out so they could let me go home?

Eventually a woman came in, a social worker. She wanted to "talk" to me. I didn't like the way she acted toward me, so I didn't say a word. I would just wait for Pablo. He got me in this mess, now he could get me out. *Where was he???*

After the social worker left, I started to wriggle my hands free. They were tied by restraints made of nylon material. I finally managed to free one hand. Then I untied the other one. What a relief!!

I reached down and untied my feet. Then I got up and stretched. Was Pablo ever going to rescue me?

I peeked out from behind the curtain. Everybody was busy tending to their different jobs. Good! Nobody was watching me. It was time to take take things into my own hands. Pablo may never find me in here. Besides, he may be locked up, too, by now.

Suddenly, I realized that the two big guys had taken my keys! How would I get out of here? Grandma! She could come get me. I left my cubicle and found a phone on the wall. I got the hospital operator, asked for an outside line, and dialed Grandma's number.

"Hello?" I was relieved she had picked up.

"Grandma? You have to come get me. I'm at Mount Sinai Hospital in the emergency room. I'll explain later. I had to bring Pablo here for the drug problem, and now they won't let me go."

"Is anything wrong?"

"I just need a ride. Can you come soon? The hospital is in Miami Beach, off the causeway. Do you think you can find it?"

"I'll try. Mount Sinai Hospital? I'll leave right now."

"Yes. Thanks, Gram. See you soon." I hung up. Grandma should be here within the hour.

Miss Social Worker spotted me. "And just what do you think you're doing?"

"I'm waiting for my grandmother to come get me."

She looked at me like I was a very sad case, indeed. Then she took me by the arm and led me back to my cubicle. "You are not going anywhere. Now, how did you get out of these?" she asked, shaking the restraints at me.

"It was easy."

She stared at me like I really *was* crazy.

"I still don't know why you are keeping me here," I said. "I came to the hospital to drop off my husband, Pablo Garcia. Where is he anyway?" I asked.

The social worker looked at me pathetically and shook her head. "You have to stay right here in this cubicle or I will have to have you restrained again," she said firmly.

"Why do I have to stay here?" I was beginning to really dislike her.

"You have to be evaluated," she said and then left.

Behind the curtain, I heard a patient calling for a nurse. She had been calling out for some time now, and I wondered why nobody was helping her. I went over to check it out. I might as well be useful while I waited for Grandma.

"Hi! What's the problem?" I asked, drawing back her curtain. She was about eighty years old and very thin.

"Oh, thank you," she said, introducing herself. "Finally, somebody will listen to me! I need to contact my doctor. He doesn't work in this hospital. I need to be transferred, but nobody will listen to me. Will you call my doctor for me?"

I thought about the phone on the wall. "Okay. I'll try."

After I made the phone call for the woman to be transferred, she opened up her purse. "Oh, thank you! I'm so grateful. Please, let me repay you," she insisted.

"You already have," I told her. *By letting me help you. By needing me and talking to me like a human being.*

I figured that Grandma would be arriving soon, so I went out the electronic doors and entered the waiting area of the emergency room. I didn't see Grandma, so I continued out the last set of doors, leading to the parking lot. Wondering if Pablo had left the hospital, I ran around to the other side of the building where we had parked the Jeep. It was still there! Pablo must be inside. He had decided to stay! I couldn't believe it.

I went back to the emergency room parking area. This is where Grandma would probably come to find me. I sat down on the curb to wait. I played with my wristband and read the name again: Jane Doe. Grandma would get a kick out of that! As I sat there waiting, I noticed two security guards coming out of the emergency room doors. They were heading toward me very quickly. Now, what could they want?

I started to get up, and when I did they broke into a run. They reached me and grabbed my arms.

"What do you want?" I asked as they started to handcuff me.

"You have to come back inside."

"Okay! I will. Don't put those on me, please. I'll come back in. I was just making sure my grandmother would find me."

When we got back inside, Miss Social Worker was waiting for me. "I told you not to leave. Now I'll have to keep a watch on you," she said, sounding annoyed. She nodded to the two security guards.

"I was just waiting for my grandmother," I explained as she walked away. The guards sat me down in one of the chairs in the waiting room.

"Can you believe this?" I asked the guard. "I come in here to have my husband admitted, and they won't let me go!"

I picked up one of the magazines, wondering what was going on in the outside world.

"Karen?"

Someone knew my name! *Grandma!* She had arrived at last!

"Grandma!!! Thank God you're here!!" I got up, ran over to her, and gave her a big hug before the guards could stop me. What a relief!

"I've been looking all over for you," she said. "Now, what's going on?"

The two guards got up from their chairs. They were ready to grab me if I tried to make an escape.

"Don't worry," I said to them, "You guys probably have better things to do than to babysit me. This is my grandmother."

Grandma smiled and held out her hand to shake with them. She probably thought these two guys were impressed by her "jockey" granddaughter and wanted to meet her, too!

"I'm Karen's grandmother," she explained, winking at me proudly.

"That's nice. My name is Phil," one of the guards said, looking amused. He shook Grandma's hand, which made her very happy.

"Well, Karen, you ready?" Grandma said, as if we could just leave.

"You have to come with me," said Phil. At least now everyone was acting civilized—thanks to Grandma. Now I had somebody to stand up for me. I thought Pablo would have come to help, but maybe they had locked him up, too.

Grandma and I followed Phil out of the waiting room and down a corridor. "Grandma, I'm worried about Pablo," I said.

"Oh, Pablo is fine," Grandma said. "I just saw him. I went up to the drug floor. I thought you would be up there with him."

"You *saw* Pablo?" I couldn't believe he was out and around—and hadn't come to rescue me!

"Yeah. He was standing by the desk, joking with the nurses. He's fine."

"Did you talk to him?"

"Yes. I asked him where you were and if you were all right. I was worried about *you*, not him."

"But—what did he say?"

"He said, 'Hi, Mrs. MacKinney. How are you?' as if nothing was out of the ordinary."

"What did he say about me?" Pablo knew I was in trouble. He had seen them take me away!

"When I asked where you were, if you were okay, he said, 'Oh, she's fine. Don't worry.'"

"Did he know I was still in the hospital?" I asked, not believing my ears.

"He told me to come down here."

He knew I was still here? And he hadn't come to rescue me???!!!

"Grandma, are you *sure* you saw him? Are you *sure* he said that?"

"Oh, don't you worry about Pablo. He's fine. He was laughing like I've never seen him before."

I was trying to get over the feeling of disbelief. Phil, the guard we were following, stopped in front of an open door to an office. The social worker was sitting inside with a doctor. She looked up.

"Now can I leave?" I asked the social worker.

"Who is this?" she asked, looking at Grandma.

"This is my grandmother."

Grandma smiled. "Now, why won't you let me take Karen home?"

"She can't go home until she is evaluated. It could take a few days."

"But I am fine," I said, not giving up. Besides, I felt fine—even strong—now that I had my grandmother's support. She believed in me. She would tell them I was fine, too.

"Yes, *Karen* is fine," Grandma said. "It's *Pablo* that needs to be in here. *He's* the problem."

"Well, we have to send her to Palmetto General Hospital for an evaluation. We don't have the facilities here."

"Can my grandmother take me there?" Grandma was the only thing that stood between me and a loony bin, where I could be locked up for days!

"No. We are having the ambulance take you."

Oh, brother. Did they have to keep treating me like I was crazy? As long as Pablo wasn't around, I felt fine, sane. Karen the jockey was still somewhere inside me: the strong one, the fighter. The seeker of truth, the one who wanted to make sense out of things that made no sense.

"You can wait for the ambulance in the waiting room," the social worker said, instructing Phil to go with us.

While we waited, I made a quick plan and whispered it to Grandma. "As soon as the ambulance comes, go get your car and get right behind us. Follow the ambulance to the other hospital. Don't lose us. Stick close. Once we get there, this crazy social worker will be out of our hair and we can make our getaway."

Grandma smiled slyly and nodded with conviction. Wasn't she the best?

Chapter 66
The Great Escape

Phil and I talked on the way to Palmetto General Hospital. I told him about my riding career. I think it was more to reassure myself of who I was (without Pablo), than to tell him anything. He probably thought I was just another lunatic who imagined stories about themselves. I'll bet he had heard a lot of those. He just smiled and nodded.

"How do you get from the Palmetto Hospital to Palm Springs North?" I asked casually, changing the subject. Phil gave me directions, which I quickly memorized so that Grandma and I could make a quick getaway. I needed to get back to the condo to get the spare keys for the Jeep.

I hoped that Grandma was following us, but was afraid to look out the back door window. Phil might think I was trying to escape and handcuff me. I would need my hands free once we got to the new hospital.

At Palmetto General Hospital, the entrance lobby was packed. "Wait here," Phil said as he went to check me in. I guess he trusted me. A few minutes later, Grandma came through the entrance.

"Grandma, you made it!"

She came over to me. "It wasn't easy. But I stuck right behind that ambulance. I wasn't letting you out of my sight," she said, giving me a reassuring hug.

"Listen, as soon as the guard leaves, I'm sure we can make a break for it. They don't know me here. They won't be watching me."

Grandma smiled and nodded. I think she liked the excitement. My grandmother, my accomplice. Wasn't she great?

Phil came back over to us. "They want to see you inside. Come with me." Oh, no.

"I'll be right back, Grandma. If not, come and find me, okay?"

"Okay." Grandma looked worried now.

I decided to act completely normal so they would trust me without a guard. If they left me unattended, it would be easier to get away.

I sat down in a little room, and Phil bade me farewell. "Well, my job is done now. Good luck."

"Bye." *Leave, leave, so I can escape.*

Too late. A woman entered the room. "Hi. We're going to evaluate you, but we're very busy. You're going to have to wait a while. Would you mind waiting outside in the waiting room until we call you?"

Would I mind??? I would LOVE it!!!

"No, that will be fine." I left the room casually. I spotted Grandma waiting for me and slowly walked over to her. I didn't want to raise any suspicions.

"Let's go slowly, Gram." Phil was gone, and nobody was watching for me. Everyone seemed preoccupied. "Okay. Now. Nice and slow."

Grandma and I left through the same doors I had come in. It was pitch black outside. When we hit the parking lot, I broke into a run. "Where's your car, Gram?"

She stuck right by me. “Over there.”

We reached her car and got in quickly. Grandma was a bundle of nerves. I must say, I was a bit shaky myself. I kept expecting some massive guards to come running after me.

“Where do we go?” Grandma asked, starting the car and backing out.

I scrunched down in my seat. “Just get out of the parking lot and onto the highway. Then it will be safe.”

When we go to the highway, I sat up and sighed. What a relief! Following my memorized directions, we made it back to the condo in one piece.

“Come upstairs with me, Grandma. I’ll get the spare set of keys for the Jeep. Do you think you could run me back to Mount Sinai Hospial to get the Jeep?”

“Okay.” Grandma wasn’t too keen on my housekeeping. “Karen, you have to keep the house straightened up. What if somebody stops in?”

“I know. But nobody ever visits. Things have been so crazy anyway. I haven’t really cared about housekeeping recently.”

“If you want to keep a man, you have to keep the house nice,” she said simply.

“I know, Grandma. I haven’t done a very good job lately—of keeping a house or Pablo.”

I pulled Grandma away from the dishes. “Come on. Let’s go. I’ll do the dishes when I come home.” Grandma seemed happy about that. And I promised her I would clean up the whole apartment, for good measure. I honestly didn’t care about the mess; it was a statement of my life.

When we arrived back at the hospital, it was late. I got the creeps. I hated the place. “Grandma, I’m afraid they may still be looking for me. They may have someone watching the Jeep. They may know by now that I escaped from the other hospital.”

She looked worried again.

“Listen. This is what we’ll do,” I said. “Pull over.”

Grandma pulled the car over, waiting to hear my idea.

“I will sneak over to the Jeep. Don’t go any farther. Wait here until

I pull out, okay?"

"No, Karen. I'll do it. They may be watching for you, like you said. They won't be watching for me. I'll get the Jeep and bring it around to you."

"You would?" She was definitely the best grandmother in the whole world. She was the greatest friend I could have right then. She believed in me, and that's what I needed to restore my faith in myself. That's what I needed more than anything.

"Yes. Now, is there anything I should know about driving it?"

"No. It's an automatic."

Grandma got out and I moved into the driver's seat of her car. I gave her last minute instructions. "I'll back the car up and meet you on the other side of the building, by the traffic light. That's where we'll make the switch. You don't know how much this means to me, Gram. I don't know what I would have done without you." I leaned out the car window and kissed her. Then she turned and snuck off toward the Jeep. My heart pounded as I watched her sneak between the rows of cars. I kept seeing her head pop up as she looked around in the dark. *I'll bet she's more nervous than I am....I should have done this...what if they catch her? I guess she can always say that she came to get the Jeep and that she doesn't know where I am...at least they won't lock HER up....*

The Jeep was parked near the building. The bright lights from the hospital windows illuminated my grandmother as she nervously fumbled with the keys. *What's taking her so long to get the door unlocked?* I sighed with relief as I watched her get up into the Jeep. If it weren't for my nerves, the situation might have been funny. My heart pounded as I prayed. *Please, God, don't let them catch us!*

Now she had found the headlights. They went on, piercing the darkness of the parking lot. *Oh, God, hurry up!!!*

Now the Jeep was backing slowly out of the parking space. Good! I drove to the other side of the building where we would meet. At the light, I pulled over and looked in my rearview mirror. Grandma was right behind me, pulling over, too.

I got out and went over to her. She was shaking from the excitement of our little adventure.

"Oh, Karen, I was so nervous. I kept thinking they would see me."

"You did great, Grandma. Now, go home and don't worry about a thing. I don't know what I would have done without you!" (I'd be locked up in Palmetto General Hospital with nobody to rescue me!)

"Call me when you get home, Karen, so I'll know you're safe."

"I love you, Grandma. You're the best!"

"This was the most exciting thing I've done in ages," she said, smiling. "Now, get going!" She nudged me to get up into the Jeep. "Hurry up, so they don't come looking for us. And call me the second you get home." She kissed me, and I watched her get back into her car. The light turned green, but she didn't go. I flicked my headlights to signal that I was right behind her. Mission accomplished, we both moved out.

On the way home, I did some thinking. I was so lucky to have Grandma. There was nothing like someone who knew me and believed in me. Family. It was worth everything. I never appreciated that simple fact before. I thought about Mom. I missed her. She had always believed in me, too, but Pablo said...

I shuddered imagining what it would be like to be alone in this world. But then it hit me. I *was* alone. Pablo was gone.

Chapter 67
Financial Fiasco

I woke up the next morning to the phone ringing. Maybe it was Pablo??!!

"Hello?"

"Hello. Is Pablo Garcia there?"

"No. Who's calling?"

"Will he be in soon?"

"Why? Who's calling?"

"I have a little problem. Maybe you can help me. I own the tack shop at the track. I've been cashing Pablo's checks, you know, for his barn help, and they have all bounced."

"What?" What did he mean? What was he saying?

"All the checks that I cashed are no good. I'm out a lot of money. I need to speak to Pablo."

"Uh, he's away."

"When will he be in? He has put me in quite a jam..."

"I don't know. I..."

"Is this his wife? Can you come down?"

"Yes." I suddenly remembered what Pablo had told me before he went into the hospital. *Don't pay any bills.* It seemed like years ago, now. "I mean, no. I can't come down. I... really don't know anything about his account."

"Well, have him call me the moment he gets in."

"Okay." I hung up the phone. I wondered if he could wait twenty-eight days to get his money. Well, Pablo will be in touch with me soon, I thought. Then all this will be straightened out. It was all probably just a misunderstanding, anyway.

I wasn't off the phone five minutes when it rang again. This time it was the feed man. It seemed that Pablo had not paid the feed bill for the horses the whole time we had been in Florida, and then the day before yesterday Pablo had given the feed man a check—for three and a half months' worth of grain and hay—but this check had bounced, too. The phone rang all morning. It was more of the same. What was going on?

I went to where Pablo kept his papers. There was a huge stack of...bills. Hadn't he paid any of them?

I heard a knock on the door. It was Mr. Garcia.

"Where is Pablo?" he asked, eyeing me suspiciously.

Did he owe his father, too???

"Umm. He's not here right now."

"I see the Jeep outside. Didn't he go to work?"

"I...no...he's not here, though."

Mr. Garcia pushed me aside, shaking his head. He went into the kitchen yelling, "Pablo? Pablo?"

He went from room to room, looking for Pablo. I stood by the door, dumbfounded.

"Where is he?" Mr. Garcia asked, sounding very upset. "He owes everybody. My phone hasn't stopped ringing all morning. He has to pay these people so I can get my horses out of Florida. We're shipping out in a few days, and now this!!!"

I stood there, silent.

"Where is he? I can't take my horses out of Florida until all these people are paid." Mr. Garcia stared at me, waiting for an answer.

I had none, so I shrugged. He left me standing there helplessly and went back out and down the stairs. I heard him shut the door to their apartment below.

God, what was happening? I had to call Pablo. I had to tell him about all that was happening. He would flip if he found out what was going on! He had to straighten out this giant misunderstanding.

I called Mount Sinai. To my astonishment, they wouldn't give me any information about Pablo. In fact, they couldn't even confirm that he was a patient there!

"What do you mean? Is he or isn't he there?" I asked again.

"That information is confidential, ma'am."

"I am his *wife*. I have to know if he is there."

"I'm sorry. We aren't allowed to say if a person is admitted in the drug rehabilitation center. It protects the identity of our patients."

"I know. I know. But I am his *wife*. I left him there yesterday. Did he leave? Is he in the detox? He is in danger of dying if he is in the detox, and I..."

"Sorry. I'm sure someone from the hospital will contact you soon."

"There is nobody else I can speak to?"

"I'm very sorry. It's hospital policy."

I hung up the phone, feeling torn. Was Pablo still at the hospital? Was he dying in the detox? Or had he left and gone to some Federal Express depot to pick up more methadone? I was worried sick, and there was nothing I could do about it. Not knowing was the worst. My imagination was running wild.

There was a knock on the door. I didn't want to talk to anyone. Where was Pablo? Was he still alive? And now everything at the barn was going haywire. Resigned, I went to the door and opened it. Mr. Garcia stood there.

"Karen, you have to tell me where he is. Jim (Pablo's assistant trainer) told me he went away for a few days. Where did he go?"

"I'm not supposed to tell you. Not yet. And anyway, I'm not even sure if he is where he is."

"You have to tell me. It's my business to know. He is in charge of my horses, and now he just disappears!"

I desperately wanted to tell someone, to share my situation and get support or understanding. I didn't want to be alone in all this. Oh, what could it hurt to tell them now? Anyway, they couldn't even contact Pablo. If I couldn't reach him, then surely they wouldn't be able to. Here goes. Oh, forgive me, Pablo.

"He is in the hospital."

"He is *where*? What happened to him?"

"He checked himself into a hospital."

"Why? Why didn't he tell somebody..."

"It's for drugs. He's trying to get off a drug."

"I knew it. I *knew* it! I knew he was messing with that stuff again." Mr. Garcia shook his head in disgust.

What did he mean, he knew it???

"What do you mean, you knew?" I asked, astonished that Mr. Garcia knew anything about Pablo and drugs.

"Oh, I suspected he was back on something, you know."

"You knew about... before?" I couldn't believe Mr. Garcia knew about Pablo's past drug problem. Pablo told me he kept everything from his parents. I just assumed they never knew. After all, Mr. Garcia and Dubai trusted him with a top stable of horses. Pablo had told me *never* to tell his parents anything—that the less they knew about him, the better. He acted as though his parents were part of a conspiracy that was out to get him.

"What hospital is he in?" Mr. Garcia asked. Just like that.

"You mean, you aren't mad that he is in a hospital? Pablo said that if you knew, you would say that he didn't belong in a hospital and that you would try to get him out."

"The hospital is the best place for him right now. I just wish he had told me so that I could make arrangements for the horses."

I was so glad Mr. Garcia was taking it so well. I thought it would come as a complete shock to him.

"He's at Mount Sinai Hospital, hopefully. That's where I left him. But, I just called and they won't give me any information about him.

I guess they'll call me. They said they would."

"We have to straighten out this mess with the bills," Mr. Garcia said, sounding sympathetic.

Finally, someone understood!

That night, I couldn't sleep at all. I was so worried about Pablo. In the morning, Mr. Garcia knocked on the door again.

"You have to come down to the bank with me," he said firmly.

"Why? What can I do?"

"You have to get the check signing privileges for Pablo's account. Then we can pay the help and all the people Pablo owes."

"Now? Do I have to come now?" I felt like a wreck. I needed to take a shower and change.

"I'll wait for you downstairs. The bank opens soon, and I want to get in and out. Then we have to take a ride to the track to pay the barn help. I'll need your signature on the checks."

"Okay. I need to change. I'll be down in five minutes." I threw on some clean clothes, my sunglasses, and went downstairs to meet Mr. Garcia. Then we drove off together in his Cadillac. I felt like the tide was sweeping me away.

At the bank, I signed some papers. I didn't really care. Not about money. Mr. Garcia was in charge now, wasn't he? He would take care of everything. Suddenly, I felt ill. I remembered Pablo's warning: *My old man will try to make you do things. Don't pay any bills.*

"Wait. Pablo doesn't want me to do this," I said in the middle of all the transactions.

"Well, you don't have a choice. These people *must* be paid. The only reason they let Pablo run up his bills was because I have good credit. I'm not letting him ruin that, too. Go on, sign here." He handed me the last of the forms and I let out a deep breath. Pablo would understand. He would have to. I had no choice.

I finished signing the papers, and then Mr. Garcia and I headed off to Hialeah. At the barn, it was more of the same. I signed checks, tons and tons of checks. "Won't these checks bounce?" I asked Mr. Garcia. Everyone had been calling about the bounced checks.

"No. Yesterday I went to the races and took the money out of the horsemen's account. That money should cover some of these bills."

"The money from Gotham?" I asked, feeling a pit in my stomach. Pablo would *kill* me.

"Yeah."

"How did you get his money out?" I asked. I was supposed to make sure the money from Gotham wasn't taken out of the account.

"It's *my* money!! Half of that horse was mine. And the rest of that money Pablo owed me anyway. But it should cover these bills. If not, we'll have to call his bank back in New York. How much money does he have in that account?"

"I don't know," I said honestly.

"You *don't know?*" he asked with disbelief.

"No. Pablo gave me a check every week. I put it in a separate account at my bank. His business account is different. Maybe ask Andy, his accountant."

We left the barn. I must have signed thirty checks: this week's payroll, last week's payroll, etc. etc.

Back at the condo, Mr. Garcia went through the stack of unpaid bills that Pablo had. "This is unbelievable," he commented angrily. He got on the phone and was yelling at Pablo's accountant. "He *what*? I can't believe this."

Mr. Garcia explained the situation to me, only because I happened to be standing there, a lost soul. "Andy said Pablo sent no money back to New York. Not since he's been down here. Where the hell has all my money been going??? He doesn't have any money in the account up there. They're as confused as I am. He still owes the feed man, the tack man—everyone! According to these bills, it's several thousand dollars! And these people *must* be paid." Mr. Garcia looked at me. I didn't know what to say.

Mr. Garcia continued to think out loud. "I must get in touch with Pablo at the hospital. I'll pay these people myself. But Pablo will have to get me that money. I'll sell his racing yacht. That ought to be worth something." Then he walked out, leaving me alone once again.

Sell Pablo's racing yacht? His baby? His pride and joy? No way. Pablo wouldn't let that happen. He would die before he sold his yacht. Mr. Garcia couldn't sell it without him knowing, could he? No. There was a title on it, wasn't there? It would be safe.

The phone rang. I dreaded answering it. But it might be the hospital, or Pablo himself. I picked up. "Hello?"

"Hello? Is Pablo there? This is Ed, from the docks."

It was the sailboat agent.

"No. Can I take a message?"

"Is this Karen?"

"Yeah. How are you?"

"Fine. Look, he got his price for the boat. They'll take a hundred and sixty (thousand). It's low, but I finally convinced them to take it. And I'm cutting my commission down to almost nothing to help you guys out. I know you really want this one. It's a bargain, at the price. I need a check for the down payment so we can hold the boat. Then I can go ahead and have the boat checked out. I'll need money for that, too. If it doesn't pass the inspection, you'll get the down payment back, and the contract will be voided. Unless you want to fix it up yourselves. I've had a look at the engine and all the parts of the boat, though, and it looks to be in good shape. Can you bring me a check?"

The boat. I had forgotten all about the sailboat. Did Pablo still want to buy the sailboat??? We kind of liked the one he was talking about. What should I do???

"Can you wait a few days? Pablo is in the hospital, and he really can't make any big decisions right now."

"Oh. What happened? Was he in an accident?"

"Sort of. No. He's just really sick."

"Can I talk to him?" the boat salesman asked.

"No. He's much too sick to talk to anyone now. I can't even bother him."

"Oh. I'm sorry."

"Can I get back to you after I talk to him? Like, in a few days?"

"The boat may be gone by then. Until we sign the contract, they can sell it to someone else."

What should I do? What would Pablo have told me to do? Oh, why couldn't I reach him???

"Okay," I said. "Here's what I'll do. I'll try to talk to Pablo today or tomorrow. If he still wants the boat, I'll bring you a check."

The salesman continued, "He loved this baby. I'm sure he'll want it. At the price, it's a steal."

"I'll get back to you soon, okay? Thanks. Bye." I hung up. What next?

Looking back, I honestly don't know what happened to my logical brain. Obviously, Mr. Garcia told me that Pablo had no money. Did I not believe him? I don't think it sunk in. Had I been reduced to not being able to think for myself? Did Pablo still have that much power over me? Could I only think my brainwashed Pablo thoughts and not my own??? Sadly, that seems to have been the case.

Chapter 68
Pushed Aside

I was in turmoil. I still hadn't heard from Pablo. Four days and no word. Was he alive or dead? Had he left the hospital because he couldn't stand the pain? They said when he checked into the hospital that it was voluntary—that he could check out before the twenty-eight days were up—but that it wasn't recommended.

Oh, where was he? Why hadn't he called me? Was he dying? If he was dying in the hospital, would they even bother to tell me?

I decided to go see my, or rather Pablo's, friends at AA. They would know about these things. When I got to AA, I couldn't believe my ears. Bill had seen Pablo! In fact, two people from the "group" had seen Pablo at the hospital! They had been at a meeting in the hospital with him. Why hadn't anyone told me? Why hadn't Pablo told Bill to call me, or just called me himself???

"Bill, why hasn't Pablo called me?"

"Oh, he probably isn't ready yet."

Isn't ready???

"You don't know what I've been going through," I explained. "The worrying about whether he is alive or dead. The hospital wouldn't tell me *anything* about Pablo!

"No?"

"No. They wouldn't even tell me if he was still there!!"

"Well, he is there. And he is doing fine."

"How can I see him? Can I talk to him?"

"He's still in the first phase, the hardest part, the detox. He is only allowed to go out of his room on certain occasions, like for the meeting I was speaking at. That was how I came to see him. But next week, I told him, we're all going down to visit him, right?" Bill smiled at everyone in the group.

Why was I being left out???

"Can't I see him or call him?"

"You have to understand. This is a hard time for him. There is no phone in his room. If he wants to call out, he'll have to use the pay phone during special hours. Maybe he has tried to call you and you haven't been home."

Now I was mad. I was home. Home just like he told me to be. He hadn't called. *He knew I would be worried.*

I shook my head. "Bill, I've been home. He hasn't called."

"What about his counselor? Has he called you?"

"No. Nobody has called me. Nobody at the hospital will tell me anything. Except now, you. I was beginning to really worry."

"I see." Bill rubbed his chin. I don't think he believed me at first. But now, maybe he did. "I'll see Pablo and have him call you, all right? Or if he doesn't feel up to it, I'll have his counselor call you. You should be a part of this, too."

"Thanks, Bill." I left the group feeling more shut out than ever before. How could Pablo talk to Bill and not me???

When I got home, I called Mount Sinai Hospital again. This time I got someone new. I think all the people who answered the phones knew me by now. I had called so many times over the past four days!

"Mount Sinai, how can I help you?"

"Can you give me the phone hours for the patients in the drug rehab on the third floor?"

"Hold on, please. I'll connect you with the desk there."

Oh, no. The people at the desk knew my voice.

"Hello, how may I help you?"

I took a deep breath. "I'm waiting for a phone call from a patient and I just wanted to know the phone hours on your floor." There. Now all I could do was hope they would help me.

"Noon to one. Five-thirty til nine in the evenings."

Phew! Finally, I got some information. I would make it a point to stick by the phone during those hours, just in case. Where else would I go, anyway?

The Garcias invited me downstairs for dinner. It was awkward for all of us. Mrs. Garcia was convinced that Pablo had a drinking problem, not a drug problem. Mr. Garcia seemed much nicer to me than he had been in the past. Maybe he felt sorry for me.

We were making small talk until Mrs. Garcia brought the conversation around to the inevitable, Pablo. "I just can't believe poor Pablo. I should have known. Once I saw a bottle of scotch in the back of the car."

"It wasn't the scotch," I said, and tried to explain.

"I knew it," she continued, not listening to me. "He was always so tired. Drinking will do that to you if you drink all day. He must have had a drink in the morning. Do you think he drank at the barn?"

"When did you see a bottle of scotch in the car?" I asked politely.

"Before we came to Florida," she said, putting one of the crab claws onto her plate. We were eating stone crabs, Pablo's favorite.

I thought back. I told Pablo to give his assistant trainers a Christmas present, and he had suggested the scotch.

"I think the scotch you saw was a Christmas present for the guys at the barn," I offered.

"Ramon, when are the horses leaving?" she asked, changing the subject.

"When I saw Pablo," Mr. Garcia said, "we agreed to have them shipped out tomorrow. I got him to sign over the title to the yacht, so at least now I know I'll get some of the money back that I'm putting out."

"What? You *saw* Pablo?" I was flabbergasted. "Where? When? He's *selling* his racing yacht? No way! You *saw* him?"

"Yeah. I've been down there a few times. We had to get this financial mess straightened out."

I was numb. Pablo had been seeing everyone *but* me! I tried to remain calm, but I was losing the battle. "How did you get to see him?" I said, feeling my throat tighten up in a knot. Tears were beginning to well up in my eyes. I looked down at my crab. I couldn't taste anything anymore.

"His counselor called. Then I went down. Oh, and we're supposed to go to a meeting in a few days, a meeting for families of the patients. That's what his counselor told me. Of course, I had to get this financial mess straightened out."

I couldn't take it anymore. His counselor had called *them* and not *me*??!! I was crying now. I had to leave.

"Excuse me," I pulled out my chair and headed for the door. I didn't want them to see me cry.

"Karen, where are you going?" Mrs. Garcia asked. "Please stay and finish your crabs. Or, would you like to take them with you?"

"No. Thank you for dinner," I managed to say before letting myself out the door. I wanted to explode in a flood of tears. Pablo hated me. Why was he doing this to me? Why was he leaving me out? Even if I had gone to the hospital, they wouldn't have let me see him. Why hadn't his counselor called me? Why hadn't his counselor called me to tell me about this "family meeting?" It just didn't make any sense.

I went upstairs and cried into my pillow. Pablo didn't love me anymore.

BRRIIING. The sound of the phone nearly knocked me out of the bed. I had forgotten that I turned the ringer way up loud so I wouldn't miss his call. I reached for the phone on the night table. Maybe it was Pablo!

"Hello?"

"Yes, I need some cigarettes." I didn't recognize the voice.

"Who is this?"

"I was told to call you for cigarettes." Was this some sort of a joke?

"Who is this?" I asked, totally confused.

"Can you bring me my cigarettes?"

"Who are you? Do you know Pablo?"

"Yeah, he told me to call you. He took my cigarettes, and he told me you would bring me a new carton."

"Where is Pablo? Can he come to the phone?"

"No. He told me to call you—to bring the cigarettes."

I was angry now. Pablo and his cigarettes. He knew this would upset me. Why was he doing this to me? And, who was this character on the phone?

"Can you come down with them?" he asked again.

"No! I don't even know who you are! And why didn't Pablo call me himself? What is your name?"

"I'm Joe. Pablo smoked all my cigarettes. Now I need more. I like Camel, but any brand will do, really. I need a smoke."

What was this all about? What was going on?

"Where is Pablo? Bring him to the phone, please."

"Bring the Marlboro brand, okay?" Joe said.

"Is Pablo there?" I knew that Pablo liked to smoke Marlboros. "Joe, is Pablo telling you to ask me that? Did he give you this number?"

"Camels. I like..." Click. Someone had disconnected us.

I felt like I had just been stabbed. Pablo knew the cigarettes bothered me. Why was he hurting me like this? I was crying and couldn't stop. Set on inflicting physical pain, I started cutting myself with a knife. I got out the vodka. Weak and alone, I knew I was in a bad place. If I continued on this way, I was in real trouble. Who could help me?

Mom? No, Pablo said she wanted to see me miserable.

My sister, Susan? No, Pablo said she would only make things worse.

Grandma? No, Pablo didn't want me staying with her.

Who was left?

My father! Pablo had never spoken badly of him because he wasn't involved much in my life. I would call my father. Pablo would be okay with that.

Crying and a mess, I called my father. I couldn't stop sobbing. "Please come down, Dad. I need you."

Dad could tell I was in crisis. He said he would get a flight out in the morning (he lived in New Jersey). Hoping I would last that long, I got drunk and remembered no more.

I awoke to a knock on the door. It was morning, and Mrs. Garcia was inviting me downstairs for coffee.

I felt like I was in the twilight zone. Crazy me. The Garcias seemed fine. They were taking Pablo's hospitalization in stride, as if it were no big deal. What was wrong with me??? They didn't understand. But at least they were being kind to me. Kinder than Pablo. What was he trying to do to me? Was I going insane?

I told the Garcias that my father was coming down. I was glad that Dad was coming. It had been a long time since I had seen him. Would he think I was crazy, too? Or would he see things my way?

I drank my coffee, thinking about all that had happened in the last few months. It seemed like forever, living in hell. The methadone, the lies. Coming to Florida. Things not being what they had seemed, and now being pushed aside. I thought about the day Pablo went into the hospital, the day our bubble had finally burst. I was lost, somewhere between reality and the twilight zone. I was no longer a "with Pablo," my role in life gone. He had shut me out of the only place I belonged...with him.

Surely, our life would pick up where it had left off—before he went into the hospital. And then I would feel normal again, a "with Pablo." Then all this could be forgotten, in the past.

But what would Pablo be like when he came out of the hospital? Who was this man, Pablo? Who was the man I had married, really, off drugs??? I had only known him on drugs. Would he be the same Pablo? Would I still love him? Would he love me? Would he need me? Would he want me? Or, would he just desert me? I wanted to go back in time. I wanted it to be like it was before. But somewhere inside me I knew that "we" were dying. Life with Pablo as I knew it was over. And the death of this part of me was torture. The way that Pablo was cutting me off, pushing me away...what was to become of me/us?

As I sat in the Garcias condo thinking about all this, I made a decision. I would stop throwing up. Now that Pablo was gone, there was no reason for me to throw up, to show him how bad I was. So, in the midst of all the craziness, I made a commitment.

"Karen?"

Mrs. Garcia pulled me out of my thoughts.

"Yes?" I answered, trying to focus on her.

"A policeman has been calling, looking for you. Here is his number." She handed me a paper. "Maybe when your father gets here, you can call him."

I looked at the name written on the paper: Sergeant Striker. "Did he say what he wanted?" I asked, a little confused. I hadn't done anything illegal, had I?

"He just said that he is trying to locate you. He said you were on a missing persons list."

Missing persons? Me? Why? Why would anybody think I was missing? Who was looking for me? Pablo? No. Pablo knew where to find me. Hmm.

Mr. Garcia came back from the track, where he had been trying to clean up the mess Pablo had left behind. He handed me a document. "Do you know what this is?"

I started to read it. It was a contract for the new sailboat. I didn't know what to say. Pablo probably hadn't told his father about the sailboat because he owed so much money and Mr. Garcia wanted him to sell his racing yacht. "Umm. Yeah. Did you ask Pablo about this?"

Mr. Garcia shook his head.

"Well, it's for a ninety-foot sailboat. Pablo wanted to buy a sailboat, and I guess this is a contract."

"A big sailboat?" Mr. Garcia laughed cynically. "Now why in the hell would he want another boat? Damn. I've got the racing yacht sold. He's not going to go and buy another boat. That money is going back to me for all those bills I paid." He got up and put the contract in the waste paper basket.

Well, I guess that settled it. I was glad somebody made a decision about the sailboat. I would have to tell Pablo, though. As soon as he would talk to me.

"Have you talked to Pablo recently?" I asked Mr. Garcia.

"Yes. We are supposed to go to a meeting tomorrow, a family meeting. That's what his counselor suggested."

Once again, I felt left out of the loop. I wish Dad were here. Then somebody would be on my side, for once.

Around eleven-thirty Dad showed up at the condo. He had flown into Miami International Airport and rented a car.

"Dad!" I hugged him. I was so glad to have somebody dependable around. I did my best to fill him in on the details. As I was explaining all the events that had happened since I found out about the methadone, he got up and drew the curtains back from the window of our condo.

"It's so dark in here," he commented.

"I know. It doesn't help to open the curtains, though. This room is the brightest one in the apartment. Oh, and I forgot to tell you. A police sergeant called. He's looking for me. He says I'm a missing person or something. Maybe you should call him."

My father called the policeman and then told me the situation. "It seems you were supposed to be at Palmetto Hospital, but you disappeared. You were put on a missing persons list. They had to trace you down, and it took them a few days to find the Garcias' number. We have to go down there and straighten this out. Sergeant Striker seemed real nice. You may still have to go back to Palmetto Hospital, but maybe not. We'll see."

"I really don't want to go. I'm afraid they will lock me up."

"We have to go," Dad explained logically. "It's the law. You're a missing person and until they see you, you'll remain on a list. Come on. We'll stop and get something to eat and then go meet the officer."

Dad was so practical. He thought everything could be done by the book. I guess being a teacher made him that way. Or maybe he became a teacher because he was so sensible. Anyway, how could I explain that, down here, nothing made sense? Nothing was as it seemed. I didn't trust anyone. Not the police, not the social workers, and certainly not the hospitals or counselors. He would see. Or maybe he wouldn't. Maybe it was the way I was seeing things. Maybe I really was crazy.

Well, as long as I was with Dad and away from Pablo, I felt sane. But I still longed for Pablo. I felt like an empty shell. I was just putting on an act, being the daughter my father knew. The only living part of me was somewhere in a South Miami Beach detox unit, going through methadone withdrawal.

We ate lunch at the Burger King down the road. I decided on a salad from the salad bar. I didn't want to be tempted to throw up, and salad was non-fattening.

I was on an emotional roller coaster. On the one hand, I felt good around my father. But more than ever, I missed my Pablo. I went from happy to sad, normal to depressed. Dad could only see me from the outside. He could only see the daughter that he once knew. He couldn't see my inner turmoil as I drifted in and out of my "with Pabloness." I guess I couldn't expect him to understand how I felt. I was hurt, confused, and rejected by my one and only. Still, I needed Pablo. I felt like Humpty Dumpty.

Humpty Dumpty sat on a wall.
Humpty Dumpty had a great fall.
All the king's horses and all the king's men
Couldn't put Humpty together again.

Who could put me back together again? Oh where, oh where was my Pablo?

"Dad, if everything goes well with this policeman, can we go visit Pablo?"

"Let's just wait and see."

Only Pablo could understand me, the real me. He knows me. He understands me. He could put me back together again.

Sergeant Striker was nice. He heard my story and was very sympathetic. He was in AA, so he knew the insanity that goes along with marriage to a drug addict or alcoholic. He said, "It's a family disease. Nobody goes unaffected." He agreed to release me into the care of my father.

Before we left, Sergeant Striker said to me, "Karen, if you ever need anything, or just need to talk, here is my number. Call me—anytime, anywhere." I would remember that.

Now that I had two people I could count on, Sergeant Striker and my father, I should have been happy. But I only wanted one—Pablo. I needed my Pablo to continue to live. I needed him to survive. Karen Garcia was dying and needed to be plugged into her life support...and soon.

As we left the police station, my mind went right back to Pablo. "Dad, do you think we could take a ride down to Mount Sinai Hospital to find out what's going on with Pablo? I'm worried about him. The Garcias have seen him, but nobody has called me. Maybe if we go down there, we can find out about this family meeting tomorrow."

"I don't know if that's a good idea," he said hesitantly. "Sergeant Striker said we should get your mind off all of this."

"But Dad, I *have* to find out about Pablo. I have to know. Come on, let's just go."

Dad was thinking. He mumbled to himself. I hoped he would listen. *I just had to see Pablo.*

"Oh, okay. If you think it will make you feel better," he finally said.

We drove to the hospital. My insides were doing flip flops as I remembered "Code White." I held my father's hand as we got off at the third floor and went over to the desk. What if Pablo's doctor spotted me? Would he have me locked up again?

"We're looking for Pablo Garcia," Dad explained. "My daughter is his wife. It has been nearly a week, and she has had no word from anyone about him."

Dad and I were taken to a room where a man asked some questions. "You say you are his wife and you have had no contact with anyone, not even his counselor?"

I nodded to the man who seemed like he was trying to help.

"I don't understand. That's not the way the program works," he said. "The families are supposed to be involved, unless that's a problem. Wait a minute. Mrs. Simon, the head of the program, has been on vacation. She came back yesterday. I'll get her for you."

I was glad my father was there with me. I needed someone to believe in me, to know that I wasn't crazy.

After ten minutes, a huge, mean looking woman marched into the room, looking annoyed. "Can you wait outside, please?" she said to Dad. It was more of an order than a question.

Dad looked at me and shrugged. "I'm not supposed to leave her..." he started to explain to the overbearing commander-in-chief, "but I guess it's okay." He got up sheepishly from his chair and left the room.

I was now alone with the Gestapo.

"Now, what's all this I've been hearing about you?"

"What?" I suddenly felt guilty.

"I've just come back from my vacation—and now this," she said, glaring at me.

"I left my husband here about a week ago," I explained, "and nobody has contacted me. My husband's parents have been called, but nobody will tell me anything." I tried to sound logical, unemotional. It was hard not to show my feelings of abandonment. *Don't cry. Stuff the feelings. Don't break down. Don't! They might have you locked up again.*

"And what drug are *you* on?" she asked, throwing the accusation out at me from left field.

"What? I'm not on drugs. You don't even know me. Why..." I did my best to hold back the tears.

"Everyone at the racetrack is on drugs," she stated with conviction.

"Why do you say that? That's not true. You don't even know me! How can you say that to me?" I felt attacked and outnumbered. Why did everyone at the hospital dislike me so much?

She shook her head as if she was wasting her time with me.

"I came here to find out about Pablo," I repeated. This was not about me, was it? "What's going on here?"

The Gestapo eyed me closely, putting her large face right up in mine. I melted back into my chair. "I don't know what's going on," she said defiantly, "but I intend to find out. If you are as you say you are, then his counselor will be able to explain everything to you."

"I don't even know his counselor," I said quietly, almost to myself.

"What? Speak up. I don't have time for this. I'm very, very busy, you know."

"I said I don't know his counselor."

"And why is that, I wonder?" she asked snidely.

"I don't know. Ask Pablo. He would know. He knows about everything. Could you get him for me? I really want to see him."

"His counselor hasn't been in touch with you?" She raised her eyebrows suspiciously. I could tell she didn't believe me.

"No. Get Pablo. He'll tell you, if you don't believe me."

"Hmm. Wait here. I'll have to see about this."

I was relieved when she turned and stormed out of the room. The floor quivered under my feet from her weight as she left. She'll see. Pablo will fix this mess. It's just a giant misunderstanding. Pablo's counselor probably forgot to call me, and Pablo probably thought I didn't love him anymore because I didn't come see him. And all because of his counselor!

An anxious thought suddenly crossed my mind. Why did she say that I was on drugs? And how did she know that I was from the racetrack? What was going on???

Thinking back on this, what was Pablo telling everyone at the hospital about me??? Why had they locked me up and treated me like a criminal??? Why did they shut me, his wife, out of the decisions from the very beginning, when he was admitted? Why didn't his counselor call me? Why wasn't I included in the family meetings?? What was Pablo saying?

Within a few minutes, Mrs. Simon came back in the room. Pablo was behind her!

"Pablo!" I cried out, happy to finally see him. But he looked...different. His head was hanging. He shuffled his feet as he came into the room. He didn't even seem to notice that I was there. "Pablo, I've been trying to figure out how to get in touch with you!" I kissed him as he sat down next to me, in the chair that Dad had been sitting in. I moved my chair closer to him, secretly wishing I could sit on his lap.

"I've called him out of a meeting," Mrs. Simon said. "Normally I don't do this, but I want to find out what's been going on."

I nodded happily. "Pablo will explain everything. You'll see that I'm not crazy or on drugs." I put my arms around Pablo and planted a kiss on his cheek.

Pablo was distant. He spoke like a ghost of the man I knew and loved. "What is it you need?" He addressed Mrs. Simon, not even glancing my way.

"Karen says she hasn't been contacted, and I was wondering why. You would know, Pablo. What's the problem?" The big woman looked at Pablo and then back at me suspiciously, like Pablo was going to say what a horrible wife I was. Well, she was wrong. Pablo *loved* me.

"Uh, I don't know," Pablo muttered softly, not looking at me.

"What do you mean, Pablo?" I blurted out. He had to know! He had to come to my defense! "Your parents have seen you, why not me?" I asked. Why couldn't he explain to her, make her see that I wasn't crazy and that nobody had called me!

"Um. Probably my counselor forgot," Pablo offered with no emotion whatsoever. "Or, yeah, he was sick last week. Another guy took his place and I guess there was a mix-up or something."

"See?" I said to Mrs. Simon, relieved.

"Huh." She shook her head. "I don't understand this happening. Not at *my* facility. I'm going to have to straighten this out. This should never have happened to you," she said, sounding apologetic and nodding in my direction.

Pablo looked so detached, so far away. It seemed like he couldn't wait to leave me and Mrs. Simon. What was wrong with him? Did the lack of drugs make him forget how much we loved each other? Didn't he miss me? Didn't he need me?

"I have to get back to my meeting," he said, emotionless, staring blankly at the door.

Mrs. Simon smiled at her perfect patient, Pablo. He couldn't wait to get back to his meeting?!? And away from me!

"Okay, Pablo. You can go," she smiled and gave him permission to leave.

"Wait! Pablo, when can I see you?" I held onto his arm as he got up from his chair. *Please don't do this to me, Pablo. Don't just ignore me...*

"I don't know," he answered coldly.

I wanted to cry. This wasn't my Pablo. Was he mad at me?

"It seems this was a misunderstanding," Mrs. Simon said to me. "Look, there is a family meeting tomorrow at four o'clock. You should be here. And I will make sure Pablo's counselor calls you and keeps you informed. That's all." She turned and left the room.

I stood there, feeling rejected and more alone than ever. Was I supposed to feel better? I didn't. I felt worse. Pablo was pushing me away. Why? Why didn't he want me around him???

Dad came back into the room. "Are you feeling better now?" he asked me.

I got up and hugged him. "I don't know what I feel, Dad. I don't know anything anymore." But I did know what I felt. Alone, unwanted, and confused. This wasn't what I expected at all. Pablo was somehow *different*. Maybe I liked him better on drugs. What an awful thing to think...

Instead of going back to the dark, depressing condo, Dad and I checked into a Ramada Inn. Our room was on the seventh floor. I went out onto the balcony and looked down. If I jumped, where would I land? How would I splatter, or would jumping seven stories be enough to make me splatter? Would it kill me, or just break my legs?

I felt so alone and rejected. Even the presence of my father couldn't undo the five years I had spent alone with Pablo. A week without him and I was going through withdrawal. I was so depressed. Reality was starting to set in: Pablo didn't love me anymore. He had abandoned me for meetings, hospitals, and complete strangers. He never called. He hated me.

Just like Vince. He was supposed to care about me! Instead there was total rejection and complete apathy for my state of mind and future. Emotionally, Pablo and Vince's behavior affected me the exact same way. It didn't matter to Vince/Pablo if I killed myself!

Measuring the distance, I imagined the jump. Would I die or just become paralyzed? What about Dad? He would feel so guilty for not preventing it...

"What are you thinking about?"

I turned around and saw Dad joining me on the balcony.

"Nothing."

"We're up pretty high," he commented. "Come away from the edge."

"Do you think if I jumped it would kill me?"

"Don't talk like that. Come on. Let's go out. We'll see a movie or something."

I followed my father back inside. Lifeless, hopeless me.

That night at the Ramada Inn, I had trouble sleeping. My mind just wouldn't rest. Here I was with my father, a "normal" person, and all I felt was more abnormal than ever. I felt like a fish out of water. I had forgotten how to think and act like a normal person. I wanted to get back into my life with Pablo. My mind and soul were still attached to him and his way of thinking. I had depended on him for survival. I didn't know how to exist without him. Who was I and where was I going without Pablo to guide me? Why couldn't things just go back to the way they were before? I dreaded my future. Without Pablo, there was no hope for me. He was the only one in the world who knew me, understood me, and loved me anyway. What would I do, now that he seemed to be rejecting me? Pablo knew I was unworthy, but he had loved me anyway. Now, his love for me seemed to have grown cold. Still, I wasn't giving up. All was not lost. The family meeting was tomorrow. Things would be better. Pablo could still love me again.

Dad and I went back to the condo in the morning. There was a sudden turn in the Garcias' attitude toward me. They had gone through all my stuff in the condo and taken the keys to the Jeep and some other things. I felt like I had been violated. Why had they done this?

"Dad, I'm going to go downstairs to get my keys back. I don't know why they would have taken them."

I went down and knocked on the Garcias' door. Mrs. Garcia was very cold and distant towards me, not like she had been before. She did not invite me in. She acted as though she knew nothing about my missing stuff or the keys. She told me to ask her husband about it.

I wondered what had caused her to suddenly change. What had happened to make her act this way? What had I done?

Mr. Garcia was out front hitting golf balls. I sensed that he didn't want to talk to me, either. For some reason, they both disliked me now. I decided it might be better if I sent Dad to get the keys back.

I watched through the window as Dad approached Mr. Garcia. They appeared to be talking, but Mr. Garcia never looked at my father. He had his head down and just kept swinging his golf club. Dad finally turned and came back to the condo.

"Did you get the keys to the Jeep?" I asked him.

Dad shook his head.

"Why *not*?" I felt like everybody was against me now. Only Pablo understood me and believed in me. "*Pablo* would have gotten the keys for me. He would have *made* Mr. Garcia give them back!"

"I'm sorry, Karen. Mr. Garcia didn't want to give them to me."

"And you *listened* to him??? Pablo would never have listened to his father. He knows how to handle him. I can't believe you listened to him!" I was so mad at my father at that moment. I was mad that he wasn't Pablo. I needed Pablo. I needed Pablo to love me, to stick up for me, to save me.

"I'm sorry," he repeated. "Maybe I was wrong. I didn't know it would upset you that much. I should have gotten the keys. Oh, why doesn't anything make *sense*? I wish I could make you feel better."

"You do, Dad," I said, feeling like maybe he was on my side. Maybe he did care. Soon we would go to the family meeting, and then everything would be better.

Chapter 69
Bad, Bad Me

Dad waited outside while I went into the family meeting. There were about twenty people at the meeting, sitting in a circle. They were mothers, fathers, husbands, wives, and adult children of the patients in the drug and alcohol rehabilitation program at the hospital. I spotted Mr. and Mrs. Garcia at the other end of the room.

The woman running the group explained how drug and alcohol addiction was a "family disease." (I could vouch for that!) I listened as some of the spouses of addicts told their stories. There was one thing that we all seemed to have in common: all of us had been lied to, in one form or another.

As I heard the stories, I felt a little better, a little less alone. This group was geared toward helping the *families* of addicts, not the addicts themselves.

I sighed with relief at the end of the hour. Things were going to be better now. Finally, I didn't feel so alone in my suffering. Maybe the others hadn't gotten as upset as I had when Pablo was first admitted to the hospital, but everyone seemed to have suffered in varying degrees.

I left the room and saw Dad in the hallway, pacing back and forth nervously. He had his head down and was mumbling to himself. I could tell he was really concerned about me. Over the past few days I had mentioned not wanting to live anymore, which I think worried and confused him.

"Dad! I feel so much better! You wouldn't believe how many other people feel like I do!" I said with relief, hugging him.

"I'm so glad you feel better. I was so worried. I feel so helpless."

As we hugged, I heard a voice behind us. It was Mr. Garcia.

"YOU'RE the one with the PROBLEM!!" he said, pointing his finger accusingly in my face. Mrs. Garcia stood a little behind her husband, nodding in agreement. I was taken off guard and started to feel horrible again.

Looking back, what was Pablo telling his parents about me? Why the sudden change in their behavior toward me?

"What do you mean?" Dad asked Mr. Garcia, quickly stepping between us as he sensed that I would get upset again.

"She's the problem," Mr. Garcia said bitterly.

What had I said or done to make him so mad??? Maybe he was right. Everyone hated me. Everyone but Pablo...

Before the meeting, the people at the desk had told me where to find Pablo's room so Dad and I could visit him after the meeting. I had to see Pablo before his parents did. He would stick up for me! Pablo would tell his parents that none of this was my fault!

I turned and ran down the hallway, choking back the tears. Pablo's room was at the very end. I pushed the door open and saw him lying on a bed, smoking a cigarette.

"Pablo, your parents are mad at me. They say that everything is my fault!" I went toward him, but he shrank away from me. He looked at me like I was crazy. He looked different. His eyes were blank.

"Pablo, tell them. Tell them it isn't *my* fault."

Pablo cowered away from me even more, tucking his legs up so he was as far away from me as possible in the bed.

"What's wrong?" I pleaded, confused. "Why don't you love me anymore? Why didn't you call me?" I started to cry, seeing my Pablo so different. He was so cold to me. I noticed that the drawer to his nightstand was wide open, revealing a carton of Marlboros. "And, who called me about those cigarettes?"

"Uh, that was my roommate."

"Why did you do that to me, Pablo? You knew I would get upset over the cigarettes." I was so confused.

"Uh, my roommate did that. He's crazy."

I took a pack of cigarettes out of the carton and opened them up.

"Don't. Those are his," Pablo said.

"You're smoking them, aren't you?" I asked, without waiting for the obvious answer. Now I was just plain angry. Pablo preferred the cigarettes, the lies, the people in the hospital, and his parents over *me*. Well, I would be part of his conspiracy, then. I would be just like him.

I put a cigarette in my mouth. "Gimme yours." I reached for Pablo's lit cigarette. He handed it over to me and watched. I held Pablo's cigarette to the end of mine to light it. Then I inhaled deeply. I hated him.

Flashback...Vince did the same, inhaling his cigarette deeply, the same way he inhaled his pot. Vince, the betrayer...I hated him.

I inhaled the hatred and wished I would pass out. Let me die already. I'm just so tired of all this. I smoked and smoked that cigarette, inhaling it as if it were life itself. All I hated was wrapped up in that little Marlboro, and I was sucking it in. I flicked the ashes purposely, flick, flick, with my thumb and watched them spill all over the floor.

Flashback... Vince did the same, flick, flick, with his thumb, not like Mom, who tapped the cigarette gently with her index finger.

I smoked, inhaling long and hard. I didn't even cough once. Mind over matter.

Dad had come into the room. He watched me and didn't say a word.

"Give me another one, Pablo. These are great," I said mockingly. "I just love to smoke, more than life itself."

I reached into the pack and got another one, grabbing Pablo's lit cigarette away from him again to light my own. "What's the matter, Pablo? Can't you inhale it any deeper?"

Flashback... inhale deeper, like Vince.

I lay down in the empty bed next to Pablo's. I was dizzy, but I didn't care. I wished the cigarettes would kill me. But I knew they wouldn't. Why was I doing this?

"How many of these do I have to smoke to become addicted, like you?"

Pablo said nothing.

"A whole pack? Let me have another."

I smoked five cigarettes before I finally stopped. I didn't really want to get addicted, did I? Oh, what was the point to anything anymore? What was wrong with me??? I must be crazy; whenever I'm around Pablo, I go insane.

My emotions and hurt were overwhelming me. However, I still had no idea where these strong feelings of betrayal and anger were coming from. I believed they all came from Pablo. Until I could consciously make the connection and deal with the profound hurt caused by Vince, I would keep going off the deep end like this.

The Garcias came into the room. They talked with Dad and tried to ignore crazy me. Then they went over to Pablo. The three talked so nicely while I lay there on the bed, finishing my last cigarette. Dad went over to the window and started pacing.

"Pablo, can we talk to you alone, outside?" Mr. Garcia asked. Pablo was being so attentive, so wonderful with his parents. Just one big happy family—without me. I was the crazy one, remember?

Just like Vince always told Mom. I was the crazy one with the temper tantrums. Trouble, that's all I ever was. Bad, bad me.

The Garcias, Dad, and Pablo left the room to talk. Why didn't they just lock me up, instead of Pablo? I'd be better off. Maybe then they would sympathize with me and not shut me out.

Pablo came back into the room. Dad and the Garcias were still outside in the hallway, probably discussing my fate. Crazy, impossible me. The nut job. Wasn't Dad on my side anymore? What were the Garcias telling him? Why didn't *they* like me anymore? Bad, bad me.

Pablo sat back on his bed again. He didn't say a word. He just looked at me like I was pathetic.

"Why don't you love me anymore, Pablo?"

Pablo shook his head, "I don't feel anything anymore."

I wanted it to be like it used to be. Why wouldn't he hold me, hug me? Or should I be supportive of him? How could I be when I had so much anger?

I am such a failure. What's wrong with me? I can't even love my husband and give him support when he needs it most! It's all my fault. If I wasn't such a problem, he never would have been in here...and I ruined Mom's life. I am so bad. So bad.

I wanted to kill myself. Right then. But I had to do it quietly, calmly, so nobody knew I was doing it until it was too late.

Dad came back into the room. "I have to use the bathroom," I said, disappearing into the private bathroom off Pablo's room.

I could hear Dad and Pablo talking. I went to lock the bathroom door, but realized there was no lock on the door. Darn. *I'll have to be very quiet and very quick*. I looked around for Pablo's razor, but all I could find was an electric razor. *Darn! I guess one of these hospitals is the worst place to try to kill yourself. There is nothing sharp anywhere. Okay. Now what should I do?*

I was getting a little frantic because I didn't want them to suspect anything. *I know! I'll drown myself.* I started to fill the tub. *No. They'll hear it. And it will take too long. I'll use the sink!*

There was no plug for the sink. The drain was covered with a fixed metal plate with holes in it. I grabbed some paper towels to stop the water from going down the drain and turned the sink on full blast. The sink was shallow. I put my face into it and breathed in the water. I coughed and my face came out of the water. Darn! Why couldn't I do this? I put my face back in and tried again. I felt a hand on my shoulder and lifted my face back out. "Don't try to stop me!" I said in desperation. The water was leaking down the drain faster than it was filling up. I realized I was defeated. This wasn't going to work.

"Don't do this," I heard the voice behind me say. It was Dad. Why couldn't it have been Pablo who wanted to save me? Why not Pablo? He was too confused to help me, right? He had his own problems. I couldn't help him, either, but at least now he had outside help.

"Please don't," Dad pleaded. I turned around and saw my father crying. He hugged me. I sat down on the tile floor, exhausted and out of breath. Dad sat down right next to me. He held me tightly and whispered, "I don't know what to do. I love you. I want to help you, to be there for you the way I wasn't in the past..."

I looked into my father's eyes. They were filled with tears. He sniffled. He looked so sad. *Was he really on my side? Did he love me, or would he turn against me, too?*

I felt bad that he was suffering because of me. "I love you, too, Dad. Thanks for coming down. I needed... someone...I don't know what's wrong with me."

Dad talked about the past, when I was very young. He brought up the old, happy memories, like when he used to tell my sister and me our favorite bedtime story, "The Adventures of Susan and Karen," which, of course, he had created. He told me how much he missed us when he left Mom, when Vince came around.

"I didn't want to leave you two. I wanted to take you with me. But I couldn't separate you from your mother. If I had known about Vince being so...ugh...I never would have let you stay there."

Dad looked so upset. I hadn't seen this emotional side of him—except for that day he cried when he left us so long ago. I never thought it had bothered him after that day. And I never thought he had considered taking us with him! I thought he loved his new family more: his new wife and her three kids. Back then, he didn't need Susan or me, but he had still come every weekend to see us. I thought he had done that out of responsibility, not love.

"Dad, don't cry. Don't feel bad. We wouldn't have gone with you anyway. You did the right thing. You didn't know about Vince. None of us did."

"I should have...done something..." He shook his head in sorrow.

I felt so much better sitting there on the bathroom floor with my dad. He cared. He really did. I could tell. I could *feel* his love. *He* wasn't lying to me.

"Come on, Dad. Let's go. I'm so glad you're here with me." I stood up, leaning on my father for support. We came out of the bathroom and suddenly I felt strong. Somebody believed in me. Somebody loved me.

Through this whole ordeal with Pablo, I had been so alone. Whenever I got the support of Grandma, Dad, or the people at AA, I felt stronger—for a while.

As we came out of the bathroom, I saw Pablo cringing in his bed. I spotted his favorite Dunhill pipe on the window sill and picked it up. The anger I had previously felt and had turned inward on myself was now suddenly directed at Pablo. *He was the cause of all this, wasn't he?* I winged the pipe at his head. It missed and shattered into the wall behind him.

"Good," I heard my father say. "Get mad. Let it out."

"Come on, Dad. Let's go."

Dad and I left Pablo, passing by the Garcias in the hall. They didn't look too thrilled with me. Of course, they believed all this—Pablo's addiction—was my fault. Poor Pablo, they were probably thinking. Their poor son, the victim of a crazy wife.

As Dad and I walked to the car, I became depressed. As usual, I turned the anger at Pablo back on myself again. I shouldn't have broken his favorite pipe. I wanted Pablo to love me.

Dad put his arm around me. He really believed everything was all better now. To him, it was black and white. Good guys and bad guys. Justice triumphs and that sort of thing. But it wasn't that simple.

"I'm so glad you finally got angry at Pablo, and not at yourself. *He* is the one putting you through all this. And, of course, the Garcias will stick up for him, not you. Pablo is their only son. They'll believe you're crazy and he is fine."

Was I dreaming to think things could ever be the same? Pablo seemed so different in the hospital, off drugs. Would he ever get back to his old self without the methadone? He had always been so in control, the authority on everything, including me, and now...What future did I have without the Pablo I knew?

"I don't feel any better, Dad. I wish I was dead."

I still wasn't aware of the subconscious connection my ancient, buried emotions had with the present. The "love and attention" and then rejection by Vince was emotionally connected to my present situation with Pablo. I believed that the whole problem was Pablo, so I couldn't understand my irrational behavior. The "bad me" feelings I had tried to bury for so many years were coming to the surface, erupting from their hiding place and trying to destroy me once again.

"I don't know what to do," Dad said, as we drove away from Mount Sinai Hospital.

"Maybe I belong in a hospital, like Pablo." I figured if I was just like Pablo, maybe it would make us one again. Maybe then he would love me, and I would have a reason to live again.

We went out to eat and then spent a last night at the Ramada Inn. In the morning, we headed back to Palm Springs North. I was becoming very concerned about my stuff. Everything was in the hands of the Garcias. After all, they had gone through my things. As we approached the condominiums, a sense of urgency came over me. I just had to get back to my belongings. They were the only thing left to hold onto. They were my identity.

We got out of the rental car, and I broke into a run. Up the stairs, onto the landing. I stopped in horror at what I saw. There, sitting by the side of the condo, were six filled black garbage bags. Not only that, I was locked out! What was going on here? Had they thrown away all my stuff? What right did they have to do this to me???

Dad came up the steps and saw my dilemma.

"Looks like they've cleaned house and locked us out."

"Dad, I can't stand it anymore. Let's get out of here. Let's pack up these bags and go back to New York."

"That's a great idea!! I've been waiting to hear you say that!"

"Dad, the Garcias still have the keys to the Jeep. You'll *have* to get them back. Tell them we're leaving, driving back to New York. That should make them happy."

Everything in my life was gone: my husband, his yacht, and his horses. (I overheard Mr. Garcia telling Pablo in the hospital that he was giving the horses to Jim, the assistant trainer, to train.) My riding was long gone, and Mom didn't love me. What was left? The Jeep. If Dad managed to get the keys, I would have that. And hopefully, I would have some of my stuff. I could only hope all my things were in the garbage bags, and not gone forever. I was going home, to Oyster

Bay. Sort of home, I think. What would it be like there, the abandoned house, without Pablo? It seemed like a lifetime ago that Pablo and I had lived there.

Dad came back smiling, keys in hand. “When I explained that we needed the Jeep to get back to New York,” he said, “they gladly handed over the keys. Follow me in the Jeep to the airport to return the rental car, and then we’ll make the trip north.”

We threw the garbage bags into the Jeep and left the condos for the last time. As I followed Dad’s rental car out of the parking lot, I sighed with relief. There would be no more waiting for the Federal Express truck to appear around this corner. I was so glad to finally be leaving Florida behind.

Chapter 70
Home Alone

After we returned the rental car, Dad drove the Jeep all the way to the northern part of Florida. Then we pulled over and switched places. Ah, behind the wheel at last. I stepped on the gas and felt exhilaration. Back in control of my destiny. Me and all my stuff, racing out of Florida as fast as I could.

I drove the rest of the way home. It felt so good to have a purpose. I finally had a tangible goal: crossing the border of each state as we traveled north.

I dropped my father off in New Jersey, and then headed for Long Island. I didn’t want to think about where I was going; I just wanted to get there.

When I got to Oyster Bay, I pulled into the driveway and stopped in front of the house. Memories of how things used to be flooded back. Suddenly, I dreaded going into the empty, cold, deserted place. What was wrong with me? Had the place changed? Was it different? No. It was me. I was different. I knew too much. I knew that our old life here had been one great big lie. What was left for me here?

I sat in the Jeep. Maybe I would live in the Jeep. Drive around the country. I could just drive and drive until Pablo got out of the hospital, and then things would be...how *would* they be?

I got out of the Jeep and opened up the house. When I went in, a creepy feeling came over me. Dark, deserted house. House of lies. House of Pablo.

I went into the kitchen and opened the blinds. There were mice droppings everywhere: on the counters, in the drawers, and among the silverware, pots, and pans. It was disgusting, but I didn't have the stomach to set any mouse traps. Oh, where was Pablo when I needed him?

I decided my first mission was to kill the mice. I went to the hardware store and found some sticky glue traps, "mouse motels" as they were called. The mice would go into their motels and die. Well, this way I wouldn't have to actually see the mice. They would die inside the cardboard motel, and I would just throw the whole thing away.

With the traps in the kitchen, I sat alone in the den. I turned on the television for company. After a while I could hear the mice in the glue traps. Dying mice. Ugh. I didn't want to think about it, so I turned the television up to drown out the sound.

I decided to call Mom. She sounded happy to hear from me and said she was glad I was back in New York. She wanted to see me, so I told her I would come by later. I told her things had been going badly with Pablo, and that he was still in Florida.

After hanging up the phone, depression started to set in. I thought about Pablo. How he used to sit in his chair. How much I needed him and missed him. Yet, things just weren't the same anymore. I got a knot in my stomach when I thought about all that had happened since we left New York. Where was Pablo when I needed him?

Eventually, I forced myself to get up and turn off the television. Except for the scratching of the mice, the silence was deafening. I've got to get out of this house. I'll go see Mom.

I crept past the kitchen, and then bolted out the door. I got in the Jeep and immediately felt better behind the wheel.

Mom and Amy gave me a warm greeting. I felt like an alien landing from Mars. Here I am, folks. What is it you are saying? Greetings. I wish I could speak your language. I wish I could think and feel like a human being.

The fact that they treated me like the old Karen made things even more difficult for me. Had I been an alien, it would have been better. We could have started from scratch. But they already had it in their heads who I was. I wished I could be Karen again, but I had forgotten how. I needed Pablo. I desperately needed Pablo. I couldn't cope. I was just an empty shell.

"So, Pablo is still in Florida?" Mom asked.

"Yes. I didn't know it, but he was on drugs. He is in a drug rehab." How did I go about explaining everything? It was no use. She didn't love me. Or maybe she did. But she wouldn't understand. All I could hear was Pablo's voice in my head, warning me about my mother. *Your mother will use whatever you say against us. She doesn't love you. She'll be happy you are miserable.*

Pablo wouldn't have wanted me here with Mom. He definitely wouldn't approve. I felt so uncomfortable. Mom didn't love me, did she?

"Mom, I can't stay. I have to unpack the Jeep." I couldn't wait to get back behind the wheel again.

"Okay. Come by soon. Amy and I have missed you."

I drove back to Oyster Bay, feeling even worse than ever. Life just kept getting more real, more dreadful with each step forward I took. I felt empty and depressed as reality set in. There was no place to go to escape. I had left Florida, but nothing had changed. It wasn't going away, my life. I hate the present, and the future looks worse. I wish I could go back in time. No. It's no use. I know too much now. I wish I were dead.

I opened the door to the house and peeked into the kitchen. I saw one of the mouse cartons move slightly. The other three boxes were in different places than where I had left them. I guessed the traps had worked. What an awful way to go, dying in a sticky mouse motel.

I went into the den and stayed on the couch. I felt somewhat comfortable there in my misery. I didn't want to go upstairs, didn't want to sleep in "our" bed, and I didn't want to go past the kitchen morgue again. Maybe this feeling would go away and I'd feel better in the morning. Nights were always so depressing. I'd feel better in the morning, wouldn't I?

I didn't sleep well. I had nightmares—too real and too many. I woke up very depressed and as I looked around the den, the emptiness of my life really sunk in. There was no escaping this horrible reality. Mornings were usually my best times, so if this was as good as it got, I couldn't go on. Not like this. I wouldn't make it through another depressing day. My life, *this* life was real. Pablo didn't love me anymore. Maybe I would call him. Hearing his voice might make me feel better.

I had the number of the pay phone at the hospital where the patients could take calls. I called it and was told Pablo couldn't come to the phone. This depressed me further still. He didn't even want to talk to me. I didn't want to be alive. There was nothing to live for anymore. I would just stay in the house and rot. Like the mice.

I checked the liquor cabinet. What the heck. I'll get drunk. I always wanted to get drunk when I was around Pablo, to show him. Yeah. I'll drown my sorrows away. Maybe it will kill me. I was dying slowly anyway.

I sat on the couch drinking Pablo's favorite scotch. I hated scotch, but I wanted to be like Pablo. I wanted to be a drug addict like him. I wanted to be in the hospital with him. I belonged with him, didn't I?

The scotch depressed me even more—if that were possible. I felt like killing myself and wondered if Pablo's guns were handy. He had so many of them. Maybe I would just use one and end it all. Knowing my luck, it wouldn't kill me, just maim me for life.

I went over to the safe by the window. How lucky was I? The safe wasn't locked! And his favorite pistols were inside. Which one should I use? His "antiques" had never been fired. That could make for an interesting story in the newspapers. Nah. They weren't loaded and I wouldn't even know where to find the bullets. How about this little pistol? I took out the small handgun. It was quite heavy, considering its size. It must be loaded. I turned the pistol gently in my hand. There was a little monogram of a horse by the handle. Ah, this must be the Colt. Pablo's Colt 45. He raved about how great a pistol this was. He loves this little gun. Yeah.

I sat on the couch pondering my situation. Should I? Would this little pistol do the trick? Should I put it to my temple or put it in my mouth? Pablo said that the best way to do it was to put it in your mouth and aim up, at the back of your brain. The cavity of the throat would allow the bullet to penetrate the softest spot, going directly to the brain. According to Pablo, if I put it to my temple, I might just end up a vegetable.

Maybe it wouldn't be powerful enough. This pistol wasn't like the ones I had fired in the basement, when Pablo was teaching me to shoot. Those pistols were heavier, more powerful.

I think I'll call Pablo again. Maybe he'll talk me out of it. Maybe he'll say he still loves me. If he did, then I would have a reason to live.

I called Mount Sinai again. Pablo came to the phone!

"Hi, Pablo. I'm so depressed. I miss you. Do you miss me?"

"I'm kind of busy right now."

"I have your loaded Colt 45 in my hand. Should I kill myself?"

"I really have to go."

"Don't you care about me, Pablo? I have a gun. You don't believe me, do you?" I pointed the gun low at the wall by the big television. *Let's see how powerful this baby is.* I pulled the trigger. The explosion that followed stunned me. It was a very powerful little gun. The bullet had blown a hold into the wall by the radiator. "See, Pablo. I'm not kidding. I have your gun, and I'm going to kill myself." He must have heard the explosion. I know he did. Now, he'll stop me. He'll say he loves me. He'll beg me not to do it...

"I've got to go to a meeting now. Bye." Click.

He hung up!

It took me a moment to digest this fact. Why did he hang up on me in my moment of need? Surely his meeting wasn't so important, was it? Didn't I count for anything?

I put the gun to my temple and imagined my brains being blown away all over the cabinet, all over the couch. What a mess for whoever would find me. It wouldn't be Pablo. He was still in Florida. I couldn't put Mom through that. She hated blood.

I picked up the phone again. Sergeant Striker cared about me. He would talk to me. He would understand. I had his number in my pocket, just in case something like this should happen. Deep down, leaving Florida, I knew this would be my fate.

The phone was ringing. Would he hang up on me, too?

"Hello?"

"Is this Sergeant Striker?" I asked.

"Yes. Who's this?"

"This is Karen Garcia. I was on the missing persons list, and I came to see you with my father. Remember?" Oh, *please* remember. *Please* care.

"Yes. How are you?"

"Uh, not too good. I'm back in New York. I've got a gun. I'm going to shoot myself."

"Wait a minute. Wait. Where is your father?"

"He's back home, in New Jersey."

"You're alone?"

"Yes. I called my husband, but he hung up on me. He doesn't care about me anymore."

"You're at your home? What town is that in, Karen?"

"Oyster Bay."

"Could you hold on a second? Just a second. I've really got to go to the bathroom. Hang on, okay? I'll be right back. Don't move. Promise me, okay?"

I aimed the gun at the cabinet where Pablo always hid his cigarettes on me. I pulled the trigger and watched the cabinet splinter. The force of the bullet had popped open the cabinet door, revealing an old empty pack of Marlboros. There was a hole in the wall behind the cabinet, where the bullet had disappeared. Yes, this little Colt 45 could do the job all right.

"KAREN?? KAREN???"

Oh, yeah. Sergeant Striker. What must he think, hearing the sound of a gun? Maybe he would care. He probably thought I was dead.

"Yeah. I'm still here."

"Oh." He sounded scared. "Hold on. *Promise* me."

"Yeah. I'll hold. I'm not going anywhere."

I waited for Sergeant Striker to use the bathroom. He was so nice. I waited. And waited. Finally, he came back on the line and I told him about my situation with Pablo. He was so understanding. While we talked, I heard a knock on the door. Who could that be? Maybe Pablo had called somebody to come and rescue me??!!

"Hold on a sec. Someone is at the door," I told Sergeant Striker. I put the phone down. Then I saw Mom at the window of the den. What was she doing here? She was peering at me, pointing toward the front of the house. I got up and went to the front door. The police were there, the Oyster Bay police. There were three of them. Pablo must have called the police and told them to come and save me!! He *did* love me!! He did!!

I smiled, opening the door for them. "Come on in. I'm so glad to see you." Cops, the good guys. Pablo loved me! Pablo loved me! I wanted to scream it out to the world.

"Where is the gun?" one of them asked.

"Oh, it's in the den. In here." I led them into the den.

One of the police picked up the phone and was talking to Sergeant Striker. How did the policeman know who was on the phone?

Mom came in and hugged me. "I was so worried about you!"

"Pablo called you, too?"

Mom shook her head. "No."

"He called them, didn't he?" I pointed to the police. "Who called you guys? Pablo, right? From Florida, right?"

The cop talking to Sergeant Striker hung up. "No. Who's Pablo? This fellow, Sergeant Striker. He called us."

I went numb. *Pablo hadn't called???*

"But, Pablo, my husband, he must have called," I said hoping, praying that he had. One of the cops was bending down, examining the fresh bullet holes in the wall. I watched him run his fingers over the cabinet searching for more holes.

"There are only two. Two bullet holes. Anyway, I just wanted Pablo to care..."

I give up. I don't care about my life anymore. Pablo doesn't care. A stranger, Sergeant Striker, had cared more about me than my own husband? Surely Pablo cared. He was just preoccupied, that's all. Busy. If he hadn't been busy, he would have talked to me or called the cops. Maybe he did call them, but they were already on their way here. But Pablo had those meetings to go to, those important meetings. How could I have been so selfish to expect, to want to take him away from his meetings? I was so selfish. Selfish me. Always so bad. Bad, selfish me. Ruining everything again. Lock me up, already. Take me away.

"Any more guns around?" the cop that seemed to be in charge asked me.

"Yeah. Pablo has loads of guns. He collects them."

"Where are they?"

"All over the house. Do you want me to show you? Will you take them away?"

"Yes."

"Pablo would kill me if he found out. But, I guess you have to, huh?"

"Where are the rest of them?"

"Will he get them back?" I asked, worried that Pablo would really be upset with me now.

"If these guns are registered to him, yes. He'll get them back. If they're illegal, he won't."

"Oh, they're legal all right. He has a gun permit."

I gladly gave the men in uniform a tour of all the places where Pablo kept his guns. When I showed them the closet, one of them whistled.

"Just look at that crossbow. That's one dangerous weapon."

I remembered the story Pablo told me about the crossbow. "Yeah, Pablo says they're good for hits. You know, hit men can use them because they can't trace any bullet to any gun. And they're silent. One of those darts could kill a man easily."

The cop seemed alarmed at what I had said. "Come on, show us the rest."

I opened the other closet and showed him the rifle case. "That's Pablo's favorite rifle, though. Take special care of that one."

"Look at this!" The youngest of the three cops was in another closet. I had never been in that closet before. It was behind the couch in the den and we never used it. "He's got a shell maker in here! This guy, is he for real? He must make his own bullets."

"Oh, yeah," I added. "He told me he had one of those, too."

The senior officer shook his head in disbelief. "Where else?" he asked me. The third cop was emptying all the guns out of the safe.

"Oh. Well," I continued, "in the basement I think he keeps a few more. That's where we shoot at the target. Come on. I'll show you."

Two of the cops followed me down the basement stairs as the third took the guns back to their car.

"Gee, I'm getting the creeps down here," the young officer said. "Find any dead bodies yet, boss?"

I laughed. But he wasn't being funny. Mom looked shocked by the whole ordeal.

"Come on, Bob. I've seen enough. Let's get out of here," the older cop said.

"I don't know where any other guns would be," I explained. "But if you want to keep looking, I'll show you some more closets."

"No, that's okay."

"Hey, thanks, you guys. I probably messed up your whole day with you having to come all the way out here. I'm really sorry."

The two of them looked at me funny. The one called Bob said, "That's okay. All we ever get to do around here is look for a lost dog now and then."

"Really? That's all?" Pablo had told me about all the neighborhood robberies and how his house had been broken into. That's why he always slept with a gun under his pillow.

"Oyster Bay is a pretty quiet neighborhood," the other one agreed as we headed back up the basement steps.

"I thought there were a lot of houses getting robbed. That's why Pablo taught me how to shoot."

"Don't tell anybody he taught you how to shoot," Bob whispered to me, out of earshot of the other policeman who seemed to be in charge.

We went outside and stood by the police cars. The sun felt good. It was so cold and dark in the house. No wonder I had been depressed.

The senior officer was writing on a pad. "Listen. You would normally be taken in for this. However, seeing that your mother is here and you seem to be all right for now, we'll let it go. But only if your mother takes you to a psychiatric hospital for evaluation. There are a few good hospitals around. Brunswick House is one."

"Yeah," Bob agreed. "That's probably the best in the area."

I didn't want to go into a hospital, but where else did I belong? If I went into a hospital, a good one, then I would be like Pablo. If I went into a hospital, he might love me again. Then I might understand him better, too.

Mom agreed to call Brunswick House right away. The two police cars left as Mom and I got into her car.

"I'm so tired, Mom. I don't know what's wrong with me. Maybe the hospital *is* the best place for me."

I sat defeated, slumped in the passenger seat of Mom's car. I didn't care about anything anymore. I was a hopeless case, wasn't I? Suddenly, I wondered why Mom had come out to Oyster Bay. I hadn't called her.

"Mom, what made you come out here?"

"Your father called me."

"How did he know?"

"That policeman called him from Florida."

And I thought Sergeant Striker had been using the bathroom. All that time he was calling Dad and the Oyster Bay police. Calling for help. Why couldn't Pablo have done even *that* for me?

Chapter 71
Living in Limbo

I checked myself into Brunswick House Hospital. I could check out anytime if I wanted to, but I decided to give it a good try and stay for a while. Maybe they would have some answers for me.

I had some of my things with me, and whatever else I needed Mom brought me later in the day. I made it a point to bring my Bible. I had read some parts in Florida and was trying to understand it. God seemed so far away from me though. I was so caught up in my present dilemma that I had pushed Him aside. That was a big mistake. Live and learn. I knew God was real from my near-death (out-of-body) experience and from the presence I felt when I prayed, so why had I been ignoring Him? God was there all along, just waiting for me to come back to Him.

God gave me a nudge in the form of a nurse. She saw my Bible and sat down next to me. She started telling me at length her experiences before she relied totally on God. Her life was falling apart until she let Jesus take over and be Lord of her life. She told me how her husband beat her up every day and she had five kids that she could not afford to take care of. There was drug abuse and sexual orgies at her house. It was sickening. But then God had changed her life. She glowed as she spoke. Even working in a psychiatric hospital couldn't depress her! I saw an inner happiness and peace as she spoke softly to me. She explained that God had given her the strength and means to leave her husband and that she had found support with her sister. She reflected that it was only a miracle that could have changed her life.

I listened, but still managed to detach. That was different, I thought. Yes, God was amazing, but I still wanted to find answers my way. I wanted God to help me, but in my way, not His.

I didn't understand about giving up the control, giving it totally to Him. Not yet. As long as I looked to Pablo or myself for answers, I would continue to fall again and again.

I enjoyed being around other people at Brunswick House. I found myself turning back into Karen the jockey. Karen the jockey thought *I don't belong in here!* I stayed up at night and sat around with the others. We played cards and told jokes. They all convinced me that I was fine. (Who was I kidding?) After hearing my tales of Pablo, they said it sounded like Pablo was the problem. (But why did I keep looking to Pablo over and over again? Why was I so insecure, deep down?) The real me, the bad me, had gone into hiding again. Yes, Karen the jockey was fine. Everyone agreed that I should go back to riding.

"You were a good jockey," the people who followed racing told me. This made me smile.

On my third day at the hospital, I started to get anxious. Originally, I had wanted to stick it out for a month, like Pablo. But now I wanted out. I considered signing myself out, but Pablo wouldn't be home yet. Where would I go? I didn't belong here in the hospital, did I? Yeah, I seemed fine now, away from Pablo.

Late that morning, my decision was made for me. Because the

billing department was closed on the weekend, they had admitted me. Now that it was Monday, the hospital realized I had no insurance coverage. I called Mom right away.

"They're releasing me! Pablo's Blue Cross bill hasn't been paid, so they won't cover me. Can you come and get me? I feel great." I really believed I was fine, too.

"Amy and I will be down in about an hour. Oh, I'm so glad you're getting out and that you feel better. You can stay here with us."

I packed up my things and waited for Mom. I thought about what she had said about staying at the house. I guess it would be all right to stay with her and Amy. They were all I had right now, and they did seem to care. I could stay with them until Pablo got out of the hospital.

When Mom picked me up, she mentioned that jockey Frank Lovato had a band that played at a nearby bar on Monday nights. The "OTB Band" was made up of jockeys and others from the racetrack. Mom thought it might be good if I got out and saw some people that I knew from my riding days. I couldn't wait.

Although I had looked forward to going, when we got to the bar I felt out of place. It had been four years since I had ridden. Four years! Most of the people I knew greeted me warmly. But there were lots of new faces, mostly young Irish guys who had come to this country recently to work at the track. I danced with a few of them. They asked me my name and where I was from. They were surprised to find out I had been a jockey. Still, it was nice to know that they had asked me to dance without knowing who I was (or had been) and just for me alone. Up, down. Up, down. My life was a roller coaster. Here I was out dancing when just that morning I had been in a mental hospital!

That night I stayed on the couch at Mom's. I felt empty. I couldn't fathom the way the rest of the world went about their business, working, keeping busy, and doing all the things I used to do before I met Pablo and was trained to do nothing. How did the rest of the world do it? How did they function? Surely, it was an act. Pablo said...

Pablo, Pablo, Pablo. He was always front and center in my thinking. In fact, I started to wonder if I could have a thought that wasn't influenced by him. How would I cope without him? I couldn't. Not anymore. I was lost without him.

Mom was baffled. “Karen, I can’t understand it. You had such a good time last night and this morning you are so depressed.”

I couldn’t explain it to her. I didn’t understand it myself. Maybe I knew Pablo wouldn’t have approved of me going out last night. He wouldn’t have approved of any of this: staying at my mothers, hanging out with people who worked for a living, or being with the “bad” people from the track. He was always right.

Pablo would have been mad at me. I was so bad. Would I ever feel better? Where was Pablo when I needed him?

I was finding it harder and harder to cope without him. It was like culture shock. Mom and Amy were so energetic. I was used to lethargic Pablo. What was wrong with me? Why couldn’t I just be like them? Why was it so hard for me to just function, to get through a minute, an hour, a day? Why did I wake up every morning sensing impending doom, not knowing the reason for my existence? Something inside me was terribly off balance.

Mom explained it like this. “It’s as if you are two people. You have such severe ups and downs. Your good moods are always followed by severe depressions.”

Until Mom pointed this out to me, I hadn’t realized that my darkest depressions always followed a time when I felt happy and free. Although Pablo wasn’t around, he still controlled my thoughts and behavior. I would reach a certain point, almost to freedom, and then it was as if Pablo himself yanked me back down to being the real me, the bad me—the one that Pablo approved of and loved.

I had to talk to Pablo, so I called Mount Sinai Hospital. They told me he was gone and that was all they could say. But the twenty-eight days weren’t up yet?! Oh, where had he gone? Was he out getting drugs? Had he run away? I couldn’t get any information from the hospital, so I panicked. Maybe he was back. I drove out to Oyster Bay several times, but he wasn’t there.

Two days went by and still no Pablo. He never even called me to tell me he was out of the hospital. I was worried. Where had he gone? Would he ever return home, to me?

I decided to call the Garcias in Florida. I doubted that they would know anything. Pablo never wanted them to know what he was doing.

But at least they could share my concern.

"Hi, Mrs. Garcia. I'm worried about Pablo. He's not at the hospital, and I was wondering if you had heard from him."

"Karen? Ah, no. Wait. Hold on."

A few minutes went by.

"Karen? Yes, Pablo is here. He is staying with us."

"What? He is?" I couldn't believe my ears! He was staying with his *parents???*

"Can I talk to him? Is he okay?"

"He's out at the moment."

"Can you have him call me when he gets in?"

"I'll give him the message. Bye."

I hung up, still in a state of disbelief. Why had Pablo suddenly taken to his parents???

He was shutting me out again. Bad, bad me.

Two more days went by. Pablo didn't call. I spent my time driving back and forth to Oyster Bay, hoping that he had decided to fly home. I couldn't take it anymore. I had to know what was going on. I called the Garcias again.

Mrs. Garcia picked up. "No, Karen. He's not here. He is at his AA meeting with Bill. They are so nice. They are so good to him."

"Is Pablo still staying with you?"

"Yes. He's sleeping on our couch."

"Have him call me when he gets back."

"Bye, now."

I stood there holding the phone. Since when did Pablo stay with his parents on the couch? Why didn't he stay in the upstairs condo, or find a hotel somewhere? And he was going to AA meetings? That didn't sound like my Pablo. Was he so different off the methadone? If he was off it, the withdrawal hadn't killed him like he said it might. Huh.

All I could do now was wait. Wait and see for myself what Pablo would be like when he got back. I made at least four trips a day out to Oyster Bay to see if he had returned. And I continued to stay with Mom and Amy, sleeping on the couch.

I hated living in limbo.

Chapter 72
Lies, Lies, Lies

I had more bad dreams. These ugly, ugly nightmares. Sometimes I didn't know which was worse: the reality of my life or the reality of the ugly dreams. Vince/Pablo dreams. Death dreams. And I would wake up in a sweat. I would want Pablo to comfort me, to tell me everything was all right. But he wasn't next to me. I was alone.

Who was I? Where did I belong? Mom and Amy were going through life so easily, so normally. What was wrong with me? I couldn't conform. I was a shell of a human being going through the motions, like sleepwalking. My life didn't feel real. What was happening to me? I would flip back and forth from "acting" the way everyone else did—faking it (which I couldn't keep up for long), to miserable depression and loneliness. I believed that only Pablo could understand me, but he didn't seem to care about me anymore. I wanted to isolate. I was much more comfortable in my real condition: depressed. Who could comfort me? I had forgotten about God. Although I had vowed not to throw up and wasn't doing that, there was always something. Alcohol. Suicide. The devil wasn't through with his schemes yet.

I wanted to get drunk, so every night I did. There was no way out anymore. I tried to blank out my feelings, but I couldn't. I tried to numb the pain, but it was everywhere I turned. I tried to forget my situation, to no avail. All I felt was impending doom. Just die already. Get it over with. I can't go on like this. Oh, where was Pablo? And so, I continued to drink myself into oblivion.

During the day, I talked with Mom a lot. I filled her in on everything that had happened. I had no one else. My feelings toward her were so mixed-up. I was angry that she didn't care about me, although she acted as if she did. I couldn't express my anger because it seemed so crazy, so unfounded. Therefore, I suppressed my anger, and it became severe depression. Mom tried to be helpful, to understand what I was going through as best she could. We talked and talked, trying to figure out what was wrong with me.

"It seems like whenever you have contact with Pablo, you go off the deep end," Mom explained. "Maybe you shouldn't go back to Oyster Bay. Can't you just forget about Pablo, like he doesn't exist? He's bad for you. I mean, all he ever did was lie about everything."

Mom was right. Was she on my side? Or did she want me to be away from Pablo so I would be alone and miserable? What was her motive? Oh, why did I have to think so pessimistically, the way Pablo would? Just try to be rational. She loves you. She does. Maybe.

"You don't understand, Mom. It's like Pablo and I were in a different world. We didn't function like other people. We didn't go anywhere or do anything. But we were happy. We had each other." Thinking about it depressed me even more. The past was gone. Even if Pablo wanted me back, I wouldn't be content to be a "with Pablo." Because now that I knew he was a liar and a drug addict, it could never be the same.

"You were happy? It didn't sound like you were very happy," Mom remarked, shaking her head.

"Well, I believed I was happy. Pablo told me we were happy, and so I thought I was."

"But you said he slept a lot. And you told me when you got depressed after he would fall asleep, you would take his gun down to the basement and contemplate suicide. When were you happy? It doesn't make sense to me."

I didn't have an answer. I didn't know. I thought I was happy when I was with Pablo. Did she want me to be unhappy, like Pablo always said? Was she tricking me?

"Mom?"

"Yeah?"

"Did you ever come on to Pablo? Like in the kitchen, when Pablo and I first dated? He told me you tried to kiss him. He said he always had to send Amy up to my room to get me because you wouldn't call me to come down."

"*What? No Way!* I can't believe he told you that!"

"Well, Pablo knew me. He knew I was always worried that you...uh..." It didn't hurt to be honest. I had nothing to lose. Nothing more. I looked down, ashamed. "Well, that if I ever fell in love with a man, I was sure that you would take him away, like I took away Vince from you." There. I said it.

"Karen, you didn't 'take away' Vince. He did something terrible to you. It had nothing to do with our (Vince and Mom's) relationship. You were only a child. You've got to stop blaming yourself."

Why couldn't Mom have told me that a long time ago? Because I wouldn't have believed her, that's why. Maybe we did talk about it a long time ago, like she said we had. She said that when she found the letter from Vince we had talked all through the night, but I didn't remember. I blanked it all out, just like that. I didn't want to hear her blame me, so I never heard a word of what she had said back then.

Maybe she didn't blame me. But that didn't stop me from blaming myself. Oh, it was all too painful, too painful. It's still my fault. But, no matter. I'm only bringing this up now because I'm at a total loss and I have to find out the truth about Pablo...Pablo. *He's* the problem, isn't he?

With intense effort, I stuffed back the mixed-up emotions from my past. *Focus on the present*. Yes, on Pablo.

"It doesn't matter about the past, Mom. The point is, did you come on to Pablo? Did you try to kiss him?"

"No way. I can't believe he said that. Think about it. It's kind of strange."

I tried to think like a normal, rational person. Would a mother come on to her daughter's boyfriend? It was kind of strange. But not to me. Pablo knew this. He knew it was one of my greatest fears. I told him that I was resigned to the fact that if I ever fell in love with a man, my mother would take him away. And Pablo had laughed! But still, Pablo could have made up the story about Mom coming on to him, knowing that I would believe it and get upset with Mom. Or upset with myself, believing that she was only doing to me what I deserved.

Still, I was confused. Then again, I didn't remember Amy ever coming upstairs to get me.

Mom shook her head. "I just can't believe he made up a story so ridiculous."

Yeah. Maybe she was right. It was ridiculous.

Mom really did try to help me. Every day we talked, trying to get to the bottom of my depression. We both thought Pablo was the problem, but I still wanted to go back to him to make it work. Mom seemed confused. I didn't want to dig too deeply into the past for fear of what we both might find: that I really was bad, that I had ruined her life, and that everything really was my fault. That was my biggest fear. Then she would reject me, blame me, disown me, and throw out disgusting me. How could I ever risk revealing the truth, so I could finally find out if she accepted and loved me—the real me, the bad me? Now, more than ever, I needed Mom. I needed her approval of me as Pablo continued to push me away. I couldn't afford her rejection, too. Not now. No way. She was all I had left. I didn't want to face the truth about myself and my past, let alone share it with her. Besides, where would I find this "truth," even if I had wanted to?

My "truth," the "bad me," was buried and hidden long ago when I was ten years old and saw Mom and Vince kissing at the window. In order to survive, my mind had built a protective barrier or wall to hide this "truth" from me and others forever. The bad me was the one who caused all the trouble and wanted Vince to love me and not Mom. From that time on, I knew that deep down I really was bad; I knew that there was something wrong with me, something hidden away that I could not access, nor did I want to. I didn't want to think about it—ever. Now, the protective wall had outlived its usefulness for my survival and it needed to come down. If I didn't get behind that wall, I would remain confused and locked out of a place I desperately needed to revisit in order to heal. I would stay on a collision course in my present life no matter what I did or who I turned to. This invisible wall had kept me alive as a child and teenager, but if I didn't find it and tear it down soon, it would surely be the death of me. Until I got behind that barrier, revisited that time period and exposed what I perceived as the bad me ("the truth") to myself and to my mother, I could never ever really believe she loved me—the real me. And I could never, ever accept or forgive myself.

Dealing with Mom was a catch-22. As much as it helped to have her support, it was a source of emotional frustration for me. For all appearances, she seemed to care and love me, yet no matter what she said or did, I couldn't really believe it.

Vince's words, long forgotten as his words and instilled into my young impressionable brain as my own thoughts, continued to echo in my head. "Your mother doesn't care about you."

And then I would feel crazy and mad at myself for thinking this absurd thought when she acted as though she cared. It was impossible to understand where my irrational and contradictory feelings toward Mom were coming from. I couldn't explain what I didn't understand. Oh, where was Pablo to make sense of things? Oh, why was I such a mess? Maybe I was going insane.

I opened the door to the house in Oyster Bay. It was one of the many trips I had made, looking to find myself. The first thing that hit me was the familiar sound of the television. Could it be? Was he back? Was Pablo home???

Pablo must have heard the door, because he appeared from out of the den.

Was he a ghost? Was he real? I looked down, afraid to face him. I felt a strange mixture of emotions. Love was not one of them. This shocked me.

"Ahem," Pablo uttered, clearing his throat. Yes, he was real. He was really standing there.

I felt an evil, dreadful chill come over me. Doom. Fear. Apprehension. I told myself there was nothing to be afraid of. Then just as suddenly and unexpectedly, anger flooded over me. Pablo, the liar. Hurtful, hateful Pablo. Liar. *Traitor!* Oh, your wicked lies...but you are my Pablo...Who are you? All the anger I ever felt started welling up in me, about to explode.

For the first time in weeks there was an inkling of a human being inside me, a strong one. I felt angry and defiant. But I stopped short, easing into the attack which I hadn't planned on—or expected—from myself. No. I mustn't make him angry. I must act happy to see him. I must try to act loving.

But I couldn't contain my anger. It was far too strong for me to handle. All the anger at the lies, the deception, and the rejection...all the rage I had turned inward was about to come out. I could feel it. A flood of emotion, out of control, finally unleashed, unharnessed, and not directed at me. *Yes!*

Think. Think *first*. Now, how did I feel again? Suddenly, I was small and weak below the towering Authority of My Life.

"Um," I said softly, "When did you get back?"

"Last night."

Suddenly, with the realization of how he had ignored me for so long, I was very angry again. Stay in control. Don't lose it. Don't let it out. *Don't.* "When...why didn't you ever call me?" I asked, trying to get my thoughts together.

"I was a mess. How have you been?" Pablo continued. "Are you staying at your *mother's?"* he asked, looking very smug.

"Uh, yeah. Well...did you see all the mice that lived here over the winter?" I had to make an excuse for my weakness.

"Yeah. I had to throw away those glue traps you set. They really aren't any good, you know. The other kind of trap is better. The mice had to suffer in those boxes," he said with a stern look of disapproval.

"I didn't know what else to do. I didn't want to look at the mice."

"Well, don't worry. I got rid of them. Come on in." Pablo started back into the dark den, shuffling along in his slippers.

I felt unwanted. He didn't love me anymore. I was confused and getting very depressed. Why did I feel so unwanted, so unworthy?

I gathered up all my courage. I was still standing by the front door. "No. I can't stay."

Pablo stopped and turned around. He came back toward me.

"Why didn't you ever call me, Pablo? Why didn't you ever let me know what was going on? I was going crazy."

"It was so difficult for me," he explained. "I didn't even know what I was doing. It was a very hard time for me."

"Well, it wasn't exactly easy on me, either."

"So, how's your mother?"

"The same." Now, why did I say that? Mom was trying to help me figure out my life. What was wrong with that? Pablo was a liar. *He* was the one that was bad for me. Mom and I were getting along just fine.

"Your mother will never grow up," Pablo said with disgust, shaking his head.

The comment made me angry again. Who was he to judge my

mother?

"And what about *you*, Pablo? Mr. Perfect, huh? Mr. Straight, after what, twelve years? Or was it longer including all those years you 'experimented with every drug on the face of the earth'? *Heroin!* God, I married a *heroin addict*. And you never even told me."

"That was a long time ago."

"Was it? Did you ever get off the heroin yourself, like you said? Or did you just go straight to the methadone? Was all that about the cabin in the woods a lie, too?"

Pablo didn't say anything.

"You lied so much, Pablo. I found out. Everything you said..."

"It was the drugs. The methadone."

"The drugs made you *lie?* And now you're all better? Is that it?"

"Look, Karen," Pablo said as turned to go back into the den, "I'm not going to stay here and listen to you cut me down."

"Fine. Just walk away. Like nothing ever happened. And what about Mom coming on to you? That's what you said. You said she tried to kiss you. Was that what happened?"

Pablo looked at me and nodded. "Yeah, she did."

"She says you made it up. Did she or didn't she try to kiss you?"

"I said that because I was on the methadone."

"But you just now said she did try to kiss you. So are you lying now, or did you lie then? And you're off the methadone, I presume?"

"I'm not going to take this," Pablo said angrily.

I didn't want him to walk away from me. Not yet.

"How do I know you're really off the drugs, Pablo? You could be lying about that, too. I'd never know. I never knew you one day off drugs."

"I can see no matter what I say, you're going to twist it, turn it around on me."

"No, Pablo. I just want the truth. For once."

"I'm straight. Really, I am."

"So now you'll tell the truth about things?"

Pablo nodded.

"Pablo, I wish I could believe you."

"Listen. I'm not all up to this. It's hard for me to deal...straight."

"I can tell."

"Why are you asking me so many questions?"

I answered his question with another one of mine. "How long will it take for you to be better, Pablo? To not lie anymore? I was talking to someone from the track who has known you for a long time. They said you are a pathological liar. Is that true?"

Pablo stormed off, disappearing into the den.

I felt awful. I didn't want to accuse him of lying, to blame him. I wanted to trust him, but I couldn't help myself. I couldn't help my anger. I felt worse now than before. I didn't *want* to cut him down, but I couldn't stop. I had to know the truth. As I accused him, I was also tearing myself apart. That part of me that used to be connected with Pablo, my old comfortable identity, was being sliced to pieces.

"Pablo?" I followed him into the den. "It was so hard on me. All of this. And you left me alone to deal."

"Well, what do you think I was going through?" he countered from his usual place in his chair. "It was no picnic, believe me. I was lucky I didn't die from the withdrawal."

I felt really awful now. Why couldn't I be understanding, sympathetic? Because I was horrible. A bad, unloving, unforgiving wife. Ugh.

"I thought it took a long time to come off the methadone," I said, still trying to understand and get the truth.

"Yeah. It could take me a few years to be normal."

"What? A few *years*? How will I know?"

"I'm lucky to be alive."

I sat down on the arm of the couch. Pablo reached under the coffee table and pulled out a manila envelope. He tossed it over to me.

What was this? I opened it. It was the prenuptial agreement. Was he trying to tell me something? Did he want a divorce??? And, his ring...his wedding ring was no longer on his finger! I was horrified at what Pablo was doing. Why was he doing this to me???

"What are you trying to tell me, Pablo? That you want...a *divorce*?"

"I thought that's what *you* were trying to say."

"Then, why don't you have your ring on your finger?"

"Oh. I had to take it off in the hospital. It's somewhere around here." He shrugged and turned back to the television.

I wasn't comfortable. Not with this Pablo. This stranger. This...liar. He just looked like the Pablo I once loved. But the Pablo I had loved is dead. Gone. Would he ever come back?

"I wish it was like before, Pablo. I liked you better on drugs."

Pablo looked at me cynically. "Thanks *a lot.*" He grabbed the remote and turned up the television.

I thought back to when I was here before, just back from Florida. I was sitting right here on this couch with his gun, missing him being in his chair. Now, there he was, just like I had wanted him to be, sitting in his chair, watching television. Only it wasn't the same.

"Pablo, why did you hang up on me when I had the gun?"

He didn't acknowledge my question.

"Sergeant Striker—a total stranger—a cop in Florida cared more about me than you did."

"I already told you. I was a mess. I am in no shape to deal with anything."

"Yeah, I guess so." I didn't like attacking Pablo this way, uncovering his lies, but I couldn't stop. "And the time I passed out from all the vodka and the Excedrin PM pills. Why didn't you do anything for me then?"

"I did. I prayed for you."

"Well, you should have called a hospital to have my stomach pumped."

"I did."

"You called a hospital?"

"Yes. They told me you would sleep it off."

"So then you prayed for me?"

"That's right."

"Are you just making this up, now? Saying whatever I want to hear?"

"I can tell we're not getting anywhere," Pablo said, shaking his head in disgust.

"I guess not. So why don't you just finish me off, Pablo? Huh?" I was working myself up. All the anger I felt at him, I directed back on myself for causing him to lie. I wished I was dead. *Dead. Dead!*

Pablo looked at me sadly.

"I know, Pablo. I'm just such a pathetic mess, aren't I? So why don't you just kill me?"

Pablo picked up a pack of cigarettes. He shook one out. Lit it up. Inhaled. He looked calmly at the television, ignoring me. Pushing me away. Again. Well, go ahead and smoke. I don't care. I don't care about you or your lousy cigarettes anymore.

I turned and left the den. I would do it for him. I would kill myself. I had nothing left anymore. I couldn't even hold onto the dream of us being together anymore; I was shattering that dream right now, right before my very eyes.

I ran out the front door and jumped into the Jeep. My hands were shaking as I worked myself up into a suicide mission frenzy. I put the key in the ignition and stepped on the gas as hard as I could. Then I roared down the driveway, heading straight for the woods, straight for the trees.

I bounced off the seat as the Jeep swiped the trees and struggled through the deep going. The wheels spun as the Jeep, stuck for a moment, kicked up some angry mud.

"DO IT! DO IT!" I didn't realize it, but those words were coming out of my own mouth. They sounded like someone else's, instructions to head straight for the biggest tree, words of encouragement, egging me on. "DO IT! DO IT!" I stepped on the gas harder as the Jeep finally broke free and headed for a big tree. *Yes!* Hit it *hard!*

My head hit the windshield. I was dizzy, but still conscious. The Jeep sounded like it was dying. It sounded like I felt. Still hanging in there, despite its wounds.

I opened the door and got out. The front and side of the Jeep were damaged. I must have hit several trees before I hit the one that eventually stopped me.

I started walking back toward the house. Pablo was standing there in the driveway, watching me, crazy me. The Lunatic. I was the problem, wasn't I? Not Pablo. No, it was never Pablo. He was always so calm. So normal. So right.

I walked up to him, still dizzy. "I guess I wrecked the Jeep." There. Maybe that would show him. Maybe that would show him how much he was hurting me, how crazy he was making me.

Pablo stood there, silent. I walked back into the house and headed for the kitchen phone. I felt sick. Who could I call?

What was I doing? Maybe I'll get drunk. My head was spinning. What is the matter with me? I must lie down. I saw a bottle of scotch on the kitchen counter. I'll drink it and show Pablo just how bad I am! I wanted to die. I wanted to hurt myself until there was no more pain. I took a swig of the scotch. And another. I drank it down. Then I dialed Dr. Davis. Maybe he'd help me. I don't remember what happened next.

I woke up in a hospital room, alone. Hmm. How did I get here? My head hurt. Suddenly, I remembered. The accident. I wrecked the Jeep. I must have passed out and...Pablo! Pablo was back and he must have brought me here to the hospital! Yes, Pablo *did* love me!

I smiled, picturing Pablo bringing me here to save me. Waiting, worried, and probably pacing in the waiting room right now.

Dr. Nolan, who had treated Pablo when he almost died, came through the door. "Well, hello, Karen. How do you feel?"

I must be at the same hospital where Pablo had been! Surely, Pablo was just outside the door.

"Dr. Nolan! I feel fine. Can I see Pablo now?"

"Um. You had quite a bang to your head. The concussion knocked you out. Wait here a moment."

I waited, anticipating seeing a new, more loving Pablo. The Pablo I had pictured sometimes as I waited for him to return from Florida. The Pablo I loved and who loved me and cared about me.

The doctor came back into the room. With Mom.

"Where's Pablo?" I asked, totally expecting him to be right behind them.

Mom came over and gave me a hug.

"Where is he? I want to see Pablo," I repeated.

Mom looked hesitant. Then she gave me the bad news. "I'm sorry, Karen. Pablo is back at the house watching television."

"What? What do you mean? He brought me here, right?"

Mom shook her head sadly.

"Then, how did I get here?" I asked, confused, disappointed, and now totally disoriented with my situation.

"I brought you here," Mom explained softly.

No! It couldn't be. I felt an empty pit in my stomach. Pablo hadn't brought me here? That was all I wanted. That was all I needed. I needed him to care. I didn't want Mom or any doctor. I just wanted Pablo. I needed him to care, to save me.

"How did you...Where is Pablo, then? How did you know?"

"I got a call from your father. He got a call from Dr. Davis saying you were in an accident. I came as quickly as I could."

"Where was Pablo?"

"He was in the den watching television."

"I remember calling Dr. Davis and then..." The scotch. Drinking on top of a concussion. I must have passed out.

"I found you passed out," Mom explained. "I asked Pablo where you were and he said you were 'sleeping.' Well, I knew it wasn't like you to be sleeping in the middle of the day and Dr. Davis said you were in an accident, so I looked for you in the house. Pablo stayed in the den. I had to call him to carry you out to the car."

"Pablo carried me out to the car?"

"Yes. I told him to, so he did. He got up from his chair, put you in the back seat of my car, and then went back into the house."

"Did he know I was hurt?"

"Karen, you were unconscious."

"Oh. Well, maybe...he said he couldn't deal. He told you I was sleeping?"

Mom nodded. Then she put her hand on mine to comfort me, to ease the shock of it all. "Karen, he's like...well...he isn't human. I couldn't believe my eyes. He just acted like nothing was wrong."

Huh. He must have been confused. After all, he told me he wasn't "normal" yet. He just didn't know how to deal with me, that's all. I was being too hard on him. He had just come out of the hospital. I should have been more loving. I shouldn't have wrecked the Jeep. Now, I really did it. He must be really mad at me. I deserved it, anyway.

In the evening, Dr. Nolan released me from the hospital. "Get lots of rest and stay with your mother. Stay away from Pablo," he advised.

Huh. I thought he liked Pablo.

I was sick to my stomach that night and the next day, too. I was told it was the effects of the concussion. I stayed in Mom's room in her bed. It reminded me of when I was very young and had wet the bed. Mom would let me stay in their bed while she changed my sheets. I was such a nuisance, yet she had loved me anyway. I felt secure now, in her bed. I was physically sick, but was almost comfortable this way.

Of course, my mind went right back to thoughts of Pablo. Why hadn't he taken me to the hospital? Then I thought about the million ways that he was good and I was bad. I was being so inconsiderate of him, of his needs, and focusing only on myself. Selfish me with all my crazy, angry feelings.

I took the phone off the nightstand and dialed Pablo's number. I wanted to apologize to him, but more than that, I wanted to find out why he hadn't taken me to the hospital.

"Hello?"

"Hi, Pablo? It's Karen."

"Oh, hi."

"What did you think happened to me?" I asked.

"I don't know. Your mother came and got you."

"Did you know I passed out from a concussion?"

"NO! Did you have a concussion? Oh, I'm so sorry to hear that, honey."

"Well, you put me in the car. What did you think happened?"

"I thought...you were just sleeping. You were upset, you know."

"Well, I had a concussion and have been throwing up all day from it."

"I'm sorry to hear that. I hope you feel better."

"Didn't you worry about me?"

"Oh, I called the hospital. The doctor said you weren't there anymore, so I didn't come down."

"You knew Mom was taking me to a hospital and you didn't even come with her?"

"Listen, I'm late for an AA meeting. I have to go now."

Mr. AA. Mr. Wonderful. Wasn't I so awful? Drinking, wrecking the

Jeep. Bad, crazy me. And he was so good.

"Oh, okay. Bye." I hung up the phone, feeling rejected and hurt once again. Pablo did not approve of me at all. Oh, why did I have to feel so bad? He had a meeting. That's all. He cares. Yesterday when he put me in the car, he thought I was sleeping. He didn't know. Well, then again, he did say he knew that Mom was taking me to the hospital. But he did call, and I had been released.

The creep.

Oh, why did I always doubt what he said to me? Why couldn't I just forget that he ever lied to me and start over? Why did I have to be so bad and keep ramming the past down his throat? Why did I keep condemning him and doubting his motives? Why did I have to continually test him? And why, oh why, couldn't he pass any of my tests?

I should stop acting like this. Just accept him and believe in him. Not question him. But he was pushing me away, wasn't he? He didn't even go to the hospital when Mom took me and he *knew*. He's never even asked me to come home to stay with him. He doesn't care. Yes, he does. This is all my doing because I can't seem to forget the past. This is all my crazy fault. It's *me* who keeps testing *him*.

Still, I couldn't shut my eyes now that they had been opened. I still doubted his love for me.

Doubted his love for me? Wasn't it obvious? I just couldn't accept the truth; I kept making excuses to myself for his actions because I didn't think I could live without knowing he loved me.

Chapter 73
Forget Him, Already!

After a few days, my headache was gone and I didn't feel sick. Because I needed a car, I convinced Mom to take me out to Pablo's again—just to get the Cadillac. I had a spare set of keys for the car, and so I just drove it out of his garage.

I went out every night. I was looking for something or someone to fill my Pablo void, for some reason to exist. I hadn't given up totally on Pablo yet. However, if I postponed seeing him, I was postponing certain disaster. I just had to look elsewhere for validation; at least, for the time being.

I was in the strangest state of mind. There was definitely something wrong with me, but I didn't know how to fix it. So, I went out looking for answers. I was friendly, going to the local bars where people from the racetrack hung out. But I couldn't get Pablo off my mind, and my conversations always ended up being about him. I wanted to know what others thought about my situation. Should I go back to him? Should I leave him for good? Should I trust him? Could he ever change? The answers varied. Most people agreed that he would never change: once an addict, always an addict.

Anyway, even if he was off drugs, did I want to spend the rest of my life watching television?

I thought about the advice I was given. My head spun. Realistically, I knew that going back to Pablo was not a good idea, but emotionally I needed him. For some reason, I needed Pablo's constant approval of me, even if it was the bad me.

In all the places I looked, I couldn't find another person like Pablo. Everyone was just too busy with their own lives and their own problems. If they were out at a bar, it was to forget about problems, not to find answers.

One night I met a guy who took a special interest in me. He "understood" me and my situation—a little too much so. He said he knew about drug addicts and how they manipulate people, especially someone young and vulnerable like me. I was thrilled to finally talk to someone who listened, who cared, and who seemed to have an understanding of what I was going through (although I was sure nobody could really understand).

He said, "I know their games. If someone wants to play games with me, watch out. I can play them better."

That, right there, should have been a warning to me. I should have run as fast as I could in the other direction, but I didn't. He reminded me too much of Pablo. He was smart, convincing, all-knowing, and macho. I felt right at home with him.

I spent several hours talking to this guy. He filled my Pablo void almost perfectly, so I embraced him with eagerness. I told him my innermost feelings and felt very close to him. After talking all night at the bar, I never heard from "Mr. Wonderful" again! (That is, until I made a comeback to riding races. Then he claimed to be my boyfriend!) When he left me that night he said, "Don't ever look for me. Don't ever call me at work." Isn't that reassuring? What a guy!

Now, I really felt bad about myself. I certainly was unlovable and messed up. I had trusted someone, let them get to know me like Pablo did, and was rejected again! I could never be normal. Nobody could ever love me. Nobody but Pablo.

So back I went, looking for my savior, once again. I drove to Oyster Bay. As I sped up Mill River Road in the Cadillac, I spotted the Jeep coming out of the driveway. Instantly, I took my foot off the accelerator and wished I was invisible. I felt so low. Why did I feel this way whenever I sensed Pablo's almighty presence?

The Jeep headed towards me. Now there was no going back. There was no place to hide.

Pablo slowed down as he approached. I tried to seem together as I stopped the car next to him on the road. He rolled down his window.

"What do you want?" he asked.

"Well, I just wanted...to talk."

"Come by tomorrow." Pablo said cheerfully. "I miss you."

"Okay," was all I could muster. Pablo rolled his window up and continued on down the road. I watched the Jeep disappear in my rear-view mirror. What was Pablo doing with his life now, anyway? Was he really getting better? And, why did I still feel so awful around him?

Was Pablo treating me like he did his parents? He always told me he couldn't stand them, yet he was nice to them. I couldn't bear the thought that he felt the same way about me. He said himself that he missed me. I needed to believe it was true. Yes, he loved me. I would go see him tomorrow, and we would work it out.

The next day I went back to see Pablo. I kept my bitterness at bay. I was going to try to make it work. We sat on the living room couch. Pablo showed me all the hair that had grown on his once bare chest. I was shocked. It was really strange. Was this proof that he was off drugs, or at least off the methadone? He said it was.

"The methadone did some terrible things to my body," Pablo explained. "That was why I was sterile, or had little sperm, if any, before."

He pulled me towards him like a teenager and put my hand on his pants. I quickly withdrew my hand in horror. He had never gotten so excited so quickly before. Surely he was off drugs, at least the methadone. Wait a minute! *He had been sterile???* And I had blamed myself all that time for not getting pregnant!!??

I felt so betrayed. "I can't believe this, Pablo."

All the love from before wasn't real. He hadn't been normal. I had loved a drug zombie! I had been tricked! *This* was the real Pablo. Who was this man?

"*Now* you could get me pregnant?" I asked, still in disbelief of what I was seeing firsthand, still in shock of what I was learning right before my very eyes.

Pablo had a big smile. "Yes."

But now, I didn't want him to get me pregnant. I didn't want *him*. Not now. Not ever. He had tricked me! He was a liar.

"You lied to me. I thought we were going to have a baby, and you *knew*. You knew you couldn't get me pregnant, and you let me believe that you could?!"

I thought about the three years of disappointment, trying to get pregnant. All those pregnancy tests. Up, down. Up, down. All that time I had hoped, and then I had blamed myself. "Why didn't you tell me, Pablo? Why?"

"I knew how much it meant to you."

"So you let me believe it was possible when you *knew* it wasn't?"

"Something like that."

"How could you do that to me?" I asked, astounded.

Pablo got up from the couch. "I'm leaving," he said.

I felt awful. Why did I have to cut him down again? Couldn't I be good, just for once?

"Where are you going, Pablo?"

"I have to go to a meeting with my friends."

"AA?"

"Yeah."

Suddenly, I felt very unimportant. Pablo didn't care about me. All he cared about was his other friends, people I didn't even know. And his meetings. I used to come first. Now I was finishing a bad last.

"Can I come with you? Can I meet your friends?" I asked, feeling like a lowly beggar. Begging for him to accept me back into his life.

"No. Maybe some other time."

Pablo went out the side door that led to the garage. I got up feeling numb. I heard the garage door open and went to the window. I waited, expecting to see Pablo pull out of the garage driving the Jeep. What I saw instead shocked me. He appeared on a big old motorcycle, with his feet sticking way out in front of him like a hippie. He buzzed out of the driveway, a drug hippie in a leather jacket, riding his hippie motorcycle. Who was he, really? Was he regressing to his old days? What was the name they called him back when he "ran drugs" on his motorcycle? Rider. Yeah. That was it.

Maybe he was lying again. Maybe he had no meeting and was just driving around in order to get me to leave.

I wandered through the house looking at his things. He had all his old hippie records out, and there were tons and tons of cigarettes everywhere. Cartons, packs, and overflowing ashtrays full of them. He must be smoking a lot these days.

This evil, wicked place! House of Pablo, house of lies.

I had to get out of there.

I drove home promising myself to leave Pablo behind. Forget him, already! Just *forget* him! I was miserable whenever I was around him anyway. Mom was right. He was bad for me. What was it that compelled me to keep going back to him?

Looking back, it seems so insane the way I kept returning to Pablo. In writing my story, I was shocked by the number of times I kept going back to him, but felt it was necessary to include this obsessive irrational behavior pattern so that others in similar situations could identify. I found out later that it is not unusual for someone who has been emotionally abused as a child to do everything in their power to keep an abusive relationship going as an adult. It is so difficult to break the ties, and the need for some kind of warped approval by a manipulative spouse is beyond comprehension. These kinds of unhealthy relationships can be as toxic as drug or alcohol addiction and just as difficult to break.

Chapter 74
Lost and Alone

I decided to look for an apartment to rent. If I was on my own, maybe I would feel better, a little less like a nomad staying on Mom's couch or in my car. If I had my own place, I would belong somewhere, finally. I would have to get my things out of Oyster Bay. Yeah, get all my stuff. That would make it official. Once my things were out of Pablo's, I would be me again, wouldn't I? Anyway, I wasn't comfortable staying at Mom's. I didn't belong there. There was just no place for me anymore. Anything was worth a try. Nothing else seemed to be working. Yeah, I'll get a place of my own. It doesn't have to be anything permanent, just a place to put me back together again. I need some kind of identity. If I had my own place, maybe I would find myself. Pablo didn't want me anymore. His house was no longer our home. I didn't want to be with him anyway. He just made me crazy. I felt bad and acted irrational whenever I was around him.

Mom helped me look for a place. She was behind whatever decision I made—as long as it didn't involve going back to Pablo. Mom gave me more credit than I deserved. She treated me like the old Karen who had just been done in by Pablo. She had faith in me. There was no way she could fathom the magnitude of my confusion—of what I was feeling inside. I felt like the most mixed-up, lost, incompetent person on the face of the earth. Mom didn't accept that. Sure, I was a little mixed-up, Mom said, but anybody would be if they were around Pablo for five years.

"Just stay away from him," she said. "Then everything will be fine."

Yeah. Maybe.

I found a cute little house for rent in Elmont. It was only a few miles from Mom and Amy, and the rent was low for a small house. I hadn't planned on renting a whole house, but I did have lots of stuff, and some of the furniture in Oyster Bay was mine. This would be a good place to put it. I had money saved from riding, and I remembered that the prenuptial agreement had stated that should we separate, Pablo would pay me $600 a month. What could he say? Pablo obviously didn't want me staying with him, and he didn't like me living with my mother, either. He would have to help me with the rent.

I moved all my stuff out of Pablo's. I left nothing behind. I didn't want any excuse to return; it was hard enough for me to stay away as it was.

Well, it was finished. I was all moved into my new little house. I had everything one could possibly need: a backyard with a barbeque grill, a garage, a basement, a storage room, and an office for my desk and my scrapbooks. There was even wall space for my unhung win photos. All the furniture fit nicely. I should be happy now, shouldn't I?

But somehow something was still missing, and I couldn't find it in the perfect little house. It wasn't found in my stuff, either. It was part of me that was missing. Was it Pablo? I wasn't sure. It was something. I felt hollow inside. The house was great, but it was just window dressing. It was what was inside of me that was still wrong. But, what was it? What *was* it???

I continued to go out every night, searching, searching, but never finding that missing something to make me whole. Pablo wasn't around, yet I still felt crazy. I had no apparent excuse for the way I felt. I didn't understand it, and I couldn't fix myself. I was getting desperate.

Mom and I continued to have our talks, piecing together everything that had happened since I first met Pablo. We figured out that Pablo had convinced me that everyone at the track was against me, which led to my decision to quit riding. He had put me on horses that made me look bad. He had lied about Mom wanting to kiss him, and so many other things. Basically, everything he had done and said brought down my self-esteem—although I had been unaware of it while it was happening. I had trusted and believed Pablo all along. Why wouldn't I? It was hard now to hear and accept this new reality. I was torn between what I now knew to be true about Pablo and what I wanted to believe was true about the man I had loved and married.

Outwardly, I agreed with Mom, that Pablo had said and done some terribly deceptive things, but inwardly I forgave him and blamed myself for our failed marriage. I was miserable. The more truth I uncovered, the more despondent I became.

I listened to music and got depressed. I drank. I didn't want to face life without Pablo. He was all I had lived for!

Pablo had trained me to be totally dependent on him. He knew that I was suicidal, stemming from my unresolved conflict with Mom and Vince. He continually baited me, probably hoping I would follow through with killing myself. For whatever reason, he obviously wanted me dead. Maybe I knew too much, and this was a threat to the gravy train he had with his parents. Or maybe he wanted me dead so he could sell my house and get easy money. He was counting on me to come back to him so that he could push me over the edge. After all, I still called him on the phone. He acted as if everything was fine, that his life was never better! Any time I tried to achieve something, he criticized and belittled it, causing me to give up. Now, he had his friends and his meetings; he didn't need me, and he hoped that this fact would be the last nail in my coffin.

I played the George Michael album, *Faith,* over and over again. It had the hit song "Father Figure" on it. I cried as I listened to the words and mourned my loss. I missed Pablo so much, or maybe it was the idea of him.

Like Vince, Pablo was my "father figure." He was more than just a boyfriend or husband. Both Vince and Pablo had used their power over me, not to protect me, but to use me and then throw me away.

I had to do something. My life needed a meaning. Maybe I'd get a job. Yeah. But what could I do? What was I capable of doing? Nothing.

The racetrack didn't want me anymore. Did they really hate me, the way Pablo had said? He said all racetrackers were liars and knockers. Anyway, I could never get on a horse again. No. I was just no good anymore. Even Pablo didn't want me around. I was a total failure.

Mom was surprised to find me searching through the "want" ads, looking for a menial job the way I had when I quit riding.

I looked at the "drivers wanted" ads closely. "Mom, what do you think of me being a driver? I loved driving up from Florida in the Jeep, and I don't know what else I can do."

"Well, uh, that's okay, I guess. But, Karen, why are you looking for that kind of job?

"I need to do something."

"Why don't you go back and do something at the track. Everybody knows you and likes you there."

I shook my head vehemently. *"No, they don't!"*

Mom looked baffled. "Where did you get that idea?"

"I *know*. That's all. I know what they think of me. Pablo says the racetrack is a terrible place."

"Well, I think people like you. And you know so much about racing."

"No. I'm going to be a driver. I like driving. People will like being taxied around in a Cadillac!"

Mom changed the subject. "Why don't you have a party? That will cheer you up. Invite those Irish kids that work at the track, the ones you met when we went out that night to hear the racetrack band play. You've met some of them from going out at night, haven't you?"

"I don't know. Nobody would want to come."

"Sure they would. They like you. You have a nice little house rented, and the backyard is great. You could have a barbecue, and we could fix up the garage with music so that everyone could dance. It will be fun!"

"Well, maybe. I can cook. Yeah, I can cook a bunch of stuff like fried chicken and all Pablo's favorites. I could make potato salad and a quiche. I can even make a cake or two. I can cook everything that Pablo likes. I know people will eat that. Maybe I *will* have a party. You think I should? Would anyone really want to come?"

"I know they would! I'll bring the lawn mower over and we can fix everything up really neat."

"Okay. I'll start cooking, anyway."

Well, this was exciting. I had never thrown a party before. The house was neat, the backyard looked great, and Mom hung a revolving disco ball so that the garage would look like a dance studio. Whatever I needed, Mom provided: extra chairs, folding tables, extra garbage cans, and extra pots and pans for all my fried chicken and potato salad. She was the best.

I cooked all weekend, and at night I handed out fliers at the bars where the locals from the track hung out. Now I could only hope and pray that people would come.

People did come, and the party was a huge success. Everyone ate, drank, danced, and laughed. They raved about my cute little house. Most of them noticed my win photos hanging on the walls. "Why did you ever quit riding?" they would ask.

I would just go numb, not wanting to reflect on my riding days. That was another me, long ago. "That was a long time ago," I would say. Over four years, what seemed like an eternity.

"You look good on a horse," an exercise rider named Gerry pointed out. He was just over from Ireland and had never seen me ride. "Why don't you ride again? It looks like you did really well."

"Nah. I could never ride again."

"Why not? You could do the weight, couldn't you?"

"I don't want to anymore. It's not the same." I was no longer a young tomboy who rode races. I wasn't much over my riding weight, but I was older now. People would never take me, a "woman" jockey, seriously. Back then I was a kid.

"Who was the best horse you ever rode?" Gerry asked as we continued to look at my old win photos.

I stopped at the picture of my first stakes win, Kuja Happa beating Angel Cordero aboard Gemrock. I noticed Angel was wearing the Dubai Stables colors. Pablo never did like that picture. I gazed at the photo hanging next to it. There was Adept, giving me my first Grade 1 stakes win in the Top Flight Handicap. Good old Adept. I had two stakes winning photos of her on this wall. "I don't know who was the best. I loved them all."

Suddenly, I didn't want to look at any more pictures or answer any more questions about my riding career. "Let's go back outside," I said.

The party ended around midnight. Everyone thanked me as they left. I felt good about myself, but it didn't last. With everyone gone, emptiness engulfed me once again.

I thought more about a job. What could I do? I could cook. Maybe I'd find a cooking job somewhere. Maybe Pablo would know of one.

The next morning, I called Pablo. I was surprised that he had an answering machine. Instead of hanging up, I waited. Maybe Pablo was home and would hear my voice and pick up. No, I wouldn't leave a message. Why should he have the satisfaction of knowing I called? He probably knew I would call. Yeah, he knew I'd come running back to him eventually, to ask for his advice, to look for his approval. Suddenly, I was mad at him again. He was probably out with his friends.

Mom told me she just heard that Pablo was training two horses at Belmont. I was shocked by this news and had a hard time believing it was true. Mr. Garcia had taken all his horses away from Pablo and given them to Jim, the assistant, to train. There was no way Pablo would be at the track. He hated training. He hated the racetrack and swore he would never go back!

If it were true that Pablo was back at the track, maybe it wasn't such a bad place after all. If Pablo was working there, it must be okay. Maybe I'll go to Belmont and see what I can find out. Maybe I could do something there, too. Not ride, of course. No way. Maybe walk horses or something. Maybe.

I got up the courage to go to the track, to risk being seen in the place where I was no longer Karen the jockey. The Pinkerton stationed at the entrance recognized me and waved me through the gate. He even smiled at me!

I drove straight to the barn where Pablo was supposed to have two horses stabled. There was the Jeep! Yeah, that's the Jeep all right. The dents I had put in it still hadn't been fixed. Well, it must be true then. Pablo really *was* working here.

I hoped that Pablo hadn't spotted my car. I didn't want him to think I cared. I drove on to Liz's kitchen (backstretch coffee house) where I used to get my coffee when I worked horses in the mornings. Everyone would be at Liz's. Wait a minute. Did I want to be seen? Should I risk showing my face? I didn't belong here. I wasn't Karen the jockey anymore.

I was about to turn the car around and leave the track when I spotted Mom's car. I remembered she had said she was supposed to meet someone at Liz's about a possible painting to do.

I gathered up all my courage, parked the car, and went in. I cast my eyes down so nobody would talk to me. I didn't want anyone to ask me what I was doing with my life.

I shuffled over to Mom, who was at a nearby table.

"Hi, Karen." It was Carmine.

"Oh, hi, Mom, I was looking for you," I said, making obvious my reason for being there.

"How are you, Karen? God, I haven't seen you in ages." It was Tommy.

"Yeah, I was in Florida over the winter," I explained, looking back down at the floor and wishing I were invisible.

"How have you been?" Liz asked, coming out from her usual spot behind the cash register to see me. What could I say?

"Hi, Liz." I wanted to disappear. Maybe I'd go over to the counter and order some coffee. If I looked busy, maybe nobody would talk to me.

In the corner, at the end of the counter where the takeout orders were placed, I stopped and waited my turn.

"Light and sweet?" one of the girls asked me with a big smile. She had remembered! But I wasn't eating sugar, now that I wasn't throwing up.

"No. Light with Sweet 'N Low," I corrected her softly.

They poured my coffee and placed it on the countertop. "Here ya go. Light, Sweet 'N Low."

"Thanks, Yvonne." I picked up my cup and headed back toward Mom's table. It took all my courage not to head straight back out the door. Mom was smiling, obviously happy that I had finally made an appearance at the track. She was probably the only one who knew how difficult this was for me.

Slowly, I looked around and took in all the people that I knew. Charlie (an exercise rider) and Rooster (a valet) were at one table. Bob Ribauto (a trainer who had put me on many winners), Carmine (from the tack shop who was always telling jokes), and Lenny Goodman (who was once the agent for Steve Cauthen) sat at another table. Nobody would want to talk to me. Not anymore.

Rooster came right over and gave me a hug. “How’s my favorite rider?”

I smiled and answered, “Okay.”

Lenny Goodman reached over and touched my arm. “Where ya been, kid?”

“Hey, I got a great joke for you,” Carmine piped in as I sat down next to Mom. He started telling me a joke. Nothing had changed. Everyone was the same. Everyone but me.

I laughed quietly as Carmine finished his joke. *I must leave. They are only trying to be nice. Maybe they feel sorry for me.*

Mom said quietly, “Why don’t you do something back here? Everyone misses you.”

“I can’t. Nobody would want to hire me,” I whispered back.

“Yes, they would. You’re good. You’re good at anything you do.”

“Mom!” I didn’t want the whole world to hear her.

Bobby, an exercise rider, got off his stool at the counter and came over to me. “Hi Karen. Are you planning to ride races again?”

I shook my head. I knew someone would ask me that question. Why did I ever come in here?

“Well,” he said, “Richie O’Connell is looking for somebody good to work for him. I’ve been galloping horses for him. Do you want me to find out?”

“No. I mean, I don’t want to get on horses.”

“Well, maybe...what do you want to do?” he asked me, confused.

What *could* I do???

“I don’t know. Maybe just walk hots (hot horses),” I mumbled with uncertainty.

Bobby looked surprised. Then he offered, “Do you want me to find out for you? Richie is a great guy to work for.”

I didn’t know. I didn’t know what I wanted. I wanted Pablo to love me again. Would he approve of me working?

Mom must have noticed my hesitation and sensed that I was getting depressed again. “Why don’t you find out, Bobby?” she said.

"It can't hurt. Right, Karen?"

Eh. Who cares.

I left Liz's and swung by "Pablo's barn" once more to look for the Jeep. It wasn't there. Where could he be now? Wait a minute. He had mentioned something about AA meetings right here at the track. I knew he was very involved with those meetings and had found friends there.

I drove back to the entrance where the Pinkerton had waved me in and asked if he knew of any AA meetings on the grounds.

"You'll have to go to the main gate, Karen. There's a house right next to that entrance where they hold those meetings. I think there is one this morning."

I thanked him and headed for the main gate. Sure enough, I found the Jeep parked outside one of the buildings.

I sat in the car feeling left out. I couldn't go in. Why was Pablo going to AA meetings anyway? He didn't have an alcohol problem; he had a *drug* problem!

Not knowing what else to do, I headed back to my house in Elmont. Maybe I'll call Pablo later. Or maybe I won't. I shouldn't. But I probably will.

When I got to the house, the phone was ringing. Maybe it's Pablo! Maybe he wants me to come to a meeting with him to meet his friends and be part of his life again! Or maybe he'll tell me about his two horses. Or maybe he'll beg me to come back to him.

I ran over to the phone. "Hello?"

It was Mom. She called to tell me that Bobby had come back to Liz's to tell her that trainer Richie O'Connell wanted to hire me. I could start at six the next morning.

"I don't know, Mom."

"Try it. It will get you out of the house and around people. You can always quit if you don't like it."

"I don't feel right about it."

"Well, I don't know, then. It's just a suggestion."

"Nothing will work for me. I'm not good at anything. I can't do anything. Do you know what? I saw the Jeep this morning. Pablo was at the barn. Then he went to one of those AA meetings, right at the track. Do you think he really has changed? Do you think he is off drugs, or that it's all just an act?"

"I don't know, Karen. I wouldn't put anything past Pablo. But why can't you just forget about him? Who cares what he does? He's up to no good. Of that, I'm sure. And you get so upset whenever you see him or talk to him."

"Do I really?" I asked. I thought I still loved him. Well, maybe I did get upset when I was around him.

"How could you forget? Remember how you ran the Jeep into a tree?! You have to stay away from him."

Maybe she was right. Maybe I did get upset when I looked for him to love me and he rejected me instead. But one day he would realize that he needed me and that I was the only one he could love—just like he had told me so many times. Then he would ask me to come back. In the meantime, Mom was right.

"I'll try working for Richie. But if I'm uncomfortable, or if Pablo doesn't like it, or if they don't like me..."

"You'll do fine. It's a start."

That night I called Pablo. He actually answered the phone.

"Pablo, I heard you have a few horses."

"Yeah. Two. I'm just doing it to keep busy."

"Well, I might go to work at the track tomorrow."

"Doing what?" he asked skeptically.

"Well, not riding of course. Maybe, well, I'm not even sure what I'm going to do. You have two horses?" I reminded him, hoping that maybe he would ask me to come and help *him*.

"I'm just training until something else comes up. So, what are you doing?"

"Nothing. I just wanted to...Nothing. I have to go. Bye."

I hung up, feeling suddenly depressed. Why did Pablo always have his act so together, and why did I always feel like such a failure, such a mess?

The next morning my alarm went off at five-thirty. Overcoming the sense of dread, I forced myself out of bed. I had to do something with my life. I made some coffee, going over and over in my head what I should do next. Should I go to Belmont again? Should I go to Richie's barn? Bobby had said I could start first thing in the morning. But, what if he really didn't want to hire me? No, I wasn't going.

Oh, what the heck. It's either that or rot in this house.

Okay. Okay. Just get in the car and go. Don't think.

Okay.

Now, I'm in the car. God, please help me do this.

Once I got over the initial fear of rejection, it wasn't so bad. Richie was nice. Bobby talked to me between sets, and Shannon, the assistant trainer, was friendly enough. Did she like me, or was it just an act? Of course, she would be nice to me because she worked for Richie. And he probably hired me out of pity.

What a charity case I was.

Well, maybe the horses liked me. I walked them around and around the shed, looking down at my sneakers, glancing up only to check the clock; each horse had to walk forty minutes. So I kept turning left. Round and round the shed row, keeping to myself, not wanting to bother anyone or be in the way. After all, they were nice enough to put up with me. And as I walked, I thought about Pablo.

A few mornings later, I was leaving the track and Pablo pulled up next to me in the Jeep. "I heard you're walking horses for Richie O'Connell," he said.

"Yeah, I've been working for him for just a few days. I tried to call you, but you are always out, or something."

"That's funny. I never got your message."

"Well...I never left one. I hate answering machines."

"Oh, you should have left a message. So, are you happy now, working for Richie?"

"Well, it's okay," I said, feeling rather low.

"I miss you."

"You do?" I asked in disbelief.

"Yes. Can I see your new place sometime?"

"Um. I don't know. Maybe."

"Why don't we get together and have dinner? Or lunch, if that would be easier on you."

Yeah, I was always such a problem, wasn't I? "Okay," I answered automatically. "Maybe. Call me." Now, why did I say that?

Pablo didn't like me working at the track, where I might regain my self-esteem. He had to drag me back down again.

Up until that moment, I had been doing pretty well. Now, suddenly, I was depressed again. Did Pablo really miss me? Did he want me back or would he just push me away again? I could tell he didn't approve of me working for Richie. Maybe, eventually, I could walk hots for Pablo—if he asked me. I wouldn't ask him. He was treating me like a pathetic basket case as it was. I didn't want his charity. I wanted his love, his approval.

The next morning (Pablo never called) I was walking a horse when Richie asked me to come outside the barn. He instructed someone to take the horse I was walking. Was he going to fire me?

"Karen, I want your opinion," Richie said as I approached. He pointed at the horse he was holding. *He wanted my opinion?*

"This horse is by Newswriter. What do you think of the Newswriter offspring?" he asked.

"Huh?"

"Well, I figured you would be a good person to ask. Pablo trained Newswriter and trained a lot of his offspring, didn't he?"

"Yeah, he trained Newswriter." All of a sudden, a confidence came over me. I wasn't sure where it came from, but it felt good to be sure of something—for once. "Newswriter stamps his babies," I explained. "Most of them are slow to develop. They get really good when they're four or five years old. Most of them hate the grass, but of course, there are exceptions. They also hate the mud, for the most part."

"What do you think of their eventual breeding value?" Richie asked, stroking his mustache as he contemplated his charge.

Pablo's words came to me so easily. "Newswriter will make a great sire. And he's going to be a sire of sires, or at least a good broodmare sire."

"Thanks, Karen."

"Okay. Any time." I started back to the barn. It was then that I realized that Karen the jockey was still there, still inside me. Or was it the confidence of Pablo that was speaking, coming forth out of my mouth to answer Richie's questions? Yeah, that was it. Those were Pablo's words. I was just no good.

I took back the horse I was walking, hung my head, and continued to turn left around the shed row.

A few days later I was walking a flighty young filly named Adam's Luck. It felt strange because I had ridden and won with this filly's mother, Adam's Angel. Eight long years ago—before Pablo, before retirement—I was winning races on this horse's *mother*. As I rounded the corner, Adam's Luck lunged forward suddenly and somehow managed to kick me. The blow hurt physically, but more so emotionally. It was more than I could take. As people rushed over to help me, I hid my tears. I was good for nothing. I couldn't even *walk* a horse!

The incident devastated me. Only my leg was injured, but emotionally I felt I couldn't get any lower. The next day I didn't go to work. Nor did I go the next. In fact, I quit working for Richie. Yes, I was a quitter. I hadn't retired from riding, like everyone said. I had quit. I was a quitter, doomed to failure. Was there any hope for me? I doubted it.

"Mom, I think I need psychiatric help. Something is really wrong with me. I need to go into a hospital, like Pablo. You know how much he changed. If I spend twenty-eight days in a hospital like him, maybe I could be better, too. Two or three days at Brunswick House didn't do it for me. I hadn't even seen a doctor there. Maybe I'll call Dr. Davis and see what he thinks."

I called Dr. Davis.

"How are you doing, Karen?" he asked, sounding genuinely interested.

"Well, the good news is that I haven't thrown up in five months."

"That's great!"

"But that's about the only thing good about my life right now. The bad definitely outweighs any problem with eating." Wasn't that strange, I thought. Only a year ago, I had believed that throwing up was my only problem!

I filled Dr. Davis in on Pablo and everything that had happened since Florida. I explained that life had gone from bad to worse. Something else must be wrong with me.

"It sounds like *Gaslight*," he said after listening to all I had to say.

"What do you mean, 'gaslight'?"

"You know the old movie, *Gaslight*, where the guy marries this young girl so he can drive her mad—make her believe she is insane—so she will agree to be committed to a mental institution. Maybe you should rent the movie."

"It sounds familiar. You know, I think I rented that movie. Was it with Ingrid Bergman?"

"That's the one."

"No wonder Pablo didn't want me to watch it with him! He had seen it before and told me he couldn't bear to watch what the guy did to the girl. I can't believe it! I thought it was strange at the time that Pablo didn't want to watch it because Pablo loved all those old movies, especially the mysteries. He could watch the classics over and over again. We did end up watching it, but I never caught on. I never put it together with my own life. How could I? At that time, I thought I was the happiest, luckiest wife in the whole world."

"Rent it again," he suggested. "You might see it differently this time."

"Okay. I think I will. You really helped me, especially when I was in Florida and needed someone to talk to. You saved my life more than once. Maybe I'll write a book about it someday."

"Rent that movie. I'm sure it will help. And stay away from Pablo. You'll be fine. You're a strong person who has been through a lot."

"Thanks again."

It was nice to talk to someone (other than Mom) who knew what I had been through, and still believed in me.

Lost and alone, I decided that maybe I should go into a hospital like Pablo. If I went into a hospital for a while, then I could go back with him, and we could share our similar experiences.

I drove out to Oyster Bay to ask Pablo what he thought of me going into a hospital. As I pulled into his driveway, I noticed a little red car next to the Jeep. Company? Hmm.

Before I could get out of the car, Pablo's front door opened and he came out, followed by a young man in his twenties.

I got out of my car and started toward Pablo.

"Who is this?" the young man asked Pablo.

"It's...her," Pablo answered, somewhat disgusted.

"Don't worry, Pablo. I won't leave you alone with her," Pablo's friend said as he moved in front of Pablo and approached me. Was I that much of a problem that Pablo couldn't handle me?

"Pablo, can I talk to you?" I asked. "Alone?"

"I won't leave you, Pablo." The young man stuck his chin out defiantly.

"What's going on, Pablo? Can't I have a minute with you alone?" I looked at Pablo who pretended that nothing was out of the ordinary.

The guy started toward me.

"It's all right, Doug. You can wait inside," Pablo said calmly. "Go on inside. I can handle her."

Handle me? "What are you talking about, Pablo? What have you told him about me?"

"I'm not leaving you, Pablo," Doug insisted. "Go on, get out of here. Leave Pablo alone."

"Pablo is my husband. Don't you think this is between the two of us?"

Pablo looked down. "Go inside, Doug."

But Doug wouldn't let up. "Yeah, Pablo's told me all about you. You should get run over by a train."

Run over by a train??!!

"And who are you?" I asked. "Another Mr.Wonderful from AA?"

What had Pablo been telling people about me? *Run over by a train???*

"Get out of here," the man repeated.

Pablo stepped back away.

"You don't even know me," I said, feeling lower than low. "What has Pablo been saying about me?"

Doug glared at me, looking ready to fight.

"Okay. If Pablo can't talk to me alone, I'll come back another time." I felt like a criminal. I was so bad. I was bad for everyone. Maybe I should get run over by a train, like he said. I backed away and got into my car.

Pablo turned to go into the house, but I wasn't quite done yet. I pulled my car up closer to him. "What have you been saying to people about me, Pablo? You can call off your bodyguard now. I'm leaving. I don't know why you're so afraid of me. The two of you together outweigh me by three times." Why was I saying all this? I threw the car into reverse and stepped on the gas. The tires screeched as I backed out of the driveway.

Tears flooded my eyes as I drove away down Mill River Road. Pablo *hated* me. He was telling everyone that I was the cause of his problems. If they only knew him, really knew him, and the way he lied. But everyone believed in Pablo. Even me. Maybe I was the one with the problem. Maybe I should get run over by a train. The railroad tracks were less than a mile away.

As I sped along, I noticed the telephone poles on the other side of the road. Maybe I should just smash my car into one of them and end it all. That would make Pablo happy. But there were cars coming in the other direction. What if I hurt someone else?

I'd better pull over. I can't control my emotions. I could hardly see through my tears.

I knew there was a phone booth by the gas station near the parkway entrance. I'd call Pablo. No. What if he makes me feel worse? I'll call Mom. I need to stop these suicidal thoughts. She'll talk some sense into me.

I pulled over at the gas station and used the pay phone. "Hi, Mom? I'm out near Pablo's. He had this friend there, and the guy told me I should get run over by a train. The railroad tracks aren't far from here. I'm debating it. What's *wrong* with me?"

"Where are you? I'll come right away!"

"No, Mom. Just talk to me. Why is Pablo pushing me away? What is he telling everyone? He must want me dead. I should be dead."

"No, Karen. He is manipulating everyone the way he did you. He probably has people feeling sorry for him and made up some bad stories about you. He probably told his parents the same thing, and that's why they turned so suddenly against you in Florida. Remember?"

"You're right, Mom. It was the same thing in Florida. First that doctor at Mount Sinai hated me. Then the woman who ran the program there asked me what drug I was on because 'everyone from the racetrack is on drugs.' Now where would she get an idea like that?"

"Pablo."

"And his counselor never called me. Then the Garcias said it was all my fault. Now this guy says I should get run over by a train. And, Mom, get this. He said, 'I'll protect you, Pablo. I won't leave you alone with her.' As if I could do anything to Pablo! Two big guys up against me! It was awful."

"Forget him, Karen. Come here. Don't go back to your house. Don't be alone to think. Spend some time here. Okay?"

"Thanks, Mom. I feel better. I'll come over, I guess."

"See you soon, okay?" Mom sounded worried. No wonder. I guess she had cause to worry about me when I got around Pablo. "Come straight here," she said. "And think about something else."

"Okay. I'll see you soon."

When I got to Mom's, I was exhausted—mentally, emotionally, and physically.

"Pablo is driving you crazy," Mom remarked, shaking her head. "You can't keep going back there to see him."

Suddenly, I got very angry with her. I left and went back to my little house in Elmont. Why did I feel so mixed-up? Why was I so mad at Mom now, instead of Pablo? What was wrong with me? Mom was only trying to help. She just didn't understand. I should get run over by a train, like Pablo's friend suggested. Pablo wanted me dead, didn't he? That said it all. I was nothing but a useless troublemaker.

I decided to get drunk for the weekend. It's Sunday, Labor Day weekend, so on Tuesday I'll pay my rent and bills and then I'll go to a hospital, maybe Brunswick House. Maybe someone in a hospital could figure out what was wrong with me. I didn't want to think anymore, to be me anymore. I couldn't seem to kill myself, so getting drunk was the next best escape. I'll lock the doors and stay away from everyone.

And so, I got really drunk. But instead of forgetting about everything, I grew angrier and angrier. Why was I so miserable? Here I was, destroying myself because of Pablo. Or was it Mom I was mad at?

I went downstairs and wrote a note in case Mom came over. I didn't want to see anyone. I wanted to be alone and drunk for the next two days. I taped the note to the side door: Mom, do not bother me. Karen.

I went back upstairs. Pablo kept coming into my mind. My head was spinning. I had drunk enough to sink a ship. All the liquor from the party was now in my system. I would drink until I died, or at least passed out. I didn't want to go to a hospital. I just didn't want to live anymore.

There was a knock on the door. *Go away!*

I stayed there in bed. Please, go away. Leave me alone. I want to just slip away into oblivion. The knock grew louder until it was a banging. I got out of bed and saw Mom's silhouette through the curtain of the side door at the bottom of my stairs. *Darn! Couldn't she just leave me alone??!!*

I went down and opened the door, "Couldn't you read my note?"

"I was worried about you. I called and you didn't answer the phone."

"I'm drunk, and I want to stay that way. I don't want to see you and I am so angry at Pablo and at you."

"Karen, I don't know what to do."

"Don't do anything. Leave me alone," I said, full of hatred and anger. "I hate you."

"Why do you hate me?" Mom asked.

"Just because. You remind me of how much I hate myself."

There. I had said it.

"Why? Can't we talk?"

"No! I'm warning you. If you don't leave, I'll kill myself," I screamed.

I shouldn't have threatened that. But I wanted her to go away and leave me alone. "Please leave!" I was so *angry*.

When I wasn't drinking, it was hard to feel anger at Mom. My anger had been repressed for all those years since Vince came around and twisted my emotions. I didn't want to feel or acknowledge this anger at Mom, but with all the alcohol in my system, I had lost control and it came flooding out.

Mom hadn't seen me this angry since I was ten. I think it scared her. “Karen, wait,” she said as I ran back up the steps.

“Leave me alone,” I called down and went to the bedroom window. It felt like I was fourteen again and back on our farm. I had gone to my bedroom window, got on the roof, and wanted to jump to end all the pain. Back then, everything was wrong. Everything was crazy. I had ruined Mom’s life with Vince. Here I was again, thinking those same thoughts. *What was wrong with me???*

“Please leave me alone,” I called down to her, the same way that I had so many years ago. “I’m by the window and if you don’t leave, I’ll jump.”

“Okay. Don’t jump.”

I went over and got into my bed again. Good. Now she’ll leave. I listened for the door. I wanted to be someone else, somewhere else. I hated myself so much, now for pushing Mom away. I wished she loved me, but she didn’t.

There was quiet. Maybe she left. Good.

“Karen, why don’t you go into a hospital?” Mom called out from the foot of my stairs.

Darn! Why hadn’t she left?

I got out of bed. “I will and I am! I’m going on Tuesday, so please just leave me alone,” I yelled. Now, I was really angry. It was *my* idea to go to a hospital. Now she was making it out to be her idea. Why did she have to be the one to tell me I was crazy? I already knew that. She didn’t have to *tell* me.

I went down the steps. “Mom, I have to pay the rent for September and some other bills. Then on Tuesday, I’m going into a hospital, the way Pablo did.”

“Why don’t you let me take you now? Before you do something bad to yourself?”

“I already told you. I want to be alone and get drunk. I’ll go in to the hospital on Tuesday.”

But it was too late. The police were outside the door.

“Mom, what have you done to me now?” I said, crying. I felt so betrayed. Why hadn’t she listened to me? Why did she have to call the police and have me locked up, committed? I was so angry at her for not believing in me, for not loving me.

"I'm sorry. I called the police. I was afraid. I was afraid you were going to hurt yourself. Or jump from your window. I didn't know what to do."

"Why couldn't you be on *my* side, just for *once*?" I said, sobbing.

Looking back, when I would get drunk, all logic was replaced by emotion. Wanting to jump out the window at the farm, thinking I was bad, and believing that Mom wasn't "on my side" were all part of these emotions from the past.

"I'm sorry. I was scared," Mom said, trying to explain.

I ran upstairs as Mom let the police in. I heard them coming up to get me.

"I'm not going anywhere!" I yelled. "I'm going to the hospital on Tuesday *after* I get my things done. It's Labor Day tomorrow. I have to pay my rent. You can't make me leave."

Three big cops came into the bedroom and grabbed me. I struggled with them. "You can't take me. You can't!"

But they could, and they did. They handcuffed me and put me in an ambulance. I was taken to Holliswood, a psychiatric hospital. I was checked in and given a cup of decaf coffee. After a few minutes, Mom arrived. She came over with hesitation and sat down beside me. I didn't want to talk to her.

"Karen, I'm sorry. This seems like a nice hospital. I heard all good things about it."

"Of course, it sounds good to *you*. You don't have to be locked up in here. I'm the crazy one, remember?"

"If you need anything, I'll bring it for you," Mom said.

"I wouldn't have had this problem if you had let me pack my own suitcase and come in two days. Then I could have paid my rent, gotten everything in order, and planned this out better."

"Well, now you're here."

"Thanks to you. How long do you think I'll be in here?" I asked Mom.

"I don't know. As long as it takes, I guess."

"I'll never be better. I don't even know what's wrong with me."

"You can't keep going the way you've been going."

Why was everything always *my* fault? Why was I always the one with the problem? In anger, I threw my coffee on her. I don't know why I did it.

Although I hadn't acknowledged it, deep down I had anger at Mom. I believed she didn't love me. My anger at her for all the problems Vince had brought into my life had been long repressed. Now, I was angry at her for not believing in me, for "turning" on me, and for calling the police.

As soon as I threw the coffee, I regretted it. "I'm sorry," I said, feeling more mixed-up.

Mom looked very upset. I wished she would just go away. But I needed her. She would be my only contact with the outside world. Unless I called Pablo.

Before I was taken upstairs to my room, a man brought in some forms for me to fill out. If I admitted myself as a "voluntary" patient, I could leave after they evaluated me, which would take a few days. Even though I signed myself in this way, I planned to stay twenty-eight days, the same amount of time that Pablo had been in his hospital. It had worked for him. Maybe it would work for me. Could I handle it? I had no choice; it seemed like the only option left. Mom was right. I couldn't keep going the way I had been. At that rate, death was inevitable.

"Don't worry about your daughter," the admittance man reassured Mom, who still appeared to be very upset. "She's in good hands. Holliswood is a complete hospital. We have the best doctors, counselors, and facilities available. We're expensive, but it looks like the insurance will cover the cost."

I was happy to hear that Pablo's insurance was covering my stay. His father must have paid the premium.

"You ready?" he asked me.

Would I ever be ready? I wanted to cry. I said goodbye to Mom and to freedom and followed him into the elevator.

Chapter 75
Professional Help

The immediate benefit to being in the hospital was that it kept me from drinking and from going out to Oyster Bay to see Pablo. I was put on a mixed unit, which meant some of the patients were here for psychiatric reasons, but most were just normal people with substance abuse problems. With all the drinking I had done, I could certainly fit into either category. Anyway, we were all in here because our lives were basically a mess, "unmanageable" as they called it.

I liked my doctor. The first few times I met with him I focused on the craziness of my life with Pablo. The doctor listened, but he seemed to think my problems went deeper than Pablo. He asked me about my childhood, which I didn't think was relevant. The next time I met with him, I went into detail about my childhood and how I rode races to escape the problems of Vince and my mother. I still didn't think it had much relevance to my current condition.

"Are you angry with your mother?" he asked me.

"No! I was just mad at her for making me come to the hospital before I wanted to. But, she was only trying to help me."

The doctor rephrased his question. "I mean, from the past. From when your stepfather was around. Are you angry at her for not doing anything to protect you from him?"

"No! How could I be? She didn't know!"

The doctor was reaching for those buried feelings from long ago. "You feel no anger at your mother? Most patients do have anger, but they won't allow themselves their feelings. Give it some time. I want you to write about how you feel towards your mother. Try to feel things, not to think them, okay?"

Was he trying to trick me into being angry at my mother? I couldn't allow myself to do that. She was all I had left. I didn't hate her, did I? I was mad at her for calling the cops and bringing me to the hospital on her terms, but that was all there was to it.

The doctor kept on about the past. I still didn't see the relevance to my present situation. "Why can't we talk about Pablo? If he would just love me again, I would be fine."

"The problem with most patients, I have found, is not their present involvements. It goes deeper than that. Sure, there are problems with present relationships, but the reason usually goes back, way back to their childhood. Usually people put up with abusive spouses, drug addicts, or liars because of their own low self-esteem. Some patients disguise their low self-esteem by becoming overachievers, such as yourself when you were riding. People who have lived through a very troubling childhood—especially surviving the trauma of incest—often end up suicidal. They can become extremely depressed and turn to substance abuse or self-mutilating (cutting or burning themselves) as a way to escape their feelings. Or they can find a new identity through someone else, becoming a candidate for something we call "co-dependency." That means depending on another, for example a spouse, for identity because their own self-worth is so low.

"There are also, but these cases are much more unusual and severe, instances of split personality or multiple personality disorder. All this is a result of coping with some greater underlying problem, from surviving the trauma of the past.

"Making it even more difficult to pinpoint the area of trouble, or root of the problem, is that often the patient has memory loss associated with and around the traumatic event or events that took place. As a child, one isn't equipped to cope, so the mind takes on other ways to diffuse the pain. The situation with your stepfather has had a much greater impact on you than you would like to think. You must have survived some very traumatic events."

It couldn't have been that big a deal. Pablo was the problem, wasn't he? That's when my life turned upside down.

"Tell me more about your relationship with Vince, was it? Your stepfather? Did you love him?"

"*No!* How could you say that?" The thought repulsed me.

"Very often patients won't admit they ever had feelings for the abusive parent. But children want to be loved and accepted by their parents and stepparents. Not love in the way two adults would love each other. More of a protective kind of love. Children want and need attention. Did you ever seek his attention?"

Suddenly, a flood of guilt overcame me. I didn't want to think about it. I had taken Vince away from Mom precisely because I *had* wanted his attention. But I couldn't admit that. I was *bad.* "Um. I don't know."

"All kids seek the approval and attention of the adults around them, especially from their parents or caretakers. Children want to be held and loved. They need adults' approval of who they are. This is how we form our self-esteem. Usually, a positive childhood experience guided by loving parents produces high self-esteem. The adults in your life during childhood and adolescence have a huge impact on what you think of yourself, your self-worth or self-esteem."

Yeah, and mine was zero.

"Feeling love for Vince," he continued, "would have been a normal emotion for you, given the situation. He came into your life as a substitute dad, a 'father figure.' Your mother loved him and you also wanted to be loved and accepted by him. You trusted your mother's judgment. She brought him into the family. Remember that. You didn't. You may have sought his attention, but you didn't ask to be abused by him. What he did wasn't love. It was abuse. No child is guilty when they are abused."

"It wasn't my fault, even if I did want his attention?" I asked. This was hard for me to believe. If I had wanted Vince to love me, it still wouldn't have been my fault??? No. That was impossible. It had to be my fault. Of course it was my fault.

"That's right. It isn't your fault. We have a great deal of trouble trying to get patients to believe or accept this fact. It takes time. Years of blaming yourself, possibly even hating yourself, cannot be undone so easily. The effects of child abuse are far too vast to understand, even today. It's a whole new field opening up to us and explains a lot of the difficulties adults have later on in life. The greatest problem is that the adult patient doesn't want to, or possibly cannot remember or access the memories of the childhood trauma. The mind can block memories in order to protect the child from extreme pain. It could take months for a patient to be ready to access the memories. It usually takes much longer than a hospital stay for patients to deal with the pain of the past and start to feel better about themselves."

"So, you think all my troubles have to do with...back then? It doesn't seem possible, although I did have trouble mistaking Pablo for Vince. They were even the same person in my dreams! Isn't that weird?"

"Not at all. It's very common, as a matter of fact. You very well could be looking, subconsciously of course, to fix the past and all its pain through the relationship with Pablo. The trouble with that is Pablo is Pablo. He is not Vince. He may even have a different set of problems that you can't even see because you perceive him as Vince. The problem with this behavior is that, even if you don't go back into a relationship with Pablo, you will seek out another man and repeat the behavior. You will find another Pablo to take Vince's place. And he will be very similar in personality to both Vince and Pablo. He'll give you the attention you seek, yet behind this will be lies and manipulation. You'll end up back here again. Do you want that?"

I shook my head. It didn't seem possible.

"Well, then, I suggest you try going back to the past. Otherwise, you'll end up in another unhealthy, and possibly more devastating relationship. I've seen it happen over and over again. If one doesn't resolve the deeper issues, he or she is bound to repeat them. Women divorce alcoholic men only to marry another alcoholic. Most of them had alcoholic fathers. They hated this fact, but marry similar men, subconsciously trying to heal the hurt from their past. They crave the unconditional love they never received as children from their own father, and yet, they end up enduring more abuse. The mind is a strange and fascinating thing. We can repeat our mistakes, or we can learn from them."

I wanted to get better. I didn't want to end up like this again. I had enough of hospitals, enough of hurting.

"So, how about the anger at your mother? That has to be dealt with, too. That may be an even bigger issue than the other."

"I don't have any anger at her," I said, believing my own words. "She has done everything for me."

"Write about how you felt about her when your stepfather came around. Just try, okay? Try to really feel your feelings from back then. It may be hard. Years of stuffing away those feelings can make them hard to access. I'll speak with you again next week. Work with the counselors and participate in the group sessions. Write what you are feeling. You can either work at getting better in here, or you can waste your time. When you go back out into the world, it won't have changed. So, you have to."

I thought about what he said. I wanted to get better. But I didn't know where to start. Anger at Mom? I didn't have any, did I? The part about Pablo and Vince made sense: the Vince/Pablo man. It was comforting to know that I wasn't alone in this strange way of thinking and dreaming.

How do I go about changing my subconscious? How would I stop myself from being attracted to someone who was "bad for me?" How depressing. Maybe I was doomed for life.

I got a pen, but I couldn't write. At least, not about anger at Mom. As far as I knew, it didn't exist.

When I was ten years old and believed I was Vince's girlfriend, I had terrible bouts of jealousy and rage over Mom and Vince's relationship. At the time, I came to the conclusion that I was crazy and bad. It was wrong to be angry with my mother. So, I had stuffed the feelings and hid them away, never to be revisited. Those memories and feelings were behind an invisible wall that I didn't know existed. If I didn't know a wall existed, how could I ever tear it down?

Time dragged in the hospital. I only saw the doctor a few more times. He explained that until I could remember and acknowledge anger at my mother, he wouldn't be able to help me move forward. Except for the episode that put me in the hospital, I didn't think I had any anger towards my mother. I grew depressed and frustrated.

Wanting to do something productive, I began reading the 1130 page novel, *Hawaii*. Maybe I would finish it by the time I got out. I started praying again, which took some of my anxiety away. It took my focus off Pablo and back on God—where it needed to be all along. Why had I ever forgotten God? He was waiting for me to start depending on Him again.

I didn't think the "group therapy" sessions were of any value, except to help the time pass more quickly. I couldn't talk about myself. All I talked about was "us"—meaning Pablo and me. Had I lost myself that much? Everyone in the group seemed to think so.

"Why don't you concentrate more on yourself and less on Pablo?" the other patients suggested repeatedly. I had to become a separate person again, not just a "with Pablo." Was that possible? I hated who I really was.

Whenever I could, I did exercises alone in my room. If I got fit, maybe I'd feel better about myself. And, in the very back of my mind, the thought of riding again occurred to me. However, I told myself, it was just a thought, not a reality. Getting fit couldn't hurt, though. I did deep knee bends, push-ups, sit-ups, and back exercises. I kept getting on the scale in the hall to see if I was back to my riding weight.

I didn't throw up, but it was hard. Food—as much as I could possibly want—was readily available. I talked about my eating disorder in group therapy. Although I had not thrown up in six months, it was still a struggle. I felt heavy at 114 pounds, ten pounds over my old riding weight. But, who was thinking about riding, anyway? I had to get my life together. Was I getting better? I didn't think so. Still, everyone in the hospital seemed to like me. I was getting things done, like reading and praying and getting fit. I wasn't drinking, I hadn't seen Pablo, and I was determined to finish *Hawaii* by the time I got out. All this had to be helping my self-esteem.

Well, if Pablo got better in a twenty-eight-day hospital stay, then I was determined to stick it out for the same amount of time. As much as I disliked being locked up, I wanted to do it the right way. I slowed my reading down so that I would finish *Hawaii* on day number thirty. In some way, this gave me control.

With my guard down and feeling better about myself, I called Pablo from the pay phone in the hall. As he talked to me, I felt the urge to smash the phone into my brain and kill myself. I knew that if I tried something like that, I'd be in the hospital for a much longer period of time. And, I'd have a heck of a headache. So I hung up on him instead. Then I went back to my room to sulk. Why did I always feel so bad whenever I talked to him?

Mom and Amy came to visit me. So did my father. Grandma and Susan called. Yet, it was Pablo whose approval I sought. I called him again and again, but I didn't tell anyone.

In group therapy, we watched a film and had a discussion on "co-dependency." I fit the description to a tee; I was a complete and total "co-dependent." I realized that I was as addicted to Pablo as he was to his drugs! I was simply dependent on a person, instead of a drug, for my survival. Pablo had become such a part of me that I couldn't tell where I began and he ended. The very way I viewed myself was through his lens. However, I wasn't ready to give that up. Not yet. He was, what I thought, the bigger and better part of me. Pablo had rescued me from myself. He had approved of me when I stopped riding. He had loved the real me, the bad me. Wasn't he the only one who could ever do that?

Who was I, really? When I wasn't talking about Pablo in group therapy, I slipped back into my outgoing Karen the jockey role. The other patients, especially David and Melvin, seemed to really like me. However, they didn't know the real me; they thought of me as Karen the jockey. Melvin was a big gambler and racing fan, so I had Mom bring in one of my scrapbooks with lots of win photos in it. (Big change from the shame I felt over the scrapbooks around Pablo.) Although I wasn't a jockey anymore, around David and Melvin and away from Pablo, I felt like Karen the jockey; I had my old confidence back.

I wanted to see Pablo, but wasn't sure if it was a good idea. The counselors suggested that Pablo and I have a meeting with one of them. The counselor would be there to mediate and keep things civil between us. This way we could discuss things out in the open, without assigning blame.

At first I thought this was a good idea, so they set it up. Later, I wasn't so sure. What if they took Pablo's side and were against me? He was so convincing. He would blame me for everything, and I would feel worse. Besides, it was obvious I was the one with the problem. Who was in the hospital now? Not Pablo. Me. This would surely be a disaster. I dreaded our meeting, feeling defeated before it ever began.

Pablo showed up for the meeting—right on time. Mr.Wonderful. I had mixed emotions. I was proud that he came and looked like he cared about me. But underneath I was still angry at him and hurt by all the past rejection and lies.

A counselor sat down with us in a small office. I felt bad, like I was the one to blame, the one who had caused this whole big mess. I was always the angry one, the one storming out. Pablo was so sweet as he spoke to the woman counselor about me. She was immediately mesmerized by Mr. Delightful.

"Hey, wait a minute," I interrupted. "Pablo was in a hospital, too—for drugs. It isn't just me," I pointed out, trying to get her to see the light.

The counselor scolded me. "We're not here to blame each other, Karen."

Pablo, Mr. Understanding, spoke up sadly, "She's right. I was. I guess it was hard on both of us."

"Well, then, I suggest you two try to be more understanding of each other. Get to know the 'new persons' you have both become since entering treatment. Don't try to judge each other so harshly for past mistakes. Start like you are entering a brand new relationship. Take it slow at first, like you're dating. See each other just once or twice a week for only a few hours. That way you can get to know the new person and you won't be jumping into a full time marriage again," she said, smiling at Pablo.

Was that possible? To pretend he was somebody else and not a liar? But he still lied, didn't he?

"I'm willing to try," Pablo said to the counselor, smiling back at her.

I was the bad guy.

"I guess so," I said, looking down. Why doesn't Pablo just take the counselor out on a date? He hates me anyway. Why did he even come here? To make me feel worse? No. This was my idea.

"Well, then, Karen, the two of you make some arrangements to take it slow once you get out of the hospital. Maybe a marriage counselor is a good idea, too."

Pablo left the meeting looking like Dapper Dan. The elevator doors shut behind him and he disappeared, on his way to freedom. It was so ironic.

Since when did Pablo care about me? Did he care? Of course he did. He wouldn't have shown up if he didn't.

That night I was more anxious than ever to get out of the hospital. I didn't have to be like Pablo. I didn't have to stay twenty-eight days. I wasn't getting any better. I wasn't "changed." So how could Pablo have "changed" in twenty-eight days, like he claimed? He was lying. The hospitals didn't work. I was still me. I felt so alone and depressed. Up until now, I hadn't felt this bad in the hospital and wondered if maybe it had something to do with seeing Pablo. Maybe I should just give up on us.

By the fourth week in the hospital, I couldn't wait to get out. The doctor told me the counselors said I was making progress, but he still wanted me to write about my anger at my mother. Why was he insisting on this one point? Well, if that's what it took to get out, I'd write.

I wrote what I thought the doctor wanted, and I even cried in our session. In order to cry, I imagined never seeing Pablo again. I couldn't bear the thought. I pretended I was crying over my anger at Mom. It worked. I was given the okay to leave.

I had been in for the full twenty-eight days. I still had ten pages of *Hawaii* left to read, but that was by design. I hadn't wanted to finish the book in case they decided to keep me longer. Now that I had "done my time," was I really any better?

Chapter 76
One Last Try

The lease for the little house I rented wasn't up yet. However, the owners called me to ask if they could move back in the following month as their plans overseas hadn't worked out. Maybe it was best. At that point, I could move in with Mom and Amy for a while.

When I asked Mom, she said it would be fine.

"What about the bedrooms?" I asked. "I have lots of furniture and Amy has my old room."

"I'll fix up my room and you can have it," Mom said. "We'll put in new carpeting and wallpaper for you. It's plenty big enough for your bed and dressers."

"But where will you sleep, Mom?"

"In the little bedroom."

The tiny one we used for storage? No way. Was she doing this to make me feel guilty?

"No, Mom. I wouldn't take the big bedroom. It's yours."

"No. It's okay. Really. I don't mind. You take the big bedroom."

She was definitely trying to make me feel guilty, wasn't she?

No matter what Mom did for me, I twisted it, believing she was trying to make me feel guilty. The words, "Your mother doesn't care about you," were deep within my subconscious, still affecting my perception of her.

And so, this key issue of the relationship with my mother was not resolved. The doctor had been right. There was hidden anger and feelings that Mom hated me. This was at the root of my low self-esteem. But because I couldn't face the past, the truth remained hidden. I was unaware that my beliefs about her had been so poisoned.

Having spent a month at Holliswood Hospital, I felt pretty good about myself. I didn't need Pablo's approval quite so intensely. I had lasted a whole month without it, kind of like going through withdrawal. I contemplated venturing over to the races. This would be a big deal for me, but I wanted to see if I could look people in the eye and not look down, the way I had after I quit riding. Maybe in the back of my mind it was there.... the possibility. Maybe this was a test. Could I ever be Karen the jockey again?

I got up all my courage and did it. I had a big hello for the agents as I bravely walked past the racing secretary's office. I went past the Belmont paddock and toward the grandstand. I watched the horses walk out onto the track. The jockeys seemed so small, like little dolls. From the outside looking in, they didn't seem like people, just little dolls in bright colors that appeared before each race. They seemed untouchable, unreal. Had I been like that once? It seemed impossible that I had ever been one of them. They seemed almost magical. I felt so far away from "jockeyland."

Wait a minute. What was I talking about? I knew these people.

They were just like me, or like I had been at one time. Angel. Jacinto. Robbie. Jerry. All just out there struggling to get mounts and win races. That's all there was to it. I had done this once, too.

I had done that?

I went back to the house in Elmont. Something inside me was waking up. I started doing more exercises, more than in the hospital. My weight was dropping. I was down to 110 pounds.

If Pablo was at the track, there couldn't be anything "wrong" with being there. I had the urge to call him. Maybe we could work it out. Like the counselor said, try going more slowly, like a new relationship. I was stronger now. I wouldn't allow him to make me feel bad.

Pablo had never been to my little house in Elmont. I had been too afraid to tell him where it was, thinking that maybe he would stop over. Or maybe I was more afraid that he wouldn't stop over, and that would have been such a put down to me. I was only staying here for another month. What would be the harm in inviting him over now?

I called Pablo and asked if he still wanted to try getting back together. We would take it very slow, as the counselor suggested. I asked him if he wanted to stop by and see my place.

"I'm really busy, but I could come by at around eleven, after training my horses. What is the address?"

I hesitated. Then I told him.

"See you around eleven, then?" he asked.

"Yeah, okay."

Well, it was done. If it didn't work out, then I'd just forget about him, right? It was worth one last try. I had to give it a shot, now that I was stronger and could see Pablo more clearly. I wouldn't let him stay long. Maybe an hour. Maybe.

As Pablo stepped inside my front door he commented, "This place is really small." Well, what did he expect? I didn't live in Oyster Bay anymore.

"Um. So, how are the horses?" I asked.

"Oh, they're cheap. I'm just messing with them to stay busy. I have a lot of speaking engagements to do."

"What do you mean?" I asked.

"I go to hospitals and speak to the people about getting straight. In fact, I've got to go and speak soon," he said, checking his watch.

"You do?" I felt bad that it was his idea to leave so soon and not mine. I never seemed to have any control when it came to Pablo. "Who asked you to speak at hospitals?"

"It's part of the program," he said.

"'Alcoholics Anonymous,' you mean?"

"Yeah. I've even helped several people at the track. People who used to work for me. I drive them to meetings."

Pablo *helping* people??? It didn't seem possible. "Well, that's good." I said, feeling lost and useless.

"So, how have you been doing?" Pablo asked, gazing around the living room. He noticed my win pictures and sneered at the photo of me on Kuja Hapa beating his Dubai horse. "Hung all your old pictures up, huh?"

"Yeah, I had to fill up the wall space..." I looked down at the carpet. Why hadn't I thought to take them down before he came?

"Oh. I didn't know you had so many pictures of yourself."

"Well, they're old. I used to keep them in the closet. Some people like them."

"Oh, yeah? Like who? Who has been over to see your place?"

"Well, just a few people from the track."

"Oh, the racetrack. Yeah, they *would* like win pictures. That's all they ever think about is winning races. It impresses them. So, you have some new friends? Did they come to see you in the hospital?"

"Well, I didn't want anyone to visit me there. Except Mom."

"Your *mother* came to see you in the hospital??!! Ha, I'll bet she loved that."

"Well, you came."

"Of course, honey. I love you."

I looked down once again.

"I read the novel, *Hawaii,* while I was in there," I said, wanting to sound productive.

"You read that *whole* book?" Pablo asked, amazed.

"Uhh, actually, no. I didn't quite finish it."

"I didn't know you liked to read."

"You never...never mind." I didn't want to blame him for the fact that I didn't read when I was with him. That was my fault, not his. Besides, I wasn't supposed to blame him for things in the past.

"Pablo, what's it like back at the track?"

"Same as always. Same people. Only it's changed. It's gotten worse."

"I was thinking. Uh...do you have enough help with your two horses?"

"I've got *too* much help. Carlos is my groom, and I've got another kid to help in the afternoon. I've only got the two horses, so I'm losing money."

"What about...exercise riders?"

"Maureen is getting on them. I wouldn't have anyone else but her. Remember she worked for me when I trained for Dubai?"

"Yeah. I knew her when I was galloping for you."

"Oh, yeah, that's right, you did. Then you got thrown off on the track. Or was it in the shed row? You know, when you hurt your finger and quit getting on horses?"

"Both. Sort of."

"Yeah, that's right."

I wanted to ask him if I could get on his horses—just to see if I could do it again. But for some reason I felt too down and incapable. I felt so small next to the almighty Pablo.

"Do you think I could come out and see your horses sometime?" I asked lamely.

"Sure. I'm in the barn next to the old Dubai barn. Listen, I've got to run. I have that meeting out at the hospital." He headed for the door.

"Which hospital? Maybe I could go sometime."

"Oh, you would never find it. It's way out on the island (Long Island)."

"Pablo?"

"Yeah?" He was halfway out the door, about to leave me alone, once again.

"Do you miss...sailing?" I wanted to ask if he missed me, but didn't have the courage.

"I've still been sailing, but it's not the same without the boat. I'm giving lessons out at the club."

"Oh." He sure was Mr. Busy Bee lately. And I was still a do-nothing.

"Gotta go. Call me, okay?"

I stood at the door and watched him get into the Jeep and drive away. "One Day At A Time," "Easy Does It," and other AA slogans were plastered over the back window and bumper of the Jeep. I guess he really had changed.

After Pablo left, I called Mom and told her I felt really down.

"I'm going over to the track to play volleyball," she said. "Some of the people get together to play on Tuesday afternoons when there is no racing. Why don't you come on over? Some trainers, grooms, and jockeys have a net set up on the backstretch. It's all people you know. Some of them were at your party. Why don't you come over and play? It will cheer you up."

"I don't know. I don't fit in. I don't work at the track anymore. I don't do anything."

"Nobody cares if you work at the track! They will be glad to see you. And, it's just for fun. That's all. Come on and stop over."

"I don't know. Maybe."

"Come. I'll see you there."

Mom expected me to be so cheerful, so energetic. But I was feeling so down on myself. I hadn't even finished *Hawaii.* I couldn't do anything. Suddenly, I remembered playing volleyball in the gym at the hospital with Melvin and David. Maybe I would go out to the track. If I felt like a misfit, I would just come home.

Everyone at volleyball seemed so happy. Watching them laugh and play made me feel so out of it. I figured nobody would like me now that I wasn't riding. They probably wondered what I was doing with my life. I remembered what Pablo had said. *All they ever think about is winning races.* Why was he so different? Why was he so much better than everyone else? And why did I feel so much worse?

After watching two games from the sidelines, I started to leave. Mom was huffing and puffing from her efforts as she came over to me.

"We finally won a game!" she said enthusiastically. "Why don't you take my place and get in the next game?" she suggested.

"No. I'm going home. I'll see you."

I got in my car feeling more out of it than ever. Just a few days ago I had felt so good going to the races. Now, I was so depressed. What was wrong with me? The hospital was just a temporary way to forget myself and my problems. Now I was back, right where I had left off, alone with horrible me. How would I ever get out of this depression? I wasn't even capable of finishing a book. I tried to think of something positive. There was one thing. I was getting fitter and my weight was down to 106. That gave me some comfort.

Later that day, Mom called me. She told me that Bill Leggett, a friend who wrote for *Sports Illustrated*, had called looking for me. There was a jockeys' strike at the track, and *The New York Times* wanted an article about the strike written by a jockey. Bill Leggett had suggested me. Would I want to do it?

"I don't know, Mom. I can't write."

"They'll even pay you for it," she said with encouragement. "You've got to be a better writer than some of the other jockeys. Some of them don't even speak English!"

"When do they need it by?"

"Bill said next week. Just try it. They can edit and change it until it looks good. What have you got to lose?"

"I don't know anything about the strike. I don't want to take sides. I'm all for the jocks getting more money, but I don't want to go against the owners and trainers either. They have lots of expenses."

"Why don't you go to the track and see what you can find out? Call Bill. Here's his number."

I took down the sportswriter's phone number, but I really didn't think I'd call. My mind went back to Pablo. Maybe he would know something about the strike. I called him to ask what he knew.

"The jocks make more money than anyone," Pablo said with disgust. "Who are they to strike? The owners are putting up the money. They shouldn't be bled dry by the riders!"

"But, Pablo, I didn't make that much money when I rode. Ten percent of the jocks make ninety percent of the money. If you're not Angel Cordero or another stakes winning rider, you just don't make the money. Besides, the risks involved..."

"Oh, for Christ's sake! You take the same risks driving a car!"

"I broke my back more than once."

"That's you."

"No. Most of the other riders have done the same. Most jockeys have broken lots of bones. Broken backs and necks are common. Angel broke his back. The injuries and risk factor..."

"Well, the whole strike is ridiculous. The trainers are ignoring the strike anyway and using unknown riders in races. Can you believe it? Some *exercise* boys are even riding races! The New York Racing Association is a joke. They shouldn't allow the jocks to strike. It's hurting the whole industry."

I had read a little about the strike in the paper and pointed out what I knew. "Lots of retired jockeys are making comebacks." What did Pablo think of that? Maybe I could make a comeback.

"Yeah, and those retired jockeys are about as dangerous as the exercise boys. Unfit 'has beens' trying to cash in on the whole mess. What a joke. I'm not running my horses until the strike is over."

"Pablo, your horses aren't that great." *I can't believe I just said that!*

"That's true," he admitted. "Listen I've gotta run."

"Okay."

After he hung up, I thought more about the strike. Maybe I would write the article. Or, maybe I'd make a comeback and ride. Nah. If I rode, I wouldn't want to ride with a bunch of "has beens" and exercise riders. I'd stick by the jockeys who were striking and ride with them when the strike was over. If I ever did ride races again, I would want to do it the right way. I'd have to be as good as I was before or else I just wouldn't do it. No way.

Maybe I would write the article. But not about the strike. I could write about riding in general, what a jockey goes through: the long hours, the lack of contracts, the empty promises, and the injuries. The highs and lows. The ups and downs. The thrill of victory and the agony of defeat. Who better to write this than someone who had been through it? I could write the truth and leave it up to the reader to decide whether or not the jockeys deserved a raise.

I borrowed a typewriter from Mom. She seemed pleased that I was going to attempt to write the article. But the typewriter stayed in the car. I kept thinking about Pablo and how he wouldn't approve of me writing, especially an article about Karen the jockey.

Pablo came over to see me again. I really wanted our relationship to work. I felt incapable of doing anything unless he approved of it first. I craved his acceptance, and if it meant denying myself everything but him, well, it would be worth it. If only he would love me like he used to, everything would be okay.

Pablo sat with me on the couch. He noticed the coffee table was covered with papers scribbled with handwriting. "What's all this?" he asked.

"I was asked to do an article about the jockeys' strike, and I'm trying to write it."

"What have you ever written?" Pablo asked with a laugh. "Who would care about someone's opinion that has been out of racing for five years? Besides, you just got out of a psych ward."

Maybe he was right. I wish he would love me. Take me back. Ask me to his meetings and let me hear him speak at the hospitals. I wanted to share in some part of his life again.

"I don't know what to do. I have to move back in with Mom again soon," I revealed.

"That's crazy. She doesn't want you around."

"Do you miss me?" There, I said it. Maybe he would ask me to move back in with him.

"I'm very busy with my new life. But, yes. I miss what we had."

This made me sad. Yeah, what we *had.* "I'm so miserable," I said. "I don't know what to do. I tried the hospital, but it didn't change me like it did you. I still hate myself."

"Oh, honey."

I knew it. He still loved me.

"I wish I was dead."

"Oh, honey." He gave me a hug. He loved me when I was down on myself. I remembered when he showed me how to make the noose to hang from the shower in Florida.

"I'm going to hang myself, Pablo."

"Wait a minute. I have to use the phone," he said, getting up and leaving me alone in the living room.

I looked down at my attempt to write the article for *The New York Times* and despised myself. I went into the bathroom and looked for something to use to hang myself. The only thing I could find was dental floss. I couldn't hang myself with dental floss, but maybe I could tie it around my neck.

Pablo was talking on my phone in the kitchen. He wanted me to do this, didn't he? Life wasn't worth living unless he loved me again. I tied the floss around my neck and sat in the empty bathtub.

Pablo came in. "What are you doing?"

"I'm trying to kill myself, but I can't seem to be able to figure out how." I climbed back out of the tub. "Dental floss doesn't work," I explained." I looked in the mirror and saw the red lines around my throat from pulling on the floss. I walked past Pablo and down the basement steps. He followed.

"Maybe I'll get in the dryer. Could you turn it on for me once I get in? Maybe that would kill me." I climbed into the dryer, squeezing myself into a ball. I actually don't know how I fit in there. I was pretty small from losing weight, and I was determined. "Pablo, could you shut the door and turn it on now?"

"If you want." He came over, but the door wouldn't shut and the dryer wouldn't go on. Maybe it was because of the weight. "I'm leaving. I have to go," he said.

"Pablo, where are you going? Why are you leaving me?"

"I just called Andy and I have to get a check to him."

From my sideways view out the dryer door, I watched Pablo wave to me and go back up the basement steps. Then I heard the door shut as he left the house. I turned and twisted, trying to work myself out of the dryer. It wasn't easy, but finally I did it.

I'm sick of living. I'm sick of Pablo leaving me. He wishes I were dead. Well, if the only thing I can do in life to make him happy is to die, then I'll do it. I have nothing left to live for anyway.

I went back upstairs and wrote Mom a goodbye note on the back of the half-written article. I wanted to tell her how sorry I was for ruining her life, but I couldn't put my feelings into words and undo all the damage I had done. Nothing I wrote would do. Nothing.

"Mom, I'm sorry. I love you. Please don't blame yourself. I'm sorry." Tears poured down my face as I crumpled up each sheet of paper and attempted a new note. Why couldn't I do it? Why couldn't I write? I couldn't say goodbye.

Angry and frustrated, I grabbed my win photos off the wall and hurled them to the floor. The broken glass splintered all over my face in the pictures. There. That's more like it. Broken me. Shattered. I hurled a few more of my favorite win photos just for good measure. Pablo hated me. I hated me. Karen the jockey was broken. Dead, *dead!*

Sobbing and desperate, I picked up the broken glass and cut my wrists. I cut every part of my body I hated, especially my legs. Pablo liked my legs. I must say goodbye to Mom. I must tell her I'm sorry.

Mom later recalled that when reading my suicide notes, she mistook the words "I'm sorry" and "don't blame yourself" for my attempt at suicide, not for the deeper issue which I was trying to express—I was sorry for ruining her marriage and life because of what happened with Vince.

I had worked myself into frenzy. "Do it! Finally, just *do it!*" I yelled and sliced my wrists more with the broken glass. Just let me die already.

In desperation, I called my mother. "Mom, I'm sorry."

"What's wrong? What...I'll be right there."

With tears in my eyes and blood on my hands, I tried to piece the little bits of shattered glass back into the picture frames on the floor. Mom came in and saw me there.

"Oh, my God. What...come here." Mom got a towel and cleaned me up. I couldn't stop crying.

"I tried to say I'm sorry, but I couldn't." I cried from the old, deep wound that hurt too badly for words. Hadn't I tried to say I was sorry a long time ago, when I had the out-of-body experience? Hadn't I wanted to say it way back then? *Why couldn't I do it?* What was wrong with me???

"That's all right. Was Pablo here, by any chance?"

"How did you know? He left. He left me to die. He wanted me to do this."

"How did he know where you live?"

"I told him. I'm just no good without him."

"Yes, you are. Pablo is the one that is no good. He wants you to do this so he can make you out to be crazy. Don't you see? He left you like this. He drove you to do this."

No. It couldn't be, could it?

"Why did he leave, Mom? Why did he leave when he knew I felt like this? He knew I needed him. He said he had to use the phone. He had to bring Andy a check. That was more important than me!"

"Did he know you wanted to kill yourself?"

"Yes. I told him!"

"He was driving you to this point all along. Then he leaves you here, hoping you will die. Don't you see, Karen?" Mom hugged me. That was all that mattered. The wounded little girl was being hugged by her mother. Maybe Mom did love me. And maybe Vince/Pablo was the problem, after all.

I went back to Mom's house. I had cuts all over, but none were deep enough to be dangerous. They would heal. But those deep wounds inside me, would they ever heal?

For the first time, I began to see what Pablo was doing to me. I don't know what finally opened my eyes. He never came back to the house in Elmont to see if I was okay, nor did he call. The next day, I called him to see if what Mom said about him was true. That he wanted me dead.

"Oh, hi, Karen," he said as if nothing had ever happened.

"Pablo, why did you leave me in the dryer yesterday?"

"I had to go. I told you that."

"But you knew I wanted to kill myself, and you left anyway."

"Where are you?"

"At my mother's."

"Well, I came back, honey. I came back to the house, but you weren't there."

"Yes, I was. I was there for a while."

"I came back late."

"I was there," I lied. I was testing him.

"The door was locked."

"If you were so worried about me, why didn't you climb in the window?"

"I thought you were asleep. I left a note on the door."

Liar. Liar, liar, *liar*. "Oh," I said sarcastically, "I can see you must have been really worried about me."

"I didn't want to wake you up. I've got to go now."

"Fine. Bye." I slammed the phone down, hating his guts.

He really had wanted me dead. And he conveniently left the scene of the crime. Maybe going to see Andy was just his alibi for when the cops found me dead. Oh, what did it matter?

"Mom, you were right. If Pablo really cared he would have broken into my house."

"He never would have left you in the first place, Karen. You're forgetting all those times in Florida."

"I know. I know. It just takes a while for it to sink in. I can't believe he doesn't love me, that he never loved me. How could he have?"

Mom and I talked for a long time. I told her the recent things that Pablo had been saying.

Mom shook her head in disbelief. "Pablo said I would be *glad* you were in the hospital? And that I wouldn't want you to move back in here? I can't believe the things he says to you."

I really wanted to believe she cared, that she really and truly was on my side. I had to believe this. With the beginning of my acceptance of the truth about Pablo, she was all I had left.

Chapter 77
Positive Feedback

The New York Times editor called to see if I had written the article.

"Well, I did write something," I explained to him. "It's not really put together into an article. Maybe you should get someone else to write it."

"There isn't any time left. The article is going to be in the Sunday edition coming up."

"What I wrote isn't so much about the strike as it is about riding in general," I explained to the editor.

"We'll use what you have. We don't have time for you to mail it in, so could you call us later, when it's ready? We'll have you dictate it over the phone and someone here will put it down on paper. Just do the best you can and call us back before five o'clock, okay?"

"Okay." I hung up feeling depressed and overwhelmed. Why didn't I just say no?

"Mom, they want the stuff I wrote. Did you bring those suicide notes over from the other house? I wrote some stuff for the article on the backs of the pages that said, 'I'm sorry.'"

"They are right here," she said, looking over what I had written as she smoothed out the crumpled pages. I noticed the dried blood on them.

"This is good, Karen. This is really good. You wrote a lot. You can just use this. You don't even need any more. Nobody but a jockey would be able to write what you wrote."

"Well, I'll work on it some more. But I'm really not in the mood."

"It will get your mind off of Pablo."

"I guess so."

I worked on the article some more. It was way too long. The newspaper would have to cut it down. So what? I'll call it in and see what happens. It's not like I'm a writer or anything. They would just have to understand that if they wanted a jockey's point of view, that's what they were getting.

At close to five, I held my breath and made the call. "It's longer than you guys asked for. So cut out the parts you don't want." I read the article over the phone.

"This is really good," the editor said.

"Isn't it too long?"

"No. I think we may use the whole thing."

"You can change it around if it doesn't follow."

"It's good, Karen. Thanks. It should be in the Sunday edition of our paper."

When the paper came out, I was astonished to find they had published the whole thing, word for word—unedited.

The New York Times, Sunday, October 30, 1988
Views of Sport
Inside the Jocks' Room: A Rider's Life
By Karen Rogers

My article covered three quarters of the front page of the sports section. They added a sketch of a horse and rider with a big stopwatch in the background. At the bottom of the page was a small bio:

> Karen Rogers was one of the top 10 leading riders in New York from 1980 to 1984 and the first woman to win a Grade 1 stakes race.

Reading the article got me thinking. Could I ever ride again? The strike was over. The jockeys got their fee increase, and the money was much better now than when I was riding. Besides, I really liked riding races. And, I used to be good.

It was time to move out of my rented house. I had a lot of stuff. Where would it all go? Mom and Amy helped, and we laughed at the fact that our family collected so much "stuff." At least I wasn't alone.

"We'll manage," Mom said, in her usual upbeat way. "Just put everything in our garage!"

After moving back home and feeling better about myself, I got the urge to get on a horse again. I was fit—as fit as I could be without actually riding. I decided to go to Pablo's barn and ask if I could get on one of his horses. Surely, he would let me. Yes, I would just do it.

I gathered all my courage and put on my exercise boots. It felt very strange. Had it been almost five years? I dusted off my helmet and headed for Belmont Park.

I felt conspicuous driving through the gate. What if I couldn't do it anymore? What if I had lost my touch? My boots would be a dead giveaway when I got out of the car. Then, everyone would know.

Well, what have I got to lose? Pablo's making a comeback. Why shouldn't I? He'll let me get one of his horses. I'm not making any commitments. I'm just getting on one horse to see if I can actually do it again. It will just be for Pablo. No pressure.

Okay. Here goes. I opened the car door, shaking. I watched my boots step out of the car. Was anyone watching me? I looked around, heart pounding.

Okay. Now the rest of me. I'm not bringing my helmet, not until I know I'm actually getting on a horse. I don't want to announce it to the world.

I walked into Pablo's barn, feeling very conspicuous and out of place. My boots were like blinking neon lights, broadcasting the news: "Look everyone! Karen has her boots on again!"

Carlos, Pablo's groom, spotted me right away. "Oh, now we've got a real rider!" he exclaimed.

I smiled. It was going to be okay.

"Getting on my horse, are you?" Carlos asked, smiling.

"I hope so," I answered.

Pablo appeared around the corner of the shed row.

"Hi, Pablo. Are these your horses?" I asked, pointing to the two stalls with yellow stall guards marked "P.G."

"Yeah, these are my muskrats."

I went over to take a closer look, hoping Pablo would notice my boots. Carlos was in the stall with a gray horse. "They don't look so bad," I commented. 'Is this one going out now?" It was kind of obvious as Carlos had put the saddle on him and was tightening the girth.

"Yeah," Pablo said. "The exercise boy is supposed to breeze him. He's late."

I could do it, I thought. Breezing would be great, much easier than galloping. If only he would ask me. I didn't want to seem too anxious, though. I would let Pablo make the suggestion.

"Where is that darn exercise boy?" he asked, annoyed.

"I thought you said Maureen was getting on your horses. Isn't she?" Maybe he'll let me do it. If Maureen isn't working for him, he would love to have me do it.

"No, I've got this freelance boy. He's not very good. He's terrible at breezing horses. And he's always late." Pablo looked down at his big old captain's watch, irritated. "This guy always hangs me up. I shouldn't pay him so much."

"I could save you a few bucks, Pablo," I suggested, smiling at the thought of helping him.

"What? Oh, phew. Here he is." Pablo walked away from me, toward the exercise boy. I recognized the rider. It was true. He wasn't very good. My specialty was breezing horses, yet, Pablo was choosing him over me.

Carlos came to the front of the stall. "Well, you ready?" he asked me. "Just like Egotist. Remember when you won on Egotist for me?"

Egotist. Yeah. Carlos was his groom. Dubai's horse. My first winner for Pablo.

"About time you showed up!" I heard Pablo scold the rider. "Bring him out, Carlos."

"Okay, boss." Carlos shrugged at me and brought the gray horse out of the stall.

I watched them, feeling noticeably out of place. Pablo gave the exercise boy a leg up. The horse really was scruffy. Nothing like the Dubai horses. I could have ridden him, couldn't I?

I can't stand it anymore. I left the barn and got in my car, holding back the tears.

That son of a gun. He'll never stop putting me down. Well, what did I expect from him? Why did I ever go to his barn? I didn't need him. I was a good rider, or at least I used to be. Maybe I'll just go home.

I turned the car toward the stable gate, ready to go home, defeated. Wait a minute. That son of a gun. Even Carlos could see I wanted to get on that horse!

I turned right, bypassing the stable gate. I'm not through yet! I came out here to get on a horse, and that's what I intend to do!

Who can I trust? Who will pick out an easy horse for me to get on? My heart pounded at the thought. I know! Billy Wright. I had won quite a few races for him. The young trainer had seen me recently. I recalled his words of encouragement.

"You should be riding, Karen. You're light enough. Why don't you ride races again? If you ever want to get on a horse, just come by my barn. I'll pick out an easy on for you."

Yes!!! That was it!! Billy would help me out!!

I drove up to Billy's barn, hoping and praying that he would keep his word. *Should I?* Oh, stop thinking so much. Just do it.

Billy was in his office going over a training chart. "Well, well." He grinned when he saw me. "What brings you out here?"

"Billy, you're not going to believe it, but I've decided to take you up on your offer. Remember when you told me I should be getting on horses?"

He nodded and smiled.

"Well, if you could pick out an easy one for me, I'd like to do it again. Just to see what it feels like. It's been nearly five years."

"Sure. Hold on." Billy poked his head out the office door. "Luuuiieeee!"

Luis Guidoy, Billy's head groom, came to the front of one of the stalls. Luis always called me "Chiquita," which meant "little one" in Spanish.

"Have you got that little chestnut filly tacked up?" Billy asked him, saying it so loudly that everyone could hear.

Luis came over to us. "Hello, Chiquita."

"Yeah, that's right, Luis. The Chiquita is here to get on a horse for us." Billy slapped me on the back and laughed. He walked over to a stall. "I've got the perfect horse for you. Come and get on this little filly. She's real easy to gallop."

"Thanks, Billy. It's been a long time."

"You'll do fine. You're a great rider. Next thing you know you'll be riding races again."

"I don't know. Don't get your hopes up. I'm just going out on one horse. Just to see."

"If I know you, you'll be back. You won't be able to stay away."

I wasn't so sure—until I settled onto the little filly's back. Then I knew nothing had changed. Sure, I was a little clumsy at first, tightening my girth and making a knot in the reins. But by the time I went once around the shed row, I felt as good as always.

Billy rode out to the track on the lead pony with me and the rest of his "set." It was like I had never been away. Everything seemed so normal.

"You look good, Karen. You haven't lost your touch," Billy commented as he jogged his pony up alongside me on the horse path. This was a far cry from the way Pablo had treated me.

We reached the gap at the main track and Billy gave me instructions. "Just gallop a mile and a half, once around. She's easy. You'll have no problems."

"Okay. See you in a bit." I jogged the filly off, trying to ignore the stares from the other riders.

"Is that you, Karen?" I heard trainer Mickey Preger ask from atop his lead pony. I had won a race for him once.

"Sure is," I answered confidently. What was the name the horse I had won on for him? Great Fling. Yeah.

"I'm just out here for a 'Great Fling'," I added with a smile. Then I galloped off.

Yeah, a great fling. But it was more than that. As we picked up speed down the backstretch, my confidence grew. I was born again. I had shed some heavy outer layer and grown wings.

I was back.

Karen the jockey, that is.

Chapter 78
Trust God

Not so fast. Not so fast. It was only one horse. One day, one horse. And, I had been a mess. Could I do it again? I had managed with one little filly, thanks to Billy, but she was easy. Did I even *want* to ride?

Well, I did feel better about myself after accomplishing that which I thought I could never do again. It was a baby step, but a step, nevertheless. It sure beat running back to Pablo.

Billy wanted me to gallop his filly the next morning and to come back every day to get on her if I wanted. But I was hesitant. I didn't have the confidence in myself yet, the confidence that he had in Karen the jockey. But he didn't know what I had been through.

I told Mom what had happened. "Can you believe the difference in the way Billy treated me as opposed to Pablo? It's no wonder I felt so bad all the time."

"Now are you starting to see how everyone believes in you but yourself? Can you see how Pablo kept tearing you down? It started when he first met you. You quit riding so suddenly after being with him. He really soured you on the track, on life in general. He really influenced you. Of course, I can see it now. I couldn't see it then because you said you were so happy. He continued to take everything away from you: your riding, your family, and then even *he* rejected you. He tore you down bit by bit until you were broken into little pieces."

"Yeah. I guess so. I'm going to rent that movie *Gaslight*. Dr. Davis said that what Pablo was doing to me sounded a lot like the plot of that movie. I didn't really believe him, but now, maybe I will watch it again. I saw it a few years ago with Pablo. You know, Mom, Pablo didn't even want me to watch it then. He knew exactly what he was doing to me!"

I rented *Gaslight*. Well, here goes. I'm open to anything, even if it means seeing the truth about Pablo. I need to finally accept that it's really over between us. He wasn't my loving savior, the man who would save me from...from what?

As I started watching the movie, I laughed out loud at the similar circumstances of the young bride, played by Ingrid Bergman, and myself. That was a good sign, at least. Maybe I was finally over Pablo. Getting on that horse had definitely helped. But as the movie progressed, it wasn't so funny. Her new husband, played by actor Charles Boyer, tried to make her believe she was going insane. (He wanted her committed to a mental institution so he could inherit her house and jewels hidden inside it.) By repeatedly telling her she looked ill, the manipulative husband convinced his naïve bride that she was sick. He rarely let her leave the house, and, like me, she became afraid to do anything without his approval. She had no confidence in herself because anything she tried to do, he put down. He even got a maid because "she couldn't handle the housework." (Pablo also had a cleaning woman come to "help" poor useless me. The similarities were striking, indeed!) One day she was tired of being sick and decided to go out. When the controlling husband could not persuade her to stay home, he went out with her, but first he hid his pocket watch in her purse. Of course, she knew nothing about the pocket watch (sound familiar?). While they were out, he claimed it was missing and then "discovered" it in her purse! He accused her of stealing the pocket watch and having fallen so ill that she didn't even recall what she had done! The wicked husband had convinced her that she was, indeed, going insane.

I remembered the strange "pocket watch" incident with Pablo. It was early on, when we first dated.

"Honey, have you seen my pocket watch? The last time I saw it was when I took you to the Waldorf-Astoria for your birthday. I love my pocket watch. I really miss it. Did you take it?" He had kept on about the pocket watch. The trouble was that I hadn't realized I was supposed to have taken it, nor did I know I was supposed to be going insane—not at that time, anyway.

Eerily, in order to bring down his young bride, Pablo had followed the same sinister pattern as the husband in the movie: first wining and dining her, then keeping her secluded in the house, and lastly twisting everything that happened to lower her self-esteem. The only real difference was that I had landed in a mental hospital while Ingrid Bergman had not.

I shuddered. This was no game. No wonder Pablo watched so many movies and read so many books. No wonder he was intrigued with mind control, Hitler, and Mengele. Looking back at my close calls with death, I knew I was lucky to be alive. I believed with sudden urgency that God wanted me to survive. He wanted me alive—for something. The feeling was quite overwhelming.

I felt God's presence in my life. He was walking with me. I couldn't explain the feeling, but it was as if something bigger was guiding my course of action, my destiny. I was comforted by this. I didn't feel so alone, and this truly helped me stay away from Pablo. I didn't need Pablo's approval for everything I did. God had a plan for my life, and this gave me a strange feeling of peace. No longer did I feel so weak that I would collapse under the weight of my own decisions. God was with me. He would guide me and hold me up. He had the master plan. I would go one step at a time, trust Him, and let things unfold. Just keep the faith. God had taken care of me this far. I was sure that He wouldn't let go of me now.

I thought back to my 1981 spill at Saratoga. Floating up out of my body, I had wanted to turn and go, but the urge to come back and say goodbye to Mom had been stronger. I wanted to come back to say I was sorry and...and what? I *had* come back. God wanted me here for something. There was something that wasn't finished, something I had yet to do. Surely, I hadn't come back for nothing. What was the bigger picture? *What was I missing?*

Trust God. Don't worry. Just trust Him.

I stayed away from Pablo. I didn't call him. By the end of the week I was breezing horses again. I got on four or five horses every morning. I was feeling better than ever. I wouldn't think about going back to riding races. Not yet. I would just put one foot in front of the other, concentrate on today, and pray, pray, pray.

December, 1988. Aqueduct was open for winter racing. I decided to take a trip over there and check things out. As fate would have it, jockey agent Dominick Del Vecchio was in the secretary's office, and he was looking to represent a new jockey.

"Hey, Karen! I see your getting on horses again," he said, coming over to me. "If you decide to go back to riding, I'll be your agent."

Was he for real? The thought of riding again had crossed my mind, but not seriously until now. Dominick was a seasoned agent with a good reputation. He thought I could ride again?

"Yeah, I've been getting on horses for almost three weeks now," I said cautiously. Maybe I hadn't heard him right.

"Well, if you do decide to ride races again, keep me in mind, okay?" Dominick said with enthusiasm.

I hesitated. He would really be my agent? But Dominick could choose any jockey he wanted. Why would he want *me?*

"Okay... thanks, Dominick." I left Aqueduct with a new feeling of urgency and purpose. The idea that I could ride races again was now tangible, and my heart soared at the thought. I could do it. I could do it! God willing, yes! I would ride again!

I didn't want to mislead Dominick, so before he became my new agent, I told him all about my recent fiasco with Pablo and my hospital stay. "I don't even know if I can ride races again, Dominick. I don't want to make a promise I can't keep. I might end up in a hospital again," I cautioned.

However, to my amazement, Dominick wasn't fazed one bit. He

believed in me—totally. "That won't happen, Karen. You will do fine. I promise." Not only did my new agent (and friend) have faith in my riding ability, but he believed in me as a person, as well. He was *so* sure of me.

Well, what did I have to lose? I had lost everything once. If I lost everything again, I could handle it. God still loved me.

And so, with my new openness and honesty with Dominick, I started to believe that maybe I was okay. Not just as Karen the jockey, but the person underneath. I opened my heart to my agent, and he accepted me—the whole package. No matter what crazy story I told him about my relationship with Pablo, Dominick still liked me.

My first race back was on December 29, 1988. I had wanted to wait until the first of the year to start, but trainer Bobby Lake had jumped the gun and named me on his horse, Mr. Chromacopy. Oh, what the heck. It was my chance, and I would take it. I was learning to leave my fate in the hands of God, a God who loved me and looked out for me. Whatever happened, it would be all right. Just take it as it comes.

Breaking out of the gate on Mr. Chromacopy, I thought to myself, *What are you doing this for? Are you crazy? It's been five years. Do you really want to do this again?* And then, my race riding instincts took over. After that one moment of doubt, I was on my way. My mind was made up. If I was doing this, I would do it right. I rode with all my old determination, but finished off the board. Still, it was a huge accomplishment.

Awake in bed later that night, the doubts started to creep in again. Am I doing the right thing? Can I possibly stay the course and not go running back to Pablo and fall apart? Am I capable of doing this—not just once, but day in and day out? Could I handle the cards that would be dealt to me? The trainers, the horses?

Nothing could be harder than what I had lived through. I would just go one day at a time, one moment at a time. One horse, one race at a time. God would take care of me if I'd let Him. Everything would come together if I just kept the faith. Hold onto God and don't let go. *God, please handle my life. I've made a mess of it. Now it's Your turn. I can't make it on my own.* And so, once again, I turned my life over to Him and fell asleep reassured.

They say broken bones knit together stronger. It was the same with my faith. My brokenness had strengthened it. My faith was weak before I met Pablo. It was almost forgotten, broken during those times of crisis. But looking back, I saw God's hand in all of it. When I didn't care about my life, He did. When I almost didn't make it through, He carried me. It was a miracle, to say the least.

My situation reminded me of the poem "Footprints" by Margaret Fishback Powers. In the poem, she tells about a man who had a dream. In the dream, he saw two sets of footprints in the sand during his life, one belonging to him and one belonging to God. During his most difficult times, he saw only one set of footprints and questioned God's faithfulness. It was then, God explained, that He hadn't left the man—He had carried him!

I prayed that my eyes would be opened and that I would know God more with each passing day. I was willing, for the first time, to face any truth that God would give me. Bit by bit, God would unfold the last mystery, the last truth which remained hidden and locked up inside me. However, it would take a little more time and a lot more effort on my part. I could become a whole person again; I just had to be willing to suffer through some more pain.

Chapter 79
Another Setback

Business was slow at first. But I didn't expect anything. Whatever happened, take it as it comes. I was alive. I was riding. I had survived the past few years, which was a miracle in itself.

Dominick couldn't believe my positive attitude. He was frustrated because we were riding all longshots and finishing off the board. But I didn't mind. I was riding well and felt reborn on the back of a horse. Even finishing last was great. People actually liked me. They didn't hate me, the way Pablo had me believe.

My weight was down to 103, which was light for a jockey. On just the second day of my comeback, I "tacked" 104 in the Display Handicap (an extremely long two and a quarter mile stakes race). The amazing thing was that I hadn't thrown up in nine months! Another miracle was that I hadn't called Pablo. I stayed busy. Busy, busy, busy, just like the old days. Too busy to think. Much too busy to feel anything.

I seemed to be getting along with Mom. I was just too busy to think about being back in the house and in her old room. She had wanted it that way, right? It wasn't my fault. Anyway, I wasn't going to think about it. However, if Mom was slightly bothered by anything—a friend, a painting, a customer, etc., I would go to my room angry. I would be angry, then sad, and then depressed. Why? It wasn't my fault. I was legitimate once again. I was riding. I was Karen the jockey.

I reverted to my old pre-Pablo behavior: riding, happy, smiling face at the track, yet secluded and sad in my room at home. Pablo was no longer in my life, but something was still very wrong with me.

The guy I had been attracted to in the bar over the summer, the one who blew me off, showed up one day at the races. Now that I was a "jockey" again, he was looking for me. After the races were over, I headed out to my car in the parking lot. He was standing there, waiting for me. Mr. Macho, like Pablo.

"How have you been?" he asked, smiling broadly. "I read the articles that you were coming back to ride, and I've been at the races every day since. Haven't you noticed me standing by the rail?"

I had not seen him by the rail and was surprised by this sudden encounter. So now that I was Karen the jockey again and not some loser in a bar, he wanted to see me? Huh. I'd come this far...

His words came back to me from that summer evening. *Don't come looking for me. Don't ever call me at work.*

Was he for real?

"Well, haven't you seen me? I've been here every day, rooting for you," he repeated.

"I didn't recognize you," I said lamely.

"Didn't recognize me??!! Well, huh! It must be the beard. Did I have a beard then?"

"No. You didn't. It was a long time ago."

"You lost weight," he said.

"Yeah. I'm a rider now. I guess you noticed."

"You've been getting some bad mounts. Those horses couldn't

outrun my grandmother. How do they expect you to win on those horses? Nobody could."

I kept walking toward my car.

He followed. "Hey, we should go out sometime. You should be getting better mounts. You're a good rider."

He thought I was a good rider? Well, of course I was—a good rider, that is.

"Wanna stop someplace? I've been waiting to see you for ages," he said.

"It hasn't been that long. I've only been back a week," I reminded him.

"Every day, I've been here. Every day for a week. And *you* don't even notice!!! Oh, yeah. The beard, right?" he winked.

He had been here for a week? He did that for me? I thought about home and Mom. I didn't feel like going home. I felt empty.

"Come on. Follow me. My car's over there. We'll stop and get a bite."

I better not. I was doing pretty well without anyone. "I..."

"Did you get a divorce from that crazy husband of yours yet?"

He remembered! He hadn't forgotten all my troubles, all those things I told him that night when I was so down. I had needed someone to listen and to understand, and he had.

"That guy should be locked up for what he put you through. Come on. Follow me."

I was amazed he had remembered, amazed that he cared. I watched him walk to his car. He had on a long, tweed overcoat. I hadn't recognized him. I hadn't seen him by the rail. Maybe it was the beard. Oh, what the heck. He likes me. I'll follow him. I don't want to go right home, anyway.

And so, I proceeded to do exactly what the doctor at the hospital had warned me about. *If you don't go back into a relationship with Pablo, you will seek out another man and repeat the behavior.*

I needed to fill the empty void. The real me, the bad me was calling for validation once again.

January 28, 1989. I won my first race since starting back. I should have been happy, but I was depressed. Why? Mr. Macho took me out to celebrate that night. We had been seeing quite a bit of each other. I felt bad when I was with him. It felt so familiar. And, I was drinking again. Maybe it was to numb the fear of rejection. I definitely could not handle being hurt again. No way. He was on my side, wasn't he? I told him more about Pablo, how even though Pablo did some bad things, he had been on my side, at least in the beginning. I told him about Mom and how I believed she hated me. He listened closely and seemed to understand.

still..."racing with my shadow"

I rode with determination. I had to make myself okay. Unlike Pablo, Mr. Macho approved of Karen the jockey. He wanted to see me again *because* I was Karen the jockey, because I was riding again. That was a good thing, right? He wasn't like Pablo. It wasn't like the doctor had warned. I wouldn't repeat the past, would I?

So, I continued to be Karen the jockey on the outside. And with Mr. Macho I steadily went downhill.

Needless to say, I shouldn't have been in a relationship. Not yet. But if not now, when? When would I be better? When would I stop having this feeling of impending doom and rejection whenever I got close to someone? When would I ever stop hating myself for feeling "love" for a man? Why did I want to self-destruct in a relationship, yet still feel the need to have someone "on my side?"

The bad me would destroy me yet.

I started heaving again. I used my riding as an excuse. I told myself I had to stay light. Yeah, I lie. Bad, bad me. Back throwing up after nine months of being good. What was wrong with me? *God, please help me be strong. Help me end this relationship. It's just no good. I'm no good. If I keep on like this, I will surely die.*

My suicidal feelings increased. Every time Mr. Macho came around I felt the strong urge to kill the feelings inside me, to cut them out of me. This strong emotion of wanting-love-mixed-with-self-hatred overwhelmed me.

I was bad, the bad little girl whose desire for love and attention from Vince had caused all the trouble in the first place. I had caused it. I was the problem. I was always the problem.

After the races, both before seeing Mr. Macho and again after he left late at night, I would drink, throw up, and cut my body. My thoughts would race... *Don't let that riding exterior fool you, Karen. You are damaged goods. You may try to lose yourself in riding, but you are losing the battle.*

The reality was hitting me hard; I must end this relationship, or wind up dead.

Mom watched me suffer. She was confused. And scared. I was hanging onto life moment by moment, headed down the same suicidal road I took when I was with Pablo. Only this time around it was happening at a much faster pace. At breakneck speed, I moved up the bad, inevitable ending. Instead of waiting five years for the toxic relationship to do me in, this time I hit bottom in less than five months. In May I finally ended the relationship. It had gone on far too long.

Yet all during this time, I never let my personal life get in the way of Karen the jockey. Karen the jockey felt no pain and rode her heart out. With all the late nights of drinking, she never took a day off and kept winning races. By the spring meeting at Aqueduct, I had made the leading jockey list. Less than four months into my comeback, I had reached the top again. I expected nothing less from Karen the jockey. After a five year absence, she was as strong as ever.

Nevertheless, the bad experience with Mr. Macho left me scarred and feeling like a failure as a person. Even though I continued to win at the track, I was withdrawn around people, threw up in the day, and continued to drink at night. If anyone got to know me, they would hate me.

Chapter 80
Robbie Told

One afternoon between races, I noticed an article in *Sports Illustrated* about jockey Robbie Davis, written by William Nack. Robbie was a friend and fellow jockey who was involved in the death of jockey Mike Venezia in a racing accident.

In the magazine, I noticed the photo of Robbie standing all alone in a snow bank in his hometown of Idaho. Something about it drew me in. He looked like I felt: lonely and sad.

From the article, I learned that Robbie had taken several months off due to the racing tragedy last fall at Belmont. Taking that much time off was very unusual for a jockey, so I read on to find out more. Robbie explained that the accident in which his horse struck and killed his friend Mike had such an impact on him that he could no longer deal. Although there was no way for Robbie to avoid the fallen rider, he blamed himself. Mike's death weighed so heavily on him that he just couldn't take it anymore. After the accident, Robbie had questioned why it seemed like everything bad always happened to him.

Then it told the rest of his story, the deeper reason for Robbie's depression. Robbie explained that the purpose of the article was to finally tell his secret and let it all out—that he had been sexually abused as a child by his stepfather. The article explained that most abused children blamed themselves for the abuse and often buried it. Layer over layer, Robbie had buried the pain. With the death of Mike Venezia, the old wound was opened and his deeper pain had resurfaced. Like most sexually and emotionally abused children, Robbie was in the habit of blaming himself and thought Mike's death was all his fault. Having been sexually abused, Robbie said he felt like the worst person in the world, like he was really, really bad.

I understood exactly how he felt; that could have been me, all alone in that snow bank in Idaho. Robbie had taken time off from riding. He had gone back, back to where he had grown up, back to the scene of the crime. Could what happened to me really have happened to another jockey? Robbie had fallen apart. And what about me? I wasn't so together either. Sure, I was riding again, but the rest of my life wasn't going so well. Then again, what happened to me so long ago couldn't be that big a deal. It couldn't have affected me that much. Still, what surprised me the most was the fact that Robbie told. He had more courage than me. He had more courage than anyone I knew.

Driving home from the races, I pondered Robbie's words. I felt like he said he felt in the article. And, I was remembering. For the first time, I allowed my mind to go back. The memories came in flashes, a split second at a time. *Robbie did it. He went back. He faced his ugly past. And, he talked about it!*

Robbie must be so strong. He admitted what happened. It was okay for Robbie to tell his story because it wasn't *his* fault. He told the whole world in an article, and nobody would blame him for what had happened. But, it was different with me. It really *was* my fault. But...Robbie blamed himself, the same way I did. Still, it was different with me.

I couldn't believe his courage. *Robbie told.*

When I got home, I showed Mom the article. "Mom, isn't it strange the way Robbie felt that what happened was his fault?" I watched her closely to see her response. Would she blame Robbie? Would she?

Mom was very sympathetic. "Of course it wasn't his fault. Why would he think he was to blame?"

But that was Robbie, not me. *He didn't take away Vince's love from Mom the way I did.*

The article stirred up my own deep, dark, ugly past. My own buried "secret." Mom said that what had happened "to" me was similar to what had happened to Robbie. Knowing that Robbie had been deeply affected by his stepfather's sexual abuse, Mom thought it might be beneficial to talk more about my own dark past. I only hoped I could revisit the past without falling apart completely.

We started talking about "the Vince years." Every night we revisited this topic. Sometimes we talked for hours, well into the night. I was starting to trust Mom. Weeks of talking went by, and she still didn't blame me. I wanted to talk about it as openly as Robbie, but for some reason I couldn't.

My invisible wall was still keeping me from delving too deeply.

At night, I started having flashbacks. There were more memories than I thought possible. For the first time, I remembered details. These flashbacks weren't just vague ideas of what happened to "someone else." I could clearly see what was going on, and I was at the center of it all. As my hidden memories were revealed to me and the emotions that went along with them erupted, I drank until I passed out.

Chapter 81
Ready to Remember

One night, we were having one of our usual "going back" sessions and I cut Mom off suddenly and left the room. She followed me. "Wait, Karen," she said.

"What?" I asked defiantly. I was angry and frustrated. "What do you want?" I wanted to be left alone. I had talked enough. *Enough!*

"Karen, I don't understand," she said with tears in her eyes. "We are making so much progress talking, unraveling many of Vince's lies—both to you and to me—and then all of a sudden you turn off and leave the room. It happens every time."

Mom was crying? She was that upset? I couldn't believe she cared enough to cry.

She continued, "It's like we suddenly hit a brick wall. Just when I want to tell you my version of what happened, you shut down."

I hadn't really been aware that I was doing this until she pointed it out. "I do that? Every time? I didn't know that. Huh," I said, truly baffled.

Subconsciously, I was terrified that if we continued to go down the road toward the truth, Mom would discover what I felt, deep down, to be true: that what happened with Vince was my fault, and that I had ruined her life.

Mom wasn't mad at me, just confused and frustrated. She really did care about me—she was crying! She was helping me dig for the truth, so I could get better. Did I really turn off? Why? I could only take so much talk about the past. I would emphatically tell her "my side" of what had happened and how I felt about it, always defending myself and then I would retreat. I didn't want to hear "her side" of what had taken place, did I? That was true. Why? What was I afraid of? Why didn't I want to hear what Mom had to say? Why did I get so defensive of my position, and so angry if she wanted to tell me how she felt? She obviously cared about me. Her tears were proof. I shouldn't be so fearful of her blaming me. *What truth did I not want her to know?*

Suddenly, a key memory came to me from out of the foggy, forgotten past. For the first time, I saw what I had buried so well years ago, the painful incident at the window when I was ten years old. I was remembering what I had tried so hard to forget forever—being madly, insanely jealous when I saw Mom and Vince kissing through my window. I had been so *angry*. Why had I buried this incident and these emotions.... Jealousy. Anger. Betrayal. Ugh. Just remembering now was very difficult. I did not want to remember, to acknowledge how I had felt at that time. I had stuffed those feelings so very long ago because they were *bad*. I remembered calling my sister to the window to see if she felt the same way I did—angry and betrayed by Mom and Vince kissing—but she had acted as if nothing was wrong. I realized then that it was *me. I was bad.* Those feelings were wrong and very, very bad.

Reliving this scene in my mind as I stood there with Mom got me very, very depressed. Then it suddenly hit me. That was the time—the exact moment—I had been trying so hard to forget. *That time at the window was the very moment I decided that I was bad.* That was when I became aware of what a bad girl I really was, when I first felt so alone, so different and so very, very sad. That night long ago I had made the decision to turn my feelings inward, to try to be good, and *to hide the bad me.* I realized with sudden clarity the magnitude of this memory. It was the very *moment*, at ten years old, that I had shut the real me feelings away somewhere forever, so that nobody could ever find out of who I really was—the hidden "truth" about me. Wow.

"Mom?"

"Yeah?"

"I think...I know why I have been reaching a certain point and then I don't want to dig any further. There is something I need to tell you. This is really hard for me. It's my very worst memory. I don't want to tell you because I am so ashamed of how I felt back then. I have been ashamed for years. Ever since that powerful incident, I was ten at the time, when I knew my feelings were wrong. I was bad. So I swore to myself I would never *feel* those feelings again. It was so painful that I buried that memory. I don't even know if I can tell you about it now. It's been my secret for so long." I wanted to cry. I was so sad, so depressed. Mom waited. She was listening.

I continued, "Maybe I haven't been ready to remember. I don't know. But I've had so much inner turmoil and depression that I have to find out how to get rid of it, if that's even possible. I have to know the truth. I have to know if I'm bad. I am ready to face it. You'll probably hate me, but it's time to tell you what I've kept buried for so long."

I thought about the risk I was taking. I would lose any last vestige of love that Mom had for me. So what? I couldn't keep going the way I was. Even though I was still winning races, my life was in shambles. I'd rather die than continue living like this, drinking myself into oblivion. It was time to deal with the truth, time to reveal who I was: the real me, the bad me.

"When we lived in Bridleton, you and Vince..." No. Start again. "Well, when Vince first lived with us, when Dad left, well, uh, I was kind of like...jealous of you and Vince. I hated that feeling, but I felt it so strongly. I guess it was jealousy. It was like some angry monster inside me. It was such a strong, horrible feeling. I couldn't take it. I couldn't take you and Vince being together. For some reason, I felt betrayed. One day when I saw you two kissing through my bedroom window, I went into a jealous rage. You remember how the courtyard was set up so that we could see into all the rooms from our windows? Well, I saw you two kissing in the dining room and went crazy. It is so hard to tell you this now. I hate myself for it. I have hated myself for so long." I paused. Was I breathing? I continued to pour it out. "Why would I feel like that? Why would I be jealous of my own mother? Why would I want to take Vince away from you? I was, well, I am, so bad."

There. I said it. I held my breath once again. Okay, I'm ready. She's going to hate me, now. Really, really hate me.

"Karen, Vince was manipulating your feelings. If he was sneaking into your bedroom, like you have told me, and telling you he was *your* boyfriend, well then, how were you supposed to feel? Confused, I guess. And angry."

"But I felt *so* angry. They were my feelings, not his. It was my fault. And then I went crazy throwing things in my room, and I almost broke the window. You two came running into my room to see what was wrong with me."

"Yes, I remember that."

"I was *always* the problem, wasn't I? I had forgotten what a problem I was all those years. I have spent my life trying to forget, trying to make myself okay. Now, I'm getting those memories back and it feels just awful."

"You got upset a lot back then. I never understood why. Whenever it was the four of us—Vince, you, Susan, and me—you would..."

"Go off the deep end. Yes, I know. I am remembering now. I tried to forget about all that. Like it was somebody else, and not me."

"But from all you've told me recently, Vince was causing you to feel that way. He would sneak off alone with you and tell you things."

"I don't remember exactly what he said. I do know I was very confused because he told me he loved me and not you, and then he acted like he loved you when we were all together. I didn't know if he loved me or you." *God, this was so hard, so depressing.*

"He was the one who made you confused," Mom explained. "He made you feel that way, don't you see?"

"I understand that the sexual abuse was wrong, on his part. I'm starting to accept that maybe that wasn't my fault. Still, I felt like I asked for it in the first place because I had wanted his love and attention when he first came around, when I was nine."

"Karen, you were so young when all this started. You wanted him to love you as a father would love a daughter. But he twisted it into some kind of sick boyfriend/girlfriend relationship. You were confused, and no wonder. He manipulated your feelings. What a horrible thing he did to you, mentally, emotionally, and then physically. He made you feel things which caused you to hate yourself. He confused you into thinking you were taking his love away from me, your own mother! No wonder you don't want to remember that! You didn't take him away from me. At ten years old, you just wanted his love and attention. He caused you to have mixed-up feelings by telling you he was your 'secret boyfriend.'"

"I never thought of it that way before. I always think of me now the same as me then. I've always felt responsible for my feelings and actions. I'm the one in control of what I do."

"But you were so young. You were being manipulated, made to think differently than a normal ten-year-old. It isn't your fault that you thought and felt the way you did. Vince should have acted like a responsible adult—but he was sick. He is sick. I hate him for what he did to you." Again, there were tears in her eyes. I couldn't believe she cared enough to cry and that she wasn't blaming me.

"You mean, those feelings of...I hate to say it, but of jealousy, came from him acting like he was my boyfriend and telling me I was his girlfriend?"

"You were set up. He planted ideas in your head. You probably don't remember all those times he went off alone with you. I don't know what he told you, but you became a very unhappy little girl. Then he helped you with the pony races and that seemed to make you happy. Maybe it was because you were doing something that pleased him. I don't know."

"He went off with me alone a lot? I remember whenever I was bad and made a scene, he would come and find me."

"Yes. You would always be getting so upset, and he would say, 'I'll handle her, Babe. I can handle her.'"

"He said that? I remember getting upset at dinner, especially when we went out to restaurants."

"It was whenever the four of us were together. He was making you crazy. You would get so upset and cry or throw something at him."

"Yeah. Crazy me."

"No. He manipulated your feelings. When he pushed you too far and you got upset, he would go off alone with you or out to the car, and then you would both come back smiling. He probably said..."

"That he really loved me, not you," I said, finishing Mom's sentence. "I could never understand why he would tell me that he didn't love you, and then he would act like he *did* love you when we were all together or out to dinner. That's what got me so upset. It made no sense, and it made me mad. Then I hated myself for wanting his attention, for taking him away from you. You loved him so much. I was the bad one. Mom, I wanted you to be happy, and yet I couldn't help myself."

"He is a sick person. He manipulated and twisted everything."

"But, you must have hated me," I said, trying to digest this new perspective. "And then the whole thing with sex...well, that was later at Garden State Park. But it was just proof that I caused him to leave you."

"He had already left me. He was away living at Garden State Park Racetrack, leaving me with little Amy and fifteen horses on the farm."

"And I always felt so guilty. Vince wanted me and not you."

"He was sick. He never should have told you he was your boyfriend when you were so young. I had no idea. How could I ever imagine? And then, later on, to be sexual with a child. That is the sickest."

"I thought it was my fault because at one time I had wanted his attention."

"You weren't the only one who was confused," Mom added. "Susan kept a diary from back then and has since looked at it. One of the things she had written was, 'I don't know who Vince loves—me, Mom, or Karen.' He had everyone confused. He separated us and acted like he loved each one of us in some special way."

"Really? She felt that way, too? I never knew that." I never really thought my older sister had been affected by Vince, by all that took place back then. Of course, she had to have been affected in some way. We *all* lived the nightmare.

I felt a little better that Mom wasn't blaming me, especially considering what happened later at Garden State Park. I thought back to the words of the doctor at Holliswood Hospital, which I hadn't really believed at the time. He had said, "It's normal for a child to want love and attention. What's abnormal is for the adult to abuse the child's trust for his or her own emotional or sexually perverted needs. Usually, this kind of person can't deal normally with adult relationships and very often they are victims of child sexual abuse themselves. It's no excuse, of course. The blame still rests with the adult, not the child."

"What are you thinking about?" Mom asked.

"Oh, about the things the doctor at the hospital told me. He said it wasn't my fault. And now you're not blaming me. It's hard to believe that what I thought was the bad me was the result of manipulation. It's hard to accept. I mean, it's hard to believe that I wasn't in control of what I felt. It may be true, but it's still very hard to accept."

The lack of control over my own thoughts and emotions did not seem possible. All these years I thought everything was my fault. This new view of my past was very difficult to digest. How could everything I believed about myself be wrong? I couldn't really believe it, but it was something to consider.

"Did I ever show you the play Vince wrote about us when all this was happening?" Mom asked.

"He wrote a play about it? What do you mean?"

"I'll get it. You won't believe what he wrote. He told me never to let you see it. I guess he knew what he was doing to you back then, but he didn't want you to know."

Mom went and got the play that Vince had written for a college class when he was dating Mom.

I read the play, astounded that he had the audacity to write it. I was made out to be a horrible, bratty kid who was always angry and storming off. In the play, Vince blamed my bad behavior on the fact that I hadn't won a pony race with Jack! This was so far from the truth that it blew my mind. I had lived for the pony races! They were the only thing that brought me joy. I couldn't believe that Vince could twist the truth so much and write such awful lies about me.

"You knew about this?" I asked, dumbfounded when I read it.

"Yes. I was the one who typed it for him. I didn't know what was going on with you at the time. Remember, he lied and manipulated me, too. I just typed his version of our life back then. Knowing what I know now, it looks like he was covering up how he was playing with your emotions by making you out to be a poor sport because you hadn't won with Jack. He knew what you were really upset about, and didn't want me to question your behavior. Remember, he was always the one to go and 'make you feel better' when you got upset."

The play infuriated me. I was bad, once again.

"Remember, Karen. This is not the truth. The purpose of his play was to make me think that he was annoyed with you. That would keep me from suspecting *him* of anything."

She was right. Still, the fact that he had portrayed me in such a derogatory way and that Mom had actually typed it was hard for me to comprehend. Then again, there was a lot I was finding out that was hard to grasp. I had seen and heard enough for one evening. Logically, I knew that Vince had manipulated me, but emotionally it was hard for me to believe it was true.

In order to get away with what he was doing, Vince had to separate Mom and me. Not only had he skillfully managed to keep my mother unsuspecting and away from me, but he had also kept me from confiding in her. He did this in a clever way, by telling me lies to make me doubt her love for me. It worked. Not only had I believed his lies (that my mother did not love me), I also believed they were my own thoughts. This "truth" (which had also created suppressed anger at my mother) was buried deep in my subconscious and needed to be uncovered and understood for what it was, so that I could heal.

With all our talks, I didn't know how to feel anymore. Did Mom really love me, or was she only pretending to care so that I wouldn't be so miserable? On a rollercoaster of pure emotion, I needed to get back in control. So again, I focused on riding races, my usual escape. Racing was black and white. Cross the wire first, you win. You don't, you lose. Simple.

However, to my surprise, this familiar method of escape no longer worked; I started having flashbacks during the day—even on a horse. Maybe I was allowing this to happen, like Robbie. Maybe. I don't know for sure. Because my mind was no longer blocking memories or emotions as it had in the past, the two "mes" were merging, and I was afraid that Karen the jockey would fall apart completely and topple right over. Like Robbie, I needed to take time off from racing, but knew this was impossible; I had just made a comeback after five years! What would people think??? *Please, God, give me time. I need time off to get this sorted out. I can't keep going like this. I'll fall apart and not be able to ride well.*

As if things weren't difficult and confusing enough during this time, I felt compelled to date.

Before I could discard the old truth (that I was bad) and accept the new one, I subconsciously rebuilt the triangle of Vince, Mom, and me in order to run the "test." (Was I loveable?) By going out with a man, I was subconsciously recreating the old, comfortable scenario: Mom vs. Vince (or the man I was dating). Who really loved me? The man (Vince, Pablo, etc.) or Mom? Who was "on my side?" I wanted to hear "your mother doesn't care about you" from a man I hardly knew in order for my crazy feelings to make sense, for the real me to feel loved and accepted. None of the men I dated said these words, so I got more and more frustrated. (Pablo had fit this role perfectly!) I would stop dating that person after a short time and think Mom was to blame for my "failed" relationship. She was the problem! She was the reason I was unlovable. Each time I would be so filled with anger towards Mom that I would write down how I felt. Then my anger would subside and turn to depression. Each relationship ended more quickly and left me with a deeper, more severe depression along with feelings of suicide. What was wrong with me?

On a roll – winning again at Belmont Park

My horses were winning, but my head was spinning. I was riding in stakes races and was the fourth leading jockey at Belmont Park, but I was an emotional wreck, sabotaging relationships and drinking at night until I passed out. When I drank, I would have terrible, uncontrolled fits of rage, all directed at Mom. What was going on? I was *so* angry, and yet there seemed to be no real cause for it. I felt crazy. Where was all this anger coming from? It was beginning to scare me. How much longer could I go on like this?

By now, Mom had noticed my bizarre dating pattern. Although I didn't recognize it, she pointed out that no matter who I dated, I always ended up in a bad place—depressed and suicidal, the same way I had been after relationships with both Pablo and Mr. Macho. She also noted that I seemed to be speeding up the "bad ending" with each man I dated. As she watched me suffer, she was truly baffled.

Trying to make sense of her revelation, I stepped back and read what I had written during each short relationship. No matter how different the situation or the man, my feelings were always the same: I was angry with Mom. Why was my relationship with a man connected to her? It was as if I was recreating the past, what I felt when Vince was around. Why? Why did I feel so strongly that any man I dated had to be "against" Mom in order to be "for" me? Why did there have to be "sides?"

The doctor at the hospital had warned me. If I didn't go back with Pablo, I would find another similar man to recreate the unresolved problems of my childhood. Now I could clearly see what I was doing, and I wanted to break the cycle. I knew I had a "bad script," an old script that, no matter how many times I played it out to find the answer (Was Mom on my side? Was I lovable?), it never worked. The doctor had also told me to write about anger at Mom, but at that time I believed my problems went no further than Pablo. Now that he was out of the picture, I knew it went much deeper than that. Was I angry at Mom? But, how could I be? She was trying to help me get better.

I had learned at the hospital that getting well took time. Logical answers may come quickly, but dealing with feelings took a lot longer. I had also learned that anger suppressed became depression. That was me. That was *definitely* me.

Chapter 82
The Truth Will Set You Free

One month into the Belmont Park fall meeting, I had a bad spill. This time I compressed the vertebrae in my lower back. Although this was another riding setback, my prayer had been answered: I now had my time to fall apart and wrestle with the demons of the past without having to function and perform at the track every day.

I got some paper and started to organize the flashbacks. I needed to revise the old version of me, the bad me. I must start to like myself. The real me is okay. I said it, but I didn't believe it. Writing it down helped me to remember. Seeing it in written form helped me to understand the whole picture, more as an outsider looking in as the story unfolded. I started with a small note pad, which quickly became a larger one. I wrote, and I wrote. And I wrote. Finally, overwhelmed by the mass of it all, I bought a computer and started writing this book.

I wish I could say my healing was instant, but it wasn't. There was still a missing piece to the puzzle. As much as I wrote, I had yet to believe this new version of me to be true and that I wasn't really bad after all.

It had been five months since my spill, and I was still writing about "the Vince years" for my book. It was very difficult and painfully slow. When I wrote about the traumatic events I had experienced when I was young, I was feeling emotion for the first time. When these events had taken place long ago, I had been numb lest I fall apart. Now, I was reliving each scene, feeling the emotions for the first time, and digesting the impact. Back then I was more of a bystander, not acknowledging what was really happening to me. Now, as I wrote and relived each scene, I realized it was me. It was still me, after all these years. The feelings that had been blocked were now flooding out. As usual, to deal with the pain, I drank.

One night, drunk, I went for a walk and found myself sobbing. As I went down the sidewalk I said between tears, "Step on the crack, break your mother's back." I stomped on every crack with a terrible bitterness. The anger was there, but I tried to stomp it away. I was so angry at Mom.

Your mother never loved you.

By the time I got back to the house, I had worked myself into a frenzy. I turned on the computer and pounded my fingers on the keyboard. As I struck the keys, I watched the words appear in all caps on the monitor: I HATE MOM I HATE MOM I HATE YOUR SHITFACED WAY OF DOING THINGS

Maybe because of the alcohol, my anger at Mom was pouring out like never before. I read the words as I typed, "I hate your shitfaced way of doing things." Suddenly, I realized these were not my words—they were *Vince's*. Vince often used the word "shitfaced" when speaking to me about Mom! I read the next line: YOUR MOTHER NEVER LOVED YOU.

My writing had gone from the first person, "I," to the third person, "your." I stopped suddenly, shocked at what I saw. My words were...Vince's? They were my feelings, my thoughts—but not my words. Reading the next line sealed it for me: WHY DO YOU THINK SUSAN LEFT?

Those weren't my words! Those *aren't* my words! Those aren't even my thoughts! Susan didn't leave! *We* left *her*—because of me!!! Because I wanted to go to Florida to ride, *we* left the farm. *We* left Susan. *She* didn't leave!!!

Grasping the enormity of what I saw, I was shocked. Vince was speaking through my emotions! His words were my subconscious thoughts and feelings! The sentence about Susan leaving told the whole truth: *Vince* was speaking. *Vince was the old script*. It wasn't me! Vince must have *told* me these things. Vince must have said, "Your mother never loved you." It wasn't my idea! It was linked to my feelings, but those feelings were based on what Vince must have said! Those were *his* words. *And Vince was a liar!*

My thoughts and my truth were based on a lie!!!

Those crazy feelings that made no sense were based on Vince's words—a lie. My thoughts had been hijacked. What I believed to be my own thoughts were someone else's lies! I was stunned.

"Mom!" I ran upstairs. I had to tell her—to show her—what was on the computer screen. I was still in shock over what had burst forth on the monitor. Words pounded out on the keyboard had finally revealed the source (Vince) of my mixed-up "truth." Suddenly, with this knowledge, all my anger at Mom was *gone!*

"Come look! Come see! You have to see what I wrote just now," I said, not able to contain the excitement of my discovery.

I brought her downstairs and pointed to the big letters on the computer screen. "Look! Read it. Right there, in all caps. That says it all: 'WHY DO YOU THINK SUSAN LEFT?' Mom, I never thought Susan left! Vince must have said that to me. He must have tried to convince me that Susan left because you were a bad mother! But I never thought Susan left. I thought *we* left her when we went to Florida! *Vince* must have told me that! Those must be *his* words!

"And, look at this. The part about you not loving me. If it were my thoughts, it would have continued to be written in the first person, 'I hate Mom. You never loved me.' But look at how it's written, 'I HATE MOM. *YOUR MOTHER* NEVER LOVED *YOU*.' *Vince* must have told me that! And all this time I believed those were my own thoughts! It was what I always "knew" to be true. I believed Vince's lies as if they were my own thoughts!!!"

Finally, I had found the source of my illogical beliefs. There it was, written in all caps on my computer screen. Now, finally, I knew where my "crazy" feelings were coming from: Vince's words *were* my thoughts—the reason I believed Mom didn't love me and that I was bad. The truth was written out for me now, plain as day. The bad me *wasn't* me. My thoughts *were* Vince's lies!

And all this time I had been looking for a man to verify Vince's twisted "truth," what he must have told me over and over since I was ten: *Your mother never loved you.*

For the first time, I could start to believe that maybe I wasn't bad and unlovable. In order to separate me from Mom and safeguard our "secret," Vince had repeated those hurtful words, burning them into my subconscious. My crazy feelings and irrational anger at Mom were all based on the falsehood that she didn't love me. After all, if my own mother found me unlovable, then it must be true!

As the final piece to the puzzle fell into place, Mom remembered a poem I had written when I was eleven years old. It had always bothered her, but now its meaning became clear. She went and got it out of an old box of papers.

Here is the old poem she found.

"The Hate"
A hate so bad, a hate so mean.
A hate that causes grief and greed.
A hate not wanted by this child
A hate that's bad and growing wild.
The hate is hated by all man
The hate is known and boy it can,
Make feelings keep so deep inside,
And always drifting by and by
It hurts me so to feel the hate
A hate that sticks like sticky tape.
by, K.L.R.

Reading my poem from years ago, I realized that even back then I had tried to make sense of my angry feelings. I had written this poem in an effort to express the feelings I had stuffed, the hate I felt toward Vince and his lies that were constantly being fed to me, that never made sense, but became my own twisted truth.

All these years my anger was buried under the layers and was real to me, but because it was based on lies it had been difficult to uncover and understand.

Since that day when Vince's words appeared on the computer

screen, I accepted the real truth much more easily. It finally made *sense.* It took a while for the reality to sink in—that my old truth had been a lie—but whenever I felt any doubt, I brought the words back up onto the monitor. There it was—proof positive of the deception. I had been tricked, manipulated, brainwashed, and lied to all along. My childlike trust had allowed Vince to twist my emotions and deceive me. Just like Mom said: it had been done *to* me. And just like Robbie, I was the victim. Everything I had felt for so long—the repressed anger at Mom and the self loathing—finally made sense, and now new feelings based on the real truth could replace the old ones. I was okay. My mother didn't hate me! And, the real me wasn't crazy or unlovable, just deceived.

Finally, I could accept and forgive myself for wanting Vince's attention and approval when I was young—especially since I was obviously being told that my own mother didn't love or approve of me. It was no wonder I had been so absorbed in making myself legitimate by becoming "Karen the jockey" or later, by wanting to be a "good wife." It was no wonder I hated the "real" unlovable me. Now, for the first time, I thought that maybe if someone got to know me, they wouldn't hate me. They might understand.

The End

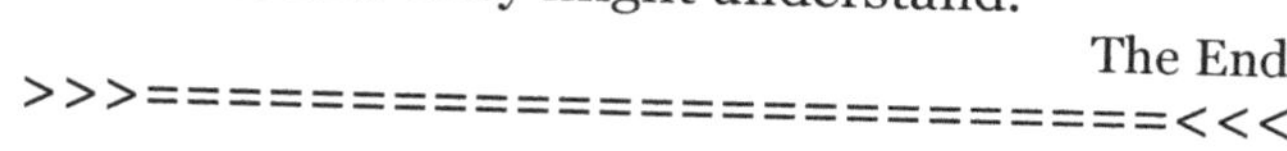

Writing this book started me on the road to freedom. It let me remember, look back into the ugly past, see the real truth, and finally let go of a lie. The bad me is gone now, but I'll never, ever forget her pain. Thank you, God. I'm finally free!

Epilogue

In the eight months that I was not racing due to my back injury, I was able to revisit the catacombs of my childhood memories and find the truth. Because of this, I was well on my way to feeling better about myself. By spring (1990) my back was better, and I began to get into riding shape. I left off writing this book at the part where I had the 1981 out-of-body experience at Saratoga because I needed more information. The memory of leaving my body was more clear than any memory I ever had, and I knew what I had experienced was real. However, others had commented that maybe I was hallucinating or under the influence of mind-altering medication given to me by the track doctor. Had I really died? Unsure of how to write about it, I turned my focus back to riding. I was still addicted to alcohol and throwing up, which really bothered me. I knew these things had to go, but I had tried many times to stop both without any lasting success.

In desperation, on May, 19, 1990, I finally gave my drinking problem over completely to God. Knowing that I couldn't help myself, but that God absolutely could, I gave up the control and said this prayer: "God, I know that alcohol will always be around and accessible, so please, take away my *desire* for it. I can't do this—but I *know* You can. I give it over completely to You, without my ever taking the control back. Just say the word, God, and I know it will be done." My prayer wasn't for God to *stop* me from drinking—but that He *take away my desire* for alcohol.

By God's grace and a total miracle, my desire for alcohol was completely gone. As I no longer wanted to drink, it was no longer a struggle! In fact, the smell so repels me that to this day I won't drink lime Coke (lime reminds me of vodka and tonic) or flavored coffee (which reminds me of Baileys Irish Cream, an Irish whiskey liqueur). That amazing answer to prayer taught me about God. He answers our prayers when we ask with complete faith; I *believed* that God could and would absolutely do the impossible for me.

Shortly after that, I prayed a similar prayer for help with my eating disorder. (However, I didn't pray that God take away my desire for food—one has to eat!) This time my prayer wasn't answered instantaneously, like with the alcohol, but soon enough my throwing up was history as well. I prayed that I could see myself as God sees me and no longer abuse my body, His temple.

> "Or do you not know that your body is a temple of the Holy Spirit who is in you, whom you have from God, and that you are not your own?"
>
> – 1 Corinthians 6:19 (NASB)

On June 6, 1990, I returned to riding races again at Belmont Park. This time there would be no setbacks. There would be no problem relationships, no self-hatred, no drinking or throwing up. No more depressions. Mom and I were close, and I knew that she really loved me. I had grown closer to God. I knew now that He loved me and wanted me to be happy. He had wanted me to find those answers locked up so deep inside.

Once again I started winning races, and even won the $90,000 Added Hudson Handicap aboard Zee Best (photo on back cover). However, I had one regret. I hadn't finished this book. What if another person was suffering the way I had? Maybe, just maybe, if my book were published it could be of some use. Maybe by sharing my story it would help someone else, the way Robbie's article had set me on the path to my own healing.

That August another miracle took place. I was back racing at Saratoga and had another terrible spill. Bruised, battered, with clothes torn and tattered, God was with me. Incredibly, not only had I escaped injury, but the spill happened at the exact same spot as in 1981—when I had my out-of-body experience! As I got up, I was surprised to find Dominick, my faithful friend and agent, standing right there beside me on the track. When he saw the horses fall, he immediately ran across the infield and jumped the hedge of the turf course to get to me! As we headed back to the first aid room in the ambulance, something suddenly occurred to me. "Dominick, maybe now I can find out what happened to me nine years ago, when I fell here! Maybe I can finish writing my book."

Dominick smiled. "Sure, Karen. You'll get that book done, yet." He knew all about my 1981 Saratoga spill and near-death experience. I had told him the story a year earlier, drawing a picture of what I had seen below me in the first aid room at this track. Who better to be with me now, as we headed back there to find some answers? *If I hadn't died and was just unconscious, how could I have seen all those details—like where my arm was up over my head and where everyone was, even on the far side of the room?*

It was a longshot, highly unlikely that I would get any information from an event that had taken place nine years earlier. Still, God was in the miracle business. Being sent to the Saratoga first aid room, the very place where I had the out-of-body experience could not have been a coincidence. This profound experience had strengthened my belief in God and was where I had left off writing my book!

I shouldn't have been surprised to discover that the doctor in the first aid room was the very same one who had treated me nine years earlier! (As I said, God was in the miracle business.) When I explained my out-of-body experience to him, I expected him to be confused or surprised by my account. Instead, he said very matter-of-factly that I didn't have a pulse for a short time. "We lost you. You died."

This confirmed what I had believed all along!

"Did you give me any medications that could have made me hallucinate?" I had to ask that question, just to put the skeptics to rest.

"Of course not. You had a major head injury. We couldn't give you anything."

I asked to see the room where I had died and told him that I remembered seeing my arm twisted up over my head. "Yes that's right. When we lost you, your shoulder had not been put back in place yet." He led us to a tiny room at the end of the hall. It looked nothing like what I had seen from above.

"Are you sure this was where I died? I saw two doctors by my gurney and some nurses in the back, around a big desk." I hoped to jar his memory so he could show me the big room that I had seen.

"Yes. There was another doctor with me. You were right here." He pointed definitively to where my gurney had been in the small room.

"But I remember the room being bigger," I said, baffled. Nothing looked as it had from up above. "Dominick, I almost wish I never came back in here. It doesn't make any sense. At least now I know that I died. But I know what I saw, and it didn't look anything like this." I shook my head. We left the room and I noticed a closed door to my right. Curious, I stopped and pushed it open. There was the big oak desk!

"This is the desk I saw!" I cried out. "Are you sure it wasn't in that big room on the other side of the hall, and I wasn't in there?"

The doctor shook his head. "No. I am sure. This is the nurse's station. This desk has been here in the nurse's station ever since I can remember."

I stepped back. Maybe I had seen it from above...maybe the two adjacent smaller rooms had been one large room!

"Was this wall here, separating the two rooms back then?" I asked the doctor excitedly. Without the wall, the room would have been big, the gurney and the desk would have been positioned correctly, and it would all make sense!

"This wall has always been here. As I said, this room is the nurses' station."

Thinking back to my viewpoint from the ceiling, I looked up. Suddenly, I realized that I couldn't have stopped floating up when I hit the ceiling; it was far too low! I had stopped way high up, and my body below had appeared small—the size of a pencil.

"Dominick, I couldn't have stopped at the ceiling because looking down at my body on the stretcher, it would have been life-size. I had to have been way up—much higher than this ceiling. Maybe I saw the two rooms as one. It would make perfect sense for the nurses to ignore me if they had been in a separate room. From that high up I either couldn't see the wall or didn't notice it. Yes! Look at where everything was positioned."

"It does make sense," he agreed, smiling.

"Something else must have stopped me from floating up and out. Maybe it only *felt* like the ceiling stopped me because I could see everything in the room, or rooms, below. Maybe the point where I stopped floating up and wanted to turn and go was some sort of barrier to cross over to the other side—to another dimension!"

Dominick smiled again, happy that I had finally pieced it all together. He could clearly see now, as I could, that my out-of-body experience had taken place exactly as I had said.

When we left the first aid room, Dominick and I went to see the film of the spill I had just walked away from. Watching it play in slow motion, I knew that God had protected me. My horse and three others had run directly over me when I fell. Thousands of pounds of horseflesh and sixteen legs had missed me somehow, each hoof managing to miss my head, my stomach, my back, my arms, and my legs. It was one of the worst racing accidents I had ever seen, yet I only sustained superficial bruises and torn clothing. It was truly a miracle and by God's design that I should walk away and find my answers, too.

Again, I was reminded of God's incredible love for me; He was there all along, through every spill and heartache, through all my troubled times, of which there had been many. I owed my life to God. I knew I had to finish my book. This story was bigger than me, full of miracles, and God had to get the glory. If knowing my story could help just one person to see God's miracles and His plan—and give them hope—it would be better than winning the Kentucky Derby, the Triple Crown, or the Breeders' Cup. For one's life to be a testimony of God's goodness—*that* was the ultimate prize.

• • • • • • • •

Update...

On October 31, 1990, I had yet another spill. This one resulted in serious injuries, which ended my riding career. However, really living, for me, had only just begun.

In 1993 I had a son, which has been my greatest blessing. I had always wanted a son, but after trying so hard with Pablo to have children and failing, I was pretty sure I could never have kids. God has blessed me in many ways. He has challenged me in ways I never would have guessed and had me do things I never would have desired or attempted without His guidance or help.

One of these challenges was homeschooling my son, Sean, as a single mom. I was against homeschooling, so when God made it crystal clear that it was His will, I was not happy about it. Eventually, I gave in to His will, and what a blessing it turned out to be. God always knows what's best for us. Through homeschooling events and co-ops, I met the most wonderful friends and families. Not only did my son get a great education, but I did, as well. God allowed me the time and opportunity to grow and learn right alongside my son. I loved learning history and sharing great books with him. A most incredible thing God did through homeschooling was to teach me grammar and writing skills which I needed to complete this book as a polished writer. In fact, I loved writing so much that I taught the subject with much success to many homeschooled kids at our co-op. (At the co-op my son learned higher math and science from other teachers who excelled in these subjects.)

When Sean went off to college, I set about using my writing skills to edit my story, which remained a complete, but unpolished first draft in dusty hard copy form since 1990. All the years that have passed since it was written until its publication in 2017 have allowed me to grow. My complete trust and faith in God have made it possible to live in freedom. The key is in giving up our control and letting God take over completely. He does what we cannot, if we will just ask and believe. These past twenty-seven years (free from alcohol, eating disorders, depression, and suicidal thoughts) not only deepened my relationship with God, strengthened me as a person, but incredibly, led me to become a more polished writer. God's timing is, indeed, perfect!

My life is proof of God's faithfulness. He helped me survive the abuse by turning my focus toward riding races. Against all odds, He allowed me to succeed with that. Then, God showed me through my failed marriage that I had never healed from my past emotional and physical abuse. When I was ready, God not only gave me the memories, but the desire and ability to write them down as well. He has given me a wonderful, supportive mother who helped me unravel the past so that together we could find the truth—that we had both been manipulated and survived a terrible ordeal. Today we are best friends. She has not only inspired me to keep at this project until completion, but was an integral part in helping me with the final edit. I thank God for all of these many, many blessings.

Finally, without knowing God, I would not have had the desire to help others. How could I not publish my story after God has freely given me so much? Though much time has passed and the people in my book have moved on, this story is still relevant. Today, many continue to suffer the lasting effects and emotional trauma of past child abuse. I hope my story will open their eyes, give them hope, and point them to God, Who desires a relationship with each one of us and wants to heal our hurting hearts.

"There is an appointed time for everything.
And there is a time for every event under heaven."
– Ecclesiastes 3:1 (NASB)

"...you will know the truth, and
the truth will set you free."
– John 8:32 (NIV)

Where they are today...

- Vince remarried and had two additional children. Although my mom and I have healed and understand the degree of Vince's deception and manipulation, we realize that others in our family and extended family have been unknowingly influenced. Vince tried to divide our whole family by insinuating to each of us that something was wrong with the other. His past manipulation and lies continue to affect family relationships to this day.
- Pablo and I divorced in 1990. He remarried and had children. As far as I know, he still lives on Long Island.
- My grandmother passed away, as did my father. My sister Susan is married with three beautiful daughters. While growing up, my younger sister Amy, watched me ride at the track and also witnessed my many spills and injuries. Because of this, she desired to save lives. Now, she is an EMT and doing just that! My mom lives close

by in New Jersey, where she is back with her first love, the horses. More than anyone else, she has encouraged me and helped me with this book.

- In 1995, I moved back to New Jersey to raise my son, Sean, close to my family. He is now grown, and I am

extremely proud of him. I have five cats, a ferret, and a big loving Rottweiler. I have saved many feral cats in the neighborhood, and my Rottweiler has won several titles in obedience as well as participated in the sport of agility. God has blessed me more than I could have ever imagined. These past twenty-seven years of living in freedom are proof that with the help of God, any one of us can achieve total victory and new life in Jesus.

For more information, please visit:
www.racingwithmyshadow.com

A Picture is Worth a Thousand Words!

I would like to sincerely thank Bob and Adam Coglianese, Dori Bassing (granddaughter of Jim Raftery), Nora Clifford (sister of Ray Clifford), Lorna Drake Giles (relative of Ted Freudy), Joe Diorio, Nik Kleinberg, Nancie Bozza, and the *Daily News* for graciously allowing me to use their wonderful photos. Also, my deepest gratitude goes to Peb and the *Daily Racing Form* for permission to reprint their materials. And, thanks to my mom for her many pictures, her pastel on the cover, and her help with the entire manuscript!

Photos courtesy of:

Freudy Photos Archives, LLC

pg 13 pg 14 pg 16 pg 20 pg 22

Jim Raftery – Turfotos

pg vii pg 44 pg 44 pg 50 pg 50 pg 51

pg 53 pg 56 pg 58 pg 58 pg 100 pg 101 pg 109

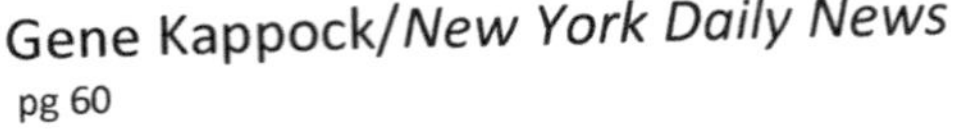

Gene Kappock/*New York Daily News*

pg 60

Nik Kleinberg

pg 113 pg 113

Ray Clifford

pg iv

pg v

pg vi

pg vi

pg 70

pg 70

pg 117

pg 158

Bob Coglianese Photos

pg iv

pg v

pg vii

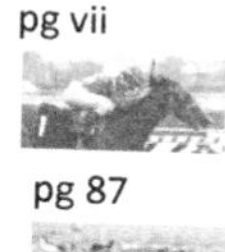

pg vii

pg viii

pg viii

pg xi

pg 79

pg 85

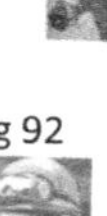

pg 87

pg 87

pg 91

pg 92

pg 92

pg 95

pg 114

pg 120

pg 123

pg 129

pg 177

pg 413

pg 426

Daily Racing Form and *Equibase Co. LLC* clipping/Jim Raftery photo

pg 66

Big M Picks Karen Rogers As '79 'Rookie of the Year'

Peb (Pierre Bellocq, artist)

pg 109

pg 115

Nancie Bozza

pg 439

Joseph V. Diorio

back cover

Made in the USA
Middletown, DE
02 September 2023

37629217R00255